D0786760

American
Historical
Pageantry

American Historical Pageantry

. . . .

The Uses of

Tradition in the Early

Twentieth Century

by David Glassberg

The University of North Carolina Press

Chapel Hill . London

© 1990 The University of North Carolina Press

Library of Congress Cataloging-in-Publication Data

Glassberg, David.
    American historical pageantry : the uses of
tradition in the early twentieth century / by David
Glassberg.
        p.   cm.
    Includes bibliographical references.
    ISBN 0-8078-1916-6 (alk. paper)
    ISBN 0-8078-4286-9 (pbk. : alk. paper)
    1. American drama—20th century—History and
criticism.   2. Historical drama, American—History
and criticism.   3. Pageants—United States—
History—20th century.   4. United States—
Historiography.   I. Title.
PS338.H56G5   1990
791.6'24'097309041—dc20   89-70586
                                                    CIP

The paper in this book meets the guidelines for
permanence and durability of the Committee on
Production Guidelines for Book Longevity of the
Council on Library Resources.

Manufactured in the United States of America

94 93 92 91 90   5 4 3 2 1

Portions of the book appeared in the March 1987 *Journal
of American History* and are reprinted with the journal's
permission.

To my father,
and in memory of my mother

Contents

. . . .

Illustrations

. . . .

Preface

. . . .

More than a decade ago, a street vendor in Philadelphia sold me the second volume of a souvenir history of the Hudson-Fulton Celebration of 1909. Upon looking up volume one, I discovered on the library shelves an explosion of commemorative events in pageant form at the turn of the century. The discovery raised a host of questions: Why did these events happen all at once? Why did they take the form that they did? Why did the pageant form die out?

My initial efforts to explain the phenomenon focused on what historians had been saying about progressivism. After all, pageantry's rise and fall seemed to correspond with that of progressive reform movements. But I soon realized that was only part of the story. While working on several public history projects in the Philadelphia area, I grew more curious about the nature of historical consciousness in America and the institutions that shape it. As I brought these questions from my public history experience back to my writing about pageantry, the book became an exploration of the changing public images and uses of tradition in the early twentieth century.

In thinking about the meaning of pageantry over the years, I especially appreciated the advice of John Higham, who commented extensively on an early version of the manuscript. His urging for clarity and precision remained in my mind through subsequent drafts. I also learned much from conversations in the early stages of this work with Tom Jacklin, Kathy Jacob, and Sally Griffith, in the middle stages with John Alviti, whom I met shortly after my arrival in Philadelphia, and toward the end with John Bodnar, who shared his unpublished material on patriotism in the Midwest. Criticism on an early draft of the manuscript from Seymour Mandelbaum and Thomas Bender confirmed my decision to reconsider the focus of the book; perceptive comments from Roger Abrahams and Michael Kammen helped me put the story back together. I have benefited greatly from their combined knowledge of folklore, public celebrations, and the place of history in American culture.

My debt to the dozens of archivists and librarians will be obvious from looking at the notes. To mention a few by name is not to diminish my sense of gratitude to the others: Alice Cotten and Jeff Hicks of the North Carolina Room of the University of North Carolina at Chapel

Hill, Linda Stanley at the Historical Society of Pennsylvania, Ken Winn of the Missouri Historical Society, and above all Barbara Filipac of the John Hay Library at Brown University. I also want to thank the interlibrary loan librarians at the University of Pennsylvania and the University of Massachusetts at Amherst for their diligence.

Special appreciation goes to Arvia MacKaye Ege and Christy Mac-Kaye Barnes for sharing reminiscences, as well as their unpublished biography, of their father; to Margaret Langdon for talking with me about her father's work, and for sharing her pageantry memorabilia; and to Phil Frable and Donald Groves of the John B. Rogers Company for sharing stories and materials.

I conducted much of the early research at the National Museum of American History, Smithsonian Institution, where I enjoyed the friendship of Carl Scheele and Ellen Roney Hughes in the Division of Community Life. Both the quantity and the quality of the illustrations would not have been possible without support from the Smithsonian, as well as from an Albert J. Beveridge Grant from the American Historical Association in 1985; an Educational Needs Grant from the University of Massachusetts at Amherst in 1987; and a Travel to Collections Grant from the National Endowment for the Humanities in 1988. I would also like to thank James W. Lynch for the many chores he performed in connection with the final preparation of this book.

Friends and family contributed materially to the completion of this work. Research trips were made more affordable and pleasurable through the hospitality of Julie Winch and Alice Hauck in Providence, Rhode Island; the Kadden family in White Plains, New York; the Berkovitz-Silver family in New Salem, Massachusetts; my sister Deborah Glassberg in Washington, D.C.; and the Daniel family in Charlotte, the Catlett family in Greensboro, and Claudia L. Shambaugh in Chapel Hill, North Carolina. My children Rachel and Daniel provided an important source of diversion by discovering new uses for the perforated edges that tear off computer paper.

The production of a book, like a pageant, involves many behind the scenes. I would like to bring out for a curtain call the staff of the design and production department at the University of North Carolina Press; copyeditor Stevie Champion, who left the prose in a lot better shape than she found it; and Lewis Bateman, whose wise counsel helped bring this project to completion.

But the greatest heroine of all is my wife, Joanne Fraser. The book simply would not have been written without her love, encouragement, and forbearance. I have been working on pageantry ever since we met a dozen years ago. In that time, she has contributed to the manuscript in countless ways; among them, her great knowledge of American history and culture, of the English language, and of indexing. More than anyone, Joni has eagerly anticipated the book's completion and deserves the credit for it happening. My father and mother, Sol and Eudice Glassberg, also never wavered in their support of this project; though my mother did not live to hold this book in her hands, I hope that at least some small measure of her influence and example are evident throughout.

*American
Historical
Pageantry*

Introduction:
History into Ritual

. . . .

The idea of history itself, special kinds of
historical studies, and various attitudes
toward history always play—whether in-
telligently conceived or not—a major
role within a culture. That strange collection of assumptions, attitudes, and
ideas we have come to call a "world view"
always contains a more or less specific
view of the nature of history. Attitudes
toward the past frequently become facts
of profound consequences for the culture itself.
—Warren I. Susman, *American Quarterly*,
1964

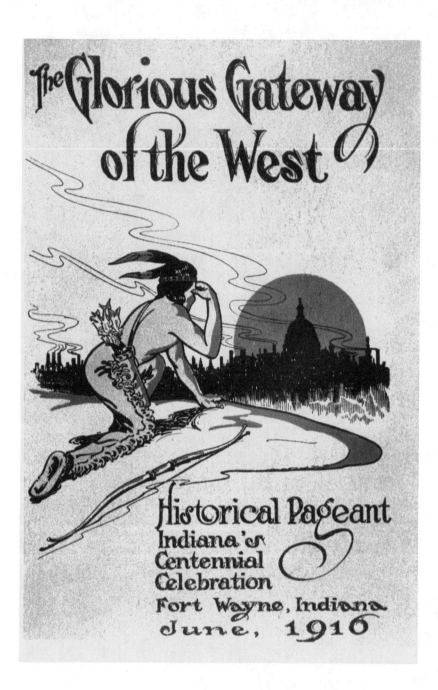

Pageant poster of an Indian viewing modern progress, Ft. Wayne, Indiana, 1916. (Brown University Library)

Where do Americans get their ideas about history? What public images shape our perception of the past and the relation of that past to the present and the future? How do particular versions of history become the public history, and how is this public history used, interpreted, understood, and changed over time?

The following chapters seek to answer these important questions by examining the pageantry craze of the early twentieth century. At the height of the craze, thousands of Americans in hundreds of towns from Portland, Maine, to San Gabriel, California, joined in civic celebrations by acting out dramatic episodes from their town's history. Historical pageants ranged in size from a cast of a few hundred to the one in St. Louis in 1914 with a cast of 7,000 and audiences of nearly 100,000 at each performance. But the appeal of historical pageantry proved as ephemeral as it was pervasive. Though some pageants, especially holiday pageants for children, remain popular, the use of pageantry as the centerpiece of an elaborate civic celebration, as in St. Louis, was over by World War II.

Historical pageantry entered a landscape at the turn of the century that was dense with historical imagery. Many of the themes it expressed were like those in other media—museums, monuments, murals—that also put forth versions of the public history. But the historical pageant, as a dramatic public ritual chronicling local community development, also had unique features that accounted for its sudden growth and decline in the period. Pageantry's story is part of the larger, essentially untold history of popular images and uses of tradition in America, as well as part of the somewhat more familiar history of the conflicts and movements that transformed American society and culture in the early twentieth century.

Public historical imagery is an essential element of our culture, contributing to how we define our sense of identity and direction. It locates us in time, as we learn about our place in a succession of past and future generations, as well as in space, as we learn the story of our locale. Images of a "common" history provide a focus for group loyalties, as well as plots to structure our individual memories and a larger context within which to interpret our new experiences. Ultimately, historical imagery supplies an orientation toward our future action.[1] Historical imagery provides categories for understanding experience, delineating what we call traditional and what we call modern, what we think is timeless and what we think can be changed, what we consider inevitable and what we term accidental, what we dismiss as strange and what we know is mere common sense. Public historical imagery, by giving recognition to various group and individual histories, also suggests categories for our understanding the scale of our social relations and the relative position of groups in our society. It delineates what is public and what is private, who belongs to the public and who does not. Finally, historical imagery suggests the relationship of these categories for understanding experience to one another: whether it is possible to maintain tradition and keep up with modernity, to retain the intimacies of community and join in mass society, or whether tradition and modernity, community and society are fundamentally opposites. As such, public historical imagery is both a reflection of the larger culture, and its prevailing ways of looking at the world, and a major element in the shaping of that culture. Since every way of seeing the world—past and present—excludes hundreds of alternatives from view, the power to define what particular version of history becomes the public history is an awesome power indeed.[2]

Fortunately, this power is not absolute. Public historical imagery, like other aspects of culture, does not speak with a single, consistent voice. It is not simply a collective representation or an expression of the culture speaking for itself. Even a casual look at how a "collective" historical representation is created reveals struggles between competing groups over the definition of the public and its history. These struggles often are resolved according to the relative political and economic power of each local group, which largely determines its access to public forums for presenting its version of history to a wider audience. Not everyone is asked to organize a parade, paint a mural, or give a historical oration. Nevertheless, as will be shown in the case of historical pageants, the desire to display the illusion of consensus through mass participation sometimes leads civic officials to include dissenting voices in their public historical representations. These voices, in turn, can subvert the overall impression the officials are trying to communicate.[3]

The power of public historical imagery to define a common understanding of experience also is limited by the varied backgrounds of the audience. An image of George Washington means something different to a member of the Daughters of the American Revolution than to an Italian immigrant, despite the former's attempt to shape the perceptions of the latter. Audiences can not only affirm what they see and hear, but also challenge it (privately or publicly), ignore it, or, most commonly, misinterpret it. While those who create public historical imagery attempt to place elements from past, present, and future within a particular tradition, and thus provide a particular context and meaning for experience, each member of the audience brings other contexts, and thus attaches different meanings, to the public images they see. Historical images arranged to present a particular interpretation of the past can also remind the audience of other interpretations. Audiences learn these alternative meanings to attach to public historical imagery from other sources of tradition, such as the customs and tales that circulate among their family, fellow workers, friends, and church. Public culture is not the only culture; public historical imagery is but one of many sources of tradition, or ways of representing the past and ordering the present, that shape the way we view our world.[4]

Public historical imagery as an element of culture handed down from generation to generation, and often from an elite to the masses, is not only subject to struggle over definition and interpretation but also is subject to change over time. One generation's understanding of history is not the same as that of the next, despite the affirmations of continuity regularly woven into commemorative rituals. Even as images of the past provide a framework within which to interpret new experiences, the meaning of the images subtly alters as it stretches to incorporate those experiences. Old categories and images acquire new meanings. Thus the historical representations and categories for understanding experience that constitute the public history change with time.[5]

To understand the meaning of historical pageantry, we must explore not only the ideas of its creators but also the other ways that history—the relation of past, present, and future—and tradition—the continuous elements within a culture—were represented in public in the early twentieth century. Reconstructing these other ways that history and tradition were displayed from the world of genteel, popular, ethnic, and working-class culture can help to explain how various audiences might have interpreted the public world that the pageant directors created on stage.

This book examines American historical pageants in terms of their creators' explicit purposes and symbols; their implicit depiction of the nature of history, of society, and of social change; and the patterns of social relationships entailed in producing "collective" historical imagery in public. Chapters focus not only on the common images and uses of history across America in the early twentieth century, but also on the common processes through which the ideas and images were formed and communicated. They examine public celebrations of history in their local context, as well as the efforts of several national organizations to reform the conduct and content of these celebrations and, by extension, reform the communities where the celebrations took place.

While *American Historical Pageantry* explores the larger question of how public versions of history are created, disseminated, understood, and changed over time, it also concerns the particular uses that Americans saw for history in the early twentieth century. Some uses of historical imagery in pageantry—as a form of local boosterism, patriotic moralizing, and popular entertainment—were like those in public celebrations of other periods. But one use of history was unique to pageantry and to the early twentieth century: the belief that history could be made into a dramatic public ritual through which the residents of a town, by acting out the right version of their past, could bring about some kind of future social and political transformation.

The perception of historical pageantry as a ritual of social transformation in the period necessarily involves an examination of progressivism. Indeed, though the historical pageant originated among the same conservative self-appointed guardians of tradition who usually orchestrated public ceremonies in the late nineteenth century, it was progressive reform movements in public recreation and the fine arts that gave American pageantry its distinctive form. Historians in recent years have had difficulty with the concept of progressivism, largely because the content of the diverse set of proposals and movements—religious, political, bureaucratic—that they have labeled "progressive" had little in common. Nevertheless, the form of the proposals owed much to a common type of historical imagery and rhetoric. Essential to the progressive appeal was the use of historical imagery to discover or invent an appropriate tradition in support of reform. Even movements that depicted themselves as new—the "New Nationalism," "New Freedom," "New Country Life," "New History"—also represented the new society they envisioned as a natural outgrowth of the society of the past and the new techniques they advocated as in line with traditional ideals. The extensive use of images of history and tradition by reform movements of the period was not only rhetorical but also intrinsic to the worldview of the reformers and their audiences, who sought a sense of continuity as a psychological keel amid recent social changes. Examining the world of the "pageant-masters," and why they thought that they could change society by staging historical pageants, illuminates many of the ideals as well as characteristic modes of persuasion of progressive reform movements.[6]

If a focus on historical pageantry as an instrument for the creation and dissemination of a public tradition in the early twentieth century necessarily concerns the appeal of progressivism, it also concerns the appeal of what has come to be called "antimodernism"—the desire to reject the present in favor of an idealized past. Images of a preindustrial golden age of handicraft and undoubting religious faith, embodied in scenes of Medieval and Renaissance Europe or Colonial America, contributed greatly to the universe of imagery employed in historical pageants. But these images, originally created in the late nineteenth century as a dissent from modern industrial society, often appeared in historical pageants as stages in the inevitable evolution of that society. In a sense, historical pageantry flourished at the intersection of progressivism and antimodernism and placed nostalgic imagery in a dynamic, future-oriented reform context. Not until after World War I, when the progressive contexts in which this premodern imagery had been placed grew less common, did historical pageantry become more closely associated with antimodernism and the use of tradition as a bulwark against modernity.[7]

Each of the following chapters will consider historical pageantry in terms of the various uses of tradition in the early twentieth century: as patriotic and moral education, as popular entertainment, as civic boosterism, as a tool to reform Americans' use of leisure, as a means of rejuvenating rural society, as a way to revolutionize the American theater, as propaganda on behalf of a program of urban political reform, as a way to mobilize society for world war, as a way to define an American folk identity, and, finally, as a retreat from the consequences of modern industrialism. Some of these uses of tradition continue to shape our own public categories for understanding history later in the century. If to modern Americans the past has become a "foreign country," seemingly distant from our present, then this book is a study of how it became that way.[8]

1 *Influences Felt to the End of Time*

. . . .

Morgantown must celebrate its centennial. Every sentiment of citizenship demands it. Every feeling of town pride demands it. Every claim of public spirit demands it. Our self-respect demands it. Our one hundred years of history demands it. It would be disgraceful to let the occasion pass without some adequate manifestation of our interest. To do so would damage our reputation abroad, and humiliate us at home. Our neighbors would point the finger of scorn at a people who were so dead to every sentiment of local pride as to "make no sign" on such an occasion in our history. Besides, our centennial year is more full of interest and hope for our town than any other period of our history. Our railroad will be open. We will have waterworks and gas. Our population is increasing and new buildings and improvements are appearing on all sides. These things give additional inspiration to the desire for a centennial jubilee.
—Morgantown (West Virginia) *New Dominion*, July 4, 1885

Midnight, July 4, 1876. Artists' representations of civic celebrations in the nation's larger cities shaped local notions of the appropriate commemorative activities on holidays. This drawing chronicles the fireworks, torchlight processions, and banners that accompanied Philadelphia's celebration of the nation's centennial. (Harper's Weekly, *July 22, 1876, p. 593; Library of Congress*)

By the end of July, a seven-man committee began meeting at the Morgantown courthouse to lay plans for the municipal centennial celebration in October. Like hundreds of other celebration committees across America that were planning commemorative programs, the Morgantown committee had an intuitive sense of the appropriate ways to celebrate an important civic anniversary—a sense developed from growing up attending July Fourth celebrations year after year. They knew that a public celebration would not be a celebration without parades, speeches, picnics, band concerts, and fireworks. Indeed, the activities that towns such as Morgantown customarily scheduled to commemorate their history seemed timeless.

Yet public commemorations of history, ceremonies explicitly designed to represent continuity and tradition in the Gilded Age, were changing. They changed as program committees watched innovations in neighboring towns and read accounts of the period's larger public ceremonies, such as those that accompanied the U.S. Centennial in 1876, the U.S. Constitution Centennial in 1887, and the giant international expositions. They also changed as committee members tried to satisfy the expectations of various local constituencies: politicians who wanted to demonstrate their political popularity; merchants who wanted to show off their commercial supremacy; new fraternal, ethnic, and labor organizations eager to assert their place in the community; and crowds of spectators who each year demanded bigger and better amusements.

What were the customary elements of civic celebrations in the late nineteenth century? How were they changing? And what problems did the direction of those changes pose for the customary guardians of local tradition that compelled them to seek a new form of public celebration?

Following custom, program committees made the historical oration the centerpiece of their celebration programs. They invited a public official, college professor, or clergyman, sometimes coming from great distances, to deliver the address. Set like a sermon amid a program of invocations, hymns, and benedictions, the historical oration explained the sacred as well as the worldly significance of past events. In an official public culture suffused with spread-eagle nationalism and Christian piety, the speakers' religious and patriotic rhetoric reinforced the authority of their historical narrative and offered a common language to address their diverse audiences as a united community of believers.[1]

Nowhere was the blend of Protestantism and nationalism, theology and history, more evident than in the hundreds of historical orations delivered in towns across the thirty-eight states in 1876 to commemorate the centennial of American independence. Centennial speakers laced their orations with biblical references comparing the sacred destiny of America with that of ancient Israel. C. E. DeLong in Gold Hill, Nevada Territory, described the Declaration of Independence as the American "Ark" and "Covenant"; Robert C. Winthrop in Boston identified its author Thomas Jefferson with Moses, "slow of tongue, like the great law-giver of the Israelites." The Reverend R. S. Storrs proclaimed to his audience in New York City that the declaration gushed from Jefferson's pen "like a river from the rock." God had entrusted America, like ancient Israel, with a mission. The nation's history unfolded as more than a mere chronicle of earthly events; it was evidence of progress toward the fulfillment of a divine calling. Thomas Alvord of Syracuse, New York, explained, "We have evidently been chosen by an over-ruling Providence to do the great and final work for man's elevation to and permanent enjoyment of the highest civilization to which human nature can attain."[2]

Orators pointed to the nation's territorial and population expansion, material abundance, and technological innovation—especially the harnessing of steam power into factories and locomotives and electricity to the telegraph—as evidence that local residents as Americans had been divinely favored. Centennial orations such as "The Destiny of the Republic" or "Our Success—Our Future" boldly looked forward to more such growth. John Wade Watts, the oldest son of the former Confederate governor of Alabama, predicted in Montgomery that by 1976 the nation would encompass one hundred states and four hundred million inhabitants, stretching from Panama to the Hudson Bay. Judge Isaac Smith of New Hampshire suggested that his auditors use the occasion of the nation's centennial to look back and gird themselves for "future upward progress." U.S. Secretary of State William Evarts assured his audience in Philadelphia that "we have taken no steps backward." Even the Civil War furthered American progress, as, in the words of Judge John Dillon of Iowa, "a fiery ordeal which purged the nation of the sin of slavery. In its blood the robes of the Republic were washed white." Orators projected that the nation's future would be essentially an extension of its prosperous present, just as its present was an extension of its recent past.[3]

Centennial speakers employed the religious celebration of America's progress to add force to their jeremiads against Gilded Age political corruption and materialism, advancing a strain of republican political ideology potent since the Revolution.[4] Thomas Alvord, in the same address in which he trumpeted American progress and destiny, complained of Gilded Age "extravagance" and "the lower scale of public and private morality." In an address entitled "The Grand Mission of America," Reverend Joseph Twitchell warned his Hartford,

Connecticut, audience, "If we forsake our calling, God will take away the crown He has given us. The Kingdom of God will be taken from us and given to another nation which shall bring forth the fruits thereof." Reverend Morgan Dix presented his audience in New York with a similar admonishment: "Every good man is a reason in God's eyes why he should spare the nation and prolong its life; every bad man . . . a reason why God should break up the whole system." Religious metaphor charged the audience as a congregation, lending additional authority to the speaker's vision of common national destiny. Speakers explained that a divine logic existed in the sequence of historical events, and that the present and future were comprehensible in terms of a covenant that bound local residents strictly in adherence to the moral principles and sacred obligations assumed at the nation's founding.[5]

History in these orations unfolded both as a sacred text chronicling the nation's divine mission and as a practical guidebook of moral instruction to outline how local residents should behave in the present. Speakers enjoined their auditors to emulate the behavior attributed to the Founding Fathers as paragons of morality, piety, patriotism, self-sacrifice—the components of stalwart Victorian character necessary to reform a corrupt age.[6] Charles Francis Adams declared of the life of George Washington: "Whatever misfortunes may betide us, of one thing we may be sure, that the study of that model by the rising youth of our land can never fail to create a sensitive force potent enough to counteract every poisonous element in the political atmosphere." Vermont's Lucius E. Chittenden spoke in Burlington on July Fourth, 1876, on "The Character of the Early Settlers of Vermont—Its Influence Upon Posterity." Chittenden reasoned: "Surely it will be to our advantage if we can find out the causes of their success. In those causes we may find the secrets of some of our failures." His address contrasted the settlers' virtues—promptness, kindness, courteousness, and a strong sense of public duty—with the partisanship and greed he felt permeated his America of the late nineteenth century. Chittenden lamented, "We have departed from the ways of our fathers. We no longer act upon the principles through which they achieved success." He then urged his audience to exercise again the virtuous qualities of Vermont's early settlers so that they might bequeath that heritage to their posterity and guarantee their community's future development. Centennial speakers emphasized that past generations continued to sit in judgment on how well the present generation followed their "path" and insisted that bountiful progress would continue only if local residents dedicated themselves to the ideals that speakers attributed to past generations.[7]

Even in southern towns, historical orators employed the religious

themes of a chosen people judged against the standards of their forefathers to bind the fate of locale and nation—though southern orators
often focused their auditors' allegiance on the recently departed Confederate nation rather than on the present federal government. The
southern "religion of the lost cause" in the decades after the Civil War
developed its own pantheon of heroes, rituals, and holidays. Southern
towns commemorated Confederate Memorial Day on June 3, Jefferson Davis's birthday; by 1900, Robert E. Lee's birthday (January 19)
also became an official holiday throughout the South.[8] Despite claims
that the U.S. Centennial in 1876 would lead to an orgy of reconciliation between North and South, white residents in southern towns still
commemorated the holiday lukewarmly, especially compared with the
enthusiasm of local black and ethnic populations.[9] In Atlanta, the
Irish Literary Society sponsored the city's principal commemoration
of the nation's centennial. In Portsmouth, Virginia, the principal celebration was at the Benjamin Banneker Lyceum, where John Mercer
Langston of Howard University delivered a centennial oration calling
for an end to the segregation of public schools. Charleston, South
Carolina, whites in 1876 preferred to celebrate the centennial of the
Battle of Fort Moultrie on June 28 and left the July Fourth ceremonies
to blacks. The pattern on the Fourth was the same in Charlotte, North
Carolina, where in the words of a local newspaper headline, "The
Whites Don't Celebrate Worth a Cent, But the Colored Brothers
Threw Themselves Away Upon It." White speakers in southern towns
that commemorated July 4 in 1876—many for the first time since
Secession—interpreted the Civil War as another trial in the sacred
history of a distinct southern nation that had failed to achieve independence, and ultimately to redeem American nationality, from a
federal government that had fallen into tyrannical and corrupt hands.
A centennial speaker in Memphis, Tennessee, equated the injustices of
Reconstruction with those of British colonial rule; one in Mobile,
Alabama, contrasted the virtues of constitutional government with the
recently departed martial law. Although speakers in public historical
ceremonies in southern towns demonstrated more concern with rally-
ing a sectional as distinct from a national identity, they paralleled
speakers in other parts of the United States in their use of history as a
medium through which to communicate their concerns about the
present state of morality and politics, as well as their prescriptions for
how local residents should behave in the future.[10]

Alongside this soaring rhetoric of sacred national destiny, the historical orators consistently argued a more concrete, local message—
the importance of being alert to every opportunity for local community development. Especially at ceremonies marking local historical

The Fourth of July in the country. This engraving by Thomas Worth regis-
tered his disapproval of July Fourth celebrations in the South during Recon-
struction. Note the drink and disorder, the cannon marked 1776 buried in the
ground, and the audience's lack of attention to the long-winded speaker, who
*bears a more than passing resemblance to John Brown. (*Harpers' Weekly,
July 11, 1868, p. 448; Library of Congress)

anniversaries, speakers surveyed each stage in the town's growth, me-
thodically tracing the development of local religious, financial, educational, and municipal institutions. In Morgantown in 1885, former
U.S. Senator Waitman T. Willey began his historical oration with the
arrival of the first white settlers—"stalwart, sinewy men, . . . uncor-
rupted by the luxuries of wealth." He then described the successive
generations that subdued the wilderness, laid out the streets, founded
the courthouses and schools, and brought the present generation to
the brink of a new century of municipal progress. Throughout the
narrative, he attributed the local community's success to its residents'
ability to seize the main chance, as well as their adherence to timeless
moral principles, and held up prominent local residents of the past as
exemplars for the present generation.[11]

In tracing the path of local community development, historical orators capitalized on the burgeoning interest in local history in the late
nineteenth century. Between 1870 and 1890, the number of state and

local historical societies in America more than doubled from 140 to 300. The new societies commissioned local histories and assembled artifact and document collections. These materials, newly uncovered and accessible, enabled holiday speakers to embellish their retelling of familiar historical incidents with detailed references to concrete local facts and artifacts—though original historical research was secondary to the overarching patriotic, religious, and moral framework of the oration.[12]

As presented in holiday orations in the late nineteenth century, history provided a source of timeless, universal moral principles that could be summoned rhetorically to guide the present, as well as a source of particular local tales that could anchor a unique community identity. A sweeping, romantic-nationalist vision, similar to that appearing in school history textbooks and the works of popular historians such as George Bancroft, coexisted in the holiday historical oration with the story of a particular community held together by unique local characteristics.[13] Speakers employed narratives of local community development alongside the religious rhetoric of nationalism to forge a united community of believers out of residents with diverse ethnic, class, and regional backgrounds. Such addresses identified local residents' unique place in a succession of past and future generations, as well as distinguished the unique character of local community ties from other kinds of social relations.

Local committees planning commemorative programs surrounded the historical oration with a host of elaborate ritual elements to underscore the importance of the day and, by extension, the particular version of history and communal identity they were commemorating in public. At the centennial celebration of General Burgoyne's surrender at Schuylerville, New York, in 1877, church bells, factory whistles, and cannon sounded at dawn, marking off celebration day from everyday and signaling the stoppage of ordinary business. The local historical society marked structures and places associated with what it deemed significant events and persons from the town's past, transforming everyday surroundings into a ceremonial landscape imbued with sacred significance. Wooden arches festooned with greenery, paintings, and slogans also transformed the town into a ceremonial center for the surrounding region and attempted to illustrate the moral lessons of history in vivid and colorful form.[14] A giant banner depicting Burgoyne surrendering his sword to the American General Gates stretched across Schuylerville's main street. On the roof of a dwelling across the street stood a life-size representation of the "Goddess Liberty," her starry crown and skirt fashioned from an American flag.[15] Crowds walking through town became actors on an elaborate stage set designed to focus their attention on the lessons of the day; they not only heard of the timeless virtues of their ancestors but also saw them represented symbolically before their very eyes.

The public exhibition of artifacts from the town's past also served to put the lessons of history in tangible form as well as authenticate the historical account presented in the oration. Civic officials called upon local families to loan heirlooms to a community relic display, housed in a public building or historic house, and cataloged the objects in souvenir programs to demonstrate both the quality and the quantity of local history. These displays could be quite eclectic. An exhibition in conjunction with the 1888 centennial celebration in Marietta, Ohio, displayed, alongside local artifacts such as a one-hundred-year-old rolling pin, a "piece" of Plymouth Rock, an Indian necklace, a fragment of a battle flag from Bull Run, and a model of a Honolulu surf boat.[16] Schuylerville's celebration of the centennial of Burgoyne's surrender in 1877 featured a "relic tent," erected between the two speakers' platforms, in which was displayed a sword alleged to have once belonged to Burgoyne. The sword bridged the century between the Revolutionary generation and that of the present. Also given honored places in the Schuylerville ceremonies were the three oldest men of the town, identified as former neighbors of General Philip Schuyler, one of the heroes of the battle. President-of-the-day Charles S. Lester introduced the trio to the crowd in much the same role assigned to Burgoyne's sword—as a "connecting link between present and past."[17]

While the public display of relics helped civic officials make tangible the connection between the town's past and present, the creation of a monument as part of a civic celebration made tangible the link between its present and future. Building a monument testified to future generations the present residents' dedication to the timeless moral principles they associated with generations past. One form of monument was the official celebration souvenir program book, which usually included the order of the day, the text of the day's speeches, and the names of the organizations, if not of each individual, participating in the event.

A ceremonial tree, stone tablet, statue, or shaft formed a second, more imposing form of civic monument to the community's future. The Schuylerville, New York, monument rose in the form of a shaft replete with Gothic features found in church architecture of the period. It contained niches on all four sides for bronze busts representing each of the four heroes of the Saratoga campaign—Philip Schuyler, Horatio Gates, Daniel Morgan, and Benedict Arnold—but the monument's planners intentionally left Arnold's niche empty as a warning against treachery for future generations. The monument's cornerstone contained a time capsule crammed with contemporary newspapers, a Bible, an American flag, and a wide array of public documents such as the annual report for 1876 of the New York Canal Commission. The stone monument, like the souvenir book, served as permanent evidence of the celebration and marked the attempt by those celebrating to enter themselves into the history they commemorated.[18]

The principal opportunity for local residents to participate in the historical ceremony occurred in the procession to the speaker's stand for the oratorical exercises. Demonstrating tangibly the virtues of organizational loyalty, townspeople marched as members of groups rather than as individuals. By the late nineteenth century, the multiplicity of civic, industrial, commercial, military, fraternal, religious, ethnic, and labor organizations present in even medium-sized towns made these processions quite lengthy.[19] Civic officials, clergy, soldiers, municipal employees, volunteer firemen, employees from local businesses, veterans, and members of fraternal organizations all marched in their finest raiment, often accompanied by their gleaming brass band and a carriage or placard trumpeting their group's identity and contributions to the community at large.[20] Twenty-three separate divisions marched in a civic and industrial procession in Philadelphia to commemorate the centennial of the U.S. Constitution in 1887, including a local assembly of the Knights of Labor, various ethnic beneficiary societies, the Kensington baseball club, and the Pennsylvania Society for the Prevention of Cruelty to Animals. Groups associated their particular traditions with a larger public one by carrying physical remnants of their past in the town-wide procession. In Philadelphia in 1887, members of the Carpenters Company displayed the same Grand Federal Edifice float that their members had pulled through the streets a century before to commemorate the ratification of the Constitution. Some Schuylerville veterans' organizations in 1877 marched in Revolutionary period uniforms. In the centennial procession of Morgantown, West Virginia, in 1885, a contingent of local residents dressed in "ancient costumes" joined a caravan of "ancient vehicles," mostly farm implements and wagons, and a brigade of citizens over seventy years old.[21]

Groups in the civic historical procession further identified themselves with local and national history by sponsoring wagons laden with tableaux vivants. Tableaux vivants were a popular form of parlor entertainment in which costumed figures frozen in place imitated famous scenes from painting, sculpture, literature, and history. By the centennial in 1876, Benjamin West's *Penn's Treaty With the Indians* and

This 9' × 12' banner painted by C. V. Atkinson was carried at the front of the Civic and Industrial Procession in Philadelphia in September 1887 marking the centennial of the U.S. Constitution. The female figure at the center of the banner integrates scenes of past and present. (Hampton L. Carson, History of the Celebration of the 100th Anniversary of the Promulgation of the Constitution of the United States *[Philadelphia: J. B. Lippincott, 1889], 2:frontispiece)*

The Death of General Wolfe, John Trumbull's series of paintings depicting the American Revolution, including *The Declaration of Independence*, Asher B. Durand's *Capture of Major Andre*, John Chapman's *The Baptism of Pocahontas*, Emanuel Leutze's *Washington Crossing the Delaware*, and Archibald Willard's *Spirit of '76* were already among the popular national icons reproduced in magazines and school history texts. Numerous guidebooks emerged in the 1870s and 1880s recommending local residents present these patriotic and historical scenes, along with historical genre scenes such as "The Puritans on the Way to Church," "Off to the War," "Tenting Tonight," and "Soldiers Return," as tableaux on local holidays.[22]

The guidebooks also recommended allegorical tableaux vivants to represent abstract virtues of the state or nation. Such tableaux offered women, who generally were excluded from the line of march, their major opportunity to appear in public celebrations, seen but not heard as they adorned floats pulled by their fathers, husbands, sons, and brothers. J. A. Hill's suggested "Grand National Tableau" for July Fourth consisted of women draped in classical garb representing "Columbia," "Legislative Power," "Executive Power," "Judicial Power," "The Army," "The Navy," and "The Thirteen Original States," along with color-bearers positioned amid patriotic slogans and a general outline of the U.S. Capitol. One float in Des Moines, Iowa's procession on July Fourth 1876, featured women posed as "Columbia" and the "Goddess Liberty" surrounded by thirteen young girls representing the original colonies. Like the giant *Liberty* statue dedicated in New York Harbor in 1886, the female figure "Liberty" in allegorical tableaux appeared in conservative guise, representing a stable equilibrium of classes and interests, rather than in the more Revolutionary incarnation displayed earlier in American history.[23]

Reunions of former residents, such as an Old Home Week, also became a part of the public holiday celebration's tangible expression of the nature of the community and its history. Civic officials touted each familiar face returning home for the holiday as a reminder of the continuity between the town of the past and the present, and as a demonstration of the strength of local ties even in the midst of the period's tremendous geographic mobility. While Senator Willey at Morgantown's centennial in 1885 warned his audience of the difficulty of maintaining "family-like" social relations once the newly completed railroad diminished the town's relative isolation, the centennial committee pointed proudly to throngs of successful far-flung former residents returning by train to participate in the centennial festivities, or sending their greetings by telegraph, as proof that the bonds of local community lasted a lifetime.[24]

*Programs of tableaux vivants intertwined classical and allegorical figures
with those from American history. Note in this poster from 1900 the "Farewell," "Writing Home," and "Return" tableaux of the Civil War at lower
right. (Library of Congress)*

The historical oration and accompanying decorations, relic displays, monument dedications, civic and industrial processions, and
reunions constituted the usual program for the public commemoration of history in the late nineteenth century. Civic officials piled
historical artifact, narrative, and image upon image in antiquarian
detail to bring the full weight of tradition to bear upon their neighbors, discharging what they felt was their sacred duty both to teach
their beliefs and values to the public and to explain the present residents' unique place in a succession of past and future residents who
together constituted the historical community. John Lewis, the speaker
at the bicentennial observance in Suffield, Connecticut, proclaimed,
"This is not therefore a mere holiday on which we have met to pass the
time in idle enjoyment, but an occasion of deep significance, based on
the realities of the past and reaching forward to modify the results of
the future, developing influences that should warm and inspire every
heart, and involving possibilities of good whose effects may be felt to
the end of time."[25]

In this 1885 tableau vivant by Naegli Studios of New York City, women in body stockings impersonate "Canymede Offering the Cup to Venus." (Library of Congress)

Despite Lewis's claim, the influences developed by these public commemorative ceremonies are difficult to determine. Even the best efforts of civic officials to construct a coherent picture of the town and its history out of diverse elements of oratory, allegory, relic, and ritual left room for misunderstanding. By the late nineteenth century, the holiday historical oration was not only a commonplace, but also a prime target for parody. Contemporary cartoonists depicted the audience listening to the succession of speakers' oratory with anything but rapt attention. Even a population steeped in fraternal ritual and allegory could become puzzled by the esoteric symbolism of tableaux vivants passing by or lose sight of how each element of the celebration contributed to the whole. Local residents could enjoy the curiosities on display in the relic tent, speculating as to their authenticity, without understanding or endorsing the particular patriotic and religious meaning civic officials sought to attach to the relics by setting them within the civil-religious context of the celebration program as a whole.[26]

Moreover, residents participated in the celebrations for many more reasons than simply the altruistic and patriotic ones attributed to them by the civic leaders who wrote the official histories of the local celebrations for posterity. A family's contribution of relics to the community

*The 250th anniversary of the founding of Taunton, Massachusetts, in 1889
brought the sons and daughters of the town back to watch a grand procession
featuring seven historical tableaux as well as floats sponsored by local industries. On this float molders from the Weir Stove Company demonstrate their
craft. (Collections of the Old Colony Historical Society, Taunton)*

display announced its wealth and social position. Similarly, the marching bands in holiday processions competed not merely to express their
civic loyalty, but often for more tangible rewards—at Morgantown in
1885, $175 in cash prizes.[27] Certainly former residents' reasons for
taking advantage of a rare holiday from work to return and visit local
family and friends existed independently from the overarching community significance civic officials assigned to the activity.

The multiplicity of meanings and motives present in public historical ceremonies becomes especially evident upon closer examination of
the giant holiday processions. What public officials viewed as demonstrations of civic unity, local residents saw as opportunities to display
their particular group identities and cultural preferences. In the civic
and industrial procession accompanying Philadelphia's celebration of
the centennial of the U.S. Constitution in 1887, many workers chose
to march in public not under the banners of their employers but
rather under the banners of newly formed trade unions, including the
Knights of Labor. Their patriotic banners replete with slogans such as

Clay Local Assembly No. 6789, Knights of Labor (Brickmakers). Four hundred men wearing blue and white march arm in arm through downtown Philadelphia as part of the Civic and Industrial Procession commemorating the centennial of the U.S. Constitution in September 1887. The local had gone public only a year before. Such demonstrations of workers identifying themselves with their union contrasted with other laborers in the same procession who marched behind their employers or with their particular ethnic organization. (Courtesy of Atwater Kent Museum, Philadelphia)

"In Union there is Strength" expressed a working-class view of American politics and the importance of upholding bonds of mutual obligation. The Journeyman Bricklayers Protective Association joined the procession not only to express their civic loyalty but also to have the public read their lengthy banner: "Honest Labor, properly organized, with arbitration as a basis for the adjustment of all grievances, is sure to command the respect and confidence of the community."[28]

Even when civic officials handpicked the groups that would be allowed to march in the public procession—in effect, determining which groups would appear as a part of the public and which would not—they had little influence over how each constituent group would participate. In 1882, Italian-American organizations invited to march in a procession celebrating the bicentennial of William Penn's arrival in Philadelphia carried a float with a representation of their own national hero, Christopher Columbus. Five years later, organizers of Philadelphia's civic and industrial procession accompanying the Constitution centennial celebration invited local black residents to ride on a series of three floats depicting black progress from slavery to freedom. While several black Philadelphians appeared on the last float displaying the achievements of contemporary black artisans, none would ride on the float that depicted blacks as slaves—even when frustrated celebration organizers offered to pay them to do so.[29]

Analysis of the entire range of historical imagery and commemorative activities on holidays, rather than only the themes expressed in the historical oration, reveals the use of history and public ritual to promote a broadly conceived but loosely defined civic ideal. Despite attempts to provide a single overarching meaning of the day's events from the speaker's platform, a variety of different formulations of the community and its traditions appeared throughout the day, displayed by the diverse groups participating. True, not every group or viewpoint had the same access to public expression. The prestige of holiday orators as respected interpreters of the public tradition, combined with the power of program committees to exclude dissent, crowded out or obscured those expressions deemed at most extreme variance from the prevailing one.[30] Nevertheless, even those groups unable to articulate a coherent alternative remained free to ignore the official version of the public history, or to interpret its component imagery in ways that made sense to them based on their particular backgrounds. While civic officials attempted to teach the mass of local residents civic virtue and piety by structuring public ceremonies in ways that called for a collective affirmation of their overarching definition of the public and its history, local residents used the same ceremonies to express their own particular ethnic, neighborhood, and occupational identities and traditions.

The expression of alternative traditions and cultural preferences on holidays was especially evident in the recreational activities and entertainment that followed the official commemorative ceremonies. For most Americans in the late nineteenth century, holiday celebrations provided time for leisure and amusement and a momentary release from the weight of the past, rather than for solemn rededication to the moral principles attributed to the Founding Fathers. Observers at the Schuylerville commemoration in 1877 noted that in the aftermath of the official ceremonies, "Broad Street took the appearance of Broadway" with gaily colored lanterns, thronging people, and the cries of street vendors. After the historical procession and orations marking the bicentennial of New Castle, New Hampshire, in 1893, the assembly retired to lunch, followed by an afternoon of track and field, bicycle, and boat races, and an evening band concert and fireworks. Residents of Hingham, Massachusetts, topped off their 250th anniversary celebration in 1885 with a town-wide dance. These recreational and entertainment elements grew especially prominent in large cities, where by the end of the century commemorative programs had expanded from a single day into an entire celebration week crammed with officially sponsored popular entertainments as well as historical ritual.[31]

Earlier in the nineteenth century, holiday recreation and entertainment had centered around individual neighborhoods, with urban residents rarely celebrating the same event together at the same place and time. Ethnic, fraternal, and labor organizations sponsored separate festivities for their members on the most commonly celebrated holidays: Christmas, New Year's, and July Fourth. Those members of elite groups such as the Society of the Cincinnati who did not leave town on July Fourth to spend the summer holiday in the country returned after official public ceremonies to private banquets, hoisting round after round of toasts in honor of their ancestors, the Founding Fathers. Working-class residents, enjoying probably their only regularly scheduled holiday all summer, also flocked to a wide variety of privately sponsored amusements. The Ancient Order of Hibernians in Worcester, Massachusetts, held boisterous picnics and athletic contests, replete with boxing, gambling, and a greased pig. Other Irish in Worcester, assuming a more respectable demeanor, attended picnics sponsored by temperance societies. In Philadelphia and Pittsburgh, similar distinctions appeared between rough and respectable holiday amusements, with the rough often taking precedence among residents for whom the holiday primarily meant milling around in the streets in drunken revelry detonating pistol shots and fireworks.[32] It was these latter aspects of holiday behavior at mid-century that prompted genteel publications to complain about the ruckus. In 1857 the *North American Review* decried Independence Day as a "nuisance," explaining: "The municipal authorities provide for it as for a lawless saturnalia; the fire departments dread its approach, as indicative of conflagrations; physicians, as hazardous to such unfortunate patients as cannot be removed into the country; quiet citizens, as insufferable from incessant detonations; the prudent, as fraught with reckless tomfoolery; and the respectable, as desecrated by rowdyism."[33] Cartoonists of the Civil War era depicted the day as rife with noisy disruption.

By the closing decades of the nineteenth century, in part in response to these direct complaints, in part as a result of municipal govern-

The Fourth of July on Boston Common. Winslow Homer's cartoon depicting July Fourth havoc appeared on the cover of Ballou's Pictorial, *July 9, 1859. (Library of Congress)*

ment's capacity to assume greater responsibility for the public conduct of all its citizens, city officials increasingly sought to bring neighborhood expressions of holiday exuberance under central control. They required parade permits, assigned new police forces to maintain order, and passed and enforced proclamations banning the private detonations of fireworks.

But in the process of expanding municipal control of holiday celebrations, city officials found themselves sponsoring a multiplicity of entertainments favored by their working-class constituents. Centrally planned amusements offered public officials a way of maintaining both public order and their political popularity. Rather than underwriting merely the historical oration and ceremony, leaving the amusement features to the neighborhoods, city government in the last decades of the nineteenth century assumed a prominent role in staging the popular carnival processions, fireworks, balloon ascensions, picnics, dances, bicycle races, and athletic contests. The city of Boston added bicycle races to its official July Fourth program in 1889. Philadelphia city councils in the 1890s organized municipal fireworks displays at several locations throughout the city as a substitute for neighborhood festivities. Pittsburgh's Department of Public Works hired a wide range of professional entertainers for its July Fourth ceremonies in Schenley Park beginning in the late 1880s. Municipal governments incorporated respectable versions of many plebeian holiday pursuits into their official programs, which grew larger and more spectacular in the effort to cater to a more diverse crowd and provide something for everyone. Large civic holiday extravaganzas made for good business, good fun, and good politics.[34]

Of all the new municipally sponsored entertainments, most spectacular were the carnival parades. Carnival parades, like many other civic holiday amusements, had their origins in various neighborhood bands and private clubs of the early nineteenth century. Mardi Gras parades in Memphis, Mobile, and New Orleans date from antebellum times, though the New Orleans Lenten carnival did not crown its first "Rex" until 1872 nor include mounted floats until 1877. Philadelphia's burlesque New Year's processions also date from the early 1800s, though the first official permit, suggesting official sanction, was issued in 1887. In the next decade, lured downtown with $5,000 in prize money, the rowdy back-street festival became an official city function—the New Year's Mummers Parade. Beginning in 1881, Baltimore augmented the annual veterans' procession commemorating the Battle of North Point with an annual carnival parade modeled on New Orleans' Mardi Gras. By 1900, carnival parades staged with the active cooperation if not direct sponsorship of city officials had become the main attraction of annual fall carnivals in St. Louis, Cincinnati, and Louisville. These carnival parades differed from civic and industrial processions in that they displayed only a few secret societies, such as Mardi Gras' Mistick Krewe of Comus, St. Louis' Mystic Order of the Veiled Prophets of the Enchanted Realm, or Philadelphia's shooters' clubs, rather than a vast array of local groups led by civic officials representing the entire community. Local residents were invited to march in the historical procession but watched the carnival parade.[35]

Just as local historical ceremonies borrowed elements from the church to inspire the community's reverence, public carnival parades borrowed elements from the commercial stage to pique a communal sense of whimsy. Carnival imagery was especially kin to the "spectacular drama"—a series of spectacular and fantastic tableaux displayed in commercial theaters. A decade after P. T. Barnum installed the "Pasha of Egypt" in New York City's Roman Hippodrome as part of his extravaganza *The Congress of Nations*, Mardi Gras in New Orleans transported its spectators to "The Arabian Nights." The fairies and forest nymphs that appeared on stage in popular theater productions such as Julia Holmes Smith's *The Butterflies' Ball* (1878) also garnished the "Fairyland" floats in St. Louis (1883) and New Orleans (1895) street celebrations. Mardi Gras' "Triumph of Epicurus," in which eighty-five figures marched through the streets of New Orleans dressed as a complete seven-course banquet, impersonating silverware, plates, and food, offered the same kind of feast for the eye as Frank Pease's indoor stage production *The Queen of Death*, which served a "Grand Ballet of Confections" featuring a "pas de bon bons." (The "Indian Ballet" in Pease's *Niagara Falls* featured a "pas de wampum.") Exotic characters from popular spectacles of the late nineteenth century such as Pease's *Ali Hassan*, Henry J. Pain's *Last Days of Pompeii*, or John Rettig's *Montezuma and the Conquest of Mexico* had little trouble leaping from indoor stage to outdoor street parade— especially since the same professional artists created the sets, floats, and costumes for both forms of amusement.[36]

Although less common than oriental and classical exotica, images from local and national history also crept into spectacular theater and carnival street processions. A nighttime King Carnival Procession in New York City in 1877 followed floats depicting "Fallstaff and His Merrie Friends" with tableaux of the Boston Tea Party, Washington and Lafayette at Valley Forge, and the Battle of New Orleans, as well as a "Reconciliation" tableau depicting Confederate and Union soldiers shaking hands, surrounded by thirteen young women in Greek gowns. St. Louis' Veiled Prophets chose "Scenes from American History" as the subject of their fall procession in 1886. Adam Forepaugh's circus in 1893 brought nine scenes of the American Revolution to its wide-eyed customers. The same year, the Auditorium Theatre in Chicago produced Imre Kiralfy's *America* in honor of the World's Columbian Exposition. *America*, like Kiralfy's previous popular extravaganzas *Nero and the Destruction of Rome* and *The Fall of Babylon*, featured spectacular scenery, special effects, and dances, as well as seventeen vivid historical tableaux vivants spanning the four centuries from Columbus's triumphant return to Barcelona to a present-day "Ballet of American Inventions" featuring modern conveniences such as Edison's electric light. These displays capitalized on Americans' growing interest in both history and spectacle in the late nineteenth century and offered audiences new standards for judging the historical tableaux they produced in their own local holiday processions.[37]

Even as historical imagery appeared on the commercial stage, carnival imagery was present in towns on days set aside for celebrations of local and national history. Every April 19 in Lexington, Massachusetts, the historical oration and procession commemorating the famous battle was accompanied by a parade of grotesquely disguised "Anticks and Horribles," a burlesque of the local Ancient and Honorable Artillery Company.[38] On July 4, 1876, Des Moines, Iowa, witnessed "a New Orleans Mardi Gras" with nearly seven hundred "fantastics" masquerading as devils and other whimsical characters. Similar "calithumpian bands" in bizarre costume joined in a torchlight parade the night

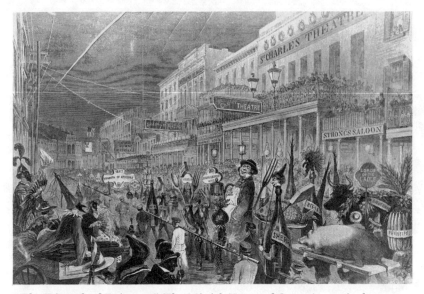

"The Triumph of Epicurus." The Mistick Krewe of Comus's carnival proces-
sion in New Orleans' Mardi Gras, 1867. The eighty-five members march in
paper-mache costumes disguised as the elements of a seven-course dinner.
(Frank Leslie's Illustrated Newspaper, *April 6, 1867; Historical New*
Orleans Collection, Museum/Research Center, acc. no. 1974.74.5)

before in Philadelphia.[39] In contrast to these amateur expressions of
carnival spirit, in October 1882, as a part of the week-long festivities
in Philadelphia marking the bicentennial of Pennsylvania's founding,
the Bicentennial Association of Pennsylvania used a mix of public
and private money to hire a troupe of professional actors to reenact
the landing of William Penn, and to import two sets of elaborate
floats from that year's New Orleans' Mardi Gras depicting "Illustrious
Women Rulers from World History" and "The Ramayana: Ancient
Hindu Epic of the East." The floats joined ten tableaux vivants from
Pennsylvania history in an evening street procession. The Special
Events Division of the Chicago World's Columbian Exposition aug-
mented its July Fourth ceremonies in 1893 with a "Wild East Show"
—a noon cavalcade of exotically garbed Bedouins, Turks, Egyptians,
Sudanese, Chinese, Dahomeyans, North American Indians, and jug-
glers from the Midway parading through the White City. That eve-
ning, the fair unveiled a giant replica of Niagara Falls in fireworks.
Three months later, for Chicago Day, the day set aside to honor
Chicago history, the fair illuminated in fireworks a four-panel, four-
teen-thousand-square-foot representation of "The Burning of Chi-

*Posters advertise a series of tableaux as part of the Adam Forepaugh circus,
1893. Such tableaux were based heavily on familiar paintings such as Emanuel Leutze's* Washington Crossing the Delaware. *(Circus World Museum,
Baraboo, Wisconsin)*

Barnum and Bailey Circus toured with Kiralfy's spectacle in 1891; two years later in Chicago, Kiralfy produced a stage version that ran concurrently with the World's Columbian Exposition. (Library of Congress)

cago"; in this sequence, the audience watched (1) a cow (2) kick over a lantern (3) starting a tremendous fire, leaving (4) Chicago in ruins.[40]

Those in the late nineteenth century who felt most responsible for preserving and transmitting patriotic ideals and moral principles in public welcomed civic officials' efforts to bring the dangerous, disorderly elements of holiday celebrations under more central control. But they worried that the growing commercialization of civic festivities and the concomitant infusion of carnival atmosphere were overwhelming the serious historical meaning of the occasions they set out to commemorate. The first families of Lexington, Massachusetts, complained that the hucksters who poured into town every April 19 were transforming the commemoration of the battle anniversary into a county fair, while attendance at the Historical Society's exercises plummeted. The *Dial* grumbled in 1893 that the periodic invasion of Midway characters into the Chicago Exposition's White City threat-

This band in women's dress and blackface won first prize in the parade of "Antiques and Horribles" accompanying the 250th anniversary of the founding of Taunton, Massachusetts, in 1889. (Collections of the Old Colony Society, Taunton)

ened to "barnumise the fair," observing that "amusement of the cheap and even vulgar sort is being substituted for education."[41]

The guardians of tradition concerned with the proper conduct of civic holiday celebrations came primarily from the ranks of the economic, educational, and hereditary elite. They stood apart from the mass of their fellow citizens not only because of their wealth, educational attainment, and family status, but also because they held positions of leadership in local and national cultural institutions. From these positions they spoke for genteel culture, voicing a shared set of concerns about American society and presuming responsibility as cultural leaders for its future. To these genteel writers, public celebrations of holidays offered yet one more example of the nation's prosaic, provincial cultural attainments and its consequent disregard for uplifting aesthetic and moral standards.[42]

Voices for genteel culture worried that different ethnic, class, and regional backgrounds undermined the extent to which local residents shared the values customarily trumpeted from the speaker's platform on holidays. The furious pace with which Americans moved from town to town, the beginnings of what threatened to become a flood of largely non-English-speaking immigrants, the rapid rise of explicitly working-class organizations such as the Knights of Labor, the explosion of vulgar commercial amusements which pandered to the lowest common denominator of mass taste, not cultivated judgment, seemed only to underscore the disintegration of a responsibly led common civic culture. Some members of the hereditary elite, despairing of public influence, suffered crises of faith, grew increasingly self-absorbed, and ultimately withdrew from public life in the presence of mass-based commercial amusements. Others, however, sought to reassert their public presence by trying to reshape public cultural forms and institutions. Like public museums and libraries, civic historical celebrations became an arena in which genteel intellectuals organized in public at the end of the nineteenth century to embrace a larger audience and reassert themes central to their beliefs and values and identity.[43]

Genteel intellectuals established new patriotic and hereditary societies to uphold proper reverence for history in their towns and across the nation. National organizations such as the Daughters of the American Revolution (DAR), Sons of the American Revolution, and Society of Colonial Dames of America launched campaigns for flags on public buildings, for legislation to create and enforce public observance of Flag Day, and for patriotic essay contests in public schools.[44] They also called upon their members to remain in town on holidays and take a more active role in the planning and staging of public celebrations. New organizations founded to encourage historic preservation, such as the American Scenic and Historic Preservation Society, staged elaborate, well-publicized dedication ceremonies at their historic sites and held annual commemorations to keep the sites' significance before the public. The Lexington Historical Society first assumed direct supervision of the April 19 battle commemoration in 1886. The Rhode Island Society of the Cincinnati, which had previously marked July Fourth with only a private dinner, held public exercises for the first time in 1895. Philadelphia's Society of the War of 1812 first assumed responsibility for arranging the July Fourth program at Independence Hall in 1896. While still not controlling the large civic holiday festivals, the hereditary and educational elite became much more involved in trying to influence their form and content, to foment "a renaissance of patriotism."[45]

Genteel intellectuals viewed public holiday celebrations as important opportunities not only to disseminate patriotism and morality but also to spread art and culture. They felt that the ways Americans usually marked their important civic occasions seemed to support European critics' barbs about the inherent drabness of American civilization—that, in the words of Matthew Arnold, their civilization just was not "interesting."[46] As early as 1857 the *North American Review*, surveying the state of the nation's holiday celebrations, lamented that, although Americans proved facile in military display and oratory, they suffered from a "national inadequacy of expression" when it came to the "language of Art." "Were a symphony as readily composed in America as an oration [and] tableaux, costumes, and processions as artistically invented here as in France . . . it would no longer be requisite to resort exclusively to drums, fifes, powder, substantial viands, and speechifying to give utterance to common sentiments." Though not wanting a civic celebration to degenerate into a "noisy carnival," the *Review* complained that America's drab "lifeless parades" and "lack of recreative zest" were symptoms of its prosaic culture.[47]

Instead of relying on commercial carnival producers, argued the genteel intellectuals, civic officials planning public festivals should consult expert historians and fine artists to ensure both the accuracy and the beauty of costumes, banners, and parade floats. Assuming that the arrangement of groups and classes in civic processions was a question of aesthetics rather than politics, Barr Ferree explained in the *Century* magazine that a civic celebration was above all "a work of art." "The moving figures in the hands of a parade designer becomes the pigment with which his picture is prepared." He described the efforts of the National Society of Mural Painters to persuade the homeowners along Fifth Avenue in New York City to adopt a uniform color scheme in their decorations for a parade honoring Admiral Dewey in 1898. Like those guardians of culture who founded art museums and symphony orchestras in the late nineteenth century, the patriotic and hereditary societies believed that fine "Art" represented pure idealism and could thus help counteract the materialism corroding American society. The American Scenic and Historic Preservation Society viewed public displays of art and history as having similar objectives. Its pamphlet stated: "The ASHPS is the first society in this country to merge Art and Historical Culture in one organization, thereby imparting an aesthetic interest to Historical work and making History, in turn, the handmaiden of Art." The patriotic ideals of history set in the elevating medium of art would merge into a conservative and uplifting force to preserve and transmit genteel values.[48]

That the public celebration exhibit art-in-motion was crucial to those who would reform civic holiday festivities. They felt that artistic civic celebrations would awaken Americans' ability to express themselves through graceful body movement as well as their dormant sense of color. Genteel families sought to improve their kinesthetic awareness by enrolling their daughters in the rhythmic training of Delsartism—a system of "harmonic gymnastics." The Delsarte system, as it appeared in college physical education courses, in "Schools of Expression" as part of dance instruction, and in manuals for holiday entertainments and tableaux vivants, called for smooth motions between dramatic poses.[49] Genteel reformers insisted that disciplined physical activity on holidays, whether men marching in formation or women gliding confidently between artistic poses in tableaux, could demonstrate tangibly the beauty and vigor of American traditions.

Making civic celebrations more artistic, colorful, and lively would not only improve the moral, aesthetic, and patriotic qualities of mass holiday spectacles, but also bolster the genteel elite's confidence in the vitality and picturesqueness of their own Anglo-American Protestant history and customs in the presence of the more lively, if less morally sturdy, European popular festivals and entertainments. While championing their Founding Fathers' heritage of piety, idealism, and hard work as the source of America's greatness, the genteel intellectuals also admitted the sobering effect of that heritage on the nation's appreciation of leisure pursuits. The *North American Review* observed that the Puritans, though "morally important," were "dry and unpicturesque." The *Andover Review* added that the rigors of settling a continent had left Americans over the past two centuries little opportunity to cultivate their artistic and playful sides.[50]

Still others blamed modern industrialism, though an integral part of American progress, for further diminishing the capacity to create and enjoy colorful, lively holiday celebrations. Though finding themselves on speakers' platforms trumpeting the official creed linking moral with technological progress, they voiced doubts elsewhere about the troubling by-products of modern industrialism—the general disengagement, emotional flatness, and passivity of the population. One writer warned of the gradual "extinction of leisure" as America's hard-driving industrial system extended its pounding rhythms beyond the workplace. Whereas past generations had resented the loss of leisure that accompanied industrialism, he noted in the *Forum* in 1889, present ones "for the most part have ceased to complain, and drag on in their accustomed places as cogs or cranks in the industrial machine as best as they may." Frederick Law Olmsted complained that visitors to the Chicago World's Fair in 1893 seemed "too business-like, common, dull, anxious, and careworn." Identifying their own drab heritage and feelings of spiritual malaise with those of the nation, the genteel reformers increasingly believed that it was just as important for them to restore to America a sense of beauty and gusto—stunted by dour Puritan origins then sapped by the industrial regimen—as it was to prevent their conception of public culture from being overwhelmed by rowdyism and commercialism. Public commemorations of history offered opportunities to revitalize the aesthetic and emotional basis of American civilization while handing down the moral principles attributed to past generations.[51]

The genteel intellectuals looked back in time beyond their Puritan forebears to Medieval and Renaissance Europe for a tradition of lively, artistic, noncommercial civic celebrations lacking in modern industrial America. Their fascination reflected a larger "American Renaissance" at the turn of the twentieth century. Architects and city planners, mural painters and sculptors, playwrights and novelists tapped Medieval and Renaissance Europe for traditions that would enrich what they felt were the thin artistic currents of the New World. Images of men and especially women in Medieval and neoclassical garb filled the paintings and sculptures in private mansions and public buildings. Works such as Edwin Austin Abbey's mural *The Quest of the Holy Grail* for the Boston Public Library and Charles F. McKim's imitation Florentine palace on Copley Square depicted closely knit communities that were inspired by high ideals and a simple, undoubting piety.[52] The Renaissance era held special appeal for those genteel intellectuals who, inspired by the writings of John Ruskin and William Morris, organized into local arts and crafts societies. The arts and crafts movement viewed Medieval and Renaissance Europe as the preindustrial golden age of handicrafts, a period uncluttered with modern machine production and the division of labor.[53] Yet most genteel artists and writers in America ignored the radical economic implications of imagery conceived by its creators such as Morris as both antimodern and anticapitalist. They looked to Renaissance Europe not to renounce the machine, but merely to appropriate the Old World's aesthetic richness and the metaphorical significance of its renaissance. They believed Renaissance Europe held out not only specific artistic traditions to emulate, but also, as an example of an era of robust pastimes and an overall blossoming in the arts, hope of redemption for drab, overworked industrial America. The Medieval and Renaissance imagery, originally created as a dissent from progress, appeared in public contexts that suggested it was evidence of progress—that the nation, heir to the best the Old World had to offer, was on the eve of its own glorious era in the arts.

The patriotic and hereditary elite hoped that local officials in the United States would model their civic celebrations especially on the colorful processions and lively folk dances of Elizabethan England—the land of their ancestors. "Pageantry and display were apparently as meat and drink to our forefathers," noted one writer in 1876. "The taste for barbaric splendor, as we somewhat lightly call it in our Puri-

The Castle of the Maidens, *a panel from* The Quest of the Holy Grail, *the mural series Edward Austin Abbey painted in the Delivery Room of the Boston Public Library between 1895 and 1901. Such representations of medieval and Renaissance tales projected a heritage of idealism and picturesqueness as a counter to drab modern American industrialism. (Photo by Richard Cheek for the Associates of the Boston Public Library)*

May Day 1900, Bryn Mawr College. Maypole dancing in Elizabethan costume flourished at women's colleges at the turn of the century. (Bryn Mawr College Archives)

tanical day, seems to have been the last thing to disappear before the breath of modern progress." Reviving Elizabethan holiday customs allowed the genteel elite to import the best from the European past without its decadence; to enjoy colorful, artistic alternatives to the drabness of modern industrialism and the wanton revelry of commercial amusements, while reinforcing social order and the nation's Anglo-American identity. To set an example for the rest of society, as well as to reinforce their own Anglo-American identity, genteel intellectuals revived Elizabethan customs of arts and play on the campuses of women's colleges such as Bryn Mawr, Vassar, and Wellesley and began incorporating them into their commemorations of local and national anniversaries as a complement to the Puritan heritage of idealism and piety that they customarily honored in their historical orations.[54]

The search for a picturesque Anglo-American past also led the genteel elite to explore the social and domestic life of Colonial America. The Colonial revival emerged in the "New England Kitchen" restaurants at international expositions; in the renewed interest in Colonial architecture, spinning wheels, and open hearths; in crafts organizations such as the Deerfield Society of Blue and White Needlework;

and in popular art, novels, and guidebooks such as Alice Morse Earle's *Home Life in Colonial Days* (1898). The romantic courtship of Miles Standish, the New England wedding, the splendor of the Colonial minuet all demonstrated that a heritage of art and play as well as piety and hard work had survived the Atlantic crossing. The new picturesque view of the American past could serve to supplement the Anglo-American heritage of Puritanism and hard work without undermining it, providing, in the words of one observer, "a delightful moss of legend and romance to cover the stony facts of our history."[55]

The patriotic and hereditary societies of the 1890s sponsored new commemorative programs which tempered the stern lessons of the past with scenes of color and romance. Figures from local and national history who had stalwartly stood watch over the community as decorations in past celebrations now gaily came to life, impersonated by their descendants in glamorous costume balls and evenings of tableaux vivants. Imagining themselves the resurgent American aristocracy, ersatz Founding Fathers and Mothers danced and played as well as performed heroic deeds in splendid settings previously reserved only for reenactments of scenes from European history. The Association for the Preservation of Virginia Antiquities reproduced for its members the court of James I for a costume ball in 1893. The Daughters of the American Revolution in Richmond, Virginia, held a ball in February 1896 where guests impersonated Generals Washington and Lafayette and their staffs. Both balls featured historic dances, such as the minuet, performed in period costumes.[56]

One evening of tableaux in 1896 received much publicity in the national patriotic and hereditary society journals. On this occasion, the Rhode Island chapters of the Daughters of the American Revolution and the Society of Colonial Dames of America cosponsored *Rhode Island Days of Auld Lang Syne* in the Providence Opera House. The societies hired Margaret MacLaren Eager, a creator of children's plays, to direct them in twelve scenes from the history of the state, and they asked Professor J. Franklin Jameson of Brown University to serve as "Historical Referee" to ascertain the accuracy of their representations. The twelve tableaux included a folk dance scene attributed to the English village from which Roger Williams left for America, Williams's founding of the Providence settlement and signing of the first deed of land with the Indians, the first commencement exercises at Rhode Island College (the antecedent of Brown University), the conspiracy to burn the *Gaspee*, a Colonial wedding, enlistment for the Revolution, a Colonial ball at which George Washington and Count Rochambeau were honored guests, a "Sewing Circle" of 1812, and three scenes of the Civil War (played by members of the local chapter of the Grand Army of the Republic [GAR]): departing Providence, in camp near Antietam, and returning home. A tableau of young women in Greek gowns arranged as the "Seal of Rhode Island" preceded the portrayal of Williams's founding of the colony, while a children's "Flag Dance" prefaced the Civil War scenes. Eager presented a similar program the following year in Plymouth, Massachusetts, under the title *Old Plymouth Days and Ways*—a "historical festival" featuring the courtship of Miles Standish and the wedding of John and Priscilla Alden; one scene depicted the children of Plymouth gaily picking wildflowers during their first spring in the New World. Such episodes displayed a history that was picturesque and domestic as well as heroic and idealistic, outlining a tradition of art and play as well as piety and hard work for their spectators to emulate.[57]

As the patriotic and hereditary societies broadened the scope of the traditions they recalled, women assumed a new role in their celebrations. Although the women of the Providence DAR still performed in the customary roles—adorning allegorical tableaux, tending hearth and home as men marched off to battle—in the creation of these historical programs it was the women of the DAR who put the men of the GAR through their paces on stage. Women in managing celebrations occasionally manipulated historical tableaux to assert a non-stereotypical image. The seventeen "living, speaking, moving" tableaux that constituted Mary A. Livermore and Cora Scott Pound's *National Pageant and Dramatic Events in the History of Connecticut* in Hartford in 1889 concluded with three scenes depicting "Women's Sphere, 1800" (a Colonial home full of parents, grandparents, and sixteen children), "Women's Crusade in 1873" (the Women's Christian Temperance Union invading a barroom), and "Women's Sphere, 1889" (a final procession of women in business, law, the ministry, and medicine across the stage to the strains of "The Battle Hymn of the Republic").[58] Although such a decidedly feminist emphasis seldom gained expression in official public historical ceremonies of the period, it demonstrates the alterations in historical imagery that were possible as women's roles expanded from primarily adorning floats and supervising refreshments to managing an important segment of the commemorative program.

As the patriotic societies increasingly highlighted the lively and the picturesque in their holiday celebrations, the events began to resemble superficially the popular commercial spectacular theatricals that the genteel reformers had attacked. Though the patriotic and hereditary societies perhaps would not have admitted it, in the search for forms of celebration that would have not only patriotic, educational, and artistic value but also, in the words of the Society of Colonial Dames of

America in 1895, "sufficient frivolity of a nineteenth century quality to appeal to the most youthful descendants of the founders of our country," they borrowed forms from the popular stage and adapted them to their own noncommercial, idealistic purposes.[59] The line between amusement and education that the genteel guardians of tradition sought to reestablish in civic celebrations continued to become blurred by the end of the century as official historical ceremonies incorporated more popular elements in an effort to draw a crowd, to exert more central control, and to maintain public order; as spectacular drama displayed scenes from American history as well as oriental exotica; and as genteel intellectuals adopted more lively visual and musical elements in their own commemorative activities.

Even though the genteel intellectuals who sought to reform the conduct of civic holiday celebrations began introducing new, more visually appealing forms for presenting history, the problem of reaching the general public with their message remained. How could they elicit the enthusiasm and cheers they imagined in Renaissance crowds without sacrificing the marrow of patriotic and moral exhortation customarily put forth in the historical oration? Despite the patriotic societies' assertion that they were staging celebrations for the public benefit, relatively few people could attend a fancy costume ball or appear in an evening of historical tableaux vivants. The genteel reformers' new, more artistic civic celebration still left most citizens spectators, not participants.

2 *The New Pageantry*

. . . .

Nothing is more likely to cement the
sympathies of our people and to accentuate our homogeneity than a cultivation
of pageants.
—*Century*, July 1910

Official program, Sherbourne Pageant, *1905. Parker's public celebration, widely cited by Americans as the first "modern" historical pageant, was full of antimodern imagery of knights in armor. (Brown University Library)*

As the patriotic and hereditary societies' campaign to persuade local municipal officials to reform the conduct of public holiday celebrations gathered momentum, its promoters heard about a new kind of civic celebration in England—the community historical pageant. In the late nineteenth century, the term "pageantry" in America had been associated primarily with the amusing carnival spectacles and burlesque parades that the patriotic societies had dismissed as of no civic value whatsoever. In 1876, the *Philadelphia Inquirer* contrasted the valuable educational features of the centennial celebration with "an idle pageant, as purposeless and profitless as All Fools' Day."[1] But the "pageants" Louis Napoleon Parker had been staging in Great Britain since 1905 seemed altogether different.

The inspiration for historical pageantry in Britain came from the arts and crafts movement. Even more than their American counterparts, members of the British arts and crafts societies of the late nineteenth century had been fascinated with revivals of Medieval and Renaissance imagery and handicrafts. Staging costumed historical revels and allegorical masques seemed a logical extension of these interests; indeed, John Ruskin had called for a revival of Renaissance "pageantry" in England in 1882. These revivals began as private affairs, offering the membership of arts and crafts societies evenings of entertainment and propaganda. In 1899, the Art Workers Guild of London presented the allegory *Beauty's Awakening*, in which symbolic figures representing the spirits of Renaissance town planning and Ruskin's "Seven Lamps of Architecture" triumphed over crass and tasteless modern industrial sprawl. In 1902, May Morris, the daughter of prominent writer-craftsman William Morris, addressed the London Society of Arts and Crafts on the subject of reviving Renaissance pageantry on a larger scale as a form of public holiday celebration.[2]

Three years later, Louis Napoleon Parker, a professional musician and dramatist, persuaded the residents of Sherbourne, England, to present a public celebration modeled on a Renaissance pageant. Parker's musical career had begun at the Sherbourne School, and he remained in touch with its headmaster, who invited Parker back to Sherbourne in 1905 to help stage a celebration in commemoration of the twelve hundredth anniversary of the town's founding. Parker devised a production that consisted of the dramatic reenactment of eleven episodes from the town's past, staged outdoors before the ruins of Sherbourne Castle. Herald trumpets announced a succession of episodes recalling the events, heroes, and pastimes of "merrie old England": St. Ealdhelm founding the local monastery in 705; the English battling to defeat the Danes in 845; the giant funeral procession in 860 on the death of Ethelbard and the accession of King Alfred; local residents ceremonially offering their produce to the Benedictine monks who assumed rule of the town in 998; William the

Conqueror declaring that the see would move to Sarcum in 1075; the laying of foundation stones for Sherbourne Castle in 1107; a quarrel between town and monastery in 1437, ending with a morris dance; the elaborate procession accompanying the founding of the local ale house in 1437; the expulsion of the monks in 1539; the procession in 1550 marking the founding of Sherbourne School; and a village Maypole dance honoring the visit of Sir Walter Raleigh in 1593. Parker's pageant concluded with a symbolic tableau in which the cast, local organizations, and delegates from neighboring towns paid homage to a female representing Sherbourne, who then led the entourage in a final march across the pageant field to the strains of "God Save the Queen" and a shower of roses.[3]

Parker described his Sherbourne pageant in explicitly antimodern terms, calling it a means to counter the "modernising [sic] spirit which destroys all loveliness and has no loveliness of its own to put in its place." Declaring the pageant "a school of Arts and Crafts," he insisted that "every article of whatever kind used in the performance must be invented, designed, and made in the town." A cast of six hundred local residents acted all of the pageant roles and made the scenery, costumes, and props. As well as the aesthetic benefits derived from the pageant's revival of handicrafts and colorful processions from the Medieval and Renaissance past, Parker touted historical pageantry's social aims as a "festival of brotherhood in which all distinctions of whatever kind were sunk in common effort." Historical pageants contributed "added brightness," "re-awakened civic pride," and "increased self-respect," and they would help bring village life in England "back to its old-time innocent gaiety." The Sherbourne pageant attracted a large audience, turning a profit, and the form soon caught on elsewhere in England. Parker created similar community dramatic productions for Warwick in 1906, Bury St. Edmunds in 1907, Dover in 1908, and York and Colchester in 1909.[4]

Parker's historical pageantry fascinated genteel intellectuals, artists, and members of patriotic and hereditary societies in the United States because it seemed to represent the culmination on a mass scale of their search for a more artistic, visually instructive way for the public to celebrate holidays. Pageantry promised to elicit popular interest without sacrificing artistic standards and the marrow of Anglo-American history so important for the transmission of proper values and ideals. Through vivid historical pageantry, the moral principles associated with the past could reach a wider audience. George Turnbull described the English historical pageant to his American readers in *World's Work* in 1907 as a "genuine folk-play" which taught history as it fostered "brotherly love" and "civic enthusiasm," and he recommended that the new form of civic celebration be tried in America.[5]

Sherbourne, England, and Sherbourne, Massachusetts. The finale of the Sherbourne pageant displayed the kinship between the town and its daughter town on the other side of the Atlantic, impersonated by Parker's daughter. The ruins of Sherbourne Castle in the background served as a symbol of continuity throughout the performance. (Brown University Library)

Court of Queen Elizabeth, Warwick pageant, 1906. Elizabeth I was far and away the most popular character in English historical pageantry. Pageant organizers depicted her reign as the last period of English history that was free of industrialism and social conflict. (Brown University Library)

Spurred on by the efforts of local historian Ellis Paxson Oberholtzer, Philadelphia was the first city in the United States to include a purportedly "English-style" historical pageant as part of a municipal celebration. Oberholtzer was born in West Chester, Pennsylvania, in 1868. His father John was a wealthy merchant and his mother, Sarah Louise Vickers was a writer active in several reform crusades, most prominently one to encourage thrift among children by establishing a system of savings banks in the public schools. She sent her son to private schools, however, and then to the University of Pennsylvania, where he remained for graduate study with historian John Bach MacMaster.

After receiving his Ph.D. in 1893, Oberholtzer worked for several Philadelphia periodicals while devoting most of his time to historical and political writing. Among his books were biographies of Robert Morris, Henry Clay, and Jay Cooke; a two-volume history of Philadelphia; a five-volume *History of the United States since the Civil War*; *Home Rule for Our American Cities*; and *The Referendum in America*. With fellow Philadelphia authors S. Weir Mitchell and Owen Wister, Oberholtzer joined the exclusive Franklin Inn Club, the base for his literary activities over the next three decades.[6]

In February 1908, Oberholtzer learned that Philadelphia's municipal government planned to commemorate the 225th anniversary of the city's founding with a week-long festival in October. To provide something for everyone, plans for celebrating "Founders' Week" included the customary assortment of events, each day featuring a different category of local organization. The planned festival week began with Church Day (Sunday), followed by a procession of soldiers and veterans on Military Day (Monday), public officials and employees on Municipal Day (Tuesday), local businesses and their employees on Industrial Day (Wednesday), and schoolchildren on Children's Day (Thursday), topped off by athletic contests on Saturday. Oberholtzer persuaded the secretary of the celebration's executive committee, George B. Hicks of the mayor's office, to add a Friday afternoon "Historical Pageant" procession to the program and to have the city foot the bill, which eventually totaled $60,000.[7]

Oberholtzer's procession displayed sixty-eight scenes from Philadelphia's past mounted on floats divided into seven "periods" from "Exploration and Settlement" through the "Civil War." Two-thirds of the episodes depicted events that occurred before 1781, including William Penn's treaty with the Indians, Betsy Ross sewing the flag, and Benjamin Franklin at the court of France—images already largely familiar to the public from decorations and banners at earlier patriotic celebrations. Pageant floats also reenacted scenes of past Philadelphians at play on festive occasions such as a street fair of 1740, the Meschianza tournament during the British occupation of 1778, First Lady Martha Washington's reception in 1794, and Lafayette's visit in 1824—the types of scenes common in elite costume balls of the period. The final floats depicted the development of the centrally administered modern city. Twenty-eight elaborately costumed high school boys marched beside a giant plaster figure of a Quakeress, symbolizing the consolidation of the twenty-eight formerly independent townships, districts, and boroughs of Philadelphia County into the city of Philadelphia in 1854. Following a float depicting the city's hosting of the Centennial Exposition of 1876, the procession ended with a symbolic float laden with young men and women draped in Greek gowns representing the role of the various arts, crafts, and sciences in remaking Philadelphia as the "City Beautiful." Oberholtzer described the last float as sounding a "prophetic note" and originally suggested that it include a plaster model of the proposed Benjamin Franklin Parkway and municipal art museum—elements of a controversial new city plan for downtown.[8] Though not in dramatic form, Oberholtzer claimed that his historical pageant followed Parker's example by enlisting Philadelphians in a single, comprehensive, illustrated presentation of their city's history,

Arrival of William Penn, Philadelphia historical pageant, 1908. Though not in dramatic form, the Founders' Week procession was billed as the first English-style historical pageant in America. (Philadelphia City Archives)

offering tangible examples of local community cohesion, moral fortitude, and artistic achievement.

The pageant, in fact, displayed a highly exclusive portrait of Philadelphia's history and population. Oberholtzer invited participating groups to demonstrate solely their identification with "the city" and not their particular occupational, district, or ethnic affiliation. Although Philadelphians customarily marched in historical processions exhibiting costumes, floats, and banners that trumpeted their particular group identity, Oberholtzer insisted that only official floats and costumes be allowed in his pageant. Violet Oakley, a muralist from the city's Germantown section, designed all of the floats in a single artistic style, while Guernsey Moore of the Philadelphia School of Industrial Art designed the leading characters' costumes, which he based on the historical costume collections of Howard Pyle, the prominent artist and illustrator from nearby Wilmington.[9] Unlike Parker's use of the pageant as a school of arts and crafts for local residents, Oberholtzer hired a commercial firm experienced in the celebration business to build the floats and supply the majority of the pageant costumes.

Benjamin Franklin at the court of France. Many of Philadelphia's hereditary elite put themselves on display in Oberholtzer's historical pageant. (Historical Society of Pennsylvania, Philadelphia)

Oberholtzer recruited groups and individuals to march in his procession and ride on his floats by personally contacting "qualified" participants—among them, members of prominent, long-settled Philadelphia families and those of the right ethnic background for the early settler floats. He assured one participant that the leading roles in the procession would go to people of "social position"—often the descendants of prominent citizens.[10] Although Philadelphia's first families were unaccustomed to marching in costume in a public street procession, Benjamin Franklin's great-grandson Henry W. Bache agreed to impersonate Franklin, and descendants of several other less well known first families eventually joined in. Oberholtzer claimed to follow Parker's pageant formula of sinking all social distinctions in a common effort, yet the social exclusivity in the lead roles made the pageant appear as little more than the hereditary elite projecting its triumphal return to the head of Philadelphia's social life, with the remainder of the city as audience.

The pageant director invited Philadelphians of Dutch, Swedish,

Welsh, German, Scotch-Irish, and English descent to play their ancestors, the early settlers of the city. But with the exception of blacks who
appeared in an Underground Railroad scene (Oberholtzer arranged
separate dressing facilities for them at the parade's point of origin),
the pageant failed to acknowledge any ethnic arrivals to Philadelphia
after the American Revolution. No Irish, Polish, or Italian organizations represented their nationality's contribution to the city's history—
though individual members of these groups may have marched in the
pageant with a unit of volunteer firemen or Civil War veterans.

Oberholtzer insisted that the public regard his historical extravaganza as patriotic and civic education, not entertainment, and refused
to permit the popular New Year's mummers' brigades to join the
parade in their usual exotic garb. Nor would he allow professional
entertainers to march in his pageant. He demanded that his performers should not be paid (beyond a free lunch at the start of the parade).
When the Canstatter Verein responded to his invitation to participate
with a list of German performers for hire, Oberholtzer complained
that the group "did not seem to appreciate the character of the procession. . . . Our procession is made up of a different class altogether."
White Cloud, proprietor of a shop that sold American Indian para-
phernalia, and Frederick "Chinese" Poole, theatrical agent for "The
Domain of the Dragon" in Philadelphia's Chinatown, met a similar
rebuff when they offered to rent to the historical pageant committee
authentic members of their respective ethnic constituencies for the
day. Rather than hire troupes of professional performers to fill out the
ranks of his pageant, in the manner of the Pennsylvania bicentennial
procession of 1882, Oberholtzer imported students from the Carlisle
Indian School for the Indian scenes, students from Temple University
and the University of Pennsylvania for the Colonial Philadelphia
scenes, and, when direct descendants of William Penn refused to play
their famous forebear, students from Haverford College to ride on
the "Penn's Treaty with the Indians" float.[11]

Carefully protecting his new form of celebration from any association with the usual assortment of commercial performers and carnival
entrepreneurs (except for the company that built his floats and rented
him costumes), Oberholtzer bristled at the discovery that the Founders' Week Executive Committee had included bandmaster Frederick
Phinney's musical spectacular *Philadelphia* in its program of official
celebration activities. Phinney's commercial production, appearing
each evening at Franklin Field, used professional actors and singers,
as well as costumes rented from a firm that had earlier failed in its
attempt to offer Oberholtzer a kickback for his patronage. Worse,
Phinney labeled his show a "pageant." Twenty operalike episodes

William Penn's treaty with the Indians. When descendants of famous personages declined to appear in the Founders' Week pageant, local college students, such as these from Haverford College, filled in. (Historical Society of Pennsylvania, Philadelphia)

traced the city's history from the first Indian settlement through the Revolution, then leapt to a five-episode finale depicting the Spanish-American War, as Sousa's "Stars and Stripes Forever" played in the background. Founders' Week General Secretary Hicks's explanation that similar spectacular musical dramas had proved to be crowd pleasers at other public festivals did little to assuage Oberholtzer's objections.[12]

Although Oberholtzer's Friday afternoon historical pageant received high praise from the press and drew a large crowd lining its route for four miles through central Philadelphia, prompting him to conclude that there was "much appreciation of the pageant from all classes of the people," many spectators probably viewed the street procession in much the same light as the bicentennial carnival procession in 1882 or the annual New Year's Mummers Parade—little more than another amusing feature of a diverse holiday program, with the costumed characters being prominent citizens rather than professional actors.[13] Even the city officials who funded Oberholtzer's show viewed it as complementing, not replacing, Phinney's popular historical entertainment. Appearing as part of a larger, week-long celebration, the historical pageant seemed less of a departure from the usual pattern of holiday fare than originally announced. This probably contributed to its popularity but, from the point of view of its planners, weakened its intended moral and aesthetic message.

Oberholtzer's experience demonstrated one way the patriotic and hereditary societies could incorporate historical pageantry into the pattern of municipal holiday activities, bringing the themes and images common in their evenings of tableaux vivants and costume balls before a larger audience. Genteel intellectuals extolled pageantry's ability to bolster the historical and artistic quality of large civic ceremonies, revitalizing the presentation of the proper version of history and definition of local community, customarily proclaimed in the historical oration, for an age of spectacle. Dramatic images from local and national history illustrated in colorful fashion the moral principles that genteel intellectuals believed bound residents together as a community through time and could guide their present behavior. This version of history also projected an overarching civic identity, modeled on an imagined deferential consensus and social hierarchy of the past, that the elite claimed could transcend neighborhood, class, and ethnic conflicts and differences.

But the genteel pageant producers' Anglocentric and hierarchical vision of society and culture limited their ability to mold opinion and behavior among a heterogeneous public oriented to a multiplicity of ethnic subcultures, or increasingly, to commercial mass entertainment. The failure of the educational and hereditary elite to elicit participation beyond their social and professional circles guaranteed that, despite their claims, their historical pageants would neither supersede the popular amusements that they felt diluted the significance of public holiday commemorations nor instill greater public appreciation for their particular version of local history and tradition.

The patriotic and hereditary elite and participants in the arts and crafts movement were not the only Americans interested in the promise of the new historical pageantry. Educators and social workers of the playground movement also considered this new form of civic holiday celebration peculiarly suited to advance their goals in public. Organized into national associations, the members of this second group to promote historical pageantry speeded its development and dissemination in cities and towns across America. In the course of appealing to civic officials to adopt historical pageantry on holidays, they transformed the genteel historical pageant form and made it their own.

Like the genteel intellectuals, educators and social workers saw the provision of wholesome leisure activities for the public as a crucial yet neglected aspect of modern life and blamed Puritanism and commercialism, as well as industrialism, for this neglect. John Dewey observed in 1902 that "recreation is the most overlooked and neglected of all ethical forces. Our whole Puritan tradition tends to make us slight this side of life, or even condemn it." Without adequate facilities for wholesome play, educators and social workers argued, the public's sole relief from the regimen of work lay in tawdry commercial amusements. Social workers complained that the ever-present saloons, the burlesque houses, and the new motion picture houses, which substituted "passive pleasure" for "active recreation," had an especially deleterious effect on children. Jane Addams warned in 1910, "To fail to provide for the recreation of youth is not only to deprive all of them of their natural form of expression, but is certain to subject some of them to the overwhelming temptation of illicit and soul-destroying pleasures." Echoing the charges of an earlier generation, the social workers sought to persuade government to regulate or close down what they regarded as dangerous leisure pursuits, while providing wholesome and uplifting ones in their place.[14]

But unlike the genteel intellectuals of the late nineteenth century who viewed recreation and play primarily in terms of its value as a relief from overwork—"the breathing space in the daily struggle for existence, without which no one of the combatants could long survive"—educators and social workers maintained that play could also make an essential contribution to education, emotional expression, social solidarity, and citizenship. Following the social and psychological theories of child development advanced by G. Stanley Hall and John Dewey, progressive educators believed that children expressed their innate curiosity, sociability, and imagination through playing together, learning about themselves, others, and the world around them. Charles Horton Cooley in 1909 declared the children's play group to be no less than one of the three "primary" groups, along with family and neighborhood, where "human nature comes into existence." Educators and social workers insisted that children "trained for life" through play and games, and that the quality of their play determined how well they developed the individual and cooperative skills necessary to become healthy, creative, productive adults.[15]

The play group, argued the educators and social workers, formed a model community in which children developed the attitudes necessary to become responsible citizens in mass society. Sociologist E. A. Ross of Stanford University warned in 1897 about the growing danger the "Mob Mind" posed to American democracy, as individual citizens, cut loose from the "old moorings of custom" and local social controls, felt increasingly anonymous and lacking in social responsibility and drifted with the latest mass "currents of opinion" rather than following the dictates of their individual consciences. Dr. Luther H. Gulick, a leader of the campaign to provide more opportunities for supervised recreation in neighborhood schools and playgrounds, held that children's successful development of the "ethical social self"—a sense of self-restraint and responsibility toward others—through playing together in groups could counter the tendency in modern mass society to rootlessness and "uncontrolled public action," which threatened the future of American democracy as the nation's citizens grew increasingly interdependent in the new century. Acting out of an optimism that they could rebuild American society from the play group up as well as out of a fear of the consequences of doing nothing, progressive educators and social workers sought to nurture loyalty to play group, to neighborhood, to town, to state, and to nation. They believed such ties would ultimately bolster citizens' awareness of their responsibilities as part of new larger-scale forms of social organization as well as their feelings of belonging to their particular local community.[16]

Since "the primary root of all educational activity is in the instinctive, impulsive attitudes and activities of the child, and not in the presentation and application of external material," observed John Dewey in 1899, it followed that the numerous spontaneous plays and games of children should become the "foundation stones of educational method." Educational reformers exhorted their colleagues to introduce more play elements—dramatic skits, songs, and dances—into their classrooms to teach a variety of subjects. They also demanded that local government and school districts recognize the playground as a major place where, for better or for worse, children learned. George Ellsworth Johnson of Pittsburgh, a former student of G. Stanley Hall at Clark University, called for local government and school districts to take a more self-conscious educational role by offering organized programs of supervised play and games on playgrounds. Johnson reasoned that, as children grew into adults, such programs helped their powerful play instinct develop into a sense of civic loyalty, teamwork, and responsible citizenship, rather than a taste for commercial amusements.[17]

Concern with the relationship between child development and play spurred the national movement to increase the number of supervised recreational activities available on playgrounds, in settlement houses, and in schools. By 1895, newly organized playground associations in

Boston, Providence, New York City, Philadelphia, and Chicago joined with working-class neighborhood and ethnic organizations to pressure local municipal governments and school districts to provide more public recreational facilities and to hire more professional educators and social workers to staff them. By 1906, these associations merged to become the Playground Association of America (PAA).[18]

The new national organization viewed civic holiday celebrations as special opportunities to put its ideas about education through supervised play into practice, as well as to publicize its demands for more public recreational facilities. Celebrations of national holidays, noted G. Stanley Hall, "have been allowed to degenerate often to rowdyism and to pleasures both dangerous and vicious." It was "high time," he declared, that they should be utilized for "pedagogic and patriotic purposes."[19]

Soon after its founding, the Playground Association launched a nationwide publicity campaign for a "Safe and Sane July Fourth" to reform the conduct of civic holiday celebrations. Armed with statistics collected by the American Medical Association testifying to the high rate of holiday injuries (several thousand annually), the Safe and Sane movement campaigned for a strict ban on the private sale of fireworks. William Orr, principal of Central High School in Springfield, Massachusetts, and one of the leaders of the movement, declared somewhat melodramatically that the rash of fireworks injuries "mock[s] the claim that our July Fourth, as at present observed, is in any sense a festal day; rather, is it a day of terror, anxiety, and dread." In 1910 the Russell Sage Foundation, a primary backer of the campaign, released a fifteen-minute movie, entitled *A Sane Fourth of July*, vividly depicting the horrors of the old Fourth and demanding, in rhetoric similar to the decade's crusades against monopoly, that aroused citizens mobilize to overcome the special interests that blocked legislation to control fireworks.[20]

Leaders of the Safe and Sane movement admitted, however, that a ban on the private sale of fireworks would not succeed without an accompanying increase in both the quantity and the quality of municipally sponsored holiday activities. Orr observed that "mere repression will, in the long run, not be effective. It is necessary to recognize and satisfy the natural instinct of men for spectacles and pleasurable excitement." Conceding that "the tastes of the children and the public have been vitiated to such an extent [by commercial amusements] that the longing for accentuated pleasures makes it difficult for those who wish to plan and carry out true festivals," the Playground Association's Committee on Festivals called for its members to seek new holiday activities with mass appeal that did not lower standards "to compete with commercialism in its devastation of public morality." Luther Gulick, head of the Sage Foundation's recreation department, told his colleagues in 1908 that safe yet appealing alternatives to fireworks explosions and street parades' "hopeless tangle and chaos of people" must be found for masses of Americans to join in civic celebrations.[21]

In the effort to create a popular, yet wholesome, holiday program, the playground workers did not want local civic officials to abandon the customary ceremonial elements—Orr counseled that a historical oration reminding the public of "the great deeds of the fathers and the present duties of the sons" added "dignity and weight" to a festival, provided that it was delivered by "someone who understands the art of addressing a multitude in the open air" and that it was not "long or labored" or overly "didactic."[22] But most of their suggestions concerned the adoption of new activities designed especially for those least likely to be reached by the historical oration: children and immigrants. Pamphlets on "The New Fourth" recommended that, in addition to holiday orations, towns sponsor giant children's play festivals on playgrounds and in settlement houses and parks, consisting of athletic contests, marching and calisthenic drills, group games, dramatic skits, and folk dances.

Folk dancing and group games represented a notably large and important part of the playground workers' model holiday program. Like the athletic drills, dancing offered children vigorous physical exercise and the opportunity to develop team spirit. Luther Gulick, who had supervised physical education for the New York City public schools before heading the Russell Sage Foundation's recreation program, proclaimed folk dancing "one of the most serviceable forms of exercise to increase organic vigor, for it involves many movements of practically all of the large muscular masses of the body." He considered folk dancing particularly beneficial for girls, who did not have the opportunities to exercise provided boys through organized school athletic programs. Gulick introduced regular folk dancing into the New York City public schools in 1905 and made it part of the schools' holiday programs.[23]

Over and above physical exercise, noted G. Stanley Hall, folk dances represented "moral, social, and aesthetic forces, condensed expressions of ancestral and racial traits." Hall explained that encouraging folk dancing, especially among immigrant children, could help reinforce the traditional moral sanctions that youth too quickly abandoned for commercial amusements. Jane Addams agreed that "the public dance halls filled with frivolous and irresponsible young people in a feverish search for pleasure are but a sorry substitute for the old dances on the village green," adding, "these old forms of dancing, which have been worked out in many lands and through long experiences, safeguard unwary and dangerous expression and yet afford a vehicle through which the gaiety of youth may flow." Folk dancing on playgrounds offered a subtle form of moral instruction.[24]

The playground workers believed that teaching folk dances, games, and crafts from the American past could also serve as a "history lesson" for both native-born and immigrant children. Acting out scenes and dances from the past enabled children to learn history by doing, rather than by merely reading about it or hearing about it from the speaker's platform. Progressive educators such as John Dewey and Charles A. McMurry stressed that children learned history, like other subjects, best through performing specific activities, such as skits, songs, crafts, and dances. McMurry, a teacher at Northern Illinois State Normal School, offered one example of how historical instruction could be combined with manual training:

> If a boy constructs a wigwam, dresses like an Indian, and makes bows and arrows to shoot with, he comes into closer sympathy with Indian life. If a child produces a miniature log-house and its surroundings, he gets closer to the reality of pioneer life. By reproducing houses and various simple products of industrial art, a child not only finds expression for his motor activities in manual effort, but he comes into a closer sympathy and understanding of the people whose fabrics and houses he attempts to reproduce. It may be said that this is only another way of repeating in the child the experience of the past, and of working it over into his physical and mental organism.[25]

History-oriented play spilled out of the classroom into extracurricular activities such as Scouting and holiday playground festivals. Eugene C. Gibney, supervisor of vacation playgrounds in Brooklyn, New York, explained that the dances selected for the "Father Knickerbocker's Birthday" celebration "were designed to entwine the beautiful story of our city about the hearts of our charges. They depict life during every important epoch in our history, and their daily production in our playgrounds has not only given healthy exhilaration and physical development, but it has installed a deep, proud, silent, patriotism."[26] Recreation workers reasoned that children learning games and dances of various periods of American history would take more interest in their other history studies, as well as absorb an American tradition of wholesome play to guide their contemporary leisure pursuits.

The particular version of history they sought to teach on playgrounds, in keeping with theories of progressive education, placed less emphasis on children memorizing the patriotic deeds of military and political figures from the nation's past and more on children acting out skits, dances, and games from local domestic and social experiences. Such a history of everyday life would help children learn about their immediate environment and their obligations as citizens. "The teacher of history, like the politician and historian, has been brought to a change of base," declared Charles McMurry in 1903. "The world is no longer chiefly concerned in the acts and privileges of rulers and kings, but in the mammoth social needs of the people." Understanding these social needs involved promoting an understanding of the evolution of contemporary society and the relation of past to present, as well as the interrelation of various elements of society in the present. According to McMurry, "The Aim of History Instruction" was "to bring the past into manifest relation to the present, and to show how historical ideas and experiences are being constantly projected into the present, are, in fact, the controlling forces in our social and industrial life." He added that history instruction should also "socialize a child, that is, to make him more regardful of the interests of others, less stubborn and isolated in his individuality," concluding that "to give a vivid and intense realization of social duties and obligations is the essence of the best history instruction."[27]

The playground workers reworked the version of American tradition handed down by genteel intellectuals and patriotic and hereditary societies on holidays to make it more usable for progressive history. The same aristocratic and Anglocentric historical imagery of Elizabethan England and the Founding Fathers at play that genteel intellectuals employed in costume balls and evenings of high society tableaux vivants found its way into the playground holiday festival, but this imagery was now invested with democratic and pluralistic meanings derived from playground workers' beliefs about the social aims of play and progressive history education. Using "traditional" American songs, dances, and games collected by folklorists William Wells Newell and Francis J. Child, playground workers guided children not only through reconstructed English morris and Maypole dances and minuets but also husking bees, quilting parties, and barn-raising dances set to tunes such as "Buffalo Gals" and "O Susanna."[28] These last folk activities, noted Percival Chubb of the Ethical Culture School in New York, recalled the times when work and play were one. Educators also recommended that local playground workers stage dramatic "story-dances," a form with origins in the Delsartian gymnastic pantomime of the late nineteenth century, to guide children's innate sense of make-believe. Dramatic dances encouraged children to act out tales from the pioneer youth of Daniel Boone, George Washington, and Abra-

Maypole Festival, Central Park, ca. 1905–9. Maypole dancing represented a wholesome Anglo-American play tradition for native-born and immigrant children alike. Playground workers incorporated various ethnic dances into the Maypole form, just as various nationalities would become "American" in a white, Anglo-Saxon, Protestant nation. (Percival Chubb, Festivals and Plays *[New York: Harper and Brothers, 1912], p. 269)*

ham Lincoln, as well as more courtly stories such as Pocahontas and John Smith, the courtship of Miles Standish, and the Maypole of Merrymount.[29]

The playground workers' holiday festival set these games and dances from the American past amid a program of dances from around the world, highlighting the folk traditions of recent immigrants as well as those of longer-settled Americans. A holiday play festival in Chicago in 1908 included dozens of immigrant dances, prompting settlement house worker Graham Taylor to praise its "cosmopolitanism" and "democratic spirit." A play festival in Pittsburgh in 1909 featured a children's history of the city, with children successively performing dances representative of the "Indians," French, British, and "newer immigrants."[30] The Maypole dance gained special popularity with playground workers because of its simplicity and open, plastic form. The addition of red, white, and blue streamers adapted it for a July Fourth celebration; Eastern European children could blend it with their traditional national dances into a "May-pole-ka." Performed by all children at the conclusion of a program of folk dances from

*The melting pot, New York City, 1914. Though holiday play festivals featured
ethnic dances, Americanization was an important part of the day's program.
This children's festival was held in the Bronx on August 19, 1914, as part of
the celebration of the New York Commercial Tercentenary. (American Scenic
and Historic Preservation Society,* Twentieth Annual Report *[1915], pl.
14)*

around the world, the Maypole dance—never quite losing its association among playground workers with "merrie old England"—represented the various nationalities eventually uniting as Americans within
the framework of a white, Anglo-Saxon Protestant nation.[31]

Recreation workers and educators believed that the playground
festival offered a model form of holiday celebration not only for
children and immigrants but also for native-born adult Americans. At
the festival, native-born adults could teach immigrants and children
about American history, art, and wholesome recreation, while learning from children and immigrants how to recapture those childlike
qualities that recreation workers felt were most lacking in modern
industrial civilization: joyous emotional expression, egalitarian solidarity, and a colorful cosmopolitanism. Recreation workers attributed
to immigrants, like children, the capacity to express a genuine communal gaiety. Mary Fanton Roberts observed in 1909 that "as a nation
we formerly played rather awkwardly and self-consciously, and we
have needed to learn something of the art of being natural from the
playing of other peoples." Mary Master Needham, a schoolteacher

and author of a handbook on *Folk Festivals: Their Growth and How to Give Them,* suggested, "When we have borrowed of our foreign Americans some of the festal feeling that they so easily express, we shall learn to play and how to observe our holidays." William E. Bohn of New York City's Ethical Culture School explained, "There is one thing which the people of Southern Europe can teach the Anglo-Saxon Americans. What we old Americans need more than anything else is to get out of our shells. We need to learn to laugh and dance and not be afraid of our feelings. We need above everything else freedom in expression." Luther Gulick commented that festivals of folk dance and games "afford one of the few avenues which exist for the expression of mass feeling" and could satisfy Americans' desperate "community need for aesthetic expression." "Self-consciousness drove out these folk arts," he declared, referring to the nation's heritage of Puritanism and hard work. "Now our conscious need of them is leading us to their restoration on a new level." Recreation workers believed that encouraging Americans to emulate the childlike spirit of play attributed to recent immigrants offered a solution to the problem genteel intellectuals posed concerning the drabness of American civilization.[32]

Recreation workers also believed that encouraging adults to express the childlike spirit of play on holidays could help heal potentially dangerous social antagonisms arising out of differences of ethnicity and class. Children instinctively played together, unconscious of social distinctions; their parents, abandoning themselves to the play spirit, might do so as well. John L. Gillin, a sociologist at the University of Wisconsin, noted that "play produces the excitement which casts off the reserve that separates men from each other." Gulick insisted, "There is no way in which a community can be brought together and made to feel and act as a unit so well as by playing together." It was this seemingly spontaneous solidarity, this seemingly effortless expression of artistic traditions in song and dance, that playground workers sought to cultivate in the mass of their fellow Americans.[33]

Civic holiday celebrations gained special significance for educators and recreation workers as the time when Americans by playing together expressed their fundamental values and ancestral traits, their deepest feelings and emotions. Like the past generations that joined in wedding celebrations, husking bees, and barn dances, Americans in the new century needed to tap these feelings to revitalize the "deep underlying communal affinities" that held their towns and cities together despite differences of ethnicity and class. Mari Ruef Hofer, a music instructor at Columbia University, explained at the PAA convention in 1907 that play based on historical and folk themes could result in "a restoring to us of an almost lost inheritance of the fundamental values of life, without which our entire social structure would crumble and fall." Like the children's Maypole dance, the holiday festival for adults could meld traditional Anglo-American communal activities and a particular childlike version of immigrant cultures into a cosmopolitan ritual of common citizenship. By reenacting the traditions associated with the childhood of their towns, as well as incorporating the culture of childlike immigrant peoples, Americans could recapture a childlike spirit of play and social solidarity.[34]

The play spirit expressed in public celebrations also represented to recreation workers a powerful medium of mass persuasion capable of molding and remolding the collective identity and personality. William Orr observed in 1909 that "the mood of the populace on a properly ordered holiday constitutes a psychological opportunity. Impressions are easily made, and ideas readily become part of the consciousness of the individual. It is as if the glow of enthusiasm and the ardor of excitement fuse the day's experience and instruction into the mental make-up of the participants." Just as children could learn about their social obligations as citizens from their peers on the playground as well as from their teachers in the classroom, adults could learn these same obligations from their neighbors in playful, artistic communal ritual as well as from the town fathers on the speaker's platform. Joining in the immediate experience of playing together supplemented hearing about past exemplars as a medium for moral persuasion. Rather than despair over the declining influence of tradition over the "Mob Mind" and the apparent truth of E. A. Ross's observation that "the multitude has now the prestige that once clothed the past," recreation workers sought to use the power of the multitude through organized play in civic celebrations to bolster the appeal of values they attributed to the past, harnessing human suggestibility in the crowd in the service of various reform causes.[35]

Recreation workers promoted the children's playground festival or immigrant folk festival as a model for adult mass participation in civic holiday celebrations. By making public celebrations for the entire community more like the immigrant folk festival, they reasoned, Americans could recapture the childlike solidarity and spirit of expressive participation that modern industrial society lacked and that spectacular carnival parades such as Mardi Gras, which PAA Secretary Lee F. Hamner condemned as "superficial" ("a show of tinsel and glitter upon which considerable money has been expended and from which there was exceedingly small return to the community"), could not provide. Summarizing the recreation workers' view of civic celebrations as opportunities for popular participation in the creation of a new common civic culture, the Playground Association's Committee on Festivals declared: "The aim of these festivals should be to involve the people in self-amusement and self-expression. The festival should be the greatest and the most characteristic form of democratic art. It should interpret the ideals of the people to themselves. It should stimulate the creative energies of the people, and bring forth the latent imagination and poetry which is in them." E. B. Mero, author of *American Playgrounds* and secretary of Boston's Public Recreation League, put it more succinctly: "The idea in back of the parade is not only to give the holiday meaning, but to reveal the city to itself."[36]

Eager to develop new forms for popular participation in public holiday celebrations, progressive educators and playground workers embraced the new historical pageantry. Members of the Safe and Sane July Fourth movement pointed especially to the historical pageant held in Springfield, Massachusetts, on July 4, 1908, as a model of how the new pageantry could revitalize civic life by gathering citizens together in joyous play. Two thousand Springfield residents marched downtown in a line stretching for blocks. Those planning the affair, unable to resist the lure of a sure, if commercial, crowd pleaser to publicize their efforts to promote a Safe and Sane Fourth, began their procession with Buffalo Bill Cody and several spectacular tableaux of "Life on the Plains" from his Wild West Show, in town that day drumming up business. Springfield's elementary school children followed, parading with floats representing scenes from local and national history such as "Puritan Maidens" and "Washington Crossing the Delaware." In the eyes of progressive educators and social workers, however, the principal feature of the procession was the "pageant of nations" in which thirteen immigrant groups paraded with floats illustrating "the characteristic qualities of each people, and the contributions each was making to national life." Most ethnic floats presented national heroes: the Italians, Christopher Columbus; the Germans, William Tell; the French Canadians, Samuel de Champlain; the Scandinavians, Leif Eriksson; and the Greeks, Socrates. Black Civil War veterans chose to reenact the Battle of Fort Wagner, in which they played a decisive role. Mary Vida Clark declared in *Charities and Commons* that "for once the contribution to American life made by the Pilgrims and the Puritans was put in its place, a large and important one, but not the whole, and some other and more recent contributions to our civilization were also given a place." She added that the pageant represented a "glimpse of the America of the future that is to come out of this mingling of races and race-ideals." In his description of the affair for the readers of *Atlantic Monthly*, William Orr concluded: "As a people, we are in the making, plastic, responsive, receptive. Such a spirit will take the best upon all the influences that bear upon it. Our civilization is in a 'nascent state,' with its power of affinity at its strongest, and its capacity for assimilation most vigorous. Such occasions as the popular festival of Independence Day constitute a rare opportunity to minister to the multitude, and rightly to shape and fashion our characteristics as a people. No more inspiring or ennobling call ever came to mankind."[37]

In the aftermath of massive, well-publicized historical pageants in Springfield and Philadelphia in 1908, members of patriotic and hereditary societies and progressive educators and playground workers adopted the new pageantry as their own and promoted it to local civic officials across the country. While both groups endorsed processions of historical floats called pageants, which they traced back to Louis Napoleon Parker in England, significant differences existed in how the two groups viewed what they were doing. Members of patriotic and hereditary societies saw the new historical pageantry primarily as a means to bolster the patriotic and artistic quality of civic ceremonies over the popular recreational elements that they felt had come to dilute the significance of public holiday celebrations. They viewed historical pageantry as an elaborate display of social position similar to the costume ball, a way to reinforce their particular definition of civic identity, social order, and the moral principles they associated with the past—to preserve Anglo-American supremacy in public life. By contrast, progressive educators and playground workers viewed the new pageantry as a way to orchestrate the popular recreational features of celebrations so that the public would not only be exposed to history and art from the podium but also learn by doing through the medium of play. To them, historical pageantry was an elaborate ritual of democratic participation similar to the playground folk festival, a way to supplement Anglo-American traditions with those of other peoples and lead all local residents in the ritual construction of a new communal identity and sense of citizenship anchored in the past, yet forged out of the underlying shared emotions generated in the present, in the immediate experience of playing together.[38] While the hereditary elite's pageants, as in Philadelphia, set forth icons of municipal consolidation and the City Beautiful, playground workers' pageants, as in Springfield, paraded the fruits of neighborhood social work efforts among children and immigrants. Both groups viewed the new historical pageantry as a medium for the reform of public behavior on holidays, as well as a medium for the dissemination of other reform ideas. Each group attempted to persuade local officials to accept its version of the new form.

Each group also proclaimed its efforts to reform the conduct of holiday celebrations a success. Though many towns had introduced ethnic processions, historical tableaux, athletic contests, baseball games, picnics, and professionally handled fireworks displays decades before the national Safe and Sane July Fourth campaign got underway, the campaign's ability to disseminate its message through national educational, medical, and social work organizations and journals accelerated the trend of municipalities to pass ordinances regulating fireworks and to sponsor diverse holiday activities. The Russell Sage Foundation announced that the number of towns sponsoring Safe and Sane celebrations increased from 20 to 161 between 1909 and 1911, while the number of holiday accidents nationwide decreased from 5,307 to 1,603. It is unlikely that all segments of the local population participated in the Safe and Sane activities—in Worcester, Massachusetts, more recently landed immigrants appeared less enthusiastic than longer-settled ones, who viewed the new celebrations as opportunities to join the mainstream of civic life. Nevertheless, the national movement bolstered the confidence of the playground workers and patriotic and hereditary societies that they could win the battle to rescue national festivals. In contrast to the hereditary elite's withdrawal from civic celebrations in the nineteenth century, the Daughters of the American Revolution's monthly magazine boasted that the apparent success of the movement to reform the Fourth demonstrated that the Daughters "can and should be a vital living influence in civic life."[39]

Yet local civic officials' understanding of the new pageantry differed from that of its national promoters. By 1909, municipalities across the United States attempting to reap for themselves the novel publicity enjoyed by Philadelphia and Springfield called virtually any kind of street procession a "pageant." Several of these extravaganzas brought together patriotic and hereditary societies, playground workers, fine artists, and occasionally commercial entrepreneurs in the creation of civic spectacle. To commemorate the combined anniversaries of Henry Hudson's landing and Robert Fulton's invention of the steamboat, New York City residents witnessed ceremonies organized by the American Scenic and Historic Preservation Society, as well as both a giant parade of fifty-four historical floats (ending with "Father Knickerbocker Welcoming the Immigrants") and an illuminated carnival parade of fifty floats created by the commercial designers A. H. Stoddard and B. A. Wikstrom of the New Orleans Mardi Gras. An estimated 300,000 schoolchildren performed in fifty parks designated "pageant districts" throughout New York City. St. Louis, Missouri, celebrated the centennial of its incorporation with a fall street "pageant" of mounted historical tableaux as well as its annual Veiled Prophets carnival parade. The Downtown Merchants Association of San Francisco, to demonstrate the city's recovery from the earthquake of 1906, staged a Portola Festival (in honor of the explorer of San Francisco Bay) with floats depicting scenes from California history. Though not in dramatic form nor based on arts and crafts principles, these parades all claimed to be part of the new pageantry, taking advantage of historical pageantry's value as "civic advertising" as much as its potential to reform public recreation on holidays.[40]

Certainly the new pageantry had its critics as well as boosters. Though Gustav Stickley of *Craftsman* magazine praised a few of the smaller American pageants, especially those sponsored by local arts and crafts societies that adhered to the English model, he blasted the attempt to expand the form to giant municipal festivals, grumbling in the aftermath of the Hudson-Fulton Celebration, "It is rather a pathetic thing for a great city to imagine that she can order the spirit of play as she can packages of fireworks, that she can make a nation gay by press-agent work; that she can create enthusiasm by electricity and commotion, and that a few conventional made-to-order parades of committees and boats and unimaginative floats can take the place in the people's minds of real merrymaking, of which they themselves are an intrinsic part." Criticizing the Safe and Sane movement, Stickley wondered, "What indeed has happened to us as a nation that we should permit ourselves to be led out 'to play' with a halter around our necks?"[41] Stickley's criticism indicates the extent to which the historical pageant in America had passed from antimodern reenactments of aristocratic Medieval and Renaissance scenes, as advanced by Parker in England, into the hands of progressive playground workers and civic boosters.

These groups drowned out such censure in waves of praise for the seemingly unlimited potential of the novel form of holiday celebration that combined mass recreation and patriotic education. Genteel publications looked to the new form of celebration to revitalize the ceremonial public affirmation of moral principles associated with the past, customarily presented in the holiday historical oration, for an age of spectacle. Paul Pinkerton Foster in *World Today* praised the revival of the "Elizabethan" pageant in 1908, declaring that "the spectacles and moving pictures of great pageants present history in tangible form and make vivid to the eye the stirring scenes which language and the pen can, at best, but faintly reflect." The *Dial* in 1909 praised historical pageantry as a means to make tangible "how firmly the present is linked to the past; forgetfulness of this fact constitutes perhaps the chief danger of our restless modern life." Writers connected with progressive education commended historical pageantry's ability to help local residents absorb the values attributed to the past through role-playing, much as the progressive educators insisted that the developing child learned through play. Mary Master Needham, describing a historical pageant in Old Deerfield, Massachusetts, in 1910, declared that, through pageantry, local residents "formed a conception of what their past was by getting inside of it and seeing how it felt." Contrasting pageants with the customary forms of presenting history in public on holidays, she added that such exercises "would mean much more to these people . . . than months and years of orations and prayers and essays." Moreover, both groups of writers praised historical pageantry's power to weld together into one "community" residents divided by ethnicity, class, and a multiplicity of affiliations and interests. Frances Maule Bjorkman in *World's Work* lauded pageantry's success in transforming American holidays "from mere individual noise-making to beautiful and social play." The *Century* remarked in 1910, in an article entitled "Pageants Better than Gunpowder," that the new celebrations were of "deep sociological value . . . in giving cohesiveness to our community life, which as it becomes more complicated, is exposed to many centrifugal forces," adding, "nothing is more likely to cement the sympathies of our people and to accentuate our homogeneity than a cultivation of pageants." Advocates of a host of causes celebrated civic officials' sponsorship of public reenactments of local history on holidays as a way to make local residents look beyond their particular group identities to a common civic identity and thus a common interest in undertaking needed reforms. In a few short years, historical pageantry had become not only a new medium for patriotic, moral, and aesthetic education envisioned by genteel intellectuals, but also an instrument for the reconstruction of American society and culture using progressive ideals.[42]

3 *The Place Is the Hero*

· · · · · · · · · · · ·

The pageant is a drama in which the
place is the hero and the development of
the community is the plot.
—William Chauncy Langdon

William Chauncy Langdon personally designed this green, blue, and white poster. The image was reproduced on stationery, postcards, and souvenir medallions. (Brown University Library)

Among the foremost promoters of the new pageantry as an instrument of community self-discovery and reform in America was William Chauncy Langdon. The author of numerous articles, bulletins, and manuals on historical pageantry, including *The Celebration of the Fourth of July by Means of Pageantry* for the Russell Sage Foundation, Langdon put his pageantry theories into practice by writing and directing several historical pageants in New England and the Midwest.

Langdon's historical pageants—especially the five "Pageants of the New Country Life" that he staged in rural New England between 1911 and 1914—combined mass participation and historical reenactment into a unique format. The form reflected Langdon's conviction, shared by many of his fellow "pageant-masters," that a historical pageant could offer local townspeople not only novel holiday entertainment and wholesome recreation, but also a stirring experience through which they could visualize solutions to their current social and economic problems. Local residents in acting out the right scenes from their town's past, present, and future would become more aware of the enduring traditions of a New England village, as well as how they must adapt those traditions to the direction of modern social and economic progress. Historical pageants would revitalize rural towns by enabling local residents to catch up with history by preserving a particular version of their traditions, helping them to recognize outmoded practices while promoting a unique local identity, sense of cohesion, and attachment to place.

The pageant-master's own background was decidedly not rural New England nor rooted in one town. His father, William Chauncy Langdon, though born in Burlington, Vermont, soon moved to Washington, D.C., where he worked in the U.S. Patent Office and helped found the local chapter of the YMCA, becoming active in its national confederation. At age twenty-eight he left the Patent Office for a career in the ministry, serving congregations in Maryland, the home of his wife Hannah Agnes Courtney, and overseas. His youngest son and namesake was born in 1871 in Florence, Italy, where the Reverend Mr. Langdon established an Episcopal church for American residents and tourists. Two years later the family moved from Florence to a new church in Geneva, Switzerland. In 1876 Langdon resumed his ministerial duties in the United States, serving successively in Cambridge, Massachusetts, and Bedford, Pennsylvania. Young William attended public schools in both Cambridge and Bedford, then St. John's Military School near Syracuse, New York. At seventeen, he entered Cornell University, where his older brother Courtney taught Romance languages. Two years later, Langdon transferred to Brown University in Providence, Rhode Island, upon his brother's appointment there. He received an A.B. degree in history from Brown in 1892, studying with J. Franklin Jameson, and an A.M. in English the following year.[1]

Upon graduation, Langdon began teaching full-time while indulging his growing interest in theater. The Brown University Opera Club performed his *8 x 8: A Comic Opera in Two Acts* in May 1893 and premiered his *Cupid '96, or Love on the Campus* three years later. In 1898 Langdon wrote *The Vision of the Throne*, a religious cantata dedicated to the memory of his father, who had died in 1895. Langdon collaborated with composer George Chadwick on the libretto to the opera *Judith* in 1901. At each school where he taught, Langdon offered courses in elocution as well as English and history and sponsored the Dramatic Club. He expected to do more of the same when, in 1902, newly married to Marion Hatheway, an artist from Boston, he accepted a position at the Pratt Institute in Brooklyn, New York, under Headmaster Luther H. Gulick. A great booster of group singing, Langdon suggested soon after his arrival at Pratt that fifteen minutes of oratorio be added to the daily chapel service.[2]

In New York City, however, Langdon's interests increasingly turned from music and drama to local politics and social work. He joined the Citizens Union, a political reform organization dedicated to the defeat of Tammany Hall, and campaigned vigorously in 1903 for the reelection of its candidate and his cousin, Mayor Seth Low, although Low lost the race. Langdon added civics and New York City history to his course offerings at the Pratt Institute. After school, he organized the Juvenile City League—a civic-oriented boys' club—in which he claimed fifteen hundred boys from Hell's Kitchen took part. Langdon modeled the league on the city's Juvenile Street Cleaning League of the 1890s, in which children earned badges for helping municipal workers to clean streets and spot violations of the sanitation laws. Through such endeavors, he demonstrated his conviction that civics could be taught not only in the classroom but also on the streets of New York City.[3]

Langdon insisted that the key to successful civic education lay in arousing local residents' "team spirit" and sense of loyalty to the neighborhood. Addressing the American Civic Association in Cleveland in 1904, he suggested that civics teachers could exploit the territorial nature of boys' gangs to instill in the groups a sense of responsibility for their neighborhood and thus an interest in the issues that affected it. Such an approach encouraged each citizen to "focus in his own locality the large questions of the day."[4] Out of local camaraderie and loyalty to place would come a larger civic awareness.

Increasingly, Langdon viewed his teaching primarily as a means of fostering civic awareness, team spirit, and local pride. His few publications appeared not in history, English, or education journals but in

Charities and *Social Service*. It was clear by the time the Pratt Institute phased out its high school program in 1903, forcing Langdon to look for another job, that a profession other than teaching would better serve his interests. Though conventionally religious, he felt no special call to the ministry, unlike his father or his older sister Florence who served as a missionary nurse in Alaska. Perhaps the influence of Luther Gulick, another missionary's son and a former leader of the YMCA, along with the example of Langdon's father's own early work with the YMCA, nudged Langdon into a full-time career in social service.[5]

When his tenure ended at the Pratt Institute, Langdon went to work in professional philanthropy and politics. In 1906, he served as secretary to the executive committee of the New York State branch of the American Red Cross, organizing new county branches and the New York end of relief for large national disasters, including the San Francisco earthquake. Langdon served the next three years as secretary to New York County District Attorney William Travers Jerome, a prominent crusader against vice whom he had helped to elect. When Jerome left office in 1910, Langdon tried to latch on with various New York area philanthropies, while supporting his wife and two young children by working for a local business, the United Lamp and Burner Company.[6]

Early in 1910, Langdon began an article on historical pageantry for his old friend Luther Gulick, now head of the Russell Sage Foundation's Division of Playground Extension, which ran the foundation's "Safe and Sane July Fourth" campaign. The new historical pageantry movement fascinated Langdon, combining his interests in history, theater, and civic education. He wrote to English pageant director Louis Napoleon Parker for information about his work and throughout the summer of 1910 attended nearby American pageants, collecting programs, pageant texts, and newspaper accounts. The more Langdon studied the new pageantry, the more confirmed was his faith in its potential civic value.[7]

Langdon hoped to establish a Bureau of American Pageantry as a nationwide clearinghouse, library, and lecture bureau for information about the new celebrations. The board of his proposed organization brought together interested artists and recreation workers: along with Gulick and prominent housing reformer Lawrence Veiller of New York City, Langdon included dramatists John W. Alexander, George Pierce Baker, and Percy MacKaye; Lotta A. Clark, a high school history teacher from Boston; publisher Walter Hines Page; and Marian Nevins MacDowell, the widow of composer Edward MacDowell. He also invited his former teacher J. Franklin Jameson to serve on the board, but Jameson declined, citing too many other commitments. Langdon, identifying himself as an "organizer and executive," intended to head the new organization.[8]

When Langdon attempted to bring his pageantry bureau to life in the fall of 1910, however, no one would fund it. Since the Russell Sage Foundation had abruptly withdrawn its financial support of the Playground Association of America (PAA) in June 1910 over a disagreement between Luther Gulick and PAA cofounder Joseph Lee, the association directors were wary about new financial commitments. Langdon then approached the Russell Sage Foundation directly. It also refused to provide funding, though Gulick agreed to hire Langdon for two months, beginning in October, as his personal secretary to answer inquiries about the foundation's Safe and Sane campaign. Langdon used this platform to seek support for his bureau idea from individual philanthropists, including John D. Rockefeller, J. P. Morgan, and Andrew Carnegie. Although these wealthy patrons supported individual pageants—in 1909, Carnegie had generously contributed to the Westchester County, New York, historical pageant sponsored by the local chapters of the Daughters of the American Revolution and the Society of Colonial Dames of America—each philanthropist turned down Langdon's appeal for money to support a nationwide bureau. Langdon answered a flood of letters asking the Sage Foundation for advice on how to stage a Safe and Sane July Fourth, yet no organization was willing to pay him to expand or even continue his work beyond November 1910.[9]

Langdon hoped to promote pageantry in America not only by establishing a national clearinghouse, but also by persuading various social service organizations to present demonstration pageants. A demonstration pageant, with adequate publicity nationwide, could stimulate public interest in the new pageantry even more effectively than a central clearinghouse. He recommended to the New York Child Welfare Commission that it hire George Pierce Baker, a drama professor from Harvard who had staged a well-publicized pageant in memory of Edward MacDowell that summer, to create "A Pageant of Child Welfare." He also suggested that the Playground Association of America sponsor "A Pageant of Play." But neither organization acted on his proposals.[10] It seemed that if Langdon wanted to demonstrate the benefits of community pageantry, he would have to produce and publicize a pageant himself.

Finally, an opportunity for Langdon to prove pageantry's civic value presented itself. Early in November 1910, Charlotte Farnsworth of the Horace Mann School in New York City had asked Langdon for advice on activities to commemorate the 150th anniversary of Thetford, Vermont, the town near the girls' camp she managed each summer with her husband Charles, a music professor at Teachers College, Columbia University. Charlotte Farnsworth had known Luther Gulick through her tenure on the Board of Management of the Girls Branch of the New York City Public Schools Athletic League, an organization he helped found, as well as through her sister-in-law's marriage into the Gulick family. Langdon suggested that Farnsworth produce a historical pageant in Thetford and, his other prospects for staging demonstration pageants having fallen through, asked if he might direct the celebration himself. Langdon assured her that his production would "set a standard in pageantry for the whole country," as well as be "vital and fundamental to the welfare of Thetford itself." Farnsworth described Langdon's plan to her friend, Mary Slade, wife of Thetford's Congregationalist minister, and sent Slade some Russell Sage Foundation brochures on the new pageantry. Mary Slade persuaded her husband, William, who in turn persuaded the Thetford Brotherhood, which he led, to invite Langdon to visit the Vermont town and discuss his pageant ideas further.[11]

Langdon arrived in Thetford during Christmas week 1910 amid a howling wind and subfreezing temperatures. He made over thirty-five visits to various townspeople, culminating in a meeting of nearly one hundred residents at Mr. Slade's church on December 28. Two weeks later, at a second public meeting presided over by Slade, those assembled voted to go ahead with the pageant, planned for August 1911. They chose a pageant committee, which eventually consisted of thirteen year-round and three summer residents, and subscribed $450 to offset initial expenses. They also formally hired Langdon to write and direct the affair, giving him copyright of the pageant book and total artistic control of the production. The town agreed to cover Langdon's traveling and living expenses at Thetford and to pay him one-third of any profits from the sale of tickets, souvenirs, and programs. But the Russell Sage Foundation, not the town, provided the bulk of Langdon's support, granting him $2,500 "to demonstrate whether or not the pageant may be used successfully as an agent in social advancement."[12]

There had been other "pageants" in the Thetford area. In 1905, the artist colony across the Connecticut River in Cornish, New Hampshire, presented Percy MacKaye's symbolic masque in honor of sculptor Augustus St.-Gaudens. George Pierce Baker's MacDowell pageant of 1910 took place not far away, in Peterborough, New Hampshire. In October of that year, St. James Church in Woodstock, Vermont, held a benefit evening of "pantomime tableaux."[13] But Langdon intended that the Thetford pageant be more than mere art or entertainment; rather, it would be a vital part of the town's social transformation.

The town of Thetford, Vermont, was actually a cluster of six villages

covering forty-two square miles along the west bank of the Connecticut River. Although farming remained a major source of livelihood
through the years, Thetford's biggest economic boost came in the late
eighteenth and early nineteenth centuries when it developed into a
center for milling lumber and grain for the surrounding region. By
1795, four sets of mills served the area, forming the nuclei of three of
Thetford's villages: Post Mills, Union Village, and Thetford Center.
Later, another sawmill helped establish the village of North Thetford.
These villages manufactured furniture, wagons, and lumber. The
area's population grew rapidly, more than doubling from 862 in 1790
to 1,785 in 1810, and continued to climb to 2,113 in 1830. A fifth
village, Thetford Hill, grew around the new Thetford Academy. A
new railroad along the Connecticut River Valley helped establish the
sixth of Thetford's bustling mid-nineteenth-century villages, East
Thetford.[14]

Like many towns in northern New England, Thetford's population
began to decline after the Civil War. New agricultural machinery enabled fewer people to work the land. Some local manufacturers could
not compete with the cheaper goods turned out by the larger factories
to the south. Townspeople left Thetford for areas with greater economic opportunities and were only partially replaced by new summer-
only residents who did not depend on the region for their livelihood.
The population plummeted, until by 1910 the town counted only
1,182 year-round residents, the fewest since 1790.[15]

Langdon hoped to help reverse this apparent spiral of economic
and social decline. He diagnosed Thetford's "problems"—depopula-
tion, isolation, lack of success in marketing its produce—as the result
of each household trying to preserve the economic independence of
the "Age of Homespun" instead of recognizing the "larger relations
and the economic interdependence of all communities in the present."
Langdon maintained that Thetford's residents needed both to recover
their sense of local solidarity and pride and to "see the larger opportunity and the greater freedom in the modern economic conditions of
community interdependence."[16] He concluded that Thetford could
not solve its problems alone. So while he worked on the script for *The
Pageant of Thetford*, Langdon also used his social service contacts to
arrange professional outside assistance for the town.

Langdon introduced Thetford residents to the "Country Life"
movement, a loosely organized coalition of social service professionals
and agricultural experts from the U.S. Department of Agriculture
(USDA) and state colleges who saw the "depleted" conditions Langdon described at Thetford as common throughout the nation's rural
areas. Country Life activists believed that if a vital rural society were to

survive in America, farmers would have to create new cooperative economic and social institutions. The U.S. Commission on Country Life, which President Theodore Roosevelt appointed in 1908, reported that the greatest need in rural areas was "a more widespread conviction of the necessity for organization—not only for economic but for social purposes." The Country Life movement hoped to improve farmers' economic position through the introduction of scientific agricultural techniques, better roads, and modern business management methods while enriching their social relations through new social clubs and a revitalized rural church. Such organization could keep rural residents on the farm by bolstering the communal social patterns Country Life publicists imagined existed in the traditional rural village "in the days of the spinning wheel" against the pull of urban-industrial society while helping rural people to share in that society's material benefits.[17]

In the months before the pageant, Langdon solicited expert agricultural and social service help for Thetford. Even before his official appointment as pageant-master, Langdon sent away for USDA pamphlets on "Teaching Agriculture in Rural Schools," "Country Life Education," and "Boys and Girls Agricultural Clubs." Through the spring of 1911, he persuaded the local grange to arrange for a professional assessment of the area's timber resources by Vermont State Forester A. F. Hawes and biweekly visits from Marshall Cummings, a professor of horticulture at Vermont Agricultural College and a Thetford native. Langdon also arranged through his brother-in-law, Dr. Milton Whitney, chief of the USDA's Bureau of Soils, for bureau representatives to visit Thetford and analyze the town's soils and farming practices.[18]

Langdon helped organize Thetford's social and artistic as well as economic life. He wrote to Ernest Thompson Seton for advice on founding a local Boy Scout troop. Langdon created a similar organization for Thetford's young females, which he called the "Campfire Girls." Luther Gulick later adopted this name for his own national girls' organization.[19] Langdon also established a Thetford Orchestra and a Thetford Choral Society, and he invited Bruce Crane, an artist from New York City, to arrange an art exhibition during Thetford's pageant week.

Langdon's efforts at Thetford echoed his earlier work with the Juvenile City League in New York City, organizing local citizens' groups as a prelude to the community's renaissance. His approach also recalled that of the urban settlement house—funneling a multiplicity of social and economic services into one area. Indeed, the Sage Foundation agreed to help fund Langdon's historical pageant precisely because it viewed his activities as rural social work. Instead of laboring to revitalize a few blocks of New York City, Langdon now worked with a cluster of villages in Vermont.

Although Langdon valued his role as a liaison between Thetford and the outside social and economic service organizations, he believed his main contribution to the transformation of the town would be his historical pageant. He insisted that "the pageant is itself part of the development work."[20] Langdon felt that the experience of participating in a pageant would help organize the town for other reform efforts. Moreover, the right pageant historical episodes could help local residents visualize the necessity for those reform efforts. A historical pageant, properly conceived and executed, could produce an ecstatic communion, galvanizing Thetford residents in the crusade for the "New Country Life."

Langdon asserted that the pageant experience would strengthen local community cohesion. As he saw it, modern vocational specialization and the absorption in work—"forces that are socially centrifugal"—needed to be balanced in leisure hours by activities that townspeople do together, which develop "the unity of the community." Working together in pageant committees, rehearsing together, and performing together unite all "as an intimate and loyal town family." "The pageant," Langdon declared, "brings people together and kindles the spirit of enthusiastic unanimity as does nothing else."[21]

Furthermore, the historical pageant would root the spirit of unanimity around a unique local identity. "In the pageant," he explained, "the place is the hero and the development of the community is the plot."[22] Langdon insisted that a pageant must be staged outdoors, in daylight, on a site with a commanding view of the whole area, so that the "hero" could remain in full view of the audience throughout the performance.[23] The presentation of pageant scenes depicting the town's development against this backdrop would reinforce local residents' attachment to their surroundings, reminding them of the special significance of their ordinary landscape. As in his previous work with the Juvenile City League, Langdon believed that encouraging territorial attachments provided the first step in civic reform.

Langdon maintained that the pageant offered local residents an opportunity not only to affirm a unique loyalty to place but also to express their dormant folk spirit. He viewed the historical pageant as a form of folk drama "done by the people rather than for the people." Pageantry called into life "the latent art-instincts of the American people which heretofore have largely failed to find expression." Langdon compared the new American pageantry with the Irish folk theater of Lady Gregory and William Butler Yeats: "The fundamental purpose of the two are the same—the development of a strong national spirit by means of a folk drama written by local dramatists and performed by the people about their own life." Pageantry enabled local residents to express their latent communal identity through art.[24]

It was up to the pageant-master, explained Langdon, to bring the process of local communal self-discovery and expression to fruition by capturing the unique essence of the town in dramatic form. "Communities have their distinct individualities, just as much as you and I have," he observed. "The object [of a pageant] is not to concoct a pretty entertainment, but to paint a portrait." Moreover, "If the pageant worker has put his soul into the task of eliciting the spirit of [the community] from its history and from its present life, he may then with hope hold up his expression of that spirit in his pageant and the people will respond."[25]

In crafting this dramatic portrait, insisted Langdon, the pageant worker had an obligation to help local residents visualize their town's current problems and their future solution. It was not enough for pageant historical episodes to be merely "picturesque" or "dramatic." "These would have little inspiration to the community for its actual life." Instead, "the incidents chosen for pageant episodes should be those which best illustrate the growing character of the community and pre-state the issues of the present and their solution in the future."[26]

Langdon described the type of history appropriate for community pageants in terms similar to the way progressive historians in colleges and universities advocated the "New History." Historical pageant episodes, maintained Langdon, should "follow the life of the town on down to the time when it ceases to be called history and is called public questions—to the present." Yet he went beyond the New History in calling for historical pageants not only to "introduce the town to the greatness inherent in its own present daily life," but also to "dramatize the future. We must represent in specific form what it will be like, what it will feel like, when those difficulties that are common to us all in our town will have been done away, when these problems have been solved, when, yes, when the millennium has come." Cautioning that the public would scoff at scenes of the future that were "vague" or merely "pretty, gratuitous imaginings," Langdon advocated that the pageant writer in conjunction with local residents carefully study the town's past and present civic, social, and industrial situation, as well as consider what new activities residents planned to undertake, in order to "compute the curve" of the development and realistically project it into the not-too-distant future. He explained that pageant scenes depicting the desired economic, educational, and aesthetic results of the New Country Life in Thetford would provide local residents with "an advance vision of what they are accomplishing, and in this way give them a clearer understanding of what they are doing and a more enduring confidence in the practicability of their ultimate complete success." The historical pageant would depict tangibly not only what the community was but also what it might ideally become.[27]

Using historical pageantry to depict an ideal future, though a departure from earlier pageant formulas as developed in Great Britain and the United States, was consistent with Langdon's philosophy of civic education. While teaching history and working with boys' clubs in New York City in the first years of the new century, Langdon complained that his fellow history teachers looked too much to a "golden past," and he recommended that "in all instruction, in all education, [we] place our ideals and our ideal time in the future, not in the past."[28]

Langdon had an immediate precedent for including a "future" scene in his Thetford pageant. In November 1910, a municipal reform organization calling itself "Boston—1915" presented *From Cave Life to City Life: The Pageant of a Perfect City* in the Boston Arena. Frank Chocteau Brown, a professional architect, and Lotta A. Clark, head of the history department at Charlestown High School, directed a cast of 1,500, primarily students from local high schools, in episodes that depicted Boston in the Cave-dweller, Indian, and Colonial and Revolutionary periods, then leapt to an allegorical grand finale unveiling the ideal Boston of the future. Symbolic figures representing the "Knights of Economy" (played by Boy Scouts) protected women representing "The City" from "Fire," "Dust," "Diseases," "Germs," "Slavery and Serfdom," "Crime and Insanity," "War," and "Strife between Labor and Capital."[29] While Langdon admired this allegorical future scene for its potential inspirational value for Bostonians, he thought that he could improve upon its vague symbolism to specify realistically Thetford's problems and their solution.

In summary, then, Langdon anticipated that his Thetford historical pageant would encourage community cohesion and loyalty to place, be an artistic folk expression of the residents' daily lives, and help the town envision future solutions to its current problems. Pageantry, he insisted, could evoke Thetford's "community spirit—the dominant, the supreme creative force of the twentieth century"—and direct it toward specific reforms.[30] A historical pageant could both organize and inspire the community toward realization of the New Country Life, publicizing future goals while it stimulated the spirit of cooperation necessary to achieve them.

Langdon also hoped that the Thetford pageant would attract a large audience of tourists, at fifty cents and one dollar per person, to help offset expenses. His pageant site near the Boston and Maine Railroad line enabled him to arrange for special excursion trains to the pageant grounds. Langdon personally took charge of pageant publicity and designed the pageant poster. Two months before the pageant, he convinced the Sage Foundation to send a secretary, at full salary, to Thetford to help him with publicity. The pair dispatched countless releases to numerous national magazines and regional newspapers.

Langdon's biggest publicity coup was his National Advisory Committee on the Development of the Town, which included the outside experts he had brought to Thetford to introduce the New Country Life—the USDA's Lawrence Dodge and H. J. Wilder, Vermont State Forester Hawes, and University of Vermont Professor Cummings—as well as Ernest Thompson Seton, Luther Gulick, Charles Farnsworth, Arthur Farwell, Bruce Crane, Columbia University domestic economist Mary Schenk Woolman, writer Ray Stannard Baker, Milton Whitney, Assistant Secretary of Agriculture Willet M. Hays, and former Secretary of the Interior Gifford Pinchot. Langdon parlayed his contact with Pinchot, which he had obtained through a letter of introduction from John M. Glenn, head of the Russell Sage Foundation, to secure a letter from former President Theodore Roosevelt endorsing the Thetford pageant. This letter became a prominent part of the pageant publicity campaign.[31]

Gaining outside support proved easier than enlisting the support of local residents. The initial $450 pledged in December stubbornly remained at that level. In March a movement to block an appropriation from the town meeting was narrowly defeated. Residents of Post Mills, the largest of Thetford's villages, grumbled that the pageant site, on the banks of the Connecticut River near North Thetford, was too far away. Ultimately, Langdon won over enough local residents by appealing to genealogy and individual village pride as well as to an overarching Thetford town ideal. He recommended that residents impersonate their ancestors wherever possible, and he assigned the casting of each of the various pageant episodes to a different village or Thetford organization, rather than casting episodes in ways that cut across existing loyalties. The cast eventually totaled five hundred—nearly half the town's year-round population.[32]

The history committee, chaired by the Reverend Mr. Slade, served an important role in drawing local residents into the pageant. Soon after his first visit to Thetford, Langdon placed notices in each village post office requesting material concerning four aspects of the town's

William Chauncy Langdon at Thetford, 1911. Hanging from his belt is a souvenir medallion with the image he created for the pageant poster. (Brown University Library)

past: political life, such as Thetford's incorporation or its residents' participation in the Civil War; work life, such as traditional techniques of farming and sheep raising; social life, such as past husking bees and fairs; and finally, colorful anecdotes about interesting individuals. He suggested that residents gather this information not only from published histories in libraries but also from trunks, attics, and the reminiscences of old people and former residents. Langdon especially encouraged local residents to search for everyday objects from the past, such as farming tools and household utensils, that could be used as pageant props. As in other aspects of the pageant, Langdon sought to connect the local residents on the history committee with outside experts, enrolling Slade as a member of the American Historical Association. He also wrote to the Smithsonian Bureau of American Ethnology and the American Museum of Natural History for information about the Indians of the region. And Langdon himself functioned as an outside expert, remaining in New York to weave the material gathered by the local history committee into his pageant script.[33]

The pattern of using outside experts to direct the activities of local residents carried over to the assignments for music and dance. Langdon selected James T. Sleeper, a student of Professor Charles Farnsworth at Columbia and a summer resident of Thetford, to arrange background music and direct the new town orchestra. For some pageant scenes, Sleeper composed original light classical music; but for most, he simply rearranged familiar themes from Bach, Dvořák, and Tchaikovsky, adding some "Indian Melodies"—romantic music popularly associated with Native Americans—and some traditional hymns. Leaving nothing to chance, Langdon wrote to the U.S. Weather Bureau asking the direction of the prevailing wind for the area in August so that he could orient the pageant grounds to ensure that his words and Sleeper's music would carry.[34]

Virginia Tanner, whose work Langdon had first seen at the Boston pageant in November 1910, directed the dancing. Born in 1881, Tanner received A.B. and M.A. degrees from Radcliffe College, where she studied drama with George Pierce Baker. She also danced professionally and taught dancing in Boston area settlement houses. The Farnsworths' summer camps in nearby Fairlee, Camp Hanoum and Camp Aloha, run by Luther Gulick's brother and sister-in-law, provided Tanner's dancers for the Thetford pageant and paid her $150 fee. Langdon announced that since Thetford contained few "foreigners" his historical pageant need not include folk dances, a typical feature of playground pageants of the period. But Tanner, Charlotte Farnsworth, and Gulick, all prominent folk dance advocates nationally, inserted several Anglo-American country dances in various pageant scenes.[35]

Yet the main form of dance Tanner taught the performers was not the traditional dancing of rural New England, but rather the new dramatic story dancing and "aesthetic dancing" pioneered by Isadora Duncan and widely, if clumsily, imitated in everything from elite tableaux vivants to children's playground festivals.[36] Langdon had seen Duncan dance several times in New York City and much preferred her style, which allowed direct dramatic expression of abstract ideas and powerful emotions, to the classical ballet of Anna Pavlova, which he claimed had no "civic value," or to the contemporary "Barbary-coast type" of popular dance.[37] He asked Tanner to model her artistic dramatic dances for the Thetford pageant on those of Duncan in order to reinforce the emotional power of pageant scenes and to carry the story line smoothly between historical episodes. Symbolic dance imparted to Langdon's Thetford pageant a thematic continuity lacking in previous historical pageants. Within a month of Tanner's arrival, bare-limbed girls from the summer camps in Fairlee romped in Greek gowns through the hills of rural Vermont, rehearsing their dances for the pageant.

A newly purchased Macy's stopwatch in hand, Langdon returned to Thetford in June to supervise final pageant production and rehearsals. Residents pulled many of their costumes from local attics; Langdon's wife Marion, up from New York, supervised the construction of any new ones. As pageant day approached, Langdon's "study of the rural problem in dramatic form" began to take shape.[38] Costumes were completed, sets constructed, and booths erected outside the pageant grounds to sell food, drink, and souvenir postcards. On Saturday, August 12, at 3:00 P.M., *The Pageant of Thetford* began.

In the pageant's introduction, Virginia Tanner's young dancers, in the guise of "Nature Spirits," frolic to the strains of an original composition by James Sleeper. The Nature Spirits continue their innocent revelry undisturbed by the Indians who slip into the pageant field but abruptly depart at the arrival of the first white man. Thetford's history now begins.

Langdon intended that the first section of three realistic historical episodes depict the "making" of the town. It begins with the coming of "Old Quail John," Thetford's first white inhabitant. He negotiates with the Indians for a place to settle, and, with an "Indian Melody" playing in the background, they smoke a peace pipe to cement their friendship. In the second scene, portrayed by the residents of Thetford Center and North Thetford, the town fights the Revolutionary War. As the Green Mountain Boys march off to battle General Burgoyne, to the tune of "Yankee Doodle," Thetford's women take charge of the family farms, stalwartly plowing fields and harvesting crops.

Virginia Tanner and dancers at Thetford. Rather than classical or folk dance, Tanner taught girls from area summer camps the dramatic style of dancing pioneered by Isadora Duncan and Ruth St. Denis. (Brown University Library)

The first section ends with the founding of Thetford's first church, when the assembled townspeople sing three traditional hymns.

As the citizens from the church scene leave the pageant field, the dancing Nature Spirits from the introduction reappear, beckoned by a "Puritan," "Ranger," "Minuteman," and "Farmer." A second group of dancers joins them, led by the "Spirit of Home"; "Her dance," explained Langdon, "is one of motherhood, of tenderness and understanding."[39] Thetford was changing from a rough frontier settlement into an established community of families. The dancers retreat, clearing the grounds for the next section of episodes depicting the town's "development."

This portion of the production displayed Thetford at the height of its prosperity in the early nineteenth century. The first scene reenacts the founding of the Thetford Academy; it was played by the people of its home village, Thetford Hill. The scene ends with all singing the school song. The next episode, portrayed by the residents of Union Village, reproduces a country fair of 1835. The Thetford of old bustles with livestock, displays of household goods, colorful vendors, and festive games. The final scene of the town's development was to have

Old Quail John and the Indians. As in most historical pageants of the period, Langdon depicted relations between Native Americans and whites as one of smooth transition rather than violent conflict. Note in these and subsequent illustrations the telegraph lines across the pageant field in full view of the audience. (Courtesy of Margaret Langdon; Smithsonian Institution)

shown the coming of the railroad. Langdon tried to borrow an early locomotive engine built in 1848 to illustrate the new way in which farmers brought their goods to market. The Boston and Maine Railroad declined to lend the engine, however, so the scene was omitted.

Dancers then return to the pageant field, interspersing their lively country dances with pantomimes of traditional household industry— threshing grain, boiling maple sugar, spinning, and weaving. Suddenly the red-clad "Spirit of War" appears, rudely disrupting their simple joyful dance. The dancers band together to confront the menacing spirit.

The symbolic coming of the Civil War signaled the third section of realistic historical episodes, tracing the "depletion" of Thetford. The Civil War scene, played by the local chapter of the Grand Army of the Republic and the residents of Post Mills, begins with soldiers marching off to war, "The Battle Hymn of the Republic" sounding in the background. The remaining townspeople then gather to hear news from the front. One dispatch arrives from "Gettysburg," when the names of Thetford's war dead are read aloud. The second dispatch, from "Vicksburg," proclaims that the Union has won the war. The scene

Off to the Revolutionary War. The Green Mountain Boys march off to fight General Burgoyne to the tune of "Yankee Doodle." (Brown University Library)

Interlude: Dance of the Nature Spirits. The spirits of the "River," "Intervale," and "Mountains" are joined by the "Spirit of Home," representing the transition from a frontier settlement to an established community of families. (Courtesy of Margaret Langdon; Smithsonian Institution)

ends as the soldiers, some wounded, return home. According to Langdon, the Civil War began Thetford's depletion by "killing many of [its] best young men and bereaving many of its best women."[40]

Thetford's "depletion" continues in the next two scenes, entitled "The Introduction of Machinery" and "The Rural Problem." New agricultural machinery drove fieldhands and small farmers off the land to seek employment in the cities. Langdon's pageant shows "Ben Farmer" buying a new mower and firing "Sam Small," who had worked for Ben to supplement the income from his own small plot. With his source of extra income gone, Sam sells his land to Ben and departs, with "Richard Towne," for the manufacturing cities to the south. Thetford reaches its nadir in "The Rural Problem." Young "Joe Edwards" sees no future in Thetford and abandons his family's farm. The depletion of Thetford is marked by discouraged youth and the breakup of the family. At this point the desolate "Spirit of Thetford"—"clad in rather dingy green and blue, so faded as to be almost brown"—slumps onto the pageant field to the accompaniment of somber chords from the orchestra.[41]

Suddenly, however, the orchestra strikes a triumphant note as the radiant "Spirit of Pageantry," danced by Virginia Tanner, wheels across the pageant field to the music of Dvořák's "Humoresque." She appeals to the dejected Thetford, who slowly rises up, "her face radiant with confidence in the future, her arms upraised to the heavens."[42] Pageantry enters into Langdon's story of the community, transforming Thetford's despair into faith.

The final section of pageant scenes presented the Thetford of the future, revitalized by the Country Life movement. The setting is a country fair of 1915. Amid the bounteous displays of farm machinery, livestock, and produce, the "Master of the Grange" (played by Charles Cook, the real master of the Thetford Grange) and "Henry West," a former Thetford farmer back for a visit, discuss the town's new prosperity, which they attribute to scientific agricultural techniques and modern methods of cooperative marketing. Troops of "Boy Scouts" and "Campfire Girls" arrive as evidence of the town's new social vitality. The boys demonstrate lifesaving techniques, the girls outdoor cooking and dancing. The whole community, as depicted on stage, then gathers for a picnic, singing "Come with a Cheer, Good Neighbors, Come," an original James Sleeper composition. As the fair scene ends, Henry West decides to resettle in Thetford.

The symbolic "Thetford," now resplendent in a vibrant blue-green robe, a pageant shield in one hand, a "sword of power" in the other, her head crowned with a laurel wreath of victory, joins the happy group on the pageant field. She summons around her all the Nature Spirits. The assembled townspeople, Thetford, and the Nature Spirits

Home from the war. The first section of episodes depicting Thetford's "depletion" gained added poignancy from aging Civil War veterans playing themselves a half-century younger. (Courtesy of Margaret Langdon; Smithsonian Institution)

The rural problem. Young Joe Edwards tells his parents that he is abandoning the family farm. (Thetford Historical Society)

Virginia Tanner as the Spirit of Pageantry. (Courtesy of Margaret Langdon; Smithsonian Institution)

The Thetford of the future. This scene depicts a country fair of 1915 in which newly organized troops of Boy Scouts and Campfire Girls demonstrate their skills. (Courtesy of Margaret Langdon, Smithsonian Institution)

then cheer the arrival of "Vermont," mounted on a white horse and lofting a green banner. Vermont in turn calls "America," also mounted and garbed in white, and riders carrying banners representing each of the other New England states. When this entourage reaches the pageant field, they raise the U.S. flag and all sing "The Star-Spangled Banner." Thetford, with the support of Vermont, her sister New England states, and the federal government, will again be prosperous and happy. The cast then parades off the field, ending the pageant.

The history presented in *The Pageant of Thetford* depicted a thriving agricultural community depleted after the Civil War but resuscitated by working together with the federal government and neighboring New England states in the crusade for the New Country Life. Langdon summarized his pageant "plot" as illustrating "a transition from the methods of economic independence on a household or town basis to methods of economic interdependence with national relations." The "future" scenes demonstrated the tangible benefits of these new national relations. Langdon declared, "The people of Thetford made this pageant not their historian merely, but their prophet."[43]

Langdon's "prophetic" format had much in common with the typical holiday historical oration of the late nineteenth century. Like the

Entrance of America and the New England states. The grand finale repre-sented federal and state representatives of the Country Life movement coming to help Thetford prosper. (Courtesy of Margaret Langdon, Smithsonian Institution)

jeremiad, Langdon's pageant lamented the community's present de-cline and promised future progress in return for heeding the "lessons of the past." Just as Lucius Chittenden in his centennial speech on July 4, 1876, praised "The Character of the Early Settlers of Vermont," Langdon intended the early scenes of the Thetford pageant to show "the character of the men and women who built the town" as inspira-tion for local residents' future behavior.[44] If past generations of resi-dents could unite to overcome hardships, the present generation could do so as well. Scenes of Thetford's social and economic progress still appeared within the essentially religious framework for history common in the nineteenth century, which emphasized townspeople's adherence to moral principles attributed to the past in order to ensure the fulfillment of their sacred communal destiny.

Yet the main lesson of Thetford's history, as depicted in Langdon's pageant, was how each generation acted to adapt to its present circum-stances and shape its own future. The dramatization of scenes from the past, present, and future represented a ritual of communal trans-formation in which local residents participated in the projection of their future history and civic identity. In the pageant, at least, the residents of Thetford not only faced the future but also mastered it. The pageant experience mirrored that of a religious revival, with the community's achievement of the "millennium," as Langdon described it, depicted tangibly in its "future" scenes rather than merely alluded to rhetorically. "Centering in the intense moment of these few days," he declared, "the whole town is re-created."[45] Local residents participated in this process of communal regeneration, guided by images they acted out on the pageant field.

In Langdon's pageant, images of townspeople playing together in traditional pursuits—dancing, singing, and frolicking at county fairs —persisted throughout this communal transformation. Scenes depicting the community's progressive historical evolution—its "making," "development," "depletion," and "future"—alternated on the pageant field with scenes depicting its timeless folk traditions and expressions of shared emotion. As Langdon put it, "each period brings community life up into a new focus, but always the same community life, the same emotional substance."[46] Folk traditions such as dancing, singing, frolicking at county fairs, and husking bees expressed the emotional substance of community life in tangible form. Langdon's historical pageant emphasized that Thetford residents' future progress depended on preserving their enduring folk traditions as residents of a New England village as well as joining the mainstream of American life— their ability to retain a primal authenticity even while embracing modernity.

The symbolic dance and musical interludes reinforced Langdon's pageant imagery of the community expressing its emotional substance while in graceful transition between periods of historical development. The abstract spirit of the community reappeared after each set of realistic historical episodes, presenting a tangible community image with which the people of Thetford could identify. Langdon's pageant form, interspersing symbolic dancing with realistic historical reenactment, displayed the powerful emotional ties of community persisting through the town's changing circumstances.

But the portrait of the evolution of a New England town as presented in the Thetford pageant reveals striking juxtapositions as well as orderly transitions. Photographs of the performance show the pageant field, even during scenes of the "forest primeval," bisected by telegraph lines, the railroad passing close by the grandstand. The sense of identification between performer and audience achieved by reenacting "their" history as a communal rite of passage was compromised by the fact that the grandstand was packed with tourists and summer residents whose ties to Thetford were very different from those of its year-round residents.

Thetford pageant grounds near the Boston and Maine Railroad. Sandwiched between the railroad tracks and the telegraph lines, spectators were never far from reminders of the modern present even during the most bucolic early episodes. (Brown University Library)

Moreover, the pageant painted a distorted picture of the town's history. Intent on portraying an ideal, closely knit agricultural community, Langdon overlooked the ethnic, class, and denominational diversity in Thetford's past. The Thetford census of 1790 included three nonwhite households. From 1805 through 1811, the town meeting ordered fifty-eight people to leave Thetford so that it would not be responsible for the relief of their poverty. Although a "Congregationalist" town, as early as 1786 one-fourth of the population worshipped as Anglicans and Baptists. The Methodist circuits first reached Thetford in 1804, and by 1812 the Congregationalist church was no longer supported by taxes.[47] None of this ethnic, class, or religious diversity surfaced in Langdon's pageant.

His production also overlooked Thetford's past economic diversity. Neither sawmills nor factories appeared in the pageant, although they were (and continued to be) a tremendously important part of the local economy, especially in the village of Post Mills where, perhaps not coincidentally, residents reportedly displayed the most reluctance to participate in the pageant. The historical episodes also neglected the growth of Thetford as a rural resort in the late nineteenth century. Entrepreneurs had begun building hotels and tourist cabins in Thetford in the 1870s. By 1911, the year of the pageant, the area boasted numerous summer homes and three summer camps.[48] Summer residents—the Farnsworths—had been the instigators of the Thetford pageant in the first place.

Langdon's pageant, in order to convince the townspeople of the need for the reforms of the Country Life movement, probably also exaggerated the town's economic decline. A detailed study of Chelsea, Vermont, in the same county as Thetford, shows that the area in the late nineteenth century experienced stagnation in its economy and population but not decline. Though few new farms were established, few were abandoned. Thetford's "Leaving Home" tableau was real, but it is likely that most farm children who did not remain on the family farm moved to neighboring towns.[49]

Thus in 1911 Thetford was not a depressed agricultural community; rather, it enjoyed a diversified economy in which local residents made their living not only from agriculture but also from tourism and manufacturing. Langdon chose to present Thetford as a homogeneous agricultural town in his historical pageant because, like many Country Life activists, he venerated the "sturdy values" of the farmer, and because this was the kind of town in which its citizens wanted to believe they lived. Both summer and year-round residents agreed to rewrite conflict and industrialism out of Thetford's past in favor of the farm town identity that would bring more tourists to the area. Railroads promoted rural Vermont as pastoral and unspoiled; Langdon and the townspeople involved in the pageant, even while introducing the "modern" reforms of the New Country Life, wanted to keep this pastoral image intact. Langdon proposed that Thetford build a new tourist hotel as part of its revitalization program but did not depict the hotel in the "future" scenes of his pageant.[50]

Ultimately, the nostalgic vision of rural New England common to the Country Life movement, coupled with local residents' willingness to market their "simple traditions" and Anglo-American homogeneity to tourists, shaped the particular version of Thetford history that appeared in the pageant as much as Langdon's future-oriented appeal for rural social transformation. Like another Russell Sage Foundation project, John C. and Olive Dame Campbell's ballad collecting in the southern Appalachians, Langdon's pageant work contained a strong element of teaching the proper version of indigenous culture to the natives; it implied that rural New Englanders' commercial amusements and ethnic or industrial lore interfered with the rediscovery of their "authentic" culture on which the New Country Life could be built. And this culture, as depicted in pageant country dances and Colonial revival spinning wheels, gave the audience a retrograde as much as a progressive vision of New England history.[51]

The Pageant of Thetford's presentation of the nostalgic aspects of rural New England culture brought in tourists and contributed to its financial success. Even with half of its final performance rained out, the sale of tickets and souvenir programs to the approximately 3,000 who attended the three performances enabled the pageant to not only recover its $800 production costs but turn a profit as well.[52] Despite the pageant's often ponderous didacticism, Thetford residents seemed to enjoy dressing up as their ancestors and presenting it, as well as making a splash outside the area. The local Bradford *United Opinion* insisted that Thetford's experience offered no less than an "object lesson" eagerly watched by the U.S. Department of Agriculture, the University of Vermont, the Russell Sage Foundation, and neighboring towns. The Rutland *Daily Herald* pronounced the affair "something more than the ordinary pageant" and noted its unique dancing.[53]

The Thetford pageant also succeeded somewhat in achieving Langdon's social goals for the town. His prophecy of Thetford's native sons returning home failed to come true—the town lost even more population from 1910 to 1930 than from 1890 to 1910.[54] But the town's orchestra and chorus, Boy Scouts and Campfire Girls continued to meet, as did the pageant committee, which as late as 1930 still debated what to do with the pageant profits. The town declared each August 12 thereafter a holiday, and in 1921 and 1937 Langdon returned to Thetford for reunions. The pageant became a part of Thetford's history: even though it did not work a social transformation, neither the event nor the local community organizations founded in its wake were forgotten.[55]

William Chauncy Langdon returned to New York City in the fall of 1911 eager to create more historical pageants. He ordered personalized stationery printed with the title "pageant-master" embossed after his name at the top of each sheet. He again suggested that the Russell Sage Foundation establish a Bureau of American Pageantry and provide him with funds to stage demonstration pageants, with all pageant profits up to the amount of the original grant to be returned to the foundation. When the foundation rejected these proposals, Langdon approached a commercial theatrical agent about being booked as a pageant-master but did not follow through when he discovered the agent's fee would be $1,000 or 20 percent. Langdon even thought that he could earn money to finance his pageant work by writing for the legitimate stage and asked English pageant-master Louis Napoleon Parker for an opinion, based on the Thetford pageant script, of his play-writing ability. Langdon admitted, "While I have always had dramatic tastes and inclinations, my work has been so much more along civic and educational lines that I do not know how to start to try to break into this new field." Nevertheless, at age forty, with a wife and two small children to support, he had given up all other work for community historical pageantry. Langdon pressed Parker: "I have no means; I have got to succeed."[56]

As Langdon's reputation spread through magazine articles about the Thetford pageant (many of which Langdon wrote himself), pageant offers from other towns finally began to arrive.[57] Leaders of the Country Life movement lauded Langdon's work as a model for how the new pageantry could transform country towns and invited him to lecture at their conferences and extension courses on rural recreation and social organization.[58] He parlayed these appearances into invitations to serve as pageant-master for several towns. After one such address at a public recreation conference in Springfield, Massachusetts, sponsored by the YMCA, he received over two dozen inquiries. The Russell Sage Foundation asked him to prepare a pamphlet on *The Celebration of the Fourth of July by Means of Pageantry* and include his own model July Fourth pageant. The foundation, though not paying him a regular salary, listed him as a "consulting expert on pageantry" and advanced him a guaranteed loan of $3,000 against his future pageant fees.[59] With this backing, Langdon assumed the direction of historical pageants in several New England towns. St. Johnsbury, Vermont, hired him to create a pageant for its 150th anniversary in July 1912. The next year Langdon staged pageants in Meriden, New Hampshire, and Darien, Connecticut. In 1914, he produced a pageant to celebrate the opening of the Cape Cod Canal in Massachusetts.

Langdon and the local townspeople billed each of the New England productions as a "Pageant of the New Country Life." Each production examined a local "problem" and projected a "solution." Langdon hoped that his St. Johnsbury pageant would stimulate the prosperous Vermont town, known for its manufacture of scales, to become a "metropolis of the New Country Life" and assume responsibility for promoting the well-being of the surrounding agricultural area. The historical pageant in Meriden, New Hampshire, commemorating the one hundredth anniversary of the local Kimball Union Academy, focused on the role of education in the New Country Life. Darien, Connecticut, was a wealthy suburb of New York City; its pageant (which cost $10,000 to produce, compared with $800 at Thetford) addressed the changing role of the small town as it became a suburb of a large metropolitan area. At Cape Cod, Langdon's pageant projected the future economic integration of the far-flung towns on the

Cape through cooperative agricultural marketing. In another pageant, planned for the Massachusetts Agricultural College in Amherst in 1917, Langdon outlined the role of university experts in easing the transition from the Age of Homespun to that of the New Country Life.[60]

Langdon's organizational strategy for his other New Country Life pageants reproduced the formula he employed in Thetford. Once contacted, he came to town to lecture on pageantry to a group of civic leaders, illustrating his talk with slides of his Thetford work. His fee for writing and directing a pageant varied; the Darien pageant paid him best—$1,500.[61] To ensure financial stability, Langdon insisted that each of the pageants in which he became involved have a separate advance subscription fund raised as a guarantee against insufficient income from ticket sales.[62] As at Thetford, Langdon assigned the casting of pageant episodes to various local community groups, while importing expert pageant production help from afar. His wife Marion supervised costuming. Arthur Farwell of New York City, listed on the Thetford pageant's "Advisory Committee," continued his collaboration with Langdon as musical adviser for the St. Johnsbury pageant and composed original music for the historical pageants at Meriden and Darien.[63] Langdon remained principal writer and director of each pageant. But as the number of Langdon's pageant projects increased, his role as liaison between local and national social service organizations for any one town faded into the background. Only at Meriden, New Hampshire, did he organize an advisory committee of outside social service experts in conjunction with the historical pageant.

The other New Country Life pageants used a format similar to that of Thetford. Each was held on a hill from which the townscape as "hero" remained in view of the audience—at St. Johnsbury, on the links of the Old Pine Golf Club. Each alternated reenactments of important events in the town's political and economic history with timeless social and domestic scenes; at St. Johnsbury between the "Founding of the Town" and the Revolution was an episode depicting "pioneer sociability"—a scene of neighbors visiting one another. Later in the same pageant came another social scene more typical of pageants on urban playgrounds, featuring French, German, Scandinavian, Scottish, Irish, and Italian children dancing in ethnic costume. Each pageant also featured abstract symbolic dancing in preludes and interludes between realistic historical reenactments depicting the evolution of the town from forest primeval to the ideal community of the future created by the reforms of the Country Life movement. *The Pageant of Cape Cod* opened with a symbolic dance depicting "The

Directing The Pageant of Meriden, *New Hampshire, 1913. Langdon directed large groups on the pageant field by means of color-coded signals on cards he lofted above his head. (Brown University Library)*

Formation of the Cape, The Pageant of Cape Cod, *1914. Beyond the dancers is the Cape Cod Canal, the "hero" which remained in full view of the audience throughout the pageant performance. (Brown University Library)*

Formation of the Cape," in which dancers clad as deep blue "waters of the ocean" and light blue "waters of the bay" surged together, leaving behind brown-clad "sand beaches." A later dance interlude featured "Fortune"—a woman clad in gold—eluding local cranberry growers until they began cooperative marketing. *The Pageant of Darien* represented the transition from country town to suburb with a symbolic dance interlude titled "The Commuters," in which men danced off to work, kissing their wives and children good-bye, then returned in the evening to their waiting families.

Each of Langdon's New Country Life pageants concluded with a finale in which the New England states, personified on horseback and led by "America" garbed in white and riding a white horse, joined the local townspeople. The St. Johnsbury finale underscored the theme of New England communities banded together in the crusade for the New Country Life through the appearance of the "Knights of St. John," each representing a town of the surrounding Caledonia County and Passumpsic River Valley.[64] The finales at Meriden, Darien, and Cape Cod added a scene where the community gathered around a Greek altar in which blazed the "Community Fire." The Medieval and classical imagery emphasized the necessity for maintaining close-knit local community cohesion in the midst of a future that necessarily also would include new outside relations.

Knights of St. John, The Pageant of St. Johnsbury, *1912. Garbed in "chain mail" outfits of lace curtains sprayed with silver radiator paint, the knights represented the Medieval idealism and spirit of unity that Langdon wanted to promote among the town's residents. Unlike similar images of knights appearing in British pageantry, Langdon placed this antimodern imagery in a future-oriented reform context. (Brown University Library)*

Though viewed by their local sponsors—the St. Johnsbury Commercial Club, the Darien Women's Civic League, the Cape Cod Board of Trade—largely as another form of civic boosterism, Langdon regarded his pageants of the New Country Life as a unique opportunity to practice civic education, history, and dramatics on a grand scale. He saw himself as an "interpretive lens" projecting a version of history that would help the residents of New England towns to act out new roles and identities, solve current problems, and envision future progress. Historical pageantry could help local residents better understand the social transformations they experienced in the early twentieth century and acquire "a clear comprehension of the history of their town as a whole, and therefore of the place of their new undertakings in the whole." Having demonstrated the apparently boundless potential of historical pageantry in New England, Langdon and his fellow pageant-masters redoubled their efforts to publicize the new form of civic celebration across the nation as a powerful tool of community revitalization.[65]

4 Community Development Is the Plot

. . . .

Pageantry is the form of art which comes
nearest to expressing the new social idea
which is already moving through one
hundred million minds, and which is
destined to make the world over in the
next century or so. . . . It may be said to
constitute, along with orchestral music,
the typical Nineteenth and Twentieth
Century Art.
—John Collier, April 1913

The art in this pageant program depicts the aboriginal past and the technological present as successive stages in local community development. (Brown University Library)

On December 2, 1910, editor Walter Hines Page of *World's Work* rejected William Chauncy Langdon's article describing the Boston civic pageant of the preceding month, grumbling, "All this cave-man symbolism can't possibly interest a reader in Oshkosh." Six months later, the citizens of Oshkosh, Wisconsin, cheered a seven-episode historical pageant presented by the local State Normal School. In the words of *American Homes and Gardens*, America was going "pageant mad." Well-known figures such as Jane Addams, G. Stanley Hall, and Ida Tarbell extolled the virtues of pageantry in the national press; so did the leaders of local school, business, and women's organizations across the nation. Support for pageantry spanned the ideological spectrum from the Daughters of the American Revolution (DAR) to the Industrial Workers of the World (IWW), the artistic spectrum from William Dean Howells to Randolph Bourne. Popular novelist Booth Tarkington even submitted his famous young character Penrod Schofield to a "Pageant of the Table Round."[1]

Local promoters billed a variety of festivities as "pageants." The term stretched to include both the Bryn Mawr College students' annual May Day fête and the Sing Sing Prison inmates' celebration welcoming back their warden after his acquittal of corruption charges. A Christmas "pageant" in Los Angeles' Exposition Park in 1915 paraded real elephants, camels, and exotically costumed extras borrowed from nearby Hollywood film studios before 15,000 spectators. Nina Lamkin, the professional recreation worker, toured a Chautauqua circuit organizing "Mother Goose pageants" for children, to be presented at the close of the show's stay in each town. *The Pageant of Darkness and Light*, produced in Chicago in 1913 to promote foreign missionary work, gathered members of 550 churches from 22 Protestant denominations. "Pageants" rallied support for causes large and small, from woman suffrage and the striking Paterson, New Jersey, silk workers to the creation of a bird sanctuary in New Hampshire. Pageants such as Fresno's *The Princess and the Magic Raisins* honored local commercial products.[2]

Commercial theatrical producing companies, which had long had a sideline in the holiday entertainment business, hustled to meet this new demand. They offered to furnish local celebration committees not only with ready-made historical costumes and properties but also with directors and scripts. One such firm, the Industrial and Historical Pageant Corporation, a subsidiary of Van Horn and Son, Costumers, opened offices in Chicago, New York City, Philadelphia, and Los Angeles. Its flyers boasted "Sane July Fourth Celebrations" as one of the firm's specialties and promised, "Any city that is progressive enough to produce an historical pageant is sure to attract visitors to its doors."[3] The firm retained A. H. Stoddard, who had made his reputation in the New Orleans Mardi Gras and New York City Hudson-Fulton Celebration, as the principal "pageant-master." In a few short

Letterhead, Van Horn and Son, Costumers, ca. 1909. Commercial producing companies hustled to meet the demand from a nation that had gone pageant-mad. (Brown University Library)

years, pageantry had become not only a popular pastime but a profitable business as well.

Social workers, artists, and dramatists who earlier promoted historical pageantry as a powerful tool of civic revitalization now worried about the speed with which the pageantry craze had ballooned. Langdon wondered whether pageantry would become merely a "temporary, superficial fad and vanish." Hazel MacKaye, an actress and director based in Boston, noted that Americans had embraced pageantry with "hot impetuousness" and warned that if "left to itself, the movement will burn out in a flaming procession of spasmodic and uncorrelated spectacles." Ellis Paxson Oberholtzer, the Philadelphia historian, cautioned further, "If those pageants are not carefully planned and wrought out by historians and artists, . . . they will be worse than useless. They will have no advantages over the vulgar carnivals and parades which we have always had." The *Nation* worried that civic pageantry, like other municipal holiday endeavors, would fall into the hands of the political machine. Moreover, the explosion of pageants had outpaced the publication of readily accessible guidebooks offering instructions on how to stage one properly. Langdon admitted to Professor James Ford of Harvard University early in 1913 that "there is no bibliography of pageantry as yet, and the material so rapidly becomes unattainable that to prepare one seems almost like sending people on a fine assortment of wild goose chases."[4]

Those interested in pageantry as a means of civic revitalization saw the need to somehow gain control of the craze: to define the term "pageant" and prevent its "promiscuous" use, to promote themselves as trained, expert pageant-masters amid the incompetent amateurs and slick commercial producers crowding the field, and to disseminate reliable information about their ephemeral specialty. Langdon's efforts to persuade the Russell Sage Foundation to establish a Bureau of American Pageantry to assume these duties had failed; so had similar attempts to interest the Playground and Recreation Association of America and the Drama League of America. Although the latter organizations, concerned respectively with the promotion of wholesome public recreation and amateur dramatics, had created "festivals" committees, neither devoted much attention to the increasingly demanding task of ensuring community pageantry's "right development."[5]

In 1913 the self-appointed guardians of the new pageantry formed their own organization, the American Pageant Association (APA). Who were these pageant-masters? What did they hope to accomplish? How were their efforts received in cities and towns across America? And how did their notions of history, of community, and of professional expertise interact with the customary ways of representing history in public holiday celebrations to shape the organization and expression of tradition in the Progressive Era?

The American Pageant Association was born during a conference on the new pageantry held in Boston under the auspices of the local Twentieth Century Club's Drama Committee. Among those present were William Chauncy Langdon, composer Arthur Farwell, and drama professor George Pierce Baker of Harvard, as well as Lotta A. Clark, Frank Chocteau Brown, and Vesper George, the trio that organized and directed the Boston civic pageant of 1910. The group organized an executive board, consisting of themselves and a few others, and elected Langdon the APA's first president. Brown announced that the new association would "protect from misuse a form of dramatic presentation or festival celebration that is inherently the property of the people, and that was—and still is—in grave danger of being commercialized and diverted from its rightful purpose." The association would "establish and define the scope of pageantry" as well as give "added authority and prestige to those pageant-masters working along the right lines."[6]

The American Pageant Association sought to guide the course of pageantry through conferences, publications, and training programs. At the second annual conference in New York City in 1914, pageant directors exchanged information, read papers on topics such as "Outdoor Festival Dancing," "The Educational Value of Festal Music," and "The Relation of the Pageant to Regular Drama," and showed lantern slides of one another's work. At the 1915 meeting in Philadelphia, four directors showed motion pictures of pageants they had created. In Boston in 1916, the APA met with the Drama League of Boston and, in addition to hearing papers, attended the performance of Virginia Tanner's *Pageant of Technology* for the Massachusetts Institute of Technology.[7]

Many of the papers read at the APA conventions were later published in the *American Pageant Association Bulletin*. From 1913 through 1916, the association published forty-three one-page bulletins, an average of nearly one per month, on the technical aspects of pageantry such as writing, costuming, dance, and music. The bulletins also contained an annotated chronological list of "recognized" pageants, beginning with Louis Napoleon Parker's Sherbourne pageant in 1905. The lists not only informed members of their colleagues' past and upcoming activities, but also attempted to define the term "pageant" by restricting its use, retroactively, only to certain types of civic events. Ellis P. Oberholtzer's Philadelphia Founders Week procession of 1908 was included in the list of previous pageants; New York City's Hudson-Fulton procession of 1909 was not.[8]

Members of the American Pageant Association also attempted to promulgate standards for American pageantry by teaching classes on the subject at various universities. Among the schools offering summer courses in pageantry were Harvard, Dartmouth, Columbia, Yale, the University of Wisconsin, Indiana University, the University of Illinois, the University of North Dakota, and the University of California. In the aftermath of Langdon's pageants of the "New Country Life," these classes enjoyed special popularity with agricultural extension departments. Pageant directors shared their expertise in drama, social work, and historical research with local schoolteachers, recreation workers, and civic boosters seeking "proper instruction" in the new way of celebrating holidays.[9]

Leaders of the APA further sought to control the pageantry movement by certifying pageant-masters. Like other fledgling municipal experts in the Progressive Era, the pageant-masters had to persuade their clients of the need for expertise in an activity customarily performed by amateurs. Although anyone could become an "Associate Member" of the American Pageant Association for one dollar, "Active

Membership" was restricted to those pageant-masters voted that status by the APA board of directors. Frank Chocteau Brown explained that active membership in the APA served the same function that restricted classes of membership served in other professional bodies such as the American Institute of Architects—as "an official guarantee as to the judgement, experience, and ability of the individual member." In 1914, the American Pageant Association published *Who's Who in Pageantry*, a twelve-page pamphlet listing pageant-masters of whom it approved, with the names of the active members of the APA printed in large type. Twenty-one of the thirty-two names listed in the booklet were active members. Each pageant worker paid two dollars for his or her listing and one hundred copies of the pamphlet.[10]

The active members listed by the American Pageant Association shared similar social, educational, professional, and regional backgrounds. Nearly all were in their thirties and college-educated and had worked in either education and social work or fine arts and theater. Significantly, in an age when women were often restricted to the lower rungs of their chosen professions, women and men appeared in *Who's Who in Pageantry* in approximately equal numbers both as technical experts and as supervisory pageant-masters. Virginia Tanner and Violet Oakley broke into pageantry as technical advisers in dance and art, respectively, but soon went on to direct their own pageants. Women's prominence in pageantry led one male pageant director in 1914 to gripe about the threat of his craft degenerating into "a self-vaunting picnic party of undomesticated feminists"—but such overt expressions of hostility between men and women in pageantry seemed the exception. More common was the response of New York dramatist Percy MacKaye, who extolled pageant directing, like teaching and social work, as "a new profession for women."[11]

Although ostensibly the APA was a national organization with active members drawn from coast to coast, in fact, most members hailed from either the Northeast or the Midwest, and nearly all of those involved in the organization's administration—arranging meetings, editing the *Bulletin*, compiling membership lists—lived between Boston and Philadelphia. The association's total membership nationwide never exceeded 250, its active membership no more than three dozen.[12] Clearly the American Pageant Association did not represent everyone in America who staged pageants, but rather a relatively small group of artists, educators, and social workers who banded together to attempt to assert technical and aesthetic standards in a wide-open field and to distinguish themselves as pageant "experts" amid the growing crowd of amateur and commercial directors.

APA members with the most to gain by promulgating standards of professional expertise were those with backgrounds in the theater. At the turn of the century, dramatists had helped patriotic and hereditary societies create their extravagant evenings of tableaux vivants, and they had been attracted to the recreation workers' playground festivals as opportunities to teach children and immigrants about American artistic traditions. But by the early 1910s, a growing consciousness among dramatists of their own professional interests and social responsibilities had evolved into an agenda for the reform of civic holiday celebrations different from that of either the playground workers or the patriotic and hereditary elite. This agenda involved using public holiday celebrations to develop themes and audiences for a new American theater, one that would revitalize the thin artistic traditions of the American stage as it overturned the dominance of commercial entertainment entrepreneurs. Significantly, the leaders of this movement were employed primarily by colleges and universities rather than the commercial stage. Borrowing rhetoric from the era's crusades against monopoly, George Pierce Baker of Harvard University exhorted his colleagues that "we must take control of the theatres out into the country at large and out of New York City." Community historical pageantry offered a vehicle for dramatists to take their art to the countryside, in the process helping both the public and their profession.[13]

Dramatists argued that pageants represented an opportunity to whet the public's appetite for quality professional theater. They became involved in the pageantry movement not only through the American Pageant Association but also through the Drama League of America, an organization founded in 1911 to help develop "a new dramatic taste for the country."[14] At the first Drama League convention, William Norman Guthrie of the University of the South emphasized the possibilities of elevating mass taste. "Crowds can be managed in both ways, upward and downward," he said. Drama League members hoped to stimulate interest in quality theater through study classes, reading circles, lectures, and amateur dramatic productions such as pageants. Hazel MacKaye observed at the third annual Drama League convention in 1913 that, just as the public's appreciation of professional baseball developed in part from "the fact that the audiences have been participators, at one time or another, in the game which they witness," support for quality professional theater could grow out of the public's widespread participation as amateur actors in historical pageants. MacKaye hoped that pageantry would make theater, like baseball, a national pastime.[15]

Many dramatists saw the new pageantry not only as a vehicle for upgrading mass taste, but also as a source of new themes for their work. Thomas H. Dickinson of the University of Wisconsin, articulating a view common among his fellow academic dramatists, described community historical pageantry as "an early expression of an art impulse springing from the soil." Pageantry's naive dramatizations of events from the local past and present offered a uniquely American form of "social ceremonial," which promised to be the precursor of other, more formal types of American dramatic art, "one stage in the development from the lowest to the highest forms of dramatic expression." Just as native folk expressions blossomed into a distinctive national artistic identity in the hands of expert dramatists in Aeschylus's Greece and Shakespeare's England, they could do the same in twentieth-century America. Baker, who had directed a pageant in Peterborough, New Hampshire, in honor of composer Edward MacDowell, proclaimed, "I believe, if properly conducted, we may make of the Pageant something as significant for our day as the Masque was for the days of Elizabeth." American dramatists saw their efforts to promote historical pageantry as part of an international movement for a people's theater, one that would revitalize the drama from the bottom up by developing a popular aesthetic different from that of commercial amusements. Dramatists believed that the new pageantry could translate the nascent American folk spirit of the twentieth century into plays of lasting beauty, in a manner similar to the contemporary works based on national folk themes that they saw produced by W. B. Yeats in Ireland, Romain Rolland in France, the Bayreuth opera festivals in Germany, and Parker in England.[16]

Playwrights claimed that the development of a new American theater based on folk themes would have political implications as well—as a "drama of democracy" articulating the emerging new society in which the dramatists felt they lived. Dickinson insisted that drama should be "socially constructive," the dramatist actively engaged in "expanding the purposes of social progress." Socially useful drama would help society to "discover itself"; historical pageantry represented "an expression of the self-consciousness of the community as a social unit." "The new art finds itself in the social discovery," explained Dickinson. "Its experiments are but reflexes of the social readjustments, the mental queries and replies, by which another order is established." The participation of skilled artists in the creation of massive public rituals such as historical pageants would give form to expressions of this emerging new order and thus shape a common public understanding of the nature of that order.[17]

Among those who shared the professional dramatists' identification of the new pageantry with artistic liberation was Randolph Bourne. In an essay entitled "Pageantry and Social Art," Bourne noted that, through pageantry, "vistas of social expressiveness are opened that we have scarcely yet begun to realize here in America." Discussing the pageant's impact on its participants, he declared, "People cannot spend months on working up the dances and the scenes and the music without becoming conscious of that immense liberation which is ours today."[18] Though the pageant form had its origins in, and drew much of its support from, the pillars of genteel culture, artists saw in pageantry's encouragement of the play spirit the seeds of aesthetic liberation and the potential to upset customary notions of social and cultural hierarchy.

Professional composers regarded historical pageantry in a similar way—as a means of upgrading mass taste, yet also, through the incorporation of folk elements, of liberating American music from genteel artistic standards. Most active among composers as a promoter of the new pageantry was Arthur Farwell, who had served on the advisory committee for William Chauncy Langdon's first two pageants of the New Country Life at Thetford and St. Johnsbury as well as composed original music for Langdon's pageants for Darien and Meriden. Farwell, born in 1872, took a vital interest in linking the search for an "American" folk music with urban social reform. In 1901, he founded the Wa-Wan Press to publish works based on "Indian," "Negro," "Spanish-American," and "Cowboy" themes. His own compositions such as the *Navaho War Dance* set Native American melodies in a romantic symphonic setting. Farwell also headed the New York City Department of Recreation Orchestra, in which capacity he sought to introduce American music to audiences at summer concerts in Central Park, and served on the Art Committee of the New York Association of Neighborhood Workers. Though his own compositions were primarily in a conservative style, he gained notoriety in 1912 for his series of articles in *Musical America* defending ragtime music, which he argued was a legitimate product of the people, reflecting their unrefined but not necessarily degraded tastes.[19]

Close examination of how the three principal groups collaborating in the American Pageant Association saw the new pageantry reveals conflicts and inconsistencies. While professional dramatists identified the new pageantry with the liberation of American theater from genteel repression, patriotic and hereditary societies identified it with the conservation of genteel standards. While educators and playground workers exalted in pageantry's recreational value, offering the opportunity for mass participation in the expression of a childlike play spirit, professional dramatists valued these folk-play elements primarily as raw material to be incorporated into the work of expert dramatists and thus transform the American theater. To patriotic and hereditary societies, pageantry promised the restoration of Anglo-Saxon Protestants to the pinnacle of the social order; to educators and playground workers, the creation of a new democratic and pluralistic society.

But such close examination never occurred between 1913 and 1916, at the height of the American Pageant Association's membership and influence. Like many of the period's reform coalitions, differences between constituent groups were submerged in vague language, unbridled enthusiasm, and the perception of a common enemy—in the APA's case, commercial producers. Convinced that the new form was endangered, members of the American Pageant Association flooded the nation with advice on the right way to organize and produce a community historical pageant—even if the advice reflected the pageant-masters' own vague notions and occasionally heated disagreements over the proper organization and form of the new craft.

Members of the pageantry movement published numerous guides to casting, financing, and organizing local productions. Their advice for casting community historical pageants emphasized above all that every local resident should be invited to participate. Margaret MacLaren Eager cautioned that "the pageant-master must be sure he is in touch with the entire town." She felt that pageant directors must go beyond contacting the local historical society, chamber of commerce, women's club, and patriotic and hereditary societies to reach every organized constituency—church groups, ethnic societies, men's fraternal organizations. One of Eager's pageants in Newburgh, New York, listed twenty-six local organizations on its program, including both the Daughters of the American Revolution and the Slovak Sokal Union. Echoing the view of the playground workers of the previous decade, Clara Fitch, chair of the Drama League of America's Festivals Committee, extolled immigrant contributions to community pageantry: "We should grasp every opportunity to make [immigrants] feel they have a place in our play as well as in our work. Until recently the immigrant has been considered of economic value only. Now we know that his invaluable social heritage of art, music, story, and dance may be ours, if only we will utilize it."[20]

While the casting recommendations emphasized the inclusion of a wide variety of local groups, they also tended to reinforce the distinctions between those groups. Rather than suggesting that pageant roles be cast in ways that crossed ethnic, vocational, and organizational lines, pageant-masters recommended that the casting and rehearsal of each pageant episode be placed under the direction of a different group, whose members already knew one another and had experience working together. Katherine Lord's suggestion that local residents impersonate their vocational forebears—for example, that a present minister play the Colonial minister, a present schoolteacher play the schoolteacher of the past—had a similar effect.[21]

The casting recommendation that most had the effect of accentuating, rather than submerging, local social distinctions was that townspeople impersonate their ancestors. Eager noted that the "participation of descendants of pioneer settlers . . . [will] bring to the pageant an atmosphere that cannot otherwise be gained."[22] Her Newburgh pageant program scrupulously demarcated DAR members from Slovaks by indicating "descendant" next to the cast members who played their ancestors. The practice of casting descendants in the roles of their ancestors followed the custom evident in historical reenactments of the late nineteenth century that displayed descendants, especially elderly ones, as living links with the past.

Pageant-masters admitted that this casting formula did not work very well for the "Indian" scenes. Though nearly every historical pageant included at least one such episode, pageant-masters realized that few towns, especially in the East, had full-blooded Indians of the proper nation living nearby or local residents willing to identify with their Indian descent. Nor could towns be expected to pay to import genuine Indians from afar, as Oberholtzer did in Philadelphia in 1908. Instead, pageant-masters suggested that local organizations with an interest in Indian lore, such as the Boy Scouts or the Improved Order of Red Men, be assigned these roles, though one pageant writer suggested that Italian immigrants' complexions made them good Indians.[23] In the New York City Hudson-Fulton procession in 1909, black children played the Indians, though organizers also had some genuine Iroquois on hand. Feeling guilty about the "whoops and leaps" that ersatz Indians, ignorant of genuine Native American traditions, tended to add to their portrayals, Virginia Tanner observed, "America has never done the Red Man justice. It remains for her in Pageantry to finish him off completely."[24]

APA guidebooks proposed that ideally the pageant should be financially self-supporting. Langdon advised that, in an effectively promoted and managed pageant, receipts from ticket and program sales would cover production costs; he cautioned that using tax money or receipts from selling advertising to businesses threatened to politicize or commercialize the affair. In fact, however, nearly all community historical pageants were subsidized at least in part by local government appropriations and the revenue from local business advertisements in the souvenir programs. Members of the American Pageant Association did not actively condemn the practice of expending public funds

Black children impersonating Indians, New York City. These children marched in the city's Hudson-Fulton Celebration of 1909. (Edward Hagaman Hall, The Hudson-Fulton Celebration *[Albany, N.Y.: J. B. Lyon, 1910], 2:1261)*

on pageantry—though occasionally local taxpayers did. The proposal of a half-mill tax in Norristown, Pennsylvania, to subsidize a historical pageant in 1912 was greeted with a headline in the local paper: "Poor Man Will Pay for Jubilee." The same year, Ellis P. Oberholtzer created a second historical pageant in Philadelphia, this time in dramatic form, in which he again cast the leading families of the city. Oberholtzer intended to finance the production by filling 20,000 specially built grandstand seats priced from fifty cents to three dollars for each of six performances. City officials allowed him to stage the show in Fairmount Park, but, labeling the pageant a "private exhibition," refused to appropriate $10,000 to bail the production out of debt when local residents, accustomed to viewing civic celebrations for free and feeling that other shows provided more for their entertainment dollar, failed to purchase tickets.[25]

In addition to proper casting and financial management, argued the leaders of the national pageantry movement, each step in the production must be carefully planned, with a clear hierarchy of authority. APA members Mary Porter Beegle and Jack R. Crawford (who taught at Columbia and Yale universities, respectively) explained that "to give a pageant or production on a large scale requires the organi-

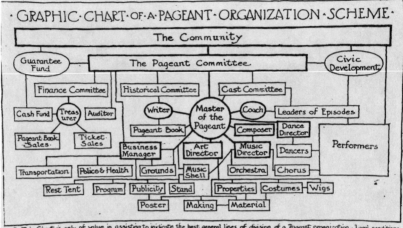

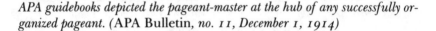

APA guidebooks depicted the pageant-master at the hub of any successfully organized pageant. (APA Bulletin, no. 11, December 1, 1914)

zation of a complex system. Only through business-like planning and preparation will the production attain artistic and financial success." One *APA Bulletin* included a model organizational chart for a "typical" pageant, containing a myriad of committees for production, financing, and publicity.[26]

At the hub of the pageant organization was the pageant-master, the supreme authority over all aspects of the production. Florence Magill Wallace of Illinois compared the pageant organization to that of an "army," in which "the best efficiency depends upon harmonious action, possible only when one general has control." Association members described the pageant-master position as similar to that of a municipal expert such as a city planner, detached from local politics. Professor Robert Withington of Smith College recommended that the pageant-master be hired from outside the local community, "so that he may use his best judgment, being tied by no local affiliations, biased by no local prejudices, independent of all local cliques." "As he has no local associations," concurred Ethel Theodora Rockwell of Wisconsin, "he is better able to harmonize all of the social groups and to secure their earnest cooperation." In effect, the APA members' insistence on tight pageant organization suggested to those who read their materials that, although any town could stage a historical pageant with widespread community participation, financial success, and artistic merit, it would require importing an experienced professional pageant-master, preferably one listed in *Who's Who in Pageantry*, to do so. APA guides for producing pageants recommended that local celebration committees budget a professional pageant-master's fee (ranging from several hundred to well over a thousand dollars, depending on the scale of the production) as a normal pageant expense.[27]

APA publications offered local celebration committees guidance not only in pageant planning and organization, but also in production techniques. The *Bulletin* discussed the role of historical research, dramatic convention, special effects, original music and dance, and abstract symbolism in pageantry. Members of the American Pageant Association insisted that the historical pageant was a unique combination of history and theater, requiring special preparation and production techniques, even if they sometimes disagreed on the form's specific characteristics.

Pageant-masters extolled the value of undertaking original historical research for a pageant, both for the scholarly benefit of supplementing and upgrading existing local histories, and for the social benefit of getting large numbers of people involved early in the production. Their research suggestions were remarkably broad based, foreshadowing many ideas of social historians later in the century. According to Margaret MacLaren Eager, "The pageant-master must discover what [local residents] know of the past; he must obtain access to the treasures of tradition which have been handed down in families, old letters, newspaper accounts of social functions carefully preserved in folded and yellowed scrapbooks." Virginia Tanner advised that those in charge of research for the pageant should make a special effort to interview older local residents in order to obtain material "not to be found upon the printed page, but genuine, homely, and traditional history, literally crying out for the recognition which pageantry was to give it." Pageant-masters noted that researching local history through such interviews simultaneously provided material for the pageant and a renewed sense of self-worth for older residents, native-born and immigrant, whose counsel seemed to be shunted aside by their children and grandchildren in the new century.[28]

They also felt that original historical research, by improving the accuracy of the presentation, increased the likelihood that the audience would accept the pageant scenes as authentic. Robert Withington of Smith College cautioned, "It is important that historical pageants be accurate in all details, so that the confidence of the audience may not be shaken, and the pageants lose their educational value." Frank Chocteau Brown, noting "The Possibilities of the Pageant as Local

Historian," recommended that towns bolster the authority of the pageant version of history by publishing a new comprehensive local history concurrently with the souvenir program and complete text of the pageant.[29]

Yet the pageant-masters of the American Pageant Association never lost sight that their productions, though socially useful and historically accurate, also must be good theater. William Chauncy Langdon advised that historical pageant writers should be sure to maintain dramatic continuity between episodes, as well as vary the setting and action according to "psychological principles" to hold the audience's attention. Francis Howard Williams, who wrote the script for Oberholtzer's dramatic Philadelphia historical pageant in 1912, told the APA in 1915 that the pageant's sequence of historical episodes should build to a climax, like melodrama. Early scenes, no matter how inherently spectacular the incidents they reenact, should not be allowed to overshadow later ones, so that the audience's interest would grow throughout the performance. Each bit of dialogue, music, and dance should be coordinated to express the same theme and emotion at the same time and contribute to a single overall dramatic effect. Thomas Wood Stevens, a dramatist from Illinois, maintained that, even if the audience could not always hear the words, pageant writers should carefully choose dialogue to provide proper motivation for the actors on stage. Arthur Farwell argued that pageants should use original rather than popular music, declaring, "It is distracting to hear familiar music laden with other associations used with a pageant which should direct attention wholly upon itself." Similarly, Mary Porter Beegle recommended the use of original dances over period dances if they better communicated the unique emotion required in a scene.[30]

Even though the pageant-masters condemned motion pictures' commercialism and encouragement of passive pleasure rather than active recreation—a position they shared with many critics of motion pictures in the 1910s—they immediately recognized the kinship between the filmmaker's work and their own as forms of "visual education."[31] Thomas Wood Stevens, though a champion of dialogue in pageantry, observed that "pageant workers can gain much . . . from a study of moving pictures, in which, of course, the interest is held entirely by action. Think your pageant through in terms of moving pictures; filter out the talk and find out how much action remains. If there remains a connected and appealing whole, the pageant should succeed." Pageant-masters suggested that books of background music written for local movie houses to accompany generic motion picture scenes could be employed to accompany historical pageant scenes as well.[32]

Although pageant directors maintained that the rules of dramatic construction bound the community historical pageant as any other work for stage or screen, they were quick to point out that "the pageant effect is different from the theatrical effect." One difference, declared Ralph Davol, was that "pageant scenes endeavor to reproduce actual occurrences more than theatrical illusions." Frank Chocteau Brown explained that the indoor theater used artificial lighting, makeup, and spectacular effects to tell its fantastic stories, whereas the historical pageant was produced outdoors in natural sunlight, "under conditions that reproduce with great reality those that might have existed at the time of the original incident being performed." Dramatists believed that the outdoor pageant should be a simple expression of a community's history in dramatic form, with only minimal special effects. Like other "back to nature" proponents of the period, such as the Boy Scouts and arts and crafts societies, the pageant-masters went to great lengths to appear without modern artifice. Their production recommendations consisted primarily of ways to employ the elaborate art of the theater to convey a "natural" impression in dance, costume, and music.[33]

To maintain an unembellished atmosphere in telling the story of the town, pageant-masters recommended that local pageant committees avoid using professional actors—though some directors did cast professionals in their pageants' lead roles. Whereas indoor historical drama focused on the triumphs and tragedies of an individual character, best played throughout the performance by a single experienced actor, historical pageants focused on the development of the community over several lifetimes, rarely requiring an individual character to appear in more than one scene. The limited speaking parts, narrow emotional range, and brief appearances on stage in historical pageantry generally demanded little of the individual acting skill that professionals possessed. Moreover, argued the pageant-masters, professional actors were steeped in the commercial traditions of Broadway; community pageantry represented Broadway's antithesis—a "groundswell," claimed William Chauncy Langdon, in which the people sought "first-hand to express dramatically their own life-hopes and life-ideals *for themselves* [Langdon's italics]." Langdon charged: "As well might Louis XVI and his friends imagine that they were qualified to embody the life-ideals of the French people, as the people of the theatre with their 30' by 50' stage traditions deep in their instincts expect to voice adequately . . . the groping uprising of the American pageant-drama."[34]

Behind the pageant-masters' careful demarcation between "theater" and "pageantry" lay the problem of devising a civic holiday celebration that was meaningful yet appealing in an age of amusing spectacle. Pageant-masters felt that, while they could borrow dramatic conventions from popular theater and film to heighten the audience's interest in the pageant "plot," they could not afford to include amusing features such as slapstick and comic relief, which would entertain at the expense of the serious historical message. Langdon stated flatly that the historical pageant "is not a vaudeville performance, it is a dramatic portrait of the town." Ralph Davol cautioned that the pageant should never "cater to the Great Broad Grin." Pageant-masters noted that sharing laughter with the historical characters on stage helped the audience to identify with the unfolding story of the community, but that scenes designed solely to provoke the audience's laughter at the characters on stage disrupted the spell of intimacy between audience and performer that was necessary for a pageant's success.[35]

Members of the American Pageant Association debated whether or not the fantastic flights of symbolic dancers also disrupted the serious historical message of the community pageant. Most educators and recreation workers, concerned with using pageantry as a medium for their reform ideas, favored abstract symbolism to make explicit the relevant "lessons" of local history. Adelia B. Beard noted that a "too realistic rendering" would "belittle" the grandeur and importance of the pageant themes. Frank Chocteau Brown cited the precedent of abstract symbolism's persuasive power in the allegorical masques and miracle and mystery plays of the Renaissance and Middle Ages. Some professional dramatists interested in pageantry as a form of experimental theater also favored the use of abstract symbolic dance, citing its kinship with the transatlantic avant-garde theater of Edward Gordon Craig, Isadora Duncan, and Robert Edmund Jones, which eschewed realistic representations in favor of presenting the emotional essence of a scene.[36]

But most dramatists in the pageantry movement, viewing community pageantry as a naive expression of local folk history, felt that elaborate abstract symbolic dance interludes obscured, rather than enhanced, the pageant's simply expressed message. Ralph Davol warned against using pageantry as experimental theater, insisting, "Cubist vagaries, futurist frills, post-impressionist anarchy . . . may be served only as a light garnish to a robust carcass of community history." Thomas H. Dickinson complained that the fantastic dance interludes and "future" scenes that were becoming commonplace in pageantry threatened to crowd out the historical "facts" with "the vaguest kind of symbolism." Robert Withington protested that allegory and abstract symbolism properly belonged only in the masque and morality play, not in the historical pageant, and correctly observed that "in America we have linked history to morality-play abstractions." Withington added that the symbolic dances in historical pageants were not only vague but also often ridiculous, remarking, "No community can be spurred to civic endeavor by frisking figures of Faith, Hope, and Charity." Over the dramatists' objections, the *APA Bulletin* continued to offer technical advice on symbolic dancing as a part of community historical pageantry. Association publications officially acknowledged the distinction between the realistic "pageant" and the abstract symbolic "masque," and that, properly speaking, it promoted local historical "pageant-masques"—but continued to call them "pageants."[37]

The debate within the American Pageant Association over whether or not to recommend abstract symbolism as a component of historical pageantry revealed the pageant-masters' inability to define the form they promoted and, ultimately, the larger question about pageantry's purpose. Members annually called for sessions on "definitions and terminology" at the APA conventions and generated elaborate typologies for community celebrations—yet three years after the APA's founding, members still could not agree on a definition of the word "pageant" among themselves, to say nothing of being able to make their definitions stick among the larger field of amateur and commercial pageant producers.[38] The pageant-masters' position of trying simultaneously to promote as well as to define a new form of civic celebration led them to claim credit and influence for celebrations that clearly lay outside the formal boundaries they had set for themselves. Langdon insisted that the term pageantry be restricted to only the "historical drama of the community," but most of his colleagues, unwilling to alienate any potential ally (except commercial pageant producers), accepted as pageants works in virtually any form and for any cause. Although members maintained that "the text of the pageant should be neither a sermon nor a propagandist document," their desire to embrace a variety of social movements going on around them led them to endorse as pageants dramatic programs for worthy causes such as woman suffrage, Irish independence, and child labor legislation. The American Pageant Association's formal categories and periodic calls for stricter definitions of the pageant form rang hollow.[39]

Members of the American Pageant Association offered local celebration committees suggestions not only on pageant organization and production techniques, but also on possible historical episodes. The pageant-masters' recommendations for historical themes, like their advice concerning pageant casting, theatricality, and abstract symbolism, contained inherent contradictions. On the one hand, the pageant-masters insisted that historical episodes must be unique to a specific locale. William Chauncy Langdon declared, "The local source of the episodes and the local application of their message give the true pageant a robust vigor that make it far surpass anything that is generally available or adaptable." He added that "the pageant spirit will not arise and sweep a town with its joyous enthusiasm simply at the sound of a formula." Ralph Davol proclaimed that no pageant prescription could be written out for a "sociological druggist" to fill. George Pierce Baker warned that one of the greatest dangers to the pageantry movement was the standardized historical pageant, which, "if slight adaptations are made in the scenes, may be used almost anywhere."[40]

On the other hand, Langdon's plea for the "local source of the episodes" appeared in the preface to his model Fourth of July pageant written to be produced anywhere. The American Pageant Association published an elaborate "Graphic Time Analysis of Three Typical Pageant Plans" which recommended durations for generic historical pageant scenes such as "Indian Episodes," "Symbolic Interludes," and "America Welcoming the Nations." Virginia Tanner's pamphlet *The Pageant of the Little Town of X* described a "main structure" for historical pageants, consisting of "Indian," "First Settler," "Colonial," and "Civil War" scenes interspersed with interludes of "story dances." Although nearly all pageant-masters echoed Margaret MacLaren Eager's insistence that only an original creation based on a town's unique history could "strike that tender local chord, which when rightly struck, binds the people of a community together as no other thing can," in fact their guidebooks and model pageants, publicized nationally, contributed to the emergence of a standard pageant formula.[41]

The community historical pageant between 1911 and 1916 became a popular genre with characteristic historical imagery, plots, and themes. The pageant-masters' notions of what to include in a production extended, however poorly and incompletely, far beyond the American Pageant Association's limited membership, the distribution of its official publications, and the relatively few towns that hired APA-approved pageant directors. Though historical pageantry first gained popularity in the Northeast, by 1920 pageants appeared in all forty-eight states. Local celebration committees got their information on how to stage a historical pageant through articles in magazines with a mass circulation; through national networks of women's clubs and educational, social work, and patriotic and hereditary associations; and through classes offered in state normal schools. They saw news and photographs of the larger pageants held in various parts of the

GRAPHIC·TIME·ANALYSIS··THREE·TYPICAL·PAGEANT·PLANS

TIME SCALE	PAGEANT A		PAGEANT B		PAGEANT C		TIME SCALE
5 Minutes			Choral Prologue	4 Min	Symbolic Prologue	7 Min	5 Minutes
10 "	Prologue–Masque	10 Min	Father Time	2	Mound Builders	4	10 "
Quarter Hour	Old Indian Trail	6	Cave Dwellers	6	Indian Epoch	8	Quarter Hour
20 Minutes	First White Men in Valley	7	Dance Interlude	4			20 Minutes
25 "	Purchase of the Land	4	Indian Life	11	Symbolic Interlude	4	25 "
Half Hour	Foundation of the City	6	Dance Interlude	2	Discovery & Indians	5	Half Hour
35 Minutes	Life at the Fort	5	The Settlers	6	First Settlers	7	35 Minutes
40 "	Indian Trading	4	Indian Battle	6	French & Indian Wars	4	40 "
Three Quarters	The Buffalo Hunt	6	Governors Reception	7	The Indian Wars	8	Three Quarter Hr
50 Minutes	Indian Forays	6	News of Revolution	5	Symbolic Interlude	4	50 Minutes
55 "	Opening of the War	7	Recruits for the War	6	Incidents preceding War of Revolution	9	55 "
First Hour	Leaving for the Front	3	Dance Interlude	4	Episodes of War	10	First Hour
5 Minutes	Life in War-Time	8	After the War	7			5 Minutes
10 "							10 "
Quarter Hour	After the War	5	Quilting & Husking Bee	8	Symbolic Interlude "Peace"	3	Quarter Hour
20 Minutes	Harvesting the Crop	7	Prosperity & Progress	6	Peace & Husbandry	10	20 Minutes
25 "	Coming of the Rail Road	6	America welcoming the Nations	14	Wedding of 1866	6	25 "
Half Hour	The Growth of the City	7			Return from War	4	Half Hour
35 Minutes	The "City Hall Gang"	6	European Contributions	6	Symbolic "Peace Pan"	4	35 Minutes
40 "	The Great Fire	7			Peace & the People of the Nation	10	40 "
Three Quarters	Reconstruction Political & Physical	8	The March Past	10	American Amalgamation	5	Three Quarter Hr
50 Minutes	The New Democracy	5	Chorus & Tableau	5	Parade Past	8	50 Minutes
55 "	The City of Today	6			Exit Song "America" full	4	55 "
Second Hour							Second Hour

A Method of Testing the comparative importance of different incidents and keeping control of length of performance. It clearly displays those characteristics individual to each pageant, and the form they are assuming in their development.

Issued as a supplement to American Pageant Association Bulletin No 19

Supplement

Though APA pageant-masters insisted that each pageant had to be a unique expression of local history, such frameworks tended to standardize historical action and imagery nationwide. (APA Bulletin, no. 19, June 1, 1915)

country in their local newspapers, in national magazines, and, increasingly in the decade, in newsreels in motion picture houses.[42] All of these media and images disseminated nationally shaped local organizers' sense of what to regard as appropriate material for a historical pageant. Through the same media, audiences learned to judge pageants, just as they had learned to evaluate the July Fourth oration and other elements of civic holiday celebrations in the nineteenth century. As a result of exposure through the national media and popular expectations raised by that media, historical pageants in different regions of the nation, places with apparently different local histories, displayed similar images of their past, present, and future. But this similarity of historical images and ritual action embedded in the pageant form also reflected concerns and desires—shared to varying degrees by the pageant-masters, their local sponsors, and their audiences across the nation—for promoting pious beliefs and virtuous behaviors, wholesome expressive recreation, local community cohesion, and a deep faith in orderly progress.[43]

In 1914, Lotta Clark told the New England History Teachers Association that "whatever our aims may be in teaching history, the final test of their success is in the conduct of our citizens."[44] Clark expressed a view common among her colleagues in pageantry, that the past could be displayed and reenacted in such a way as to offer a guide to proper behavior in the present. Historical pageants depicted local residents of the past with the virtues pageant directors and their clients, local civic officials, wanted to instill in present-day residents. Holding up the behavior of past generations as a model for the present was a customary use of history in public events, one found in historical orations and holiday decorations of the late nineteenth century. But the pageant could communicate its version of idealized behavior through action as well as through words and pictures.

Community historical pageants typically depicted past generations as religious, temperate, hard-working, and patriotic. One common pageant scene re-created a church service of the past, complete with hymns familiar to the contemporary audience.[45] Organizers of the historical pageant in Caldwell, New Jersey, in 1915 made a subtle plea for temperance through a Revolutionary War scene in which George Washington refused ale for cider and a later "Town Meeting" scene in which local residents voted to expel a drunkard. The same year a pageant in Freeport, Illinois, pointedly showed the young Abraham Lincoln turning down a drink of whiskey. Historical pageant scenes depicted early settlers bravely persevering to overcome hostile elements and disease, sometimes representing the trials of the pioneers allegorically. *The Pageant of Ridgewood*, New Jersey, opened with a pioneer family banding together with neighbors to fend off "Wildwood Creatures" and "Hostile Nature Forces." In the Holland, Michigan, pageant, families battled horrible figures representing "Hunger," "Cholera," "Malaria," "Thunder and Lightning," and "Death." *The Pageant of Lincoln*, Nebraska, depicted early settlers surviving an onslaught of ravenous "Grasshoppers." Scenes of the town in wartime exhibited past residents' spirit of patriotism, idealism, and self-sacrifice, as successive generations of minutemen and Civil War soldiers marched off to battle without hesitation, while the women bravely maintained hearth and home. Pageant-masters and local civic officials hoped that dramatic depictions of past generations' stalwart actions in times of crisis would inspire similar behavior among members of the present generation.[46]

Historical pageants also dramatized past generations bound together in times of peace and joy, in scenes designed to cultivate present-day residents' spirit of play as a supplement to their spirit of idealism and self-sacrifice. Borrowing liberally from imagery that had

Puritans going to meeting, Old Deerfield Historical Pageant, *Deerfield, Massachusetts, 1910. (Brown University Library)*

Early Puritans of New England Going to Worship, *1872. Pageant directors based their tableaux illustrating the piety of past generations on familiar images, such as this painting by George H. Boughton. (Toledo Museum of Art)*

appeared since the 1890s in elite costume balls and children's playground festivals, pageant episodes reenacted festive weddings, husking bees, and elaborate civic ceremonies of the past. The highlight of the Bennington, Vermont, pageant was the Colonial-era wedding of Governor Wentworth and Martha Hilton, at which all danced a stately minuet. Freeport, Illinois, residents in 1915 included a lively barn dance as part of their pageant's reenactment of a July Fourth celebration of the 1830s. One common pageant scene depicted an Elizabethan folk dance, set either in England just before the colonization of North America or in the New World as part of a dramatization of the incident, made famous by Nathaniel Hawthorne's short story, the "Maypole of Merry Mount," in which Puritans disrupt Thomas Morton's May Day revels. Mrs. Collona M. Dallin's historical pageant for the Arlington, Massachusetts, Women's Club in June 1913 showed Puritans sternly interrupting the Maypole dance at Merry Mount, but depicted subsequent generations in Arlington turning out for exuberant festivals honoring Lafayette in 1824 and celebrating the renaming of the town in 1867. Such historical imagery suggested that, even if America's Puritan heritage scorned playful behavior, an older, Anglo-American tradition encouraged it. Pageant episodes recounting Elizabethan, Revolutionary, antebellum, and "modern" pastimes portrayed past generations as bearers not only of a tradition of work, idealism, and sacrifice worthy of emulation, but also of a heritage of wholesome recreation and expressive dance.[47]

Besides presenting models of work and play for the present townspeople to emulate, organizers of historical pageants used history to present an idealized portrait of local social relations. Through historical imagery, civic officials outlined how local residents were to envision the nature of their community, the position of various groups within the community, and their place as a community in a succession of past, present, and future generations. Pageant directors and their clients created ideal past, present, and future communities on stage that were wholly free of class, ethnic, or racial conflict. Such imagery, they believed, would promote social harmony and evoke, in the words of William Chauncy Langdon, the "underlying public spirit" beneath social divisions.[48]

Praising historical pageantry's ability to produce "the obliteration of class lines," pageant-masters recommended that local officials present nothing that could arouse nascent class sentiment. Langdon pointedly advised the YMCA in 1911 that dramatists working with industrial groups "should avoid the labor question." Even though the epilogue of *The Pageant of the Blackhawk Country* in Freeport, Illinois, appeared to address this very question, depicting "industrial toilers, their lives

Morris dancers, Deerfield, Massachusetts, 1910. Such dancing highlighted the early settlers' origins in Elizabethan England and their heritage of colorful play to supplement the Puritan one of hard work and idealism. (Brown University Library)

Minuet, Warwick, Massachusetts, 1912. The minuet was among the most popular pageant scenes. It projected aristocratic and courtly traditions, allowing the elite who could afford the fancy silk, Colonial-style costumes to project themselves at the head of local society. (Brown University Library)

all but crushed out by the system of labor that takes its toll in human lives," the epilogue concluded with the workers' redemption, which came not by organizing to change that exploitative system, but rather by stately symbolic figures representing "Sympathy," "Understanding," "Cooperation," "Justice," "Idealism," "Conservation," "Brotherhood," and "Love" driving back other figures personifying "Greed," "Competition," "Jealousy," "Injustice," "Inhumanity," "Misunderstanding," "Hate," and "Materialism." In the pageant finale, all sing "Labor Is Joy and Joy Is Love for All Humanity." "Labor" and "Capital" also danced together joyfully in a historical pageant presented in Lawrence, Massachusetts, in 1911, six months before the bitter textile strike. The cover of the pageant program depicted textile workers, like the Indians of an earlier day, paying homage to a vision of "The City." A pageant in Buffalo, New York, sponsored by the Larkin Company, a local soap manufacturer, washed away any trace of class differences in an allegorical ballet: figures representing "Imagination" and "Cooperation" drive away "Ignorance" and "Strife," surrounded by dozens of young girls dancing as soap bubbles and bottles of perfume.[49]

The conventional treatment of the labor question in community historical pageants contrasted markedly with the treatment it received in the Industrial Workers of the World pageant staged in Madison Square Garden for the benefit of the striking Paterson, New Jersey, silk mill workers in June 1913. John Reed, megaphone in hand, directed the striking employees in scenes depicting industrial exploitation—"The Workers Dead, the Mills Alive"—brought to an end not by a joyous dance of "Labor" and "Capital" or the "Spirit of Cooperation," but by militant class warfare. Against a giant backdrop painted by John Sloan depicting the Paterson mills, employees reenacted the violence of their picket line and the recent funeral of one of their colleagues felled by company agents. Reed's pageant ended with the workers on stage joining with the audience in a mass meeting and speeches, thus combining elements from the new pageantry with the labor movement's customary forms of mass protest. Most of the New York press, while condemning the revolutionary aims of the IWW, praised The Pageant of the Paterson Strike for its realism and dramatic intensity. Rose Pastor Stokes, writing in the Socialist New York Call, went further, contrasting the "red pageant" that displayed history "fresh from the hands of its makers" with what she saw as the usual historical pageant's glorification of a lifeless, distant past.[50]

Historical pageantry's idealized portrait of a town without internal conflict extended to ethnic relations as well. In the pageant version of local history, each immigrant group peacefully joined the community in turn and encountered neither hostility nor prejudice. Pageants

Representations of labor, such as that on the cover of this program for the Lawrence, Massachusetts, pageant of 1911, depicted a community free of conflict between labor and capital. The textile worker, like the Indian of an earlier time, is on bended knee before a serene symbolic representation of the city. (Brown University Library)

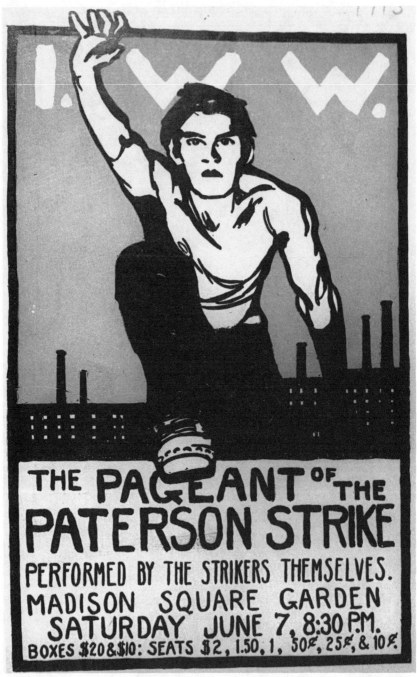

Pageant poster, designed by Robert Edmund Jones, 1913. (Brown University Library)

*Depicting the Paterson strike on stage. In contrast to the typical historical pag-
eant, the Paterson strike pageant represented labor and capital in conflict.
The pageant enlisted some of the leading insurgent artists of the day, from the
poster designed by Robert Edmund Jones to the ninety-foot backdrop depicting
the mills painted by John Sloan.* (The Independent 74 [*June 19, 1913*], *p.*
1407)

commonly depicted local ethnic relations in the early episodes, which
displayed the first groups of white settlers, impersonated by their
descendants, appearing on the pageant field in the order of their
nationality's initial arrival in the town. The Norristown, Pennsylvania,
historical pageant in 1912 began with the "successive waves of humanity" who settled in the town: the Dutch, Swedes, Welsh, English,
Germans, and Scotch-Irish. Historical pageants also frequently portrayed local ethnic relations in the grand finale, where "America" or
the enthroned "Spirit of the Community" cheerfully welcomed "later"
immigrant groups. Such finales borrowed liberally from the children's
playground festivals celebrating immigrant gifts and the melting pot.
The Boston civic pageant of 1910 ended with "America" receiving the
nations—Sweden, Russia, Southern Europe, Holland, "Hungaria,"
Italy, Scotland, England, Ireland, and Greece, each group dressed in
colorful national costume performing its native folk dance. Local civic
officials extolled the value of such pageant scenes for providing a
tangible demonstration of how disparate ethnic groups could unite
into one community.[51]

Blacks and Asians were generally absent from the pageant portrait
of the community and its history, reflecting the racism of the society in

which pageants took place. The pageant-masters most responsible for the development and dissemination of the pageant form hailed largely from the Northeast and Midwest and knew little of the history or folklore of these groups; the playground workers' cosmopolitan ideal often fell short where race was concerned. What pageant-masters did know about black history they associated with an unpleasant era of national history—the Civil War and Reconstruction—which pageant versions of the past usually obliterated in the effort to promote national reconciliation. Local civic officials seldom assigned black groups as prominent a place in a historical procession as they did in the Newburyport, Massachusetts, *Pageant of Nations* in 1913. In this celebration, blacks marched between the Historical Society of Old Newbury and the Old Newbury chapter of the DAR, pulling floats depicting harsh "Life under Slavery," "William Lloyd Garrison," "Lincoln's Emancipation Proclamation," and "Fifty Years of Progress since Emancipation." More commonly, historical pageant directors, if they depicted blacks at all, borrowed stock scenes from the popular stage of the period that displayed an idealized view of race relations in the Old South and blacks as comic buffoons. The plantation scene of William Chauncy Langdon's model July Fourth pageant, distributed nationally by the Russell Sage Foundation, showed blacks content with their plight rather than attempting to escape it. George Pierce Baker's Peterborough, New Hampshire, pageant in 1910 included a comic scene in which "Old Black Baker," pausing for a swig of whiskey while driving cattle to pasture, sees the Devil and runs off hysterically. This sort of pageant treatment prompted W. E. B. DuBois to conclude that "the American Pageant Association has been silent, if not actually contemptuous, of efforts to use pageantry as black folk drama."[52]

DuBois responded by writing and directing his own black history pageant, *The Star of Ethiopia*. It premiered in New York City in 1913 as part of the NAACP's commemoration of the fiftieth anniversary of the Emancipation Proclamation. DuBois took his pageant to Washington, D.C., in 1915 and to Philadelphia in 1916, overseeing the recruitment of a cast of nearly one thousand local blacks for each production. The pageant depicts five epochs in African and American history, beginning with prehistoric times and the black discovery of iron. It then narrates the rise of African civilization in ancient Egypt and in the kingdoms of Central Africa between 900 and 1500, just before European contact. The fourth section of episodes shifts to America and the "Valley of Humiliation" of slavery. As a chorus sings spirituals, episodes depict blacks under the lash, their toil interrupted only briefly by a lively Creole dance. But as "Ethiopia" awakens, struggles toward freedom increase. Scenes depict the actions of David Walker, Nat

Turner, Denmark Vesey, Frederick Douglass, John Brown, and, with the Haitian national anthem swelling in the background, Toussaint-Louverture. A chorus sings "The Battle Hymn of the Republic," then, as black Union soldiers stride on stage, "Marching through Georgia." The finale of DuBois's pageant depicts black progress since Emancipation, as a procession of black athletes, ministers, physicians, and teachers overcome the "Furies" of race prejudice, idleness, and intemperance to build a "Tower of Light" out of the "Foundation Stones of Knowledge." True to DuBois's vision of the pageant as black folk drama, the pageant music consisted of either traditional "sorrow songs," such as those discussed in his *Souls of Black Folk* (1903), or original compositions by black composers based on African music—with the exception of the two selections from Verdi's *Aïda* that accompanied the Egyptian episodes. The *Washington Bee* especially praised the pageant music, "which must be played accurately and absolutely on time," over the "syncopated jingling dance music" that black musicians ordinarily played. Like other middle-class observers, the *Bee* looked to historical pageantry not only to foster a greater appreciation of history but also to elevate the community's taste in amusements.[53]

In contrast to *The Star of Ethiopia* and the Paterson strike pageant, most community historical pageants depicted local class, ethnic, and race relations as a stable cohesive hierarchy. In the pageant version of local history, factory workers magically find joy in their work and do not challenge their employers for a share in the ownership of the means of production. Recent immigrants perform colorful national dances and do not vie for social and economic position with native-born Americans and one another. Though Norristown's historical pageant reenacted the coming of the early settlers, it excluded the contributions to local community development of more recent arrivals—Italians, Slavs, Poles, Jews, and blacks—even though they numbered among the largest ethnic groups in the town. These groups marched during celebration week in a procession of Norristown fraternal organizations, but not in the one that depicted local history, the community's core identity. According to Norristown pageant organizer Theodore Heysham, "The historian of another century will record the deeds of these new arrivals. It is our responsibility to speak of those of the past."[54] Despite the pageant-masters' invocation of the democratic and cosmopolitan spirit of the playground in their work, welcoming all into the embrace of the community, pageant historical imagery typically placed labor and recent immigrant groups on the community's margins. Images of local community cohesion and cheerful social interaction on the pageant field belied the genuine strife and social inequalities in the towns where pageants took place. Pag-

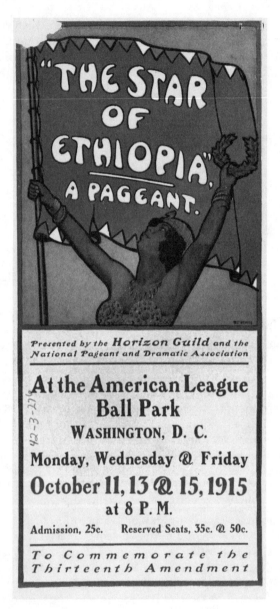

Pageant poster. After opening in New York City, this pageant of black history played in Washington, D.C., and Philadelphia. The Horizon Guild was DuBois's national organization to promote drama among blacks; the National Pageant and Dramatic Association was the local group responsible for the Washington production. (W. E. B. DuBois Papers, Archives and Manuscripts Department, University of Massachusetts, Amherst)

Dance before the Pharaoh Ra, The Star of Ethiopia, *New York City, 1913. (W. E. B. DuBois Papers, Archives and Manuscripts Department, University of Massachusetts, Amherst)*

eants represented particular local interests and ethnic groups as vague abstractions, artistic symbols that harmonized with one another to present an idealized portrait of social relations—one that local residents could aspire to and that civic officials would find acceptable.

Historical pageantry's characterization of women's contribution to local community development also upheld conventional social roles. Women, like labor and recent immigrants, were left out of scenes depicting crucial turning points in local economic or political history. Although pageant directors generally gave pioneer women their due in managing farms and fighting hostile elements alongside their men, they rarely depicted later generations of women in economic or political roles outside the home. Even community historical pageants directed by women portrayed women's work stereotypically as domestic work—though the well-publicized 5,000-member woman suffrage pageant presented in Washington, D.C., in March 1913, the day before Woodrow Wilson's inauguration, prominently displayed a scene of women workers in the professions. The author of the pageant, Hazel MacKaye, also produced a *Pageant of Susan B. Anthony* for the National Women's party. She concluded, "Women are becoming more and more alive to the fact that the working world is man-made, and that women will have to put up a good fight to get a fair share as bread-winners. . . . Through pageantry, we women can set forth our ideals and aspirations more graphically than in any other way."[55]

Woman suffrage pageant, Washington, D.C., 1913. Unlike the typical local historical pageant, this production—held on the steps of the Treasury Department the day before Woodrow Wilson's inauguration—depicted women in the professions as well as in domestic work. The tableau shown here displays "Liberty" and "Charity"; other groups represented "Justice," "Peace," and "Hope." (Library of Congress)

In most pageants of local history, however, women appeared only in episodes depicting the social and domestic side of community life. These episodes reenacted the relatively timeless events, such as a church service, a sewing circle, a festive wedding celebration, or a husking bee, in which the underlying emotional bonds of community surfaced. The pioneer or Colonial wedding, among the most popular of pageant scenes, represented the community reproducing itself from generation to generation. In the pageant version of history, women appeared as the heart and soul of the community throughout its history, in scenes reenacting the upholding of the town's timeless traditions, not those depicting its response to changing circumstances.

Women represented the emotional essence of the community not only in pageant scenes reenacting the social and domestic rituals of the past, but also in the abstract symbolic dance interludes between historical episodes. Pageant directors personified the community bound together by its historical experiences, shared emotions, and high ideals with a woman in classical garb who reappears throughout the pageant and to whom the successive generations depicted on the pageant field pledge allegiance. The pageant woman symbolizing the community resembled the idealized female image represented in public statues, murals, and posters of the period but was explicitly tied to images of both maternity and maturity through casting and surrounding imag-

*Women at the spinning wheel, Medford, Massachusetts, 1915. Despite the
many pageants directed by women, women in pageants stereotypically were
represented in scenes of hearth and home. The spinning wheel has been a
popular icon of the Colonial revival since the late nineteenth century. (Brown
University Library)*

ery. The women commonly cast in this role were middle-aged and
married.[56] The idealized Spirit of the Community thus resembled a
mother; local residents, her family; and their town, a home.

Pageant imagery representing the community through history assumed metaphorical as well as realistic and abstract symbolic form.
Representations of ancient Greece, Medieval and Renaissance Europe, frontier America, and the North American Indian appeared in
historical pageants as past examples of closely knit communities of
ideals and civic virtue which towns of the twentieth century could
emulate. Renaissance and Medieval imagery, including the pageant
form itself, proved especially popular, representing to pageant directors and their clients the height of art, of play, of handicrafts, of
community solidarity, and of responsible political and cultural leadership. Such community imagery flourished not only in historical pageantry but in other popular media of the period as well, from the
rustic chivalry of the *Boy Scout Handbook* to popular magazines and
novels.[57]

Pageant scene of a Colonial wedding, Northampton, Massachusetts, 1911. Reenactments of Colonial or pioneer weddings were among the most popular kind of pageant scene. Such ceremonies were familiar to local residents and served as a symbol of continuity between past and present. They also represented historical continuity on a deeper level, as a ritual that led to the procreation of a new generation and the community regenerating itself. (Historic Northampton, Northampton)

In addition to depicting a model of social relations, historical imagery in pageants provided a model of how social change occurs over time. Pageant-masters shared with local civic officials and their audiences a concern about the impact of recent social and technological changes on community life. William Chauncy Langdon's "Pageants of the New Country Life" most explicitly addressed this question, but the popularity of his pageant formula suggests that other pageant directors agreed that Americans would better understand the social and technological transformations of the present and future when viewed in the context of the whole of their town history. A sequence of historical episodes representing successive stages of community development from past to present could provide local residents with a kind of psychological keel that would prevent them from drifting amid a sea of recent social changes without clear identity, purpose, or direction.

Pageant depictions of orderly, stable progress appeared in the way the sequence of historical episodes unfolded. While individual pageant episodes suggested a particular "lesson" from the past—the importance of idealism, hard work, wholesome recreation, or community cohesion—the entire sequence of episodes embodied a vision of how change occurred. The succession of episodes across the pageant grounds placed past, present, and future within a single framework, offering a coherent plot within which local residents could interpret their recent experiences and envision their future progress.

Historical pageant plots portrayed social change as a nearly organic process, smoothly unfolding from forest primeval to "City Beautiful." The pageants typically began with symbolic embodiments of nature, usually gentle and feminine, frolicking innocently until the arrival of the Indians. *The Pageant of St. Johnsbury*, Vermont, opens with a dance depicting a male "Power of the Wilderness" commanding female "Spirits" of the "Mountain Tops," "Forests," "Rivers," and "Valleys," until the Spirit of Civilization lures away the Rivers and Valleys from Wilderness's domain (the local golf course where the pageant was held). Indians appeared as part of the natural landscape. Their episodes, like those representing nature, were not identified with a particular time period. Pageants displayed Indian dancing, hunting, and domestic activities as scarcely disrupting the rhythms of "Nature Spirits," who typically did not relinquish the stage until the arrival of Europeans.[58]

Chronological time in pageants began with the arrival of the first white settlers and the "inevitable" decline of the Indians. One popular pageant scene presents a "Medicine Man" foretelling his race's decline shortly before the episode in which the whites arrive. In Thomas Wood Stevens's *Pageant of the Old Northwest*, performed in Milwaukee in 1911, the Indian prophet "White Cloud" describes the "natural"

A dance illustrating the Power of the Wilderness and Nature Spirits, 1912. Unlike this opening dance in The Pageant of St. Johnsbury, *most pageants depicted the wilderness as feminine, waiting to receive successive waves of settlement. (Brown University Library)*

passing of his nation like the seasons, watching at the end as the "leafage" of his people drifts down. In the Yankton, South Dakota, pageant of 1916, it was the "Spirit of Locality" who predicted that the Indians would not remain on their ancestral land. Inevitable progress, not white conquest, brought about the end of Indian civilization. Though pageants commonly depicted contact between Native Americans and white settlers in scenes reenacting the purchase of land, and some historical pageants portrayed Indian attacks on whites as part of the early pioneers' struggles with "Nature," almost none showed whites attacking Indians.[59]

Once "history" began, subsequent pageant scenes depicted past generations' successive adaptations to inevitable technological and material progress. Institutions evolved on the frontier as naturally as the whites supplanted the Indians. Scenes in the Haddonfield, New Jersey, historical pageant of 1913 reenacted the founding of two local schools, five churches, the fire company, the public library, and three local businesses. Railroads and industry blended smoothly into the pattern of town life. In *The Pageant of the Charles River* in 1914, "Smoke" and "Cinders" from the railroad at first overpower the "Spirit of the River," but "Electricity" and the "Spirit of Invention" eventually restore her. When the "First Settler" reappears in the finale

The inevitable decline of the American Indian. In the pageant version of history, inevitable evolution, not white conquest, ended Indian dominion over the land. This program cover, depicting White Cloud's prophecy that whites would replace Indians, is from An Historical Pageant of Illinois, *staged in Evanston, 1909. (Brown University Library)*

*Purchasing land from the Indians, Westchester County, New York, 1909.
(Brown University Library)*

William Penn's Treaty With the Indians, *1771. Borrowing heavily from
familiar images such as this painting by Benjamin West, pageant directors
portrayed white displacement of Indians as a friendly, legitimate business
transaction. (Gift of Mrs. Sarah Harrison [The Joseph Harrison, Jr., Collec-
tion]; Pennsylvania Academy of the Fine Arts, Philadelphia)*

Carrying off the captives, Deerfield, Massachusetts. This scene probably is from the 1916 pageant, though a similar reenactment of the "Deerfield Massacre" of 1704 took place in the pageants staged in 1910 and 1913. (Pocumtuck Valley Memorial Association Library, Deerfield)

of the *Pageant of Schenectady*, New York, to view "Modern Schenectady," he voices unqualified approval of "Mr. Modern" and the radiant "Spirits of Light" from the local General Electric Company's manufacturing complex, confirming that the giant factory represented the logical and inevitable culmination of a century and a half of local community development. When early "Pioneers" arrive on the pageant field in one of the later scenes of William Chauncy Langdon's historical pageant for Indianapolis, Indiana, in 1916, characters in contemporary dress summon the "Police" and the "Board of Health," complaining that the pioneers are one hundred years "out of their episode"—until the "Centennial Spirit" comes to mediate between the generations and point out the essential continuity of their identity over time. The sequence of historical pageant episodes emphasizes historical continuities over dislocations and conflicts. Disparities between past and present, as embodied in pageant program art depicting an Indian viewing modern progress, appear within a single overarching context that links both scenes as successive stages in the social and technological evolution of the town, leading to the fulfillment of local residents' sacred communal destiny. Any lingering doubts about the direction town life has taken in recent years are resolved in the grand

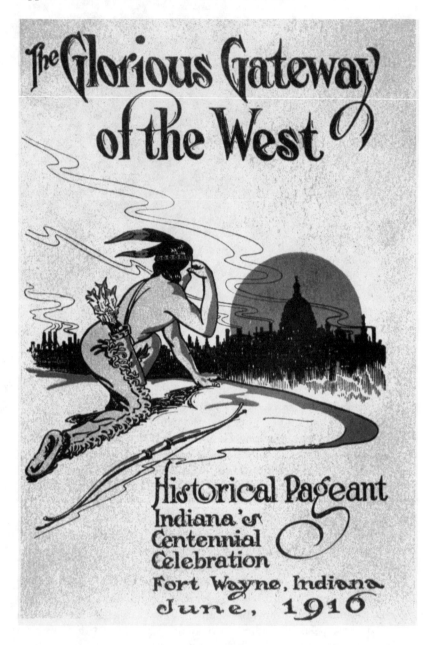

Pageant poster of an Indian viewing modern progress, Ft. Wayne, Indiana, 1916. (Brown University Library)

In this poster, the "Spirits of the Prairies" wind their way from Indian villages to the modern city, indicating the direction of local community development as well as its continuity with the past. (Brown University Library)

finale, when all of the pageant participants, attired in historical costumes representing successive generations, confidently stride forward into the future.[60]

Pageant grand finales depicted the culmination of the town's progress in the present and future. They displayed not only a vast array of local organizations and resources, but also the town's wide-ranging network of regional, national, and even international relations. Many historical pageants delineated these relations by imitating Langdon's well-publicized New Country Life pageant finales, in which abstract symbolic figures represented the county, state, sister cities, and nation. Railroads, the export of produce, and giant industries also joined local residents with the outside. *The Pageant of the Aroostook Valley* in Fort Fairfield, Maine, in 1916 featured a dance of the potato export trade, in which someone dressed as a local spud danced a "Hesitation" with Boston, a "Fox-Trot" with New York City, a "Cake-walk" with the South, and a "Spanish Waltz" with Cuba.[61] Like pageant scenes re-enacting the visit of a famous national figure such as Abraham Lincoln in Freeport, Illinois, or George Washington in Caldwell, New Jersey, these scenes boosted the town's status above its neighbors' and acknowledged its ties to a larger society. They embodied a crucial historical theme: that local residents could increase both their attachment to place and their contacts with the outside without one excluding the other. Pageant directors depicted the town's relative autonomy of the past and its present myriad links with the outside world as successive stages in a single, natural evolution through which local residents' underlying affection for one another, and for their town, remained strong.

Pageant music further emphasized the essential continuity of the different historical periods re-created on stage. Pageant-masters selected background music for its contribution to the overall "emotional structure of the pageant" rather than for its association with a particular historical period. Musical interludes offered harmonious transitions between historical episodes; particular musical motives repeated in the background music of several episodes subtly wove together diverse historical periods. Hymns familiar to twentieth-century audiences inserted in early pageant episodes underlined connections between past and present. Background music for an entire pageant appeared in a single style—generally the romantic light classical music popular at the turn of the century. The ersatz Indian melodies of Edward MacDowell and Arthur Farwell proved especially popular as background music, because they hinted at the exotic while employing the same contemporary Western-style harmonies familiar to the audience and easily blended with other parts of the pageant. At the same time that Charles Ives assembled hymns and marches from different historical periods into multi-layered, dissonant compositions that retained the discreteness of each source, composers associated with pageantry blended music from various historical periods and ethnic sources within a single harmonious score. Such musical treatment underlined the similarities rather than the differences between historical periods, as well as suggested a musical version of the American identity as a melting pot.[62]

Pageant directors also employed abstract symbolic dance interludes to represent the essential continuity of the community in orderly transition, gliding gracefully between historical periods. The flowing, rhythmic dance pioneered and popularized by Isadora Duncan and Ruth St. Denis—both of whom danced in pageants—imparted logic, grace, and rhythm to scenes of social change.[63] In Virginia Tanner's *Masque of Rockport*, Massachusetts, in 1914, the "Spirit of Nature" meekly bows in submission before the "Spirit of Civilization," signaling the departure of the Indians and the coming of the whites. In the late nineteenth century, a new commuter rail line had transformed Ridgewood, New Jersey, from an isolated rural town into a residential suburb of New York City. *The Pageant of Ridgewood* in 1915, between

Interlude: The Indians glimpse a vision of the future. "As the Indians gather about Pocumtuck, the Spirit of Vision approaches and points toward the trees, from which emerges the symbolic figure of the Pioneer Spirit. Deerfield, Greenfield, Conway, Shelburne, and Gill enter, followed by Agriculture, Industry, and War." (Margaret M. Eager, The Pageant of Old Deerfield *[1916], p. 15; Pocumtuck Valley Memorial Association Library, Deerfield, Massachusetts)*

historical episodes depicting the villagers of the Civil War era and the commuters of the present, included a symbolic dance interlude in which "Paramus" and the "Nature Spirits" heartily welcome Manhattan "City Dwellers." Through such dance imagery, pageant directors represented potentially jarring recent changes in local conditions as smooth, intelligible transitions.[64]

In many ways, the historical formula in American pageantry resembled the "New History" and progressive synthesis emerging among academic historians of the period. Like the New History, historical pageants focused on a past that included the town's development along economic and social as well as political lines; they purportedly told the story of all local residents rather than only the elite, and they extended forward to address present public questions and point the way to future reform. But unlike the progressive historians, pageant organizers took a conservative evolutionary approach to social change rather than viewing change generated out of the polarity of conflict.[65] Any dramatic confrontations in historical pageants occurred between humankind and nature, not between social classes and forces; the history ultimately had more in common with George Bancroft than with Charles Beard. "Historical and economic research and its dramatic presentation," as William Chauncy Langdon once described community historical pageantry, essentially remained within a moral and religious framework similar to the one employed by holiday orators in the late nineteenth century.[66]

In this framework, which resembled religious ritual more than original interpretation, familiarity counted for more than innovation. Everyone present knew the outcome of each scene; there could be no major revisions of local history, no surprise endings. Despite a professed commitment to historical accuracy, Francis H. Williams admitted that he included a scene of "Penn's Treaty with the Indians" in the Philadelphia historical pageant of 1912 not because he believed it occurred as Benjamin West's painting portrayed, but because the public expected to see it that way. Similarly, the Freeport, Illinois, historical pageant scene re-creating Abraham Lincoln's debate with Stephen Douglas in 1858 depicted Lincoln in his more familiar appearance with a beard, even though he did not begin growing a beard until 1860, after his election as president.[67]

As a whole, historical pageants in America presented a public version of history designed to be emotionally compelling as much as intellectually convincing. The two hours of dramatic sketches held together by abstract symbolic interludes of music and dance depicted each new stage in the community's development realistically and authoritatively, yet set within a single overarching moral and emotional structure. While the realistic reenactment of historical events within each episode advanced a pageant plot, offering "key scenarios" formulating specific orientations to action, the abstract symbolic representations of home and community in pageant dance interludes offered "key symbols" that helped catalyze feeling and provoke a strong emotional response. Together, pageantry's alternating prosaic and lyrical content served a "traditionalizing" role, framing scenes of the unfamiliar present and the unknown future within the same coherent emotional structure of familiar actions and imagery used to envelop the past. The swirling music, dance, and costume in symbolic interludes bridging scenes of the community's past development and future transformation took the form of a metaphoric rite of passage for local residents. Women on stage in Greek gowns impersonating the Spirit of the Community in transition, gliding between episodes of the past, present, and future, mirrored the audience participating in the pageant experience, celebrating the timeless local traditions and emotional bonds that would endure through its own interlude of transition into the uncertain future of the twentieth century.[68]

The pageant form resembled a classic rite of passage, or ceremony marking a transition in individual status, in its emphasis on the child-like state of the community at play and its promotion of local residents' feelings of undifferentiated love for one another—or *communitas*—at a crucial stage of their history. Nevertheless, the resemblance was not because historical pageantry represented a spontaneous expression of *communitas* in the Progressive Era, but rather because pageant-masters deliberately grafted classical, Medieval, Renaissance, and Amerindian ritual elements onto the customary holiday ceremony. The exotic language of ritual action, even more than oratory and banners, best expressed this metaphor of the community in transition and the progressive sense of the public history as a combination of social evolution and divine revelation, high art and popular spectacle, intellectual exercise and powerful emotional experience.[69]

Historical pageantry's making of history into ritual depended—even more than other forms of drama—on the audience's complete identification with the special world created on the pageant field, a world at once real and prophetic. One can see why pageant-masters jealously guarded their format from the carnival, from disruptions of ironic comedy or popular song that united the audience in collective emotional expression—laughter and singing—but at the expense of their identification with the historical plot; why it was crucial that the audience in the opening scene of *The Pageant of St. Johnsbury* saw the "Wilderness" and not the local golf course where the scene was played. Like the "jeremiad" historical oration of the late nineteenth century, the historical pageant of the early twentieth century depicted the town united in times of jeopardy and renewal, through past, present, and future. It projected local residents bound together through collective beliefs and values expressed in historical episodes presented on stage, as well as through the "play spirit" or sensation of mutual affection they supposedly experienced in their interaction as members of the cast and audience. Pageant-masters, like historical orators, proclaimed that such affirmations of continuity in the midst of social change would enhance local residents' feeling of community and attachment to place, linked, but not lost, in a widening network of relations in larger society and in a succession of past and future generations.

American historical pageantry's celebration of the future and of the local community's role in larger society set it apart from its Parkerian counterpart in England. English historical pageants, like American pageants, typically displayed the community working together and playing together free of internal conflict. The British re-created Maypole dances and colorful royal progresses, just as the American pageants re-created barn dances and receptions for Lafayette. Viewing historical pageants as a protest against modernity, however, Louis

Napoleon Parker and his British imitators abhorred industrialism and rarely reenacted historical incidents from after Elizabethan times. A scene depicting an early settler returning to approve of the modern factory, as in *The Pageant of Schenectady*, or a rural town becoming a commuter suburb, as in *The Pageant of Ridgewood*, would have been unthinkable in British pageantry. Moreover, British pageants had little thematic continuity between episodes. No plot outlined successive stages of local social and economic development from past to present; no symbolic dances smoothed the "natural" transitions between historical periods. American pageant-masters, though tracing their work to Parker and agreeing that modern industrialism made even more necessary the outlet for wholesome recreation and artistic expression provided by pageantry's reenactment of preindustrial communal pastimes, also insisted, in the words of Lotta Clark, that "interest in the past was incomplete unless through it was demonstrated the meaning of the present and the duty of the future." Pageantry's enormous popularity in the United States stemmed not from Americans' desire to escape to the past, argued Ralph Davol, but rather from their "ambition to catch up with the world which is running away from them." American pageant-masters correctly declared that symbolic interludes and future scenes were the uniquely "American" contribution to pageant art. British pageantry, in the hands of pageant-masters closely aligned with the arts and crafts movement, displayed historical imagery in a format that glorified a remote golden handicraft past; American historical pageantry, especially when in the hands of pageant-masters distinctly sympathetic with the forward-looking progressive movements around them, presented history in a setting that emphasized the continuities between past, present, and an ideal future.[70]

But how often did the historical pageant wind up in the hands of reform-minded citizens? What did pageantry mean to local promoters, performers, and audiences in towns across the United States between 1912 and 1916? A pageant derived its meaning not only from its references to historical themes and ritual elements disseminated nationally, but also from a wide variety of local circumstances. The national formula served as a general template, not a detailed blueprint, for towns seeking to bring the usual local forms of civic holiday celebration up to date. Historical pageants in rural areas resembled a revised version of a county fair; in urban areas they resembled a children's playground festival. Rather than creating a separate dramatic production, towns sometimes added pageant elements to their customary holiday street procession. The committee in Stonington,

Connecticut, in charge of planning the commemoration of the battle centennial in 1914 originally decided that producing a dramatic historical pageant would be too expensive and instead scheduled a giant military parade as the principal feature of the town's celebration. But three weeks before the event, fearing that the army and navy units it invited to march in Stonington would be sent to Mexico, the committee hired Virginia Tanner for $300 to provide "an infusion of the pageant quality" into one of the other parades scheduled during celebration week.[71] Towns staged historical pageants in conjunction with July Fourth ceremonies, county fairs, Old Home Weeks, and high school graduation exercises—other events when townspeople customarily considered their place in a succession of past and future generations. The kind of occasion in which the pageant appeared contributed to how its imagery would be interpreted.

Moreover, who performed in the pageant added another layer of meaning to the imagery. In the finale of Ellis P. Oberholtzer's second Philadelphia historical pageant in 1912, the "Spirit of Philadelphia," to whom representatives of the various neighborhoods of the city paid homage, was played by the wife of reform Mayor Rudolph Blankenburg. At the time of the pageant, Blankenburg was attempting to revise the city charter to concentrate more power in City Hall. Similarly, in October 1916, one month before the presidential election, the daughter of Charles Fairbanks, Charles Evans Hughes's running mate, portrayed the "Spirit of America" in the *The Pageant of Indianapolis*. No matter how stereotypical the historical pageant imagery seemed, these events ultimately derived their meanings from the particular local circumstances as well as national conventions surrounding their characterization.[72]

For the chambers of commerce, local governments, and myriad private organizations that sponsored historical pageants, pageantry served a variety of purposes. It provided an opportunity to boost their town in a way more spectacular than the customary historical exercises and more novel than the parade. Darien, Connecticut, residents boasted that the $10,000 they spent on their pageant in 1913 would "put their town on the map" and astound the neighboring communities of Norwalk and Stamford. Yet as well as using the pageant for reasons of boosterism, to demonstrate that their town was up-to-date, local officials in towns such as Darien congratulated themselves on what they called their "Ruskin Spirit." To Darien officials, local residents playing their ancestors in the pageant demonstrated the persistence of old Connecticut families and traditions—even if the pageant plot chronicled the town's transformation into a commuter suburb. Town officials also shared the pageant-masters' goal of promoting a sense of local community identity and cohesion amid the pull of competing affiliations. One press release from *The Pageant of Darien* claimed that the pageant experience served as "a general social leveller . . . [which] not only brings a community together in a social way, but breaks the crust of exclusiveness." Until the pageant, "there had been nothing done in a social way to draw the widely scattered residents together. Hundreds of people residing in the neighborhood of these several scattered villages knew each other only by sight, and then, mainly, when whizzing by in motor cars." But as a result of the Darien pageant, declared another press release, "people are on familiar terms who many weeks ago were oblivious of one another's existence." A "friendly spirit" emerged from the pageant, fostered by the "zest with which all are working together." Civic officials saw historical pageantry, by promoting such cheerful social interaction within their town, as a prelude to the integration of the disparate local classes, ethnic groups, and interests under their responsible leadership.[73]

For leaders of local women's clubs and ethnic groups who customarily had only minor roles in civic celebrations, the historical pageant gave them an opportunity to associate their group with the community as a whole, as well as to assert their particular concerns in public—even if the pageant structure limited the particular form of this expression. Unlike other media for recounting history in the Progressive Era, such as books, magazines, and murals, historical pageants were public performances in which the stereotypical historical images did not always appear as the creators intended. Organizers of Boston's Columbus Day Parade in 1912 did not expect that they would be staging an appeal for woman suffrage—yet, as part of the historical procession, the Boston Equal Suffrage Association pulled a float depicting "Isabella's Part in the Discovery of America" with a sign on it proclaiming "Isabella Had Equal Rights with Ferdinand in the Government of Spain." Similarly, recent immigrant groups sometimes took advantage of the public space pageantry offered to project a different image of their place in the community than that intended by local pageant planners. The Italians of Norristown, Pennsylvania, excluded from the historical procession of 1912, marched with historical floats in a procession of fraternal organizations—one of the few fraternal societies that day that paraded with historical floats. Among the Italians' five floats was one depicting George Washington and the Continental Army at nearby Valley Forge—clearly an attempt to place themselves at the center of the community's history instead of remaining in their assigned place on the periphery. The conventions of the pageant form, established and disseminated nationally, also could be manipulated to make particular statements locally.[74]

Madeline Randall and folk dancers, St. Johnsbury, Vermont, 1912. (Brown University Library)

For the mass of pageant participants, pageantry also provided a whimsical interlude in their ordinary routine, an opportunity to dress up as Founding Fathers, as well as nature sprites, grasshoppers, and dancing potatoes. Rehearsal photos reveal pageant participants mugging for the camera and striking mock theatrical poses, imitating publicity stills from motion pictures and vaudeville. Though pageant directors insisted that the place was the hero, individual participants enjoyed the opportunity to act like stars. The pageant also offered occasions for camaraderie outside of the roles defined by directors; the actors in one pageant in New York City played baseball while waiting their turn on stage.[75]

Audiences seemed to have a good time at the pageants. Hundreds, sometimes thousands, who probably had little interest in attending the customary historical oration, saw and heard the pageant historical "message"—though it is unlikely that they were as absorbed by the action on stage as the pageant-masters claimed. Although each spectator probably had at least one friend or relative in the cast, attention inevitably wandered in the long succession of historical scenes. Compared to the spectacular historical drama produced on an indoor stage, or the feature-length historical motion pictures increasingly

Madeline Randall in a more adult pose offstage. Before the pageant, Randall listed herself in the St. Johnsbury city directory as a schoolteacher. Soon afterward, she listed herself as a professional dancer. (Brown University Library)

Pageant performers offstage, Louisville, Kentucky, 1911. (Brown University Library)

Pageant performers offstage, Cambridge, Massachusetts, 1917. While pageants imposed considerable structure upon participants during the performance, photos from Louisville in 1911 and from a production of Caliban *in Harvard Stadium in 1917 suggest that an informal camaraderie prevailed offstage among both male and female participants. (Dartmouth College Library)*

common in the 1910s, outdoor pageants produced in daytime on large fields contained many distractions and offered audiences little help in distinguishing between foreground and background action.[76] In many ways, D. W. Griffith's *Birth of a Nation* resembled a pageant, with its abstract symbolism, allegorical finale, and tableaux vivants of famous historical scenes, such as Robert E. Lee and Ulysses S. Grant at Appomattox; but Griffith's film also included a romantic melodrama and action far more stirring, complete with close-ups, than anything a local town could produce.[77] Watching from the distance necessary to take in the crowd scenes, pageant spectators were bound to miss more subtle scenes and dialogue. Spectators without a program to explain the action and elaborate symbolism would be lost. Photographs of pageant audiences, like those of participants, suggest that the atmosphere surrounding the performances more resembled that of a picnic or a ball game than a serious drama.

Historical pageantry's popularity in the early twentieth century went beyond its appeal to local officials as a medium for civic boosterism and moralizing, to local organizations as a forum to associate their views with the core community, to performers as a means of playful recreation, and to audiences as a novel form of holiday entertainment in which their family and friends took part. The pageant form, and the historical themes, abstract symbolism, and ritual action embedded within it, appealed to the desire of men and women in the Progressive Era to make tangible in public their ideals, their position in a succession of past and future generations, and the emotional basis of their modern community life. Robert Withington, an opponent of abstract symbolism in pageantry, conceded its enormous appeal to a public already steeped in idealistic abstractions. "We speak of Efficiency as if he were an intimate friend," he explained. "A few years ago we personified Gold and Silver in a political campaign. Pageantry readily adapts itself to this state of mind." Like many of the decade's social and political movements, which also employed the rhetoric of "community" and "tradition," the pageant experience promoted hierarchy, discipline, and rational organization in the effort to achieve a celebration of democracy, spontaneity, and lyrical emotion. Historical pageantry's popularity represented, in the words of Helen Thoburn, "one of the heralds of a new national willingness to be lifted above materialism, statistics, efficiency—as ends in themselves." At a time when Americans' lives were increasingly shaped by their contacts with ever more distant organizations, when neighbors saw one another only when whizzing by in motor cars, historical pageants projected the town as a manageable arena for reconstructing the intimacies of community while fostering loyalty to nation, for asserting the essential continuity of local tradition in the midst of sweeping social and economic change. The historical pageant's ability to embody these larger themes, as much as its particular local uses, made it the characteristic medium for the organization and expression of a public tradition in the Progressive Era.[78]

5

To Explain
the City to Itself

. . . .

If we play together, we will work
together.
—St. Louis Pageant Drama Association,
1914

Pageant poster, 1914. This poster by Joseph C. Leyendecker was reproduced on handbills and railroad circulars as part of a national advertising campaign. (A. W. Proetz Collection, Western Historical Manuscripts Collection, University of Missouri—St. Louis)

Community historical pageants remained in the early 1910s a holiday activity recommended primarily for small towns rather than large cities. Pageant directors believed that small-town pageants could include a majority of local residents, eliciting the high level of enthusiastic participation necessary for success, yet still be staged inexpensively and coordinated easily. By contrast, the limit on the number of performers a pageant director could manage effectively worked against efforts in cities to reach out to the population as a whole and recruit participants from more than one class or section. Moreover, in cities it was more difficult to drum up interest in historical pageants given the competition of other holiday amusements. As George McReynolds, a high school history teacher in Evansville, Indiana, explained, "The small town furnishes the best soil for a pageant's growth, because in it there are fewer distracting influences. Unity of feeling and action are, therefore, more easily acquired. . . . It is impossible to bring about the personal responsibility and interest in the large city as in the village or town."[1]

To stage a historical pageant that attempted to involve all of the groups in a city required a production of unprecedented scale and expense. Organizers of the few historical pageants produced citywide—in Philadelphia in 1908 and 1912, in New York City in 1909, and in Boston in 1910—had claimed, but not actually achieved, the high level of local citizen participation often possible in the small-town pageants. Yet even these urban extravaganzas proved artistically unwieldy. William Chauncy Langdon grumbled that the Hudson-Fulton Celebration in New York City had "pretended to be a city pageant and was a miserable failure." The public's lack of support for Ellis Paxson Oberholtzer's Philadelphia historical pageant of 1912 had resulted in financial disaster, saddling the pageant association that sponsored the affair with debts that remained unsettled for six years. Even if a pageant-master were prepared to oversee the production of a giant citywide pageant, with literally a cast of thousands, few city governments or private organizations were willing to assume the huge financial risk.[2]

Despite urban historical pageantry's dismal record, civic officials in St. Louis, Missouri, decided in 1913 to spend $125,000 on an enormous pageant to celebrate the 150th anniversary of the city's founding. "Shamed" by Chicago's increasing hegemony over midwestern trade, the apparent stagnation of municipal improvement campaigns, and Lincoln Steffens's series of articles in *McClure's Magazine* publicizing the city's political corruption, St. Louis officials desperately sought to present a different civic image to the nation. They felt that a successful historical pageant would not only cleanse the city's tarnished reputation nationwide, but also advance a single civic identity around which the various peoples and classes could rally to enact reforms at home. In addition, the pageant would offer St. Louisans an evening of art, recreation, and entertainment—a "people's diversion" of unprecedented proportions.[3]

The Pageant and Masque of St. Louis, performed on the last four evenings in May 1914, proved to be the culmination of American historical pageantry. To its sponsors and creators, the thousands onstage, performing before tens of thousands of their families and neighbors in the audience, seemed to reflect the ecstatic communion of all St. Louis, galvanized for civic revitalization. The St. Louis experience demonstrated pageantry's exciting potential to create a coherent vision of the public and its history in the Progressive Era—as well as the limitations of that vision.

In late June 1913, several men and women prominent in St. Louis civic affairs approached Mayor Henry Kiel with the idea of staging a historical pageant to coincide with the 150th anniversary of the founding of the town. The group wanted something big—its leader, businessman John Gundlach, declared, "We want to give a pageant to compare favorably with those in Eastern cities and Europe." Arthur Bostwick, head of the St. Louis Public Library, added, "We want a big spectacle, with thousands of participants in costume." Within a month of its first meeting, the planning group announced plans for a civic historical pageant with a cast numbering at least five thousand.[4]

The pageant would be the third major citywide celebration St. Louis had mounted in a decade. In 1904, the city hosted the Louisiana Purchase Exposition. Five years later, St. Louis celebrated the centennial of its incorporation as a city with a week of special events coinciding with its annual Veiled Prophets Autumn Festival. Along with the Veiled Prophets' spectacular torchlight carnival parade, eighty fraternal, business, and labor organizations joined in various processions through the streets of downtown St. Louis during celebration week. The "historical pageant" parade, like Ellis P. Oberholtzer's Philadelphia historical pageant of 1908, was dominated by the city's hereditary elite—the "Old French Families."[5] The version of St. Louis history presented in public that day included seven floats displaying scenes of the early French settlers from the discovery of Mississippi to the incorporation of St. Louis in 1809, but none depicting incidents from the subsequent history of the city.

In the aftermath of the 1909 celebration, some St. Louisans complained that the centennial "pageant" parade had failed to highlight the recent history of the city, particularly reform District Attorney Joseph W. Folk's success in rooting out municipal corruption in the decade since Lincoln Steffens's "Shame of the Cities" series appeared in *McClure's*. The *St. Louis Republic* editorialized in 1909 that "the ordeal by fire through which St. Louis passed when Joseph W. Folk was circuit attorney, followed by the birth of the new municipal spirit, the farewell to the old days of lax administration and facile corruption, is a series of events of the first magnitude in the moral history of America. It is strange that its humiliation, its heroisms, and its fruition should pass unremembered at such a time." Backers of the historical pageant in 1913 insisted that their celebration would not only outshine all previous municipal festivals, but also make up for the opportunity "lost" in 1909 to tell the nation that St. Louis' corruption had been purged.[6]

Civic leaders also wanted the pageant to demonstrate St. Louis' economic vitality to the nation. The city's decline from a genuine transcontinental trade rival of Chicago in antebellum years to a clearly inferior status after the Civil War had reinforced its reputation as a sultry, "Southern" town known more for its age than its dynamism.[7] A letter sent to local business people soliciting their support for the pageant warned that, unless St. Louis advertised to the world that it could do big things in a big way, the fourth largest city in the nation would soon suffer the "humiliation" of being surpassed by faster-growing Boston and Cleveland. Even more than the Louisiana Purchase Exposition of 1904, which highlighted the achievements of the world, a giant historical pageant focusing on local achievements could help transform St. Louis' national reputation from that of a decaying river town to that of a dynamic, progressive midwestern city.[8]

Supporters of the historical pageant hoped that it would not only project a new civic image to the nation but also promote a program of permanent municipal reforms at home. Eight of the thirteen members of the committee involved in the initial planning of the pageant belonged to the St. Louis Civic League, a group of college-educated, middle-class white professionals who supported a variety of progressive causes. In 1911, the league campaigned unsuccessfully for the passage of a new city charter. John Gundlach, a prominent realtor who chaired the pageant's executive committee, served on the Civic League's City Plan Committee and subsequently on the St. Louis City Planning Commission. He was the principal voice in St. Louis for the "City Beautiful" movement. Pageant committee secretary Luther Ely Smith, a lawyer, also served on the Civic League's City Plan Committee, as well as its Open-Air Playground Committee. Dwight F. Davis was the St. Louis Parks Commissioner, while Charlotte Rumbold was secretary of the Parks Department's Public Recreation Commission, responsible for the city's playgrounds. Rumbold, a member of the national board of the Playground Association of America since 1910, had previously authored a Civic League investigation of St. Louis' deteriorated housing conditions and lack of recreational space and, along with Smith, led the campaign to establish municipal playgrounds. The pageant planners envisioned the historical pageant as a dramatic extension of their efforts to publicize their municipal reform agenda: specifically, the passage of a new city charter, the creation of a giant downtown plaza along the lines of other cities' City Beautiful plans, and the construction of a new free bridge across the Mississippi River.[9]

Pageant backers argued that the right kind of civic celebration not only could inform the mass of St. Louis residents of the need for a new charter, downtown plaza, and bridge, but also forge the citywide spirit of cooperation necessary to create them. Charles Stix, chair of the pageant's finance committee, explained that, while St. Louis residents customarily supported projects for their individual neighborhoods, they rarely did so for the city as a whole. The historical pageant could remedy this focus solely on neighborhood by promoting local residents' identification with the entire city. Choosing as the pageant motto "If we play together, we will work together," pageant organizers pleaded that if only St. Louisans could attain "that fundamental thing . . . to get together in a playful mood and get acquainted, uniting into a perfect bond—the North, South, and West Sides, every neighborhood, block, and home," then improvements that would benefit all of St. Louis—the new charter, bridge, and plaza, as well as a subway and better hospitals and playgrounds—would surely follow. Neither the Louisiana Purchase Exposition of 1904 nor the centennial pageant of 1909 elicited citywide participation or left permanent reforms and institutions (with the exception of the art museum built in 1904) in its wake. To St. Louis civic leaders, historical pageantry's invitation to playful mass participation offered a golden opportunity overlooked in previous celebrations to enlist the diverse groups and neighborhoods of the city in a comprehensive program of municipal reform.[10]

Promoters expected that a historical pageant, unlike the usual ways that reform campaigns appealed for public support, could invigorate local residents emotionally, imbuing them with a heightened feeling of civic solidarity and awareness. "It is entirely possible," remarked Charlotte Rumbold, "to have a perfectly sanitized and financially stable community, every family having a porcelain-lined bathtub and a building and loan association house, with a paved street in front and certified milk delivered at the back door, and be a spiritually, to say nothing of politically, dead community." The historical pageant would "vibrate and stir the soul of every real St. Louisan," imparting a new sense of vitality in his or her daily life. St. Louis, trumpeted one pageant brochure, would become an "Awakened City," in which every citizen would feel obligated to "do something" for the entire community.[11]

Organizers of the St. Louis historical pageant, a coalition of the city's hereditary elite, downtown businesses, and playground workers, thus intended the commemoration of the 150th anniversary of the city's founding to be a celebration of the "new" St. Louis—reformed, dynamic, united, and invigorated. They wanted an affair unlike the ones in 1904 and 1909—a civic celebration that would focus exclusively on St. Louis, enlist the participation of the city's entire population, and highlight recent municipal reforms as well as point the way to future ones. To emphasize the uniqueness of their venture, they moved the date of the proposed extravaganza from the fall of 1913, when it would have coincided with the annual Veiled Prophets' carnival procession, to the last four days of May 1914.

Soon after the pageant backers organized as the St. Louis Pageant Drama Association (SLPDA) and set the date for their production, they sent inquiries to four experienced pageant-masters: William Chauncy Langdon, Ellis Paxson Oberholtzer, Thomas Wood Stevens, and Percy MacKaye. Langdon replied quickly, forwarding the St. Louis committee copies of his "New Country Life" pageants, including the celebration at Thetford. He informed the SLPDA that "the great attraction to me in your plans is the fact that the underlying purpose of this St. Louis pageant is to bind the people of the city together into a civic unanimity."[12] Langdon visited St. Louis during the last week in September 1913, promising the local civic groups he addressed that his pageant would "eradicate dissension, promote civic brotherhood, raise the aesthetic standards of your citizenship, and introduce the finest, cleanest, and healthiest entertainment."[13] He recommended that St. Louis produce its historical pageant along the lines of his pageants of the New Country Life, under the complete control of a single pageant-master, strongly intimating that, by virtue of reputation, experience, and interest, he should be that pageant-master.[14]

While Langdon was preparing to visit St. Louis, however, Charlotte Rumbold was in New Hampshire watching Percy MacKaye's allegorical masque *Sanctuary*, directed by Joseph Lindon Smith. She reported back to John Gundlach in St. Louis that "there is no question of doubt as to either Mr. MacKaye's or Mr. Smith's genius." Rumbold strongly recommended that MacKaye be hired over Langdon, whose New Country Life pageants were "dull, to put it mildly." Although Langdon was an astute promoter, remarked Rumbold, he was hardly an artist of MacKaye's caliber.[15]

MacKaye had responded to the SLPDA's inquiry with a proposal that the city stage two productions each evening rather than one. He envisioned a twilight *Pageant of St. Louis*—a dozen realistic dramatic scenes reenacting events from local history—to be followed immediately by a *Masque of St. Louis*—a spectacular, nighttime, two-act allegorical play. MacKaye assured Rumbold that the dual production, by illustrating the central themes of the city's history through both realism and abstract symbolism, would "explain the city to itself."[16] MacKaye offered to create the masque if the SLPDA would hire someone else to write and direct the pageant.

In October 1913, the SLPDA adopted MacKaye's plan for two related productions under different authors and directors, and hired MacKaye and his director Smith to prepare the masque. Langdon, who had insisted that he would not work in St. Louis without total artistic control of the entire production, dropped out of the competition. The executive committee then chose Thomas Wood Stevens, drama instructor at the Carnegie Institute of Technology, over Ellis P. Oberholtzer to write and direct the realistic pageant.[17]

When the SLPDA Executive Committee announced the names of the pageant-masters, a protest sounded among St. Louis' professional artists and dramatists. "St. Louis Artists Slighted by Pageant Managers," charged a headline in the *St. Louis Republic*. A few days later, the *Republic* carried a letter from Dawson Dawson-Watson of the St. Louis School of Fine Arts complaining that "the East takes care of itself and we are perfectly capable of doing the same." He correctly accused the SLPDA Executive Committee of deliberately not asking local artists to compete for the St. Louis job because it wished to gain national attention and prestige. The executive committee weakly replied that merit was the sole factor in its selections but wound up having to defend the decision to hire outside directors over and over in the months ahead.[18]

Dawson-Watson's critique indeed hit the mark. The SLPDA intended its production not only to celebrate St. Louis' history and to invigorate its community spirit, but also to advance the claim that St. Louis could afford and appreciate the finest in art. Unlike Langdon and Oberholtzer, who were trained as historians, MacKaye and Stevens had acquired their reputations principally in the world of the arts. The executive committee hoped that, in addition to overseeing a historical celebration of benefit locally, the pair would create an artistic extravaganza sufficiently dazzling to attract national attention.

The offer in November 1913 to write and direct *The Pageant of St. Louis* came at a turning point in Thomas Wood Stevens's career. Until then, Stevens had been a professional fine artist and amateur dramatist, but in the fall of 1913 he reversed these roles and assumed direction of the new theater arts program at the Carnegie Institute of Technology in Pittsburgh. His appointment as Carnegie's first drama teacher and as director of the St. Louis pageant, a production projected on an unprecedented scale, were all the more remarkable because he had virtually no training in theater.

Stevens was born in Daysville, Illinois, about ninety miles west of Chicago, in 1880. His parents sent him to secondary school at the Armour Scientific Academy in Chicago, and he remained in Chicago to enter the Armour Institute of Technology's engineering program in 1897. During his schooling in Chicago, Stevens developed an interest in the creative arts, writing stories, plays, and poems as well as attending drawing classes on Saturdays at the Art Institute of Chicago. Influenced by the writings of William Morris and the British arts and crafts movement, Stevens took up printing as a hobby and, falling in with the arts and crafts circle in Chicago, began producing handcrafted poetry books under the imprint "Blue Sky Press." His parents' death in 1900 forced him to leave engineering school for a job in the print shop of the Santa Fe Railroad's advertising department, but he soon quit the railroad to work full-time on the Blue Sky Press, writing poetry himself to supplement its list of titles. When the press folded in 1903, Stevens sold its equipment to the Art Institute of Chicago and joined the faculty as an instructor in lettering and printing—though he hoped eventually to establish himself as a free-lance book illustrator.[19]

But it was young Stevens's interests in drama and stagecraft that developed most fully during his decade at the Art Institute. In 1904 he taught a course on historical costume design and collaborated with Alden Charles Noble, his former partner in the Blue Sky Press, in a five-act play, *The Spanish Main*. The next year Stevens drafted a dramatic biography of *Cellini of Florence*, as well as several shorter plays for Art Institute student productions. In 1906 he and his wife Helen Bradshaw visited England, where they saw a rehearsal of the Warwick historical pageant and met its creator, Louis Napoleon Parker. Three years later Stevens wrote and directed his own historical pageant for the Art Institute—*A Pageant of the Italian Renaissance*. Using Vasari's *Lives of the Painters*, Stevens expanded his earlier *Cellini of Florence* to include dramatic sketches of the lives of Botticelli, Titian, and Michelangelo. He wrote his exceptionally wordy pageant text in Elizabethan-style blank verse. Although few outside of the Art Institute's faculty, students, and wealthy patrons actually saw the production, it received extensive publicity in Chicago's major newspapers and further fueled Stevens's dramatic ambitions.[20]

Soon after the Art Institute pageant, Stevens accepted an offer from Northwestern University to create a historical pageant to benefit its settlement house. Staged in October 1909, *The Pageant of Illinois* was among the earliest dramatic historical pageants produced in the United States. Based largely on the works of Francis Parkman, it presented six realistic episodes from Illinois history—from the coming of Father Marquette to the Blackhawk War of the 1830s. In June 1911, Stevens produced a second version of this pageant, retitled *The Pageant of the Old Northwest*, for the Wisconsin State Normal School at Milwaukee, adding scenes reenacting the arrival of the German settlers in 1848 and the departure of troops for the Civil War in 1861. He repeated this format of episodes for a third historical pageant for Madison County, Illinois, in 1912, inserting just before the Civil War scene an episode depicting abolitionist Elijah Lovejoy's murder in Alton. Together, Stevens's three pageants of the Old Northwest, like his *Pageant of the Italian Renaissance*, featured realistic dramatic historical reenactments filled with large stretches of dialogue and little abstract symbolism.[21]

Stevens knitted together the historical episodes of his Old Northwest pageants with the poetic narration of the Indian "prophet" White Cloud, played in all of the productions by a professional actor-friend from Chicago, Donald Robertson. The narrator's lyrical poetry served as a dance of words bridging the prosaic dialogue of the historical episodes, just as symbolic dancing linked the episodes of realistic action together in other community historical pageants of the period. White Cloud's recurring prophecy before each section of the episodes, as he watched the "leafage" of his Indian civilization "drift down," also reflected the "historical inevitability" of white conquest, a common pageant theme of the period.

Stevens's burgeoning interest in plays and historical pageants in the early 1910s complemented his involvement in movements to popularize the fine arts. He joined the Chicago Municipal Art League, which arranged for traveling art exhibits in neighborhood centers, sent artists to decorate various spots in the city, and promoted art instruction in the public schools. The league also advocated that Chicago create open air theaters in its city parks for holding plays and artistic community festivals. In 1913, Stevens gave a course at the University of Wisconsin on "Civic Art." His twenty-four lectures covered topics ranging from monumental sculpture to mural painting. Stevens taught that the quality of a city's public works of art reflected the health of its community life. He included historical pageantry among these works as "an expression of the community ideal in art."[22]

While Stevens in these years still defined himself professionally as a fine artist, he clearly also wanted to break into legitimate theater. He joined the editorial board of *The Playbook*, Thomas H. Dickinson's journal dedicated to the reform of the theater, collaborating on an issue devoted to "The Open Air Theatre."[23] Stevens described his pageant work to William Chauncy Langdon as "about as interesting as anything one can find to do in the present field of art," adding that his primary interest in the community pageantry movement lay in the eventual establishment of "high traditions" in drama and fine art.[24]

Stevens felt that the giant municipally sponsored holiday celebrations popular since the late nineteenth century did little to further these artistic aims. Every year, he griped, the Chicago Safe and Sane July Fourth Association trotted out its "usual stupid and inaccurate floats." "It will take a long time," he predicted in 1910, "before anything in the dramatic pageant field will be taken up by cities directly. Its educational features and its interest are admitted, but the dramatic end scares off the people in charge of public celebrations—too much art in it, which they don't readily understand."[25] Stevens's appointment as director of the St. Louis pageant thus represented an opportunity to reverse himself and see if he could work out his strongly dramatic version of historical pageantry on a citywide scale without compromising his standards of artistic achievement.

In 1913, when Thomas Wood Stevens was just embarking on what would be a long career in theater, Percy MacKaye's place in American drama was already well established. Several of his works had played on Broadway, and he was among the best-known poets and playwrights in America. MacKaye's appointment to create the giant civic *Masque of St. Louis*, however, fulfilled an ambition he had harbored since youth.

Percy MacKaye was born in New York City in 1875, the fourth of six children of Steele MacKaye, one of the most famous actors and theatrical producers of his generation, and Mary Medbury, a playwright. All of the MacKaye children exhibited interest in literature and the performing arts. Older brothers Harold and James were published authors, as was younger brother Benton, the forester and regional planner who first proposed the idea of an Appalachian Trail. Older brother Will, who died of typhoid fever in 1889, had begun an acting career; younger sister Hazel became an actress and pageant director active in the woman suffrage movement. But among all of the MacKaye children, the dramatic shadow of their parents, especially their father, fell heaviest upon Percy.[26]

Steele MacKaye, born in 1842, acted, wrote, directed, and produced numerous plays and theatrical spectaculars in the late nineteenth century. He invented a variety of devices, including flame-proof curtains, folding theater seats, and the "Nebulator," a machine for creating clouds onstage. MacKaye's productions ranged in scale and artistic pretension from Shakespeare and experimental one-act plays to Buffalo Bill's Wild West Show, which he corralled in New York City's Madison Square Theater in 1886. His reputation for staging elaborate spectacles led several members of the committee planning the Chicago World's Columbian Exposition of 1893—Daniel Burnham, Charles McKim, Frederick Law Olmsted, and George Pullman—to commission MacKaye to create *The World Finder*, an original musical extravaganza based on the life of Christopher Columbus, to premiere at the exposition. MacKaye designed a giant, 10,000-seat "Spectatorium" on the shores of Lake Michigan for his production. The theater design, which resulted in twenty-one patents, called for twenty-five stages set on six miles of railroad track, a forestage of water large enough for Columbus to "sail" his ship, and a vast array of newly invented machinery for creating special effects. Antonín Dvořák composed the music for MacKaye's show; portions of the score became better known as the *New World Symphony*. Steele MacKaye saw *The World Finder* and the Spectatorium as the culmination of his career, incorporating all that he knew about the theater. But the Spectatorium project ran out of money before its completion and creditors ordered the structure razed before a single performance of MacKaye's "Spectatorio" had been given. Cruelly disappointed, MacKaye built a much smaller "Scenitorium" for *The World Finder*. One week after the show's premiere in February 1894, its creator caught pneumonia and died.[27]

Percy MacKaye became the zealous guardian of his father's memory. In 1909, he rushed to Chicago to rescue the original plans for the Spectatorium from destruction; two years later, he wrote a two-part sketch of his father's career for *Drama* magazine. In the piece, he recalled helping on the Spectatorium project during his vacations from Harvard and vowing, as he stood with his shattered father on the balcony of the enormous shell shortly before its demolition, to continue on the same "path" his father had "blazed" to provide "a fine art for the people." It was for this ideal, declared MacKaye, that his father had "given his life."[28]

Percy MacKaye returned to Harvard University the fall after his father's death determined to make his living writing for the theater. Unlike his father, however, Percy MacKaye created works employing abstract symbolism rather than thrilling realism. He studied the classics as well as drama, and his early plays, such as *Sappho* in 1896, brimmed with allusions to ancient mythology. MacKaye's commencement address in 1897, "The Need of Imagination in the Drama of Today," argued that it was not enough for the theater simply to mirror reality; it must also stretch the audience's imagination, which had become atrophied by the matter-of-fact drabness of modern life. The ancient vocabulary of myth, symbol, and ritual could best accomplish MacKaye's goal of transporting the audience beyond the mundane to a vivid and ennobling world of ideals.[29]

Percy MacKaye's literary reputation began to grow within a decade after his graduation from Harvard. He spent several years writing in Europe with his wife Marion Homer Morse, of Cambridge, Massachusetts, whom he had married in 1898. On their return to New York City in 1900, MacKaye taught at a private school for boys and began publishing a steady stream of poems and plays-in-verse based largely on ancient and Medieval themes. Among his works for the theater were *The Canterbury Pilgrims* (1903), *Fenris the Wolf* (1905), *Jeanne d'Arc* (1906), and *Sappho and Phaon* (1907). Advance commissions for these plays from a sympathetic producer, E. H. Sothern, enabled MacKaye to quit teaching in 1904 and move with his family to the artist colony in Cornish, New Hampshire, that had grown around sculptor Augustus St.-Gaudens. It included sculptor Herbert Adams; painters Kenyon Cox, Thomas Dewing, and Maxfield Parrish; and writers Norman Hapgood, Louis Evan Shipman, and Winston Churchill.[30] Association with this circle of well-connected artists and writers, who were responsible for the creation of many of the period's most notable public murals, statuary, and historical novels, further encouraged MacKaye's interest in writing symbolic poetic drama for the stage. In June 1905, within a year of his arrival, the group performed *The Gods and the Golden Bowl*, an outdoor symbolic masque in honor of St.-Gaudens. Describing himself as a symbolist "raising his banner boldly" to clatter "symbolic spears against the shields of embattled naturalism," MacKaye also grew close to avant-garde theater designers Edward Gordon Craig and Robert Edmund Jones, whose experimental sets substituted broad abstract landscapes for realistic scenic detail. MacKaye traveled to California in 1908 to attend the annual Bohemian Club Grove masques staged by Porter Garnett of Berkeley. By 1910, H. L. Mencken dubbed MacKaye "the best dramatic poet that the United States has yet produced"—a reputation he retained at least through 1925, the year Professor Thomas H. Dickinson of the University of Wisconsin ranked Percy MacKaye, along with Eugene O'Neill, as one of the two major figures in American drama. A fiftieth birthday dinner in MacKaye's honor attracted many of the most prominent literary figures of his generation, such as Robert Frost, Edgar Lee Masters, Edwin Arlington Robinson, Henry Seidel Canby, Hamlin Garland, and Vachel Lindsay.[31]

Accolades for MacKaye's published plays and poems failed, however, to translate into box office success. Although several college theater departments and amateur companies undertook productions of his works, MacKaye had to wait until 1906 before a professional company staged one of his plays, *Jeanne d'Arc*, which opened in Philadelphia to mixed reviews. *Sappho and Phaon* closed in New York after only seven performances. Several drama critics, and apparently the ticket-buying public, considered MacKaye's poetic dramas wordy and his abstract symbolism obscure. A reviewer for *Collier's Weekly* faintly praised *The Scarecrow*, which opened and closed in 1911, as "comparatively free of that pedantic humor which has marred so much of Mr. MacKaye's work." The *New York Times* noted that at the premiere of his comedy *Anti-Matrimony* in 1910 "the mirth was by no means unrestrained." James O'Donnell Bennett of the *Chicago Record* observed that at times MacKaye conjured "shining visions and golden voices," but that at other times, writing with "pitiful fluency," he produced only "unconscionable twaddle." Nevertheless, MacKaye's reputation for soaring symbolism and leaden humor would prove no barrier to his success writing pageants.[32]

Rather than abandon a public that did not understand his dramatic art, MacKaye redoubled his efforts to reach a wider audience through other forms. He accepted invitations to read his poetry at public celebrations commemorating historical anniversaries or recent technological achievements—in Brooklyn, on the centennial of Abraham Lincoln's birth; at Fort Ticonderoga, on the tercentenary of the European discovery of Lake Champlain; and in New York City, on the first airplane flight of Wilbur Wright, on the return of Admiral Peary from the North Pole, and as part of a festival celebrating the opening of the Panama Canal.[33] Within a month after the closing of *Sappho and Phaon* in New York, MacKaye also began lecturing to settlement houses, colleges, and local drama clubs across the United States on the need for creative artists and their supporters to wrest control of the American theater from commercial entrepreneurs and lead the public in the development of new artistic standards.

Like Thomas Wood Stevens and other dramatists influenced by the arts and crafts movement, Percy MacKaye viewed historical pageantry as a step in this process, a rudimentary form of drama that offered the public wholesome recreation while whetting its appetite for higher forms of art. Pageantry provided an outlet for mass creative expression, an essential relief from the industrial regimen. "In the vocations of modern industry," charged MacKaye, "the divorce between joy and labor has become too absolute to reconcile." Only active participation in broad-based, artistic enterprises such as historical pageants could restore this joy and quench "the demand of a people thirsting for regeneration through their leisure."[34] MacKaye extolled community historical pageantry as the forerunner of a new civic theater that would invite widespread popular participation, be publicly funded, like libraries and museums, and have creative artists, not business people, in control. As his initial contribution to the pageant form, MacKaye, in August 1909, adapted *The Canterbury Pilgrims* for a large outdoor civic holiday celebration in Gloucester, Massachusetts, casting local residents alongside the small group of professional actors who played the leading roles.

But unlike many of his fellow dramatists who were interested in pageantry primarily as a school of arts and crafts, MacKaye explicitly linked the new pageantry's potential to liberate creative artists and their audiences from commercialism and industrialism to contemporary political movements. In 1913, he described the "Wisconsin Idea in Theater" for Thomas H. Dickinson's journal *The Playbook*. The Wisconsin Idea, explained MacKaye, "involves the full scope of popular self-government; but popular self-government without indigenous art-forms is incapable of civilized expression." Community pageantry represented the art form of American democracy, "the ritual of democratic religion" in which the mass of citizens, through the intervention of expert dramatic artists, could be made socially and politically articulate.[35]

MacKaye envisioned the new civic theater as expressing a local community's political will, mobilizing public opinion on behalf of particular reform movements. He followed politics avidly in these years, maintaining a scrapbook labeled "Civic Movements and Politics." Identifying himself with the forces of "progressivism," though not the Progressive party, MacKaye corresponded with Herbert Croly, Lincoln Steffens, Upton Sinclair, and Walter Lippmann (who invited MacKaye in 1912 to create a July Fourth pageant for Schenectady, New York). Moving between the genteel world of the St.-Gaudens art colony in Cornish and the bohemian world of *The Masses* and Greenwich Village, MacKaye also grew friendly with the circle of radicals surrounding Mabel Dodge, including John Reed, twelve years his junior, whom he first met when Reed acted in one of his productions at the Harvard Dramatic Club.[36] In the midst of this political climate, MacKaye supported socialism in 1912. But he subsequently came to idolize Woodrow Wilson, whom he had met in the summer of 1913 when Wilson's daughter Eleanor performed in MacKaye's outdoor masque *Sanctuary* back in Cornish. MacKaye's politics, like his symbolic theater, was full of idealistic abstraction—that an enlightened public inspired by men and women governing according to the loftiest principles could bloodlessly transform the harsh realities of modern industrialism into something more aesthetically pleasing, fair, and humane.

The role of the playwright in advancing these progressive causes, insisted MacKaye, was that of "dramatic engineer." Leaders of movements to reform society would seek advice from expert dramatists on how best to present their programs to the public, just as they turned to engineers with other expertise for advice on sewer construction or bridge building. Whereas in the past, religion and the "flaming hell" preacher could stir the imagination and arrest the attention, in the present "age of advertising" the sermon is a "dead issue" and reform appeals must be presented in a "cheerful and picturesque form." MacKaye concluded, "It is only through the drama that reform can be made spectacular enough to interest the nervous, restless people of today."[37]

MacKaye engaged in several attempts at "dramatic engineering" for various causes before undertaking the St. Louis project in 1914. He helped Judge Ben Lindsey of Denver create *The Children at the Door*, a play advocating protective legislation for children. MacKaye assisted his younger sister Hazel MacKaye with the allegorical masque held on the steps of the Department of the Treasury Building in Washington, D.C., as part of the woman suffrage pageant procession in March 1913.[38] He probably also helped his friends John Reed and Robert Edmond Jones in staging the Industrial Workers of the World's pageant in Madison Square Garden in June of that year on behalf of the striking Paterson, New Jersey, silk mill workers. MacKaye's *Sanctuary*, the masque Charlotte Rumbold had seen in New Hampshire, was presented at the request of naturalist Ernest Harold Baynes and advocated the establishment of wildlife preserves.[39]

But Percy MacKaye had never successfully produced a civic masque based on local history, one designed to promote overarching civic commitments as well as advance the claims of particular reform groups. He had planned two elaborate Fourth of July celebrations for Pittsburgh, Pennsylvania, to be staged over 1910 and 1911. The first year's production was "to symbolize the fusion of many nationalities in the American nation"; the following year's was to culminate in a *Masque of Labor* "interpretive of the great steel, glass, and mining industries of Pittsburgh" and played by their workers. MacKaye commissioned Frederick S. Converse, founder of the Boston Opera Company, to write the music for both affairs. Three months before the debut of the first celebration, however, news of a scandal broke involving the bribery of city officials. One hundred sixteen persons were indicted, and twenty city councilmen landed in jail. Instead of seizing the opportunity of MacKaye's upcoming civic pageants to redeem Pittsburgh's tarnished reputation, local officials postponed the celebrations indefinitely.[40]

The Pageant and Masque of St. Louis gave two professional dramatists the chance to experiment on a massive scale with the role of civic art in social reform. After the disappointments of the Spectatorium in 1893 and the Pittsburgh civic masque in 1910, Percy MacKaye would at last create a giant municipal spectacle embodying his ideas of the relationship between democratic politics and aesthetic liberation. After years of advocating the extension of fine art to the masses, Thomas Wood Stevens would at last discover whether or not a large city could nurture a truly artistic public celebration. Five days after signing the contract to write and direct the St. Louis pageant, Stevens confided to Thomas H. Dickinson, "We'll either do something wonderful or something unspeakable—can't tell which."[41]

Amply funded by the St. Louis Pageant Drama Association, Stevens and MacKaye created a production of unprecedented proportions. They chose a site in Forest Park, near the grounds of the Louisiana Purchase Exposition of 1904. A natural amphitheater was provided by a hill sloping down from the St. Louis Art Museum, the only building surviving from the exposition, to a large lagoon. Stevens and MacKaye ordered an enormous semicircular stage—over 500 feet wide, 200 feet deep, and totaling 90,000 square feet—to be built on pilings in the lagoon. Workmen constructed a 40-foot-high wall at the rear of the stage as a sounding board and two towers at either end of the stage, each holding an assortment of spotlights. A system of telephones linked the lighting crew in the towers to the stage managers below. At the center-rear of the stage, against the backdrop, workmen built a pit large enough to hold the 100-piece orchestra and 500-voice chorus. Between the stage and the audience lay a 125-foot-wide band of water peeking out from the lagoon below, forming a "mimic Mississippi."[42]

Across the lagoon, extending up the hill toward the Art Museum, was seating for over 43,000 spectators. The SLPDA arranged the 1,800 seats nearest the stage into 300 boxes, which sold for fifteen dollars each. Behind the boxes, workmen placed 12,000 chairs and 30,000 bleacher seats. A 3½-foot-high chicken wire fence divided the sections of chairs and bleachers into a left and right side. The price of the 21,000 reserved seats on the left side of the fence ranged from 25¢ to $1.50. The 21,000 seats on the right side of the fence remained unreserved and were free to the public on a first-come, first-served basis. Standing room on the hillside behind the seats could accommodate an additional 50,000 spectators.[43]

The SLPDA Executive Committee assigned the production of near-

Planning the pageant. Percy MacKaye, Joseph Lindon Smith, and Thomas Wood Stevens in Forest Park with a model of the pageant stage, February 1914. In the background are pilings on which the stage would be built. (Missouri Historical Society, St. Louis)

Building the stage. The stage for the Pageant and Masque *extended out over the lagoon in Forest Park. (Missouri Historical Society, St. Louis)*

The completed pageant grounds. The skyline of St. Louis was clearly visible from the hillside where the audience was seated. Note also the tents erected just offstage which served as dressing rooms for the 7,000 performers, the signs demarcating sections of "Free" and "Reserved" seats, and the substantial standing room behind the seats. (A. W. Proetz Collection, Western Historical Manuscripts Collection, University of Missouri—St. Louis)

ly all of the music, costumes, props, and sets to local artists and businesses, in part responding to public criticism for hiring so many "outsiders" in the early stages of the pageant planning. Although Percy MacKaye imported Frederick Converse from Boston to compose the music for his masque, local musical directors Frederick Fischer and Noel Poepping conducted the chorus and orchestra, respectively.[44] The SLPDA held a local competition for pageant costume designs. Over half of the 7,000 costumes were either made at home by the participants or sewn in a special "pageant house" by volunteers. The SLPDA rented the remaining costumes from Famous-Barr, a local dry goods firm. J. V. Musick of the Veiled Prophets' Den supervised construction of the larger stage properties. The St. Louis Float and Scenic Company painted the scenery and sets.[45]

Production expenses for the *Pageant and Masque* topped $125,000— approximately what D. W. Griffith spent later that year to film *The Birth of a Nation*. The pageant stage alone cost $20,000; props and sets, an additional $15,000. The SLPDA spent nearly $10,000 for lighting and over $15,000 to provide seating and sanitation facilities for the audience. Even though more than half the costumes were homemade, fees for rented costumes (at $2.50 each) and for renting seven big tents for the performers to use as dressing rooms (two for women, five for men), totaled over $11,000.[46]

Much of the $125,000 went to pay laborers and professional staff. Percy MacKaye received $2,500 for creating the masque. His stage director, Joseph Lindon Smith, and composer, Frederick Converse, received $2,500 and $1,500, respectively. Thomas Wood Stevens could command only $1,500 for writing and directing the pageant. Although most members of the SLPDA Executive Committee donated their time, Charlotte Rumbold, who took charge of the day-to-day community organization for the pageant, drew a salary of $75 a week. She convinced the YWCA to pay the salaries of her several assistants. The St. Louis Parks Department performed much of the construction work on the pageant grounds, but the SLPDA spent $5,000 to hire additional laborers. They were union laborers—when lighting director Rolf Toensfeldt began to demonstrate a homemade dimmer to a group of visiting dignitaries, the carpenters building the stage walked out until a union electrician arrived to run the device. Although the pageant actors and chorus were not paid, the union musicians received a total of $5,000 in wages.[47]

The SLPDA handled pageant finances without a direct subsidy from city government. Donations from local businesses and trade associations paid nearly 40 percent of the pageant production expenses; individuals contributed another 15 percent of the total needed. The remainder of the $125,000 came from the sale of tickets, programs, and souvenirs. The finance committee, headed by Charles Stix, owner of a local department store, appointed representatives from each type of St. Louis industry to solicit contributions from other firms in that industry. A pageant speakers' bureau dispatched representatives to solicit contributions from church groups and fraternal organizations. Although the bulk of the money raised came from businesses and wealthy individuals, who for contributions of $100 or more were listed in a pageant "Roll of Honor," the finance committee devised campaigns to encourage smaller donations from the mass of St. Louis residents to promote a more broad-based local attachment to the affair. Over $1,000 came from the sale of pageant buttons to schoolchildren at a penny apiece. For 25¢, all who lived in St. Louis during pageant week could register their names in a book of "Native-born" St. Louisans.[48]

Unlike Ellis P. Oberholtzer's Historical Pageant Association of Philadelphia, the St. Louis Pageant Drama Association had no qualms about boosting the historical pageant's spectacular and popular entertainment value to outsiders alongside its social benefits for local residents. The SLPDA launched a $12,000 national publicity campaign run by a professional advertising firm, hoping that visitors to St. Louis would purchase some of the 23,000 seats on sale for each performance. It commissioned Joseph C. Leyendecker, of New York City, the famous magazine illustrator, to create a pageant poster. Leyendecker's art soon flooded the nation, along with postcards, railroad handbills, and shrewdly timed press releases. Comparing the St. Louis pageant to other popular diversions, one flyer boasted that the historical pageant's cast of 7,000 "are more people than are employed by all of the circuses in America combined." It assured potential visitors to St. Louis that "in both the Pageant and the Masque there will be spoken words, but whether they are heard or not, the action will explain itself, just as it does in the motion picture films." To further boost attendance from outside St. Louis, the SLPDA announced that a national Conference of Cities would convene in St. Louis during pageant week to discuss recent trends in municipal recreation. Efforts to secure envoys from every major American city for the conference also served to publicize the pageant.[49]

Although publicity aimed at drawing visitors from outside St. Louis billed the pageant as popular spectacle, local materials portrayed it as a serious commemorative event in the tradition of other municipal holiday celebrations. The SLPDA worked hard to win over local support after its initial gaffe in hiring outside artists. It scheduled a performance for Sunday so that working-class residents could attend, then deftly responded to complaints about the propriety of a Sunday show by organizing a committee of local ministers to endorse the performance as "Religious Day" at the pageant.[50] The SLPDA employed a similar approach to deflect local criticism that its May 30 performance desecrated Decoration Day by designating the performance "Military Day." To further demonstrate that the pageant belonged in the tradition of civic historical celebration rather than private show, the St. Louis Pageant Drama Association organized a relic display to run concurrent with the pageant. Significantly in a celebration managed by a middle class increasingly infatuated with consumer goods, the association housed its display of historical artifacts not in a tent or a public building, but rather on the second through fourth floors of a downtown department store.[51]

By mid-January 1914, the SLPDA had received detailed outlines of Stevens's pageant and MacKaye's masque and could begin casting its enormous production. The pageant motto, "If we play together, we will work together," outlined the promoters' goal of bringing the peoples and classes of St. Louis together in harmonious cooperation. Charles Stix declared that the pageant "will be the means of introducing thousands of St. Louisans who hitherto have been strangers to one another."[52] The cast of 7,000 "playing together" onstage would mirror the blocks of diverse peoples "working together" in the city of 700,000.

The *St. Louis Republic* predicted that the *Pageant and Masque*, like the centennial celebration of 1909, would draw upon few outside of the city's "Old French Families." The newspaper proved to be wrong, however, as the SLPDA looked beyond the city's hereditary elite to cast its production. Using Charlotte Rumbold's connections with neighborhood playground associations and settlement houses, the SLPDA invited a broad base of ethnic and fraternal organizations to participate as groups in the pageant and masque. Each group in turn selected members to act in the episode it was assigned to play. The Swedish National Society of St. Louis met for the special task of recruiting one hundred members to play hunters and trappers in one of the early pageant scenes. Serbs, Croatians, Bohemians, Greeks, Italians, Poles, Bavarians, and Hungarians all met with the SLPDA Executive Committee and took part in the pageant.[53]

Not all immigrant groups were pleased with their assigned roles. Joseph Treschi complained that his organization, the League Pro Colonia Italiana, should have been invited to represent Italy rather than the rival Circolo Silvio Pellio. Moreover, the Italian scene should have reenacted the Italian Signor J. C. Beltrami discovering the sources of the Mississippi in 1823, rather than merely showing "some peasant folks" arriving as new immigrants.[54] As in other local community historical pageants of the early twentieth century, pageant organizers assigned "recently" arrived immigrants roles playing "immigrants" on the margins of the community, rather than having them appear in scenes depicting the "making" of St. Louis.

The three largest national groups in St. Louis—the Germans, Irish, and Anglo-Americans—received no special ethnic designation in the pageant cast. Stevens had difficulty even locating the leaders of the city's Irish community. The SLPDA changed "German Day" at the pageant to "Native-born Day", in recognition of the fact that by 1914 most St. Louisans of German ancestry were second- and third-generation Americans, not foreign born. Although the pageant included one specifically "German" scene, St. Louis' Germans, like its Irish and Anglo-Americans, appeared throughout the production. Members of these groups chose to assert their identity as St. Louisans, rather than that of their ethnic origin and, unlike more recently landed immigrant groups, were allowed to do so.[55]

The St. Louis Pageant Drama Association decided not to use real Amerindians in the *Pageant and Masque*. Casting director Eugene Wilson declined the offer from William Hole-in-the-Day to bring his band of Chippewa from Minnesota to participate in the pageant, even though for the same fee the traveling troupe would have staged a baseball exhibition as well. Pageant planners instead ladled out sixteen

Painting the Indians. Sixteen gallons of copper paint transformed white St. Louisans into "Indians" for the performance. Note the half-painted man on the right. (Alice Willis photo, St. Louis Public Library)

gallons of copper-colored makeup and distributed dozens of gunny-sacks to transform local white residents into "Indians" for the performance.[56]

In addition, the SLPDA apparently neglected to include the city's large black population in the production, reflecting blacks' status as outside the boundaries of community designated by civic officials. St. Louis in 1910 had counted nearly 44,000 black residents, well over 6 percent of its total population. More blacks lived in St. Louis than any of the groups of recent immigrants whom the SLPDA especially invited to play pageant parts.[57] Six weeks before the pageant, James L. Usher, who chaired the integrated Committee for Social Service among Colored People, complained to Luther Ely Smith, secretary of the SLPDA Executive Committee, that no blacks had been appointed to any of the pageant committees nor assigned any roles in the pageant. "As this great spectacle is to be given by and for the city," Usher asked, did the executive committee intend to include black citizens in the planning or in the cast, or to set aside a section of seats for black spectators? Percy MacKaye claimed to have visited a black high school in conjunction with the production, and one black did play in his masque, but the connection of black St. Louisans as a whole to the performance was so insignificant that the question of whether to have segregated seating did not arise.[58]

The SLPDA also denied organized labor a place in the dramatic depiction of St. Louis' development. At a meeting of the Central Trades and Labor Union in March 1914, delegates from St. Louis unions heard Luther Ely Smith call for their cooperation in the pageant production. Before Smith could leave the hall, however, delegates bombarded him with questions about the pageant's contents. A Mr. Schmidt from the Butcher's Union asserted that the "history of St. Louis could not be properly dramatized without taking in the history of the labor movement," adding, "The best thing that could be exhibited in the Pageant would be the Great Drama of the Butchery of the St. Louis Police in Dealing With Organized Labor On Strike." Otto Paul, a columnist for *St. Louis Labor*, suggested only half-facetiously that a pageant episode reenacting a strike, complete with a violent clash between organized labor and the police, court injunctions, and grand jury indictments, "can't be beat for truth, realism, and popular interest." Paul also declared that the pageant should incorporate a march of 10,000 unemployed St. Louisans carrying banners and shouting aloud to protest "the beastly stupidity of an industrial system which starves the workers in the midst of fabulous wealth." The labor columnist concluded that, as written, the *Pageant and Masque* served merely to "distract the attention of the people from their miseries, in the same way that the Roman patricians made use of circuses to still the clamorings of the hungry multitude," warning that someday "the sufferings of the mob [would force] a state of affairs that will be neither a pageant, a masque, or a circus, but rather a grim struggle with reality resembling the French Revolution." Although the SLPDA eventually gained organized labor's official endorsement for its employment of union labor for construction and music, and for holding a Sunday performance so that the working classes could attend, union leaders remained unenthusiastic. Percy MacKaye's intellectual sympathy with socialism and his earlier ambitions to stage a *Masque of Labor* in Pittsburgh apparently did not prompt him to insist that the SLPDA recognize organized labor as a community group worthy of inclusion in its version of St. Louis history.[59]

As well as inviting various ethnic and fraternal organizations to join in the pageant as groups, the SLPDA appealed directly to individual citizens. The casting committee created twenty-five "Registration Bureaus" at neighborhood branches of the public library and YWCA/YMCA throughout the city and encouraged local clergy to enroll their parishioners. Residents filled out index cards giving their height, weight, sex, age, and nationality and were assigned to an appropriate

Water maidens. St. Louisans could join the pageant cast not only though their membership in local fraternal and women's organizations, but also through open registration at branches of the city's public libraries and YWCA/YMCA. (A. W. Proetz Collection, Western Historical Manuscripts Collection, University of Missouri—St. Louis)

group and role in the pageant.[60] Except for the Lafayette Ball scene, in which members of St. Louis' hereditary elite insisted on playing their forebears, the casting committee placed more emphasis on histrionic ability than genealogy in casting pageant roles. From among those auditioning for one of the few speaking roles in the *Pageant and Masque*, MacKaye and Stevens selected primarily on the basis of the would-be actor's ability to project his or her voice two hundred yards across the expanse of Art Hill. Though seeking amateurs, the committee filled a few lead roles with professionals, who possibly donated their services in return for the publicity.[61]

The pageant-masters managed their massive mélange through an elaborate system of group assignments. They labeled each group in each episode with a letter, "A" through "W," and printed blue script cards for each letter containing only its own lines and cues for entrances and exits. Newspapers announced rehearsal times by group letter.[62] Not until pageant week was either the pageant or the masque of St. Louis rehearsed in its entirety.

Thomas Wood Stevens's *Pageant of St. Louis* surveyed three centuries of local development—from the earliest "aboriginal" communities, through the Spanish and French explorers and settlers, to the American city of the mid-nineteenth century.[63] The pageant opens to the sound of beating tom-toms, as the ancient Mound Builders, the first inhabitants of St. Louis, bury their dead chief. The "Prophet" then climbs upon the chief's burial mound, foretelling that the mounds of his people will rise no higher. Subsequent episodes display the Plains Indians, the next residents of the Mississippi Valley, dancing, fighting with neighboring tribes, and reaching a peace. The section of episodes depicting St. Louis' history before white settlement concludes with reenactments of three visits to the Indians from European explorers: de Soto seeking gold, Father Marquette seeking converts, and La Salle seeking furs and skins. The Prophet from the first episode returns, narrating the further decline of the Indian civilization and foretelling the coming of a new race of settlers:

> Into the West our nations trooping slow,
> And here our council places desolate.
> The paleface rears in stone his mighty lodge,
> And sets his town upon the crossing trails.[64]

The second section of six pageant episodes traces the history of St. Louis from its founding by the French in 1763 to its acquisition by the United States in 1803. Early French settlers establish a fur-trading post, found a church, and defend their fledgling fort against an Indian attack in 1780. The section concludes with a reenactment of "The Day of the Three Flags" in 1803, when St. Louis transferred from Spanish to French to American sovereignty. The mostly French settlers of 1803 dance a lively gavotte to celebrate. Paralleling the Indian Prophet who closed the first section of pageant episodes, an American "Watchman" high in the stockade ends the second section of episodes, foretelling the growth of the American city in the new century.[65]

The third section of historical episodes, depicting St. Louis' "development," required nearly twice the number of actors as the previous two sections. Lewis and Clark depart to explore the West. Scores of pioneer families in covered wagons soon follow. Two thousand St. Louisans greet the arrival of the first steamboat chugging up the lagoon "river" in front of the pageant stage and remain to welcome Lafayette in 1824 and local troops returning from the Mexican War two decades later.[66] The first big wave of German immigrants arrive, singing, in 1849.

The final episode of the historical pageant depicts St. Louis during the Civil War. Echoing the realistic Lovejoy murder scene of his *Pageant of the Old Northwest* in Madison County, Illinois, Stevens originally drafted an episode reflecting St. Louis' divided loyalties in wartime: an angry mob parades through the streets by torchlight bearing a picture

Arrival of the first steamboat. Two thousand St. Louisans crowded on stage for this scene, the largest in the Pageant and Masque. *This and subsequent photographs were probably taken during rehearsals, including the one where a motion picture version of the pageant was filmed for commercial distribution. (Missouri Historical Society, St. Louis)*

of Abraham Lincoln and confronts another hostile crowd. On the arrival of news from Fort Sumter, the young men of St. Louis bitterly divide and depart, some to Union, some to Confederate armies. "Dixie" and "The Battle Hymn of the Republic" discordantly blare in the background. Later, at the announcement of peace, St. Louis residents celebrate the soldiers' return and the pageant closes. The SLPDA Book Committee forced Stevens to rewrite this Civil War scene, eliminating the depiction of internal discord and the jeering at Lincoln.[67] As finally performed, the Civil War episode presented only a symbolic musical clash of forces and the jubilant procession of a united St. Louis celebrating the announcement of the peace.

The historical *Pageant of St. Louis* closely resembled Stevens's earlier pageants of the Old Northwest. As in his earlier works, a narrator linked realistic dramatic scenes. The pageant presented St. Louis' "Indian times," "founding," and "development" as stages in a single natural process of local community development, inevitably unfolding from the first canoes of the ancient Mound Builders to the steamboats of the nineteenth century. Throughout St. Louis' rise, the inhabitants—French, Spanish, American, German—remained united, working together to establish the fur trade, defend the settlement against outside attack, and found the first church. They also played together, celebrating "The Day of the Three Flags" and the visit of Lafayette.

The SLPDA expunged from the pageant any direct reference to the internal discord of the Civil War era in favor of a scene depicting a reunited St. Louis celebrating the peace. The *Pageant of St. Louis*, like other historical pageants of the period, presented a model community through time working together, playing together, and remaining free of ethnic, class, and ideological conflict.

The St. Louis pageant differed from Stevens's earlier works, however, in its spare use of dialogue. The enormous cast and outdoor setting led him to simplify the action and limit speeches so that the audience could more easily grasp the events depicted onstage. But Stevens rejected the SLPDA Executive Committee's proposal that he further explain the performance by placing large placards at the base of each lighting tower, "to be changed as the action of the play proceeds, just as is done in vaudeville shows."[68] Despite the unwieldy size of his historical pageant, Stevens still viewed it as a unified dramatic work and not as a collection of amusing scenes.

The St. Louis pageant also differed from the typical historical pageant formula of the period in its lack of either abstract symbolism or a grand finale projecting the ideal city of the future. Stevens's pageant episodes, which advanced local history only to 1865, did not even show off the reformed St. Louis of the new century. Instead, Stevens and MacKaye agreed to treat these symbolic and future aspects of St. Louis history in the separate masque.

MacKaye's masque and Stevens's pageant presented St. Louis history on two different levels. The pageant, MacKaye explained, contained groups of realistic historical episodes that allowed the audience to view three hundred years of local history as if "from a hill-top, not too distant for the recognition of personalities in the groupings." The masque would "adopt another scale of outlook, and . . . relate that local life to larger national and world life." The masque would transport the audience "from its hill-top to a viewpoint of even larger vantage . . . the bird's-eye view of the horizon's rim." At this ethereal level, MacKaye noted, the dramatist and his audience soared too far above the episodes of local history to recognize them in detail and could only discern their general outlines, presented through abstract symbolism. MacKaye distilled the episodes from St. Louis history reenacted in Stevens's pageant for their "national and world significance" and presented the results in a two-part allegorical drama employing just a few symbolic characters.[69] MacKaye's theatrical plan underlined the transition from pageant to masque, from realism to symbolism, from local to cosmic significance, with the shift from day to night. Stevens's historical pageant played in twilight, from approximately 6:30 to 8:00 P.M.; MacKaye's masque began after a half-hour intermission, at 8:30, the time of the evening in late May when St. Louis begins to get dark.

By dusk of May 28, 1914, opening night, 47,000 spectators filled the amphitheater seats in Forest Park. Another 30,000 crammed in behind them. Stevens's pageant had already dragged on nearly an hour past its scheduled completion time. At last, the orchestra sounded Frederick Converse's theme introducing the *Masque of St. Louis*, as banks of spotlights dimly illuminated the stage below.

The theme of MacKaye's masque was "the fall and rise of social civilization," represented by the decline of the ancient Mound Builders and the rise of the modern metropolis. At center stage soars an enormous temple, designed by Joseph Lindon Smith and based on the Mayan temple at Chichén-Itzá. "Mound Builders," impersonated by members of the local turnverein, perform graceful acrobatic stunts at its base, complementing the innocently sensual gyrations of their "Priestess" (played by Anita Gaebler, a professional dancer) on a dais above. On the completion of their communal ritual, the stage again dissolves into darkness.[70]

Suddenly a shaft of light reveals "Cahokia," a giant puppet symbolizing "the pinnacle of the social aspirations of the Indian race, regarded ethnologically," perched atop the temple. Around him thunder the "Powers of Chaos." Tremulous rumbles (produced by rolling cannonballs down a zig-zag wooden track behind the rear sounding board) and savage yells of "Wild Nature Forces" punctuate the frenzied, dissonant music. On either side of Cahokia's mound stand grotesque carvings representing "Hiloha" and "Hoohai," the elements heat and cold, around which swirl flame and snow. Cahokia in a "bass-drum voice" solemnly narrates how these hostile elements drove his once-gentle people back into barbarism.[71]

But amid this churning chaos, Cahokia cries out defiantly that "dreams are born and rise from ruined worlds." He looks to the constellation "Wasapedan," the Great Bear, outlined above him in electric lights. The constellation promises Cahokia that a new civilization will arise to restore the cooperative arts lost with the fall of his Mound Builders. Below, rounding the bend in the lagoon "river," a canoe guided by "River Spirits" delivers a small white child to Cahokia. A colorful procession of "Discoverers" soon follows, headed by a Spanish knight, a French trapper, and a priest. The three men pay homage to the young child and the priest baptizes him "St. Louis." As Part One of the masque ends, the dying Cahokia entrusts the child St. Louis with the mission to continue the "fight with the formless void for beauty and order to triumph."[72]

Part Two of the masque begins with westward bound white settlers

Percy MacKaye and Cahokia. The giant puppet, crafted out of wire and pa-
per-mache, represented the "Indian" race at its peak at the time of the Mound
Builders. MacKaye named Cahokia after the ancient burial grounds across
the Mississippi River in Illinois. (Dartmouth College Library)

encountering the adult St. Louis, now a knight in armor "symbolic of a young crusader in the cause of social civilization."[73] No sooner does St. Louis agree to shepherd the pioneers across the prairie than their progress is interrupted by the menacing figure "Gold" and his band of enslaved "Earth Elements." The gilded figure and his multihued army of metals challenge St. Louis and the pioneers to a wrestling match. St. Louis selects a strapping pioneer to grapple with Gold on an elevated dais, while the other pioneers and Earth Elements struggle below. The pioneer defeats Gold, two of three falls, freeing the Earth Elements from their bondage to corrupt materialism so they may better serve mankind.

A new wave of settlers arrive in colorful immigrant dress, seeking the child who, "left amid wild river reeds," grew up to "lead the tribes of men." Five figures lead the immigrants, representing Europe, Asia, Australia, Oceania, and Africa—the latter played by William E. Mack, a local janitor and apparently the sole black performer in the St. Louis pageant and masque. As the new arrivals pledge allegiance to St. Louis, Gold, now accompanied by his "tool and mightiest minion," "War," again bursts onstage to threaten the community. St. Louis selects a stalwart settler to battle the crimson war demon. The settler routs the mounted invader in a Medieval-style joust and sword fight.[74]

The joy over War's defeat is quickly muted, however, by the entrance of a tattered "Poverty" and her bedraggled children, who appear at the mercy of a mysterious black-hooded figure.[75] The figure approaches St. Louis and ascends the temple (from Part One) before he reveals himself to be the nefarious Gold. St. Louis calls upon his "Brother Cities" to help him "purge the temple" of Gold. Mounted figures in Medieval garb, each representing an American city and led by "Washington, D.C.," gallop onstage to St. Louis' aid. Behind this "League of Cities" march figures representing the arts, play, dance, and the civic theater. The group remains stymied, however, until "Imagination," "a noble female form masked in serene beauty," leads "Love," a small child crowned with a garland of thorns, forward to challenge Gold. The haughty element moves to strike the child but instead falls to his knees and declares the child his "master." Poverty and her once-stricken children are now transformed and radiant. Triumphant, St. Louis proclaims to the assembled cities "leagued by love": "If we are dreaming, let us scorn to wake; or waking, let us shape the sordid world to the likeness of our dreams." In the finale, the "mighty chorus" repeats the lines first intoned in Part One when the child St. Louis received his mission from Cahokia:

Out of the formless void
Beauty and order are born,

King Gold and the knight St. Louis. (Missouri Historical Society, St. Louis)

*The World Adventurers. William Mack, a local janitor (second from left),
played "Africa." On horseback are the "Brother Cities" that gallop to St.
Louis's aid in the masque's finale. (Brown University Library)*

One for the all, all in one,
We wheel in the joy of our dance.
Brother with brother,
Sharing our light,
Build we new worlds
With ancient fire.[76]

MacKaye envisioned the masque concluding with an airplane trailing
multicolored lights flying over the stage, but this never occurred in the
performance.[77]

Percy MacKaye's *Masque of St. Louis* proclaimed to the nation the
city's solidarity and purity. Christian, Indian, and Medieval symbolism
added moral authority to MacKaye's plot depicting St. Louisans rising
up to overthrow Gold's corrupt grip on their city. Religious prophecy
foreshadowed the coming action to make "social civilization's" death
and resurrection seem inevitable. Mound Builders ritually demonstrated their social cohesion, just as MacKaye hoped that the pageant
and masque would demonstrate the cohesion of local residents of
modern St. Louis, putting aside neighborhood, class, and ethnic dif-

Gold deposed by "Love" and "Imagination." (Ralph Davol, A Handbook of American Pageantry *[1914], p. 15)*

ferences. Mighty choruses gave a single united voice to "the city's" aspirations. Other cities, leagued with St. Louis in the crusade to conquer Gold, exhibited the "one for all, all for one" chivalric spirit that MacKaye and his fellow pageant-masters hoped to rekindle in American cities of the early twentieth century.

MacKaye presented his tale of St. Louis' restoration of "social civilization" through a remarkably rich, if tangled imagery. Local residents would have recognized the knight St. Louis as a familiar civic symbol. Atop Art Hill stood Charles Niehaus's sculpture *Apotheosis of St. Louis*, depicting a knight, Louis IX, charging forward on horseback. Newspaper cartoonists of the previous decade had also used the knight image to represent the city. The *St. Louis Globe-Democrat* displayed the knight, complete with chain mail, sword, and cross, on the cover of its Sunday magazine supplement accompanying the centennial celebration of 1909, and wondered why the image had not been more prominent in the celebration's street "pageant" parade floats.[78]

The Cahokia figure, however, was much less familiar to those watching the masque. For years, St. Louis had been nicknamed "Mound City," and local residents were dimly aware of the ancient burial grounds across the river in Illinois.[79] But the weird blend of exotic Meso-American ritual and mumbo-jumbo incantation derived more from Percy MacKaye's fascination with arty primitivism than from the customary symbols of the city. Overall, despite the rather heavy-handed meanings implanted in MacKaye's script and the wide coverage the masque's themes received in the local newspapers, the symbolic *Masque of St. Louis* probably remained more dazzling than comprehensible to the majority of those who watched it.

Nevertheless, St. Louis residents flocked to the *Pageant and Masque*, enduring marathon performances lasting over five hours. Police estimated attendance for the four complete performances at 75,000, 100,000, 90,000, and 90,000, with another 30,000 turning out on Friday night only to have the performance canceled by rain. Seats for the Saturday evening performance in the "Free" section reportedly disappeared by mid-afternoon.[80]

Civic reformers and intellectuals described the massive throngs gathered in Forest Park as "entranced" by the production. Charlotte Rumbold declared that the pageant placed all St. Louis "under the spell of a unifying idealism." Poet Vachel Lindsay recalled that the performance "went deep into the imaginations of the citizens," shaking the town "to its foundation with new dreams and visions and hopes." His companion Sara Teasdale recalled a "great spirit" among the audience watching the performance. "We had, all of us, a vision of what modern life might be." Composer Arthur Farwell, visiting from

The pageant audience. Nearly 100,000 attended each of the four perfor-mances. In the foreground is Charles Niehaus's statue, The Apotheosis St. Louis. *(Missouri Historical Society, St. Louis)*

New York, exclaimed that those witnessing the event "all felt more emotional ecstasy than they had ever felt before." Four days after the final performance, William Marion Reedy proclaimed: "There passed from the stage to the assemblage on the hill a vibration as of the awe in joy that comes when we apprehend the beautiful sublime in any form. The city pulsates yet with the passion the performance evoked. The pageant and masque influenced the great assemblage on four even-ings—100,000 people at a time—as with a physical ozone of exaltation, and the enthusiasm still burns."[81]

What invigoration St. Louis' population gained from the *Pageant and Masque*, however, probably had more to do with the informal camaraderie of the crowd than with the formal action onstage. News-papers reported that pageant audiences were not nearly as mesmer-ized during performances as the pageant boosters claimed. Even when wearing "Pageant Ears"—sheets of cardboard cupped around

the ear to gather in sound—many spectators heard only fleeting snatches of dialogue. One observer complained that the noise of the crowd frequently drowned out the dialogue onstage.[82] A picnic atmosphere prevailed over that of a solemn civic ritual. Myriad St. Louis charities set up concession stands along the perimeter of the pageant grounds to raise funds. Vendors hawked hot dogs, sandwiches, ice cream, popcorn, lemonade, and soda water.[83] News of the latest development in the Cubs-Cardinals baseball game, which had entered extra innings, periodically rippled through the opening night audience.[84] Rowdy spectators on Saturday night battered down the fence separating the free and reserved seats. Pageant officials called out fifty extra policemen (in addition to the four hundred already on duty), twenty National Guardsmen, and one hundred Boy Scouts to quell the disturbance.[85] Injuries from onstage accidents, from overcrowding, and from exploding soda water bottles further flavored the proceedings.

Many St. Louisans doubtless took a more irreverent view of the pageant than its promoters described. A cartoon in the *St. Louis Globe-Democrat* depicted "Indians" sprawled atop their mound, "built by Moundbuilders Union Local No. 6," jabbering about the Cubs-Cardi-

"Sidelights on the Pageant." This cartoon appeared in the St. Louis Globe-Democrat, *May 29, 1914, p. 5. (St. Louis Mercantile Library Association)*

nals game and griping about their aching lumbago. The *Globe-Democrat*'s general enthusiasm for the pageant did not prevent its police reporter, John M. McCully, from complaining that some of the re-enacted historical scenes were hard to swallow. In all of the crowd scenes in Stevens's pageant, noted McCully, "there was not a uniform copper or a plainclothes man in sight, and nobody got socked with a nightstick." Also, he continued, "St. Louis must have been a temperance town in those days, for there was not a souse on the job in the whole show, not even when the soldiers returned from war." McCully found MacKaye's masque mildly interesting but "evidently built for highbrows who understand allegory." "Even the desk sergeant didn't know what an allegory was," cracked McCully, though "he had heard of gory bodies and gory walls."[86]

Though the *Pageant and Masque*'s forbidding length and "highbrow" pretensions did little to endear it among the masses to whom it was directed, the production did succeed in stimulating the artistic imagination of at least some local residents for several years afterward. Critics generally acknowledged that the production propelled St. Louis into the forefront of the community drama movement. The $17,000 profit cleared by the pageant went toward the establishment of the St. Louis Municipal Opera Company. Frederick Fischer's chorus for the masque formed the nucleus of the group that tackled Handel's *Messiah* in December 1914. The St. Louis Pageant Drama Association also continued to operate after 1914 and staged *As You Like It* in Forest Park in 1916 to commemorate the three hundredth anniversary of Shakespeare's death. Across from the pageant grounds in Forest Park stands a permanent outdoor municipal amphitheater still in use. Thus, although the pageant failed to awaken every St. Louisan's interest in the arts, it provided an impetus for those residents already interested in staging amateur dramatic and choral productions to organize on a larger and more permanent basis.[87]

But leaders of the SLPDA wanted the historical pageant and masque to be judged as more than a passing artistic and social success. They hoped above all that their production would leave in its wake a united public spirit that would foster the enactment of lasting municipal reforms. When the pageant ended, John Gundlach, who chaired the executive committee, asked, "Does the unanimous spirit of love for city aroused in such forceful spontaneity disclose but the beauty of froth and silver on the crest of the incoming wave, to be lost as it washes against the sands of time; or is it to be the tide of a mighty ocean of human cooperation which will carry us to a higher level of intimate human contact and subsequent civic accomplishment?"[88]

Judging by the three municipal improvements that the pageant planners set as specific goals for St. Louis—the creation of the downtown plaza, construction of the free bridge, and passage of the reform city charter that had been defeated three years earlier—the pageant achieved mixed results. Although the bridge bond passed within two months of the event, the municipal plaza failed to gain approval until 1918 and was not built until the 1930s.[89]

City officials originally scheduled the charter vote for June 3, 1914, but the procharter forces persuaded the election commission to postpone the vote for one month because so many of those active in the charter reform campaign were busy managing the pageant. Also, calculated Gundlach, if the procharter forces waited a month, the "spirit of cooperation" engendered by the pageant could "take full effect." The campaign for a new charter resumed immediately after the *Pageant and Masque*. In fact, at the final performance of Stevens's pageant, in the scene where Senator Thomas Hart Benton welcomes the troops home from the Mexican War, the actor playing Benton ad-libbed, "Now that you're all safe and at home, I hope you'll all work and vote for the new city charter." When the new St. Louis charter passed in July 1914, local newspapers credited the pageant with helping to push it through. Even *St. Louis Labor*, which strongly opposed the new charter, sneered in the wake of the charter vote, "Whenever Big Cinch

"The Lessons of the Pageant." This cartoon posed the three specific goals pageant organizers held out for St. Louis. It appeared in the St. Louis Globe-Democrat, *May 29, 1914, p. 10. (St. Louis Mercantile Library Association)*

[the city's business elite] is anxious to 'put one over' on the people, the old Roman method must be applied: Panem et Circenses—bread and plays. In St. Louis the Big Cinch can accomplish its purpose with pageant plays without bread."⁹⁰

The vision of the political process embodied in the provisions of the new charter shared much with the political vision depicted onstage in the *Pageant and Masque*. In MacKaye's masque, citizens spontaneously and unanimously affirm the inspired absolute leadership of the knight "St. Louis," rather than democratically debate the future course of their city. The new city charter called for a stronger mayor, fewer elective and more civil service positions, and consolidation of the two houses of the St. Louis City Council—thirteen members elected at large, twenty-eight elected from individual wards—into a single chamber of twenty-eight members elected at large. St. Louis' Socialists and the Central Trades and Labor Union worked hard to defeat the new charter because they felt that at-large election of city council members and a stronger mayor would doom working-class representation in city government. Cartoons in *St. Louis Labor* depicted charter leaders— many of whom, like John Gundlach and Charles Stix, were also active in the pageant—as on the leash of big business. The new St. Louis charter, like the masque, claimed to widen popular participation in citywide affairs even as it narrowed the range of issues decided by democratic debate.[91]

If the *Pageant and Masque* speeded the passage of a new city charter in 1914, it also implicitly helped secure the passage of a segregated housing ordinance for St. Louis two years later. Proposed since 1910, voters approved the ordinance in 1916 by a 3:1 ratio.[92] Those civic leaders most active in extolling historical pageantry's ability to unite their city's diverse neighborhoods and ethnic groups failed to oppose the ordinance; it was clear from their actions in 1914 that they really did not regard the local black community as a part of St. Louis. Although pageant planners claimed that their giant municipal celebration suppressed internal divisions citywide, its virtual exclusion of black St. Louis effectively sharpened the differences between black and white residents.

The reputation of *The Pageant and Masque of St. Louis* as a stupendous civic success spread beyond local borders, boosting the careers of its creators and the historical pageantry movement generally. Percy MacKaye and Thomas Wood Stevens supervised a special Saturday morning rehearsal in which a motion picture version of the St. Louis pageant was created for commercial distribution across the nation. Squabbles between MacKaye and the SLPDA, and between the SLPDA and the film company, limited distribution of the film; so, reportedly, did insufficient titling to explain the myriad scenes and symbols flickering across the screen.[93] Still, clips appeared in *Pathé's Weekly Newsreel* and proved useful for promoting MacKaye and Stevens's work to other cities planning civic celebrations. In 1916, the New York City branch of the Drama League of America called upon MacKaye to write and direct *Caliban*, an enormous civic masque held in City College Stadium to commemorate the three hundredth anniversary of Shakespeare's death. The same year, the committee planning the 250th anniversary celebration of the founding of Newark, New

Jersey, hired Stevens to write and direct a Newark historical pageant at double the fee he had received in St. Louis. Mimicking the St. Louis format, Stevens concluded his realistic dramatic work with a symbolic "Masque of Newark." Among others who capitalized on their involvement with the St. Louis production, Frederick Converse added the music he composed for the *Masque of St. Louis* to his concert repertoire and eventually recorded it.[94]

The Conference of Cities accompanying the St. Louis pageant, by bringing together representatives interested in municipal recreation from throughout the United States, also promoted the pageantry movement nationally. Many of the same envoys who met during the daytime conference carried his or her city's crest each evening while galloping to St. Louis' aid in Part Two of MacKaye's masque. Invitations to the conference listed equestrian skills among the desirable qualifications for participants.[95]

Percy MacKaye's letter inviting representatives to the conference proclaimed that "never before in modern times" had cities leagued themselves "for the explicit purpose of considering art and imagination as practical means for expressing and promoting democratic life." Conference participants, many of whom were already active members of the American Pageant Association, discussed how the new pageantry could support other civic reforms and heard papers on such topics as "Municipal Recreation: A School for Democracy" and "Humanizing City Government." The latter address, by Henry Bruere, chamberlain of New York City, explained that pageantry could improve the urban reformer's "icy" public image. "You cannot win the people to an active interest in government," he declared, "until you begin to dramatize and humanize government acts." Another conference speaker extolled historical pageantry's value not only as a tool in reform movements, but also as a developer of "civic folk-culture" heretofore lacking in urban America. When the conference ended, those assembled voted to organize into a permanent League of Cities "to promote civic drama and other forms of civic art."[96]

The Pageant and Masque of St. Louis reinforced historical pageantry boosters' extravagant confidence in their craft's awesome power to galvanize local community solidarity in the service of social reform. One month after the pageant, Luther Ely Smith announced in "Municipal Pageants as Destroyers of Race Prejudice," a paper delivered at a sociological conference in Massachusetts, "It was like a transfiguration, like a vision of heaven—of the new earth that is to be. There was no race or national antipathy then. It was destroyed not by reason or logic, but by playing together, working together." The same month Arthur Farwell described historical pageantry as a form of "community auto-suggestion," in which a town's residents, by dramatically reenacting scenes from their past, convince themselves that they can collectively attain whatever civic goals they desire.[97]

Descriptions of the pageant as a transfiguration and as autosuggestion suggest that it was the irrational elements of the St. Louis experience that most fascinated pageantry advocates. At the Conference of Cities accompanying the pageant, Arthur Bostwick introduced the session on civic holiday music in primarily psychological and political rather than aesthetic terms: "Music, like other arts, cannot prove a proposition, but it can do very much more—it can influence the emotions; and emotion plays a very much larger part in civic activity than some of our most intellectual people think. I assert that if our emotions are right, our actions will be right, and that it is our business so to influence and control the emotions of the masses that their civic activity will be along proper lines."[98]

More than any other civic celebration in America, *The Pageant and Masque of St. Louis* self-consciously attempted to manipulate the emotions of the crowd on a scale comparable only to Wagnerian opera festivals in Germany.[99] Pageant boosters credited the sense of communal intoxication created by the pageant's rhythmic chanting and mesmerizing spectacle, as much as its historical themes, for forging a feeling of community solidarity and collective purpose in St. Louis.

The particular blend of the rational and the irrational in the St. Louis pageant epitomized not only historical pageantry but also, in many ways, the aesthetics of reform politics in the decade. At the heart of many of these movements was the sense that expressions of public sentiment—whether in legislation, voting, or emotional public demonstrations—reflected an emerging new civilization, but that these democratic outpourings required expert intervention to be made articulate and to be given form. Political and social movements organized massive public gatherings as occasions when this sense of the public sentiment could surface and employed the images and rhetoric of history to forge a "common" interpretation of that sentiment. Like the art of pageantry, the art of democracy in the Progressive Era involved creating the illusion of the public appearing to speak for itself, in the process defining the terms under which particular local interests appeared as the public interest. In the words of Percy Mac-Kaye, with the help of the expert "dramatic engineer" the community could "wheel in the joy of its dance" and "imagine its own origins and destiny, its life drama," creating "beauty and order" out of the "formless void"—and thwarting the encroaching "powers of chaos."[100] "New worlds," imagined by the pageant-master/reform politician, would be built with the "ancient fire" of elaborate historical ritual linking past, present, and future; city, nation, and world.

6 Organizing the Soul of America

. . . .

So thin, so frail the opalescent ice
Where yesterday, in lordly pageant, rose
The monumental nations—the repose
Solid as earth they seemed; yet in a trice
Their bastions crumbled in the surging
    floes
Of inconceivable, inhuman woes,
Gulfed in a mad, unmeaning sacrifice.

We, who survive that world-quake, cower
    and start,
Searching our hidden souls with dark
    surmise:
So thin, so frail—is reason? Patient art—
Is it all a mockery, and love all lies?
Who sees the lurking Hun in childhood's
    eyes?
Is hell so near to every human heart?
—Percy MacKaye, "Doubt," from "Car-
nage: Six Sonnets," September 1914

Pageant program, 1917. Once the United States entered World War I, the production of pageants with standard images from national history that could play anywhere to rally support for the nation's war aims took precedence over pageants that primarily told the story of local community development. The National Pageantry Corporation, based in Cedar Rapids, Iowa, boasted A. H. Stoddard, a veteran of the New Orleans Mardi Gras and New York City's Hudson-Fulton Celebration, among its directors. (Library of Congress)

Two months after *The Pageant and Masque of St. Louis'* triumphal depiction of a world "leagued by love," the powers of chaos thundered across Europe. Americans responded to the outbreak of hostilities with appeals for peace abroad and increased military strength at home. If America's call for international peace failed to end the war, then the nation's formidable military strength would at least keep the conflict at a distance by dissuading belligerents from mounting an overseas invasion.

But the United States did become involved in the European war, sending supplies, then troops, across the Atlantic. Extensive national mobilization accompanied the formal declaration of war in the spring of 1917. Not since the Civil War had the call for military sacrifice been spread to every home. Local civic officials who entertained modest hopes of inspiring their towns to collective achievement in peacetime found themselves trying to direct a massive wave of patriotic sentiment in wartime that grew beyond all anticipation.

Pageantry became a part of this war mobilization effort. Those who in peacetime had heralded historical pageantry as a tool for promoting international understanding soon used it to rally support for American war aims and programs. Leaders of the national pageantry movement between 1917 and 1919 rode the crest of an enthusiastic swell of wartime parades, rallies, and pageants that promised to spread the gospel of expressive mass participation further and faster than ever before.

Within a year of the assassination of Archduke Ferdinand at Sarajevo, American peace societies—most not even a decade old—launched public demonstrations and pageants urging the United States to remain out of the conflict that quickly engulfed Europe.[1] Beulah Marie Dix produced *A Pageant of Peace* in Boston for the American School Peace League in May 1915, depicting a symbolic figure "War" luring away various segments of the American population until he is finally halted by a female "Peace." Another peace pageant, presented in Somerville, Massachusetts, in July 1915, recapped the events that had led up to the war in Europe, including a realistic reenactment of the archduke's assassination. The Somerville pageant then projected "The Marshalling of Forces" and "The Last Battle," an apocalyptic allegorical finale in which "Death," "Rage," "Fire," "Steel," and "Hate" run rampant until the arrival of "Peace" riding in a "winged chariot drawn by bewitching sprites." The same year, the Women's Club of Sioux City, Iowa, staged a pageant honoring famous women through world history who had worked for peace. The club women hoped that their pageant, "through its spectacular nature, would reach some minds which could not otherwise be stirred." Peace advocates, like

Pageant program, 1915. In the aftermath of the outbreak of war in Europe, some Americans used historical pageantry to emphasize the nation's alliance with the British rather than past differences. (Brown University Library)

municipal political reformers, trade unionists, and woman-suffragists of the decade, employed pageantry as one of several media publicizing their cause.[2]

The outbreak of war prompted Americans not only to appeal for peace in Europe but also to examine their defenses at home. Prominent national figures such as Theodore Roosevelt and General Leonard Wood had warned, even before 1914, that the nation stood woefully unprepared to defend its borders. The chaotic organization of U.S. forces fighting the Spanish-American War revealed the potential dangers of placing the nation's defense in the hands of several dozen separate, poorly trained state militias over which the small regular army had little control. General Wood, U.S. Army chief of staff from 1910 through 1914, sought to expand, reorganize, and centralize the military to make it more professional and efficiently administered. One proposal called for the nation's reserve capacity to be shifted from the several dozen state militias to a "Continental Army"—a name chosen for its "grand historical associations"—under direct federal control.[3] "Preparedness" as a campaign to introduce to the military the modern management techniques that existed in large-scale business organizations gained increased public support after 1914 in the face of the deadly efficient Prussian war machine overseas.

Some observers believed that the nation's lack of preparedness was a spiritual and social as well as a military problem. Critics scolded that the increasing material abundance in the half century since the Civil War had spoiled the public's capacity for disciplined communal sacrifice. Herbert Croly warned that "[America] has been too safe, too comfortable, too complacent, and too relaxed. Its besetting weakness is the prevalence of individual and collective irresponsibility based on the expectation of accomplishing without effort."[4] "Preparedness" advocates lamented that, instead of a tightly integrated network of unified communities able to respond as one to crisis, America presented a loose congeries of towns, divided by ethnicity and class, bickering among themselves and displaying little aptitude for cooperation. Groups of self-interested citizens did not act as a community, groups of towns did not act as a state, groups of states did not act as a nation. If the European war were to spread across the Atlantic and the United States suddenly had to defend its borders, the nation might not have the time to wait for the necessary wartime spirit of sacrifice and unity to coalesce.

As the war in Europe dragged on through 1915 and 1916, preparedness as a movement for personal and social regeneration soon overwhelmed its original purpose as a specific program of military reform. While bills to reorganize the military bogged down in Congress, business and professional people called for universal military training and formed new civilian volunteer groups—the National Security League, Council of National Defense, and American Legion—that pledged to enlist in the army if the nation were to go to war. These groups practiced their military skills in special summer training camps and on college campuses. In August 1915, nearly 1,300 middle-aged men spent five weeks at "businessmen's camp" in Plattsburgh, New York, claiming that their dedication would furnish "an object lesson to the whole nation." A Womens Preparedness Camp opened the following summer in Chevy Chase, Maryland. Preparedness organizations also staged awesome street parades to demonstrate their strength. On May 13, 1916, approximately 125,000 New Yorkers marched twenty abreast down Fifth Avenue in a procession that observers estimated took thirteen hours to pass. One month later, a total of 350,000 preparedness advocates marched in ten cities across the United States. Most prevalent in cities of the Northeast and among the upper and middle classes, the craze for demonstrating one's preparedness through paramilitary drills and parades grew far out of proportion to all reasonable threat of foreign attack.[5]

The social aspects of the preparedness movement tapped the same impulses for promoting community solidarity that fueled the historical pageantry movement. Preparedness parades thrived in areas of the country where historical pageants were popular and were enjoyed by the same classes of people. Preparedness advocates claimed for the military training camp experience the same benefits from participation in a model community that the American Pageant Association (APA) claimed for pageantry. The *New Republic* praised the Plattsburgh camp for requiring its participants "to behave rather as members of a community than separate individuals," adding, "Is there anything . . . that the body of American citizens needs more than a discipline of this kind? Is there anything which would do the ordinary American more good than an actual participation in a well-ordered community life?"[6] Although professional pageant directors emphasized more often than advocates of universal military training the affective rather than the solely disciplinary lessons of their respective model "community" enterprises, both movements sought to encourage the individual's emotional identification with a larger group united in pursuit of a common goal.

Unlike the promoters of historical pageantry between 1910 and 1916, who encouraged townspeople to identify their most intense feelings of "community" with their locale, leaders of the preparedness movement focused above all on fostering local residents' sense of identification with the nation. General Leonard Wood argued that universal military training would encourage Americans "to think more in terms of the nation and less in those of the individual or the small community." Herbert Croly noted that army service could provide a "source of national unity" and a remedy for "national incoherence." His *New Republic* warned that "there is a real danger of national disintegration which can be counteracted only by an equally powerful and a more authoritative organization of the American people into an indivisible political and social body." Although Walter Lippmann opposed universal military service, he praised its goal of creating an "Integrated America"—"a more highly organized nation in which the great mass of the population lives a national rather than a local life, in which we become more than ever a union of people rather than a congeries of groups, provinces, and racial stocks." While the pageantry movement encouraged local residents to assert their unique identity and solidarity as a community amid a multiplicity of national organizations, the preparedness fervor emphasized the fusing of all competing local identities into a single national body.[7]

Some pageant directors active in the American Pageant Association argued that the public enthusiasm for national military preparedness would be better channeled into the pursuit of peaceful local reforms. Looking askance at the burgeoning paramilitary movements across the nation, they believed that never had the need been greater to answer the call that William James had issued in 1910 for a "moral equivalent of war"—a peaceful public activity that duplicated war's ability to elicit a spirit of "strenuous honor" and a desire to be in the noble "service of the collectivity" but without war's violence and destruction. Percy MacKaye, in an article entitled "A Substitute for War," declared that his *Pageant and Masque* had provided St. Louis residents with such an opportunity for heroic, yet peaceful collective service. He insisted that the pageant experience in St. Louis evoked "the moral equivalent of war: self-sacrifice, solidarity, energized will, [and] militant devotion to a civic cause." MacKaye corresponded with Crystal Eastman in August 1915 about staging a pageant for the Women's Peace party. His sister Hazel, along with Lotta Clark of Boston and Charlotte Rumbold of St. Louis, joined the Committee for Encouragement of Artists, Musicians, and Writers to Productions Promoting Peace. Violet Oakley, the muralist and pageant director most active in the American peace movement, looked to community historical pageantry to further the peace movement's aims as an "outlet for the dormant but struggling corporate consciousness, and a possible aid in bringing about 'the Day' when happily Man shall no longer seek 'to find himself' by recourse to the deadly fascination of great destructive forces."[8]

MacKaye's insistence, in 1915 and 1916, that pageantry could serve as a substitute for war was based on the belief that war appealed not only to the public's hunger for collective service, but also to its thirst for color and rhythm. Echoing his earlier criticisms of the lack of opportunity for artistic expression in industrial society, he complained that modern life was so contaminated by "ugliness," "ennui," and "dulled despair" that "to millions of laborers the conditions of war seem hopeful and visionary in comparison." According to MacKaye, "Devisers of war create magnificent symbols. Under their expert control, the chaotic, drifting, meanly competitive life of everyday peace becomes transfigured by order, discipline, organization, imbued with a majestic unity of design: *the enacting of a national drama, in which the people themselves participate* [MacKaye's italics]." But the banners, bands, and flashy uniforms of war exercised a "hypnotism toward destruction." Only the community "pageant-master" as "dramatic engineer" could employ the same colorful techniques and organization to "lure the imaginations of men away from war to peace." MacKaye suggested that the peace movement could take the first step in greatly increasing its public appeal by replacing the "meek and anemic" dove symbol with a more stirring standard.[9] Although not explicitly condemning the preparedness movement, he and some of his colleagues, shocked by the carnage in Europe, sought to use their craft to direct the increasing clamor for national mass mobilization toward constructive, not military, ends.

Many other pageant-masters, however, viewed community historical pageantry not as a potential substitute for the militant preparedness fervor but rather as its extension. In 1916, Professor Albert H. Gilmer of Tufts University addressed the fourth annual convention of the American Pageant Association on "The Place of Pageantry and Drama in the Program of National Preparedness." Gilmer declared that towns producing pageants practiced the cooperation that would be required in wartime. "A well managed pageant is a thing of beauty and efficiency in its working mechanism," he explained. "With its requirements for harmony, obedience, subordination, discipline, responsibility, and loyal cooperation—as at St. Louis, New York, and elsewhere—the pageant is as demanding as is military necessity, and the schooling of the pageant in this respect applied to a system of supplies and victualling would be most helpful to any army in action." Historical pageants could help transform Americans "from an unformed social mass into an orderly, well-formed and informed body politic of power and high purpose."[10] To Gilmer, historical pageantry and military preparedness went hand in hand.

For the most part, however, the community pageantry and military preparedness movements seldom joined forces in 1915 and 1916. Those most active in historical pageantry neither staged preparedness rallies nor altered their work to address specific preparedness themes. But even before the rise of a preparedness movement, historical pageants implicitly "prepared" Americans for war through scenes that depicted past generations as at their best in wartime, exhibiting ingenuity, courage, solidarity, and a spirit of self-sacrifice.

War most often appeared in historical pageants in episodes reenacting local battles. During a pageant in 1913, residents of Saratoga, New York, dressed up as redcoats and colonists to re-create the Battle of Saratoga and Burgoyne's surrender. Deerfield, Massachusetts, faithfully reenacted its earliest white settlers' brave but unsuccessful defense against Indian attack. Each of Thomas Wood Stevens's pageants of the Old Northwest featured the same Revolutionary War scene of George Rogers Clark craftily capturing Kaskaskia on the night its defenders were holding a ball. The Revolutionary War scenes in *The Pageant of Southampton* on Long Island depicted local minutemen marching off to battle without hesitation as soon as word from Lexington arrived; after the British occupied Southampton in 1778, the townspeople could be seen performing various covert acts of resistance such as putting ground glass in the feed of the British soldiers' horses. Such historical episodes, emphasizing the cunning and courage of Americans in combat, exhibited model behaviors for the present generation to emulate. Dressed in picturesque period uniforms, soldiers reenacting the century-old battles of the Revolution and the frontier displayed the gallantry of war without its violence.[11]

No such portrayal of heroic battle accompanied pageant scenes of the Civil War, however. Instead, local community historical pageants between 1910 and 1916 almost invariably presented the conflict's domestic aspects: local volunteers marching off to war, the town receiving news from the front, and, finally, the veterans returning home. William Chauncy Langdon's *Pageant of Darien*, Connecticut, in 1913 depicted the Civil War in one of its symbolic interludes: the austere figure "Principle" slips unnoticed into a pleasant community gathering of the mid-nineteenth century. As the background music grows louder and more dissonant, foreshadowing war, the local residents one by one notice her presence. Principle's face becomes stern, her figure erect; she "raises her arm slowly in irrevocable command," pointing toward the battlefield, "along the way of sacrifice and death." Ignoring the cries of their mothers and young wives, the men follow Principle off to battle "as if fascinated in an unreasoning loyalty to her." Thundering music and the flash of lights continue, suggesting the far-off conflict. Finally the men of Darien trudge back, the body of

The Battle of Bennington, Vermont, 1911. Pageant versions of the American Revolution emphasized the cunning and gallantry of battle without its violence. (Brown University Library)

one borne upon an improvised stretcher. Principle halts the grim procession to lay a palm branch on the dead soldier's breast and raise her hand in solemn blessing over him. She also stretches out her arm to comfort the soldier's grieving family before once again disappearing into the woods whence she came.[12]

The Civil War episodes in nearly every historical pageant displayed a similar pattern of departure, sacrifice, and return. Domestic scenes emphasized the sacrifices common to both sides of the conflict, rather than recalling the specific issues that had divided the nation five decades before or the victories in battle of one side over the other. "War"—represented by an abstract symbolic figure—arrives suddenly, unavoidably, and without explanation; the men march off to do their duty, then return. Pageants rarely mentioned slavery as a cause of the Civil War. One exception occurred in a pageant in Minnesota, where a tableau of Dred Scott preceded the "Spirit of Militarism," "Spirit of Unrest," and departure of the troops. In the Brooklyn, New York, pageant, the "Spirit of Bondage"—whipping blacks tied to a tree— preceded the depiction of local troops marching off to battle. But most Civil War scenes appearing in historical pageants between 1911 and 1915—the fiftieth anniversary of the war—generally reflected the prevailing historiographical trend of the period: that neither side was to blame for the "irrepressible conflict." Vague symbolic scenes presented no explicit causes, animosities, or violence.[13]

Pageant directors invested the Civil War scenes of departure, sacrifice, and return with even more emotional intensity by casting the town's few remaining Civil War veterans in the role of returning soldiers. The "return" scene of the Caldwell, New Jersey, pageant in 1915 concluded with children garbed in white, representing the future generation, joining the Civil War veterans on the pageant field as all observed a moment of silence for the war dead.[14] In their sixties, seventies, or older, the veterans served as living symbols of their generation's sacrifice, the pageant episodes' dramatic equivalents of the monuments that local officials erected at the turn of the century to recall the selfless heroism of past generations.

Whether displaying the gallantry and ingenuity of the Revolutionary soldier in battle or the stalwart courage and spirit of sacrifice of the home front during the Civil War, organizers of historical pageants left little doubt that fighting a war was an expected duty of community life. Though not explicitly tying their productions to military preparedness, pageant-masters implicitly connected performance in war and the worth of a community, presenting the deeds and sacrifices of past generations as a challenge to the present one. Martial images in their pageants reflected Americans' thirst, in the words of Herbert Croly, for "the tonic of a serious moral adventure." Moreover, by failing to present realistic images of the combat of the eighteenth century—to say nothing of the bloody results of the type of modern mass warfare that debuted in the Civil War—historical pageants, like other cultural expressions in the early 1910s, in fact left Americans woefully unprepared for the kind of war they would soon fight in Europe.[15]

Although the outbreak of war in Europe set off a debate among pageant directors about whether their work was a substitute or a preparation for war, it scarcely affected local historical pageant themes or formats before 1917. The American Pageant Association counted nearly sixty local historical pageants in 1916, among the largest of which was Percy MacKaye's *Caliban by the Yellow Sands* for New York City's commemoration of the tercentenary of the death of William Shakespeare. Fifteen thousand New Yorkers filled City College Stadium for each of ten performances to watch a mixed cast of 2,500 professional and amateur actors portray a history of drama through the ages. Isadora Duncan danced on opening night, Robert Edmond Jones designed the costumes, and Arthur Farwell wrote the music.[16] Thomas Wood Stevens's *Pageant of Newark*, New Jersey, also in 1916, mimicked the format Stevens and MacKaye had devised in St. Louis—

following realistic reenactment with a symbolic masque. William Chauncy Langdon, pageant-master for Indiana's celebration of the centennial of its statehood in 1916, created a series of three historical pageants in Corydon, Bloomington, and Indianapolis based on the "New Country Life" formula he had used earlier in New England. Each pageant chronicled local economic growth and the development of transportation routes linking the town with the outside world and concluded with a grand procession of the states of the "Old Northwest" led by "America." Although a few historical pageants tacked on extra scenes calling for international peace, displaying local military preparedness, or expressing support for one of the combatants— Langdon intended his Bronxville, New York, Christmas pageant of 1914 to link symbolically Bronxville, Bethlehem, and Belgium—the basic dramatic form through which the local community celebrated its history remained unchanged.[17]

When the United States entered the war in the spring of 1917, however, the enthusiasm for national integration and militant organization advocated by the preparedness movement suddenly became institutionalized. Giant federal agencies formed almost overnight to coordinate the nation's war effort. By June 1917, ten million men had registered for the draft. A War Industries Board formed to coordinate industrial production. A Committee on Public Information made motion pictures, posters, pamphlets, and mimeographed speeches on various war-related subjects available to every town in the United States. The War Department established a Commission on Training Camp Activities to coordinate recreational activities for men in military training camps throughout the United States, while leaders of the Playground and Recreation Association of America created a new organization, War Camp Community Service (WCCS), to offer recreational opportunities in towns adjacent to the camps.[18] Recreation workers directed their efforts to helping the war mobilization. Although some prominent social workers—Jane Addams, Paul Kellogg —organized the American Union against Militarism and remained opposed to U.S. participation in the war as a belligerent, the National Conference on Social Work supported it.[19] Conference President Robert Woods told the convention in Kansas City that "social work today is hardened and sharpened by the inflexible resolve to which the democratic nations are committed. It must go forward steeled to its purpose no less surely than if its personnel were fighting at the front."[20] The nation created new organizations and harnessed existing ones for the task of waging war.

In this new setting, each local activity had to prove its value to the war effort. Woods declared that the community in wartime must organize "not merely for its internal well-being, but that it might rise spiritedly to a vast collective achievement." Federal agencies created an elaborate pyramid of national, state, local, and neighborhood Councils of Defense to transmit the "Washington impulse" to every town. Each new campaign for saving food, for buying Liberty Bonds, for donating to the Red Cross, for enlisting in the armed services tested local residents' ability to work together. William Chauncy Langdon proclaimed in June 1917, two months after President Wilson's declaration of war, that "American community life is going through the fire, and everything connected with it is going with it—pageantry included."[21]

Some active in the national pageantry movement saw in wartime mobilization the potential to enact reforms that towns seemed reluctant to undertake in peacetime. Langdon, an early and enthusiastic supporter of American intervention, noted that in several instances the war mobilization seemed to accomplish goals that pageant-masters had envisioned earlier for a town. He cited the example of the "future" scene in a historical pageant he wrote for Amherst, Massachusetts, in 1917 that projected cooperative agricultural marketing; before the pageant was performed the Committee of Food Supply of the Massachusetts General Committee of Public Safety had already organized cooperative marketing as part of the war effort.[22] War mobilization campaigns, tapping many of the same impulses for collective service as pageantry, could pave the way for historical pageantry to stimulate even greater collective achievements once the peace was won.

Shaped by the pressure to be of use in "organizing the soul of America" for war, however, historical pageantry changed greatly from 1917 to 1919.[23] Productions featuring a full-length, dramatic reenactment of episodes from local history, which had flourished through 1916, virtually came to a halt with America's entry in the war. The money and organizational energy that towns had previously set aside for large-scale, community-wide historical pageants now went into a multiplicity of campaigns connected directly with the war effort. Langdon's historical pageants scheduled for Amherst in 1917 and Illinois in 1918 were postponed indefinitely. He observed, "The issues of the times are the real subject of high interest at present, not historical community development."[24]

Members of the American Pageant Association concluded that, under the circumstances, they could best support the nation's mobilization efforts and keep their craft before the public through the publication and widespread distribution of short allegorical masques which a small cast could perform in one hour or less, inexpensively, and anywhere for the benefit of any war organization. Meeting in Boston in 1918, they decided that their own 250-member organization, concentrated on the East Coast, was unequal to the task of distributing pageant texts nationwide. So they called upon the Playground and Recreation Association's War Camp Community Service, which already had a staff of 3,000 workers in 755 towns near military training camps across the nation, to establish a Division of Community Drama. APA leaders proposed that the new department in WCCS serve as a clearinghouse to distribute pageant texts, lists of published pageants, and information on pageant organization, financing, and production— though reserved for themselves the role of advising WCCS on which pageants and information to distribute. They also suggested that War Camp Community Service sponsor a national competition, to be judged by qualified pageant directors, for "the creation of a pageant best calculated to express the average community's emotional reaction to the present day war situation."[25]

The pageant-masters entrusted the responsibility for promoting pageantry in wartime to the wrong agency. Although War Camp Community Service created a Division of Community Drama with well-known pageant director Constance D'Arcy MacKay at its head and assigned dramatists to local recreation staffs near training camps, it never promoted pageantry as fully as its other community activities. It distributed MacKay's *Patriotic Christmas Pageant* but turned down war pageants written by William Chauncy Langdon and Thomas Wood Stevens and never held the competition. Seeking above all to create a "home-like" atmosphere in hundreds of communities near war training camps for the soldiers on leave, WCCS chapters placed a priority on sponsoring athletics, motion pictures, and regular plays for trainees and their hosts' amusement. The U.S. War Department's Commission on Training Camp Activities expressed a similar preference in its forty-two on-base "Liberty Theatres," newly built with a $1.5 million appropriation from Congress. Rather than hire dramatists to organize patriotic pageants, it turned to commercial impresarios David Belasco, Lee Schubert, Oscar Hammerstein, George M. Cohan, and Irving Berlin to book wholesome diversions featuring popular professional talent. Franklin H. Sargent, coordinator of the Liberty Theatres for the commission, explained, "These boys don't want sentimentality. It calls up memories they are trying for the time to push aside. Neither do they want patriotism. They are living it every hour and they do not need it taught to them through their entertainment." William Chauncy Langdon conceded that he and his fellow pageant-masters, always in danger of getting "too highbrow with [their] eternal symbolism," were ill-suited to provide the comedies sought by War Camp

Community Service, the Commission on Training Camp Activities, and the soldiers they served—he confessed to Virginia Tanner that the only funny things he wrote he had not intended to be humorous.[26]

Direct competition with motion pictures also diminished the use federal agencies made of pageantry on the home front. The type of pageants that APA members recommended—allegorical masques devoid of local imagery that a small cast could perform anywhere in the nation—differed little in scale or in form from the centrally produced and distributed motion pictures over which government war agencies had greater control and which incurred fewer expenses. For the Fourth Liberty Loan drive in October 1918, the U.S. Treasury Department quickly ordered 4,000 prints of 35 different productions. Films produced to rally support for the war also featured celebrities well known to the public, such as Charlie Chaplin in *The Bond*, William S. Hart in *Bullet for Berlin*, Mary Pickford in *100% American*, and Douglas Fairbanks in *Swat the Kaiser*. The advantages of movies over pageants in terms of distribution, cost, and celebrity appeal led the federal Committee on Public Information to establish a separate division to oversee the production and distribution of war films, but not pageants.[27]

Without the help of national war mobilization agencies in promoting and distributing pageants, each pageant-master was left to respond to inquiries about his or her own work. Nevertheless, several saw their pageants performed throughout the United States to rally support for a variety of wartime causes. In 1917, Nina Lamkin's 75-minute *America, Yesterday and Today* was performed over 350 times by local amateur companies. Thomas Wood Stevens's *Drawing of the Sword*, though turned down for national distribution by War Camp Community Service, still played several hundred performances, including one with an all-star professional cast at the Metropolitan Opera House for the benefit of the Red Cross. Percy MacKaye's *Roll Call* also played across the country to help raise money for the Red Cross.[28]

Despite the fact that the public seemed to prefer war comedies to "highbrow" symbolism, pageant directors persisted in using abstract symbolism to rally patriotism and justify the nation's involvement in the European conflict. Six months after the United States declared war, Clara Fitch of the Drama League of America defined the role of pageantry in wartime as "establishing the spiritual aims of the nation, and of spreading knowledge that spiritual ideals alone can inspire men to the deeds of sacrifice and patriotism that are required to win liberty for the world." Thomas Wood Stevens explained in his preface to *The Drawing of the Sword* that "we know that we are fighting in a just cause from an intellectual point of view. The intellectual conviction may or may not bring the war to an early successful conclusion. What our people need most is to realize the situation emotionally."[29]

To elicit the desired emotional response, pageant writers created the melodramatic equivalent of World War I recruiting posters, depicting in symbolic form the events that led Woodrow Wilson to send American troops overseas. Typically, pageant-masters assigned a woman draped in a flowing classical gown to represent each of the nations involved in the war. William Chauncy Langdon's *Sword of America*, produced at the University of Illinois in November 1917 in place of the historical pageant he was originally asked to prepare, depicted "Great Britain" and "France" appealing in vain for "America" to help them fight. "Belgium," a frail woman holding aloft a broken, tattered flag, also appeals to America for aid. Seeing poor Belgium's plight, along with a battered life preserver from the SS *Lusitania* and the remains of a Red Cross flag that had been perforated by an artillery shell, "America is aroused to the extreme of fury and indignation." She takes up her sword, crying, "This is not war! This is the purging of the world." In the finale of Langdon's masque, soldiers, sailors, Red Cross workers, and Boy Scouts troop onstage to express their loyalty to America. Stevens's *Drawing of the Sword*, Percy MacKaye's *Roll Call*, and Constance MacKay's *Patriotic Christmas Pageant* employed a nearly identical symbolic format. MacKaye depicted the Red Cross battling a Teutonic-looking figure called "The Despoiler." Constance MacKay pitted a symbolic "America" against "Tyranny." The Metropolitan Opera House production of Stevens's *Drawing of the Sword* featured Ethel Barrymore as "Belgium" and John Barrymore as "The Tyrant." Each of these and similar productions outlined the reasons why America entered the war, highlighting the despoilment of innocent Belgium, and concluded with a massing of armed, loyal, and determined Americans onstage.[30]

The relatively few local historical pageants produced in conjunction with holiday celebrations in wartime incorporated the symbolic "drawing of the sword" theme in their finales. Maud May Parker's historical pageant for communities in Louisiana—dedicated to the mothers of soldiers and sailors—concludes with a common type of pageant finale depicting an enthroned "Louisiana" receiving "gift" baskets of sugarcane, rice, fruit, salt, and flowers from her subjects. Then, "America" enters the pageant field to ask Louisiana for her help in fighting the war overseas. America cites the atrocities committed against Belgium and the *Lusitania*. All pageant characters then return to the stage, the procession led by mothers in white offering their sons for battle. Wallace Rice's historical pageant in 1918 commemorating the one hundredth anniversary of Illinois' admission to the Union concludes

"America" between "Vision" and "Sacrifice" offering her prayer. In this scene from William Chauncy Langdon's Sword of America, *performed in Champaign, Illinois, in 1917, Langdon appears as the hooded figure on the right. (Brown University Library)*

with "Illinois" pledging to join "France," "Italy," "Belgium," and "Great Britain" in the European conflict. While historical pageants before 1917—such as Langdon's pageants of the New Country Life—emphasized America uplifting the local community through federal aid, historical pageants in wartime underscored the local community's obligation to the nation, as America took its sons for war.[31]

Community pageantry in wartime employed realistic historical imagery as well as abstract symbolism. Rather than dramatizing incidents primarily from local history, however, pageant writers producing works to be distributed throughout the United States used almost exclusively incidents and figures from national history. This was a reversal of the pageant-masters' previous policy. In October 1916, William Chauncy Langdon had refused to supply Clara Fitch, of the Drama League of America's pageantry committee, with a bibliography of works chronicling national history, declaring flatly that "all pageant material must be local" and that he could not think of a single instance where national history had ever helped him in his pageant writing. In a follow-up letter to Percival Chubb, also of the Drama League, Langdon insisted that creating a "Pageant of the United States" would be futile because "the more general [imagery] the weaker, the more local the more vital." He added, "No man can compress the United States of America into two hours and a half, really do it, or half do it, and be thereafter anything but a chattering idiot with only fragments of intellect left, unless he was a smiling imbecile to begin with, not knowing any better than to try it." Once the United States entered the war, however, this position changed dramatically. Pageant-masters and their clients expressed greater concern with national integration; towns wanted short, readily available, easily produced works rather than original historical dramas. Hence the prevailing historical imagery employed in community pageants changed in wartime from distinctively local to standardized national scenes and figures.[32]

Pageants in wartime presented the nation's history in a kind of shorthand, where brief extracts of familiar speeches, songs, and symbols replaced the more elaborate reenactments of local historical incidents. Portraits of George Washington and Abraham Lincoln superseded those of the town fathers; scenes of Paul Revere's ride crowded out scenes of a town's defense in the Revolutionary War. *The Glory of Old Glory*, published in 1917 by the National Pageantry Corporation of Cedar Rapids, Iowa, compiled fifteen stock scenes depicting "The Liberty Bell," "Columbus Discovering America," "The Pilgrims Landing at Plymouth," "The Boston Tea Party," "The 'Spirit of '76'," "Washington's Inaugural Procession from Mt. Vernon to New York City," "Washington's Inauguration Ceremony," "Lafayette's Visit to America," "The Bombardment of Fort McHenry," "The Evolution of the Flag," "Lincoln at Gettysburg," "Civil War Soldiers in Camp," "The Reception for General Joffre, Hero of the Marne," "Washington, Wilson, and Lincoln beneath the Statue of Liberty," and "The Lion, Lamb, and American Eagle in the 'Mission of Old Glory'."[33] In Langdon's *Masque of the Titans of Freedom*, presented at the University of Illinois on Memorial Day 1918, George Washington and Abraham Lincoln discuss the necessity for sacrifices in each generation to preserve freedom.[34] In Percy MacKaye's *Washington: The Man Who Made Us*, written the same year, George Washington goes "Over There" (as MacKaye titled the scene)—across the Delaware to New Jersey on Christmas 1776 to fight the Hessians. Scenes of the American Revolution in wartime pageants downplayed conflict with the nation's present ally Britain even as they highlighted France's role in helping America to win its independence. MacKaye's Americans fought Germans rather than redcoats; in Linwood Taft's *Progress of Liberty*, performed in seventeen Missouri towns under the auspices of the Women's Committee of the State Council of National Defense, a grateful Revolutionary America honors not only Washington but also Lafayette. Scenes of

Lafayette in America, popular in historical pageants before 1917, became even more prominent in wartime pageants as a means of reminding the audience of the nation's original "debt" to France, which American soldiers were repaying daily.[35]

Images of famous figures from American history appeared in a standardized pageant format emphasizing the nation's tradition of military prowess. Joseph Lee's model July Fourth exercises in 1918 for towns near military training camps called for only three scenes, of the "Revolutionary," "Civil," and "Present" wars. It begins with a fife and drum corps in Colonial dress parading past the audience, carrying an American flag. All pledge allegiance to the flag and sing "The Star-Spangled Banner." A speaker reads excerpts from the Declaration of Independence, then quotations from Revolutionary War heroes, who appear in a tableau at center stage. Next, veterans of the Civil War march onto the pageant field, to the music of "Tramp, Tramp, Tramp," "The Battle Cry of Freedom," and "Dixie." The assemblage hears excerpts from Lincoln's second inaugural address, then all sing "The Battle Hymn of the Republic." The costumed Revolutionary War soldiers pass their flag to the Civil War veterans, who in turn hand it to Spanish-American War veterans, who pass it on to the soldiers of the present army. The speaker reads excerpts from Wilson's war message to Congress, then all sing a medley of popular World War I songs, ending with "America." Lee's model celebration concludes with a mass recitation of the final section of Lincoln's Gettysburg Address, one minute of silence, then a bugle retreat.[36]

Unlike the pageant guidebooks published before 1917, guidebooks for staging public ceremonies distributed during World War I advised local officials to avoid extended dialogue, dancing, or dramatic scenes. Joseph Lee cautioned local civic officials that the speeches in his July Fourth program should last no more than three to six minutes.[37] Symbolic dance interludes depicting transitions between historical periods were reduced to fleeting glimpses of one generation of soldiers handing its guns down to the next. The rich gallery of colorful figures and distinctive episodes from a town's past displayed in historical pageants before the war, illustrating the community working together, playing together, and developing from forest primeval to City Beautiful, gave way in wartime to a more specifically and narrowly focused past which served primarily as inspiration to join the nation in battle.

As the dramatic and historical elements of community pageantry waned with America's entry in the war, the musical features grew more prominent. Before 1917, historical pageants wove light classical music unobtrusively into the background of historical reenactments and abstract symbolic dance interludes as a means of integrating the overall structure of the performance and focusing the audience's attention on the action onstage. Pageant directors advised towns to avoid popular music laden with outside associations and discouraged the audience from joining the chorus in song, except for an occasional patriotic hymn such as "The Star-Spangled Banner" or "America" in the finale. Public ceremonies in wartime, however, included places for the audience to sing popular songs throughout the performance.

The larger role assigned to audience singing in wartime pageantry reflected the growing popularity of a "community singing" movement in the United States. What had been a modest effort among music teachers and recreation workers at the turn of the century to organize community choruses as a form of public recreation ballooned during the war into a national craze aimed at getting Americans to sing aloud together. War Camp Community Service trained professional song leaders to work with both organized church and industrial choruses and unorganized groups in towns near military training camps. Its songbooks contained the lyrics to "traditional" tunes such as "Dixie" and "The Old Folks at Home," as well as to the new war songs: "Over There," "Pack Up Your Troubles," and "Fight Boys Fight." Several composers who had been active in historical pageantry, such as Frederick S. Converse and Arthur Farwell, promoted community singing in wartime with new songs and marches. Each state appointed a "State Musical Director" under its Council of Defense to train men and women with "magnetism, assurance, and knowledge of crowd psychology" to lead "spontaneous" outbursts of song at war rallies, in motion picture houses between features (with lyrics projected on the screen), and at specially organized "Liberty Sings." Within a year of America's entry in the war, the Connecticut State Council of Defense boasted of organizing eighty-two community choruses with an average of fifty members each.[38]

Organizers of community sings—whether as part of a historical pageant or in another setting—emphasized the importance of enthusiastic mass participation. All present sang the same words; there were to be no spectators. J. R. Jones, a chorus director in Kansas City, asked in 1918, "What can be more conducive to our solidarity than the Community Chorus, where the trained and the untrained, the small voices and the large, the rich and the poor alike can mingle together in one grand cheerful song of hope?" The tempos, melodies, and lyrics of the songs in the community songbooks were invariably upbeat. One observer, writing in *Playground* magazine, compared community singing in wartime to cheering from the sidelines in a football game. Indeed, some war songs assumed a cadence identical to football cheers, such as the refrain "Hit the Hun!" from the song "Fight Boys

Liberty Loan rally, Hartford, Connecticut. Singing offered the primary means of mass participation at wartime rallies, such as this one in front of the Pratt and Whitney Company. (Dudley Photograph Collection of Hartford during World War I, 1917–19, State Archives, Connecticut State Library, Hartford)

Fight." The volume and enthusiasm of the singing demonstrated the solidarity and spirit of the community.[39]

The other side of the attempt to elicit the cheerful participation of every local resident in one or another wartime activity was a militant insistence on uniformity of action and opinion. The Connecticut State Council of Defense's "Instructions to Town Committees in Charge of War Rallies" advised local leaders not only to "Hearten the Loyal," "Enthuse the Active Workers," and "Brace Up the Faint-hearted," but also to "Round Up the Slackers" and "Silence the Disloyal." A children's historical pageant in Illinois in 1918 depicted the "Children of the Civil War" period forcing one of their little playmates to renounce the Confederacy and kiss a Union flag. In the wartime community, declared an editorial in the *Hartford Times*, there could be no "slackers," no "dead weight."[40]

The militant insistence on uniformity of behavior as a demonstration of loyalty to national war aims appeared in some pageant directors' new attitude toward recent immigrants. Previously, historical pageants—especially in urban areas—celebrated immigrants' diverse contributions to the nation; after 1917, the leaders of many local

Liberty booth, Hartford, Connecticut. Each day from noon to one, visitors to this building in a factory district of the city learned that being an American required the use of English, as well as absolute support of the nation's war effort. (Dudley Photograph Collection of Hartford during World War I, 1917–19, State Archives, Connecticut State Library, Hartford)

organizations heeded the call that General Leonard Wood had issued two years earlier, amid the preparedness fervor of 1915, to "Heat Up the Melting Pot." Constance D'Arcy MacKay's manual of suggestions for *Patriotic Drama in Your Town*, published in 1918, began with the complaint that the United States lacked "national solidarity"—"Our American citizens have not been American enough; our foreign citizens after years in this country are still our foreign citizens." MacKay suggested that pageant directors change their customary portrayal of immigrants: "Over and over again in scenes dealing with emigration," she remarked, "the immigrant has been shown bringing his gifts to America. But very little stress has been put on what America gave the immigrant. It is high time that this should be done." In one of her proposed pageant scenes, immigrants recite the following:

> We sit here in the promised land
> That flows with freedom's honey and milk,
> But 'twas they won it, sword in hand,
> Making the nettle danger for us soft as silk.[41]

Loyalty Day Parade, Springfield, Massachusetts. This float on July 4, 1918, sponsored by the city's Jewish benevolent societies, displayed the loyalty of local Jews to the nation through a blend of Revolutionary War and ethnic historical imagery. (City of Springfield, Committee on Public Safety, Pictorial Record Collection; courtesy Connecticut Valley Historical Museum, Springfield)

War Camp Community Service and the federal government designated July Fourth 1918 as "Loyalty Day" and coordinated massive parades of immigrant groups pledging allegiance to the United States. Despite the rather heavy-handed "Americanizing" aspects of these displays, immigrants sometimes used them to assert their own national identity and goals. The Loyalty Day Parade in New York City included not only the forty-four nationalities recognized by the Foreign Language Division of the Liberty Loan Committee, but also an additional twenty units representing the national aspirations of splinter groups. Such expressions of ethnic diversity occurred, however, within the context of public officials' strong insistence on the uniformity of behavior in demonstrating support for the war effort.[42]

Blacks enjoyed more attention from national recreation organizations during the war than previously. As they moved north or joined the army, race riots in several towns—East St. Louis, Houston, San Antonio—received national publicity. Black social welfare workers used these riots to underscore their demand that the larger social

War and peace pageant, Penn School, St. Helena, South Carolina. Black participation in pageantry, as in other recreational activities, increased during World War I. This particular pageant took place after the war, in 1920. (Penn School Collection, permission to reprint granted by Penn Center, Inc., St. Helena Island, S.C.; Southern Historical Collection, University of North Carolina Library, Chapel Hill)

work community help provide public recreational opportunities for blacks as well as whites. Leaders of War Camp Community Service promoted community singing among blacks and rewrote the words to spirituals to reflect wartime themes. In *Drama League Monthly*, Constance D'Arcy MacKay described a Christmas pageant built around spirituals that was performed by local black residents in thirty cities across the United States in 1918. Yet blacks continued to be excluded from the massive demonstrations of national loyalty in most towns—in the North and South alike—and WCCS's recreational activities for soldiers in towns near military training camps remained racially segregated as official policy—what the agency described as "a parallel of hospitality."[43]

Hardly eighteen months after the United States entered the European war, and scarcely ten weeks after American soldiers in large numbers first began to see battle, the belligerents signed a truce. Division by division, the troops returned home in the spring of 1919. Towns and cities welcomed their sons and husbands with much the same fanfare used earlier to send them overseas; pageant directors wrote symbolic "victory" masques displaying much of the same abstract imagery that appeared in their wartime productions. An elaborate pageant on July 4, 1919 in Chattanooga, Tennessee, reviewed the history of the war from the invasion of Belgium to the final signing of the peace treaty. The same day, residents of Washington, D.C., witnessed an *International Festival of Peace*, while New Yorkers attended a giant *Victory Pageant* in City College Stadium. Allegorical figures in these celebrations "explained" the terms of the peace and argued for (or against) entering the League of Nations, just as pageants in years past had outlined the reasons for going to war. Linwood Taft's *Pageant of Thanksgiving* for Savannah, Georgia, concluded with an episode celebrating "The Federation of the World" at the signing of the armistice. Esther Willard Bates's *Pageant of the League of Free Nations* in 1919 depicted the various nations of the world joining a League of Nations following the victory of "Democracy" and "Truth" over "Autocracy" and "Anarchy."[44]

Despite the brevity of the nation's involvement in the European conflict, American historical pageantry changed greatly during the war years—more so than any other medium of mass persuasion. Whereas less than 20 percent of the motion pictures produced in the United States between 1917 and 1919 concerned war themes, historical pageantry became almost totally absorbed in the war mobilization effort.[45] Pageantry in wartime submerged the dramatic expression of local and regional identity in mass demonstrations of national loyalty. War mobilization agencies employed the same historical imagery throughout the country as a powerful tool of national integration. The exclusively sectional meaning of "Dixie" and "The Battle Hymn of the Republic" diminished as they entered the national songbook. Figures from national history previously thought too "general" to be of use in a community pageant were among wartime pageantry's principal components, vague enough to harmonize the nation's different interests and sections.

In attempting to draw together the diverse towns, regions, and peoples into a single body instantaneously and completely identifying with the nation's present concerns, organizers of pageants during World War I all but ignored the development of a town's unique historical identity over time. Brief bursts of song, glimpses of the Founding Fathers, and snatches of patriotic speeches outlined contemporary war themes but did little to enrich local residents' understanding and appreciation of long-held traditions. Historical pageants before the war had invited members of the audience to identify imaginatively with the entire range as well as several dimensions of the local community's historical experience; pageants during the war asked the audience to identify only with the community's present mobilization as part of the national war effort.

War songs in particular had less to do with inspiring renewed dedication to the moral principles embodied in the community's history than with sparking an instantaneous, enthusiastic solidarity. Professor John Milton Berdan of Yale University complained that the war songs were "superficial." Quoting from "Johnny get your gun, get your gun, get your gun; Johnny show the Hun, you're the son, of a gun," Berdan declared, "We are going [to fight] not because we are sons of guns, but because through our veins pulses the blood of our Puritan forefathers, men who dared to live for their freedom, and dared die for their faith."[46] That Berdan's reference to the Puritan past was a dissenting opinion in 1918 demonstrates the diminished role historical imagery played in the appeal to community solidarity in wartime and the increasing importance given to materials borrowed from contemporary popular culture. While Civil War songs such as "The Battle Hymn of the Republic" depicted war as a solemn moral crusade, World War I songs like "Pack Up Your Troubles" insisted "What's the use of worrying?" Ultimately the appeal to high idealism in World War I, evident in historical pageants, posters, and speeches, took a back seat to songs and comedies pitched more directly to the crowd's sense of playful camaraderie.

Placing less emphasis on a common history, civic officials in wartime attempted to foster community cohesion primarily by appealing to the common sensation of mass participation in a crowd. Although historical imagery and abstract symbolism remained components of pageantry, pageantry's most striking new feature was the intermittent mass demonstration uniting performer and audience. In the urgent atmosphere of war mobilization, of recurrent campaigns to save food or buy bonds, such demonstrations emphasized the instantaneous mobilization of all local residents for the war effort through their direct participation in specially planned parts of the performance. This feature of mass participation was built around the elements of a shared popular culture rather than upon the affirmation of a latent, historically based community identity expressed onstage.

The vision of local community development evident in historical pageants before the war—that towns could join with the outside agencies of modern life without sacrificing their unique local identity and traditions—became in wartime solely a vision of local residents tightly organized through their participation in national agencies. In a few short years, recreation workers went from directing the dances of carefree fairy sprites on city playgrounds—encouraging the expression of children's innate bonds of mutual affection—to discussing "The Importance of the Neighborhood Play Center in Any Program of National Preparedness for Defense."[47] Several months after the

United States entered the war, Percy MacKaye described pageantry as producing a loyalty to community aims "at once spontaneous and disciplined, for a purposeful efficiency of neighborliness."[48] Mac-Kaye's language—"disciplined spontaneity," "efficient neighborliness" —betrays how even one of the pageant-masters least inclined to war came to describe his desire to promote expressive participation in the terms of coercive mobilization. Expanding on the techniques of crowd psychology and "dramatic engineering" employed earlier in the decade in historical pageants such as *The Pageant and Masque of St. Louis*, the flurry of rallies, pageants, and community sings on the home front during World War I seemed to offer an opportunity for the fulfillment of the pageant-masters' goal of attaining spirited local community solidarity in the service of social reform. But in fact, the wartime conditions dramatically altered the public historical imagery through which pageantry would shape local residents' beliefs and feelings about their locale, their traditions, and one another.

7 *The Receding Past*

· · · · · · · · · · · ·

We of 1932 accept as a matter of course
those things which to them [our forefa-
thers] would be miracles. We have seen
the tallow candle changed to the arc
lamp, the gas burner to the electric light.
We have seen the covered wagon replaced by the railroad, the electric car by
the airplane, and the old melodeon by
the modern radio. What experiences for
a hundred years.
—Mayor George R. Cameron, Fostoria,
Ohio, September 1932

Pageant program, Manteo, North Carolina, 1937. This program cover for the first performance of Paul Green's drama depicts the first attempt at English settlement in North America. Note that the insets are images not of subsequent periods of local history, but rather of area tourist attractions: fishing, boating, swimming, hunting, and the Wright Brothers Memorial at Kitty Hawk. (Courtesy Roanoke Island Historical Association; North Carolina Collection, University of North Carolina Library, Chapel Hill)

P ageants commemorating local history regained popularity after World War I. Towns that in wartime had given their all to make the world safe for democracy could in peacetime sponsor public activities of less pressing concern. In the twenties, historical pageantry not only blossomed anew in the Northeast and the Midwest but also flourished as never before in the Deep South and the West.[1]

But the pageantry movement—the coalition of patriotic and hereditary societies, progressive educators and recreation workers, and professional artists and dramatists who saw historical pageantry as a vehicle for a town's social, aesthetic, and moral regeneration—did not survive the war. The pageantry movement disintegrated into its constituent groups, each advancing its own agenda for reform, none valuing historical pageantry as an important part of its efforts. Although recreation workers, dramatists, and members of patriotic and hereditary societies, along with commercial producers, continued to create historical pageants in the 1920s and after, they lacked the same sense of belonging to a pageantry "movement" that they had felt before the war.

In addition to losing its organizational base, American pageantry witnessed an erosion of its historical formula for tracing local community development. By the 1930s, new ways of representing history in public emerged, reflecting different beliefs about the relationship of Americans to their past and future than those evident at the height of the pageantry craze in the 1910s.

The war had left the responsibility for the promotion of pageantry primarily in the hands of professional recreation workers. Immediately after the armistice, this group sought ways to maintain the enthusiastic spirit of local cooperation that it believed wartime agencies had successfully elicited in towns across the nation. Recreation workers saw the experience of disciplined social organization in wartime ushering in an era of unprecedented peacetime reforms. Weaver Pangburn of War Camp Community Service wondered in 1920, "In helping to win the war, have we discovered the basic principles of successful community life?" He proposed that towns convert many of the new organizations they had created to assist the war effort into permanent institutions, so that the higher emotional plane and "enlarged community sense" fostered during the war would not lapse into "prewar indifference."[2]

Determined to keep their wartime recreation programs intact, leaders of the Playground and Recreation Association of America reorganized War Camp Community Service into a peacetime Community Service, Incorporated. They envisioned that Community Service would complement the Playground and Recreation Association as a federation of local agencies linked through a national bureau of public recreation experts.[3] National leaders hoped to employ the network of local recreation workers who had been active during the war mobilization to organize a permanent local Community Service chapter in every town. Launched in 1919 with a grant of $200,000 from the Laura Spelman Rockefeller Memorial Fund, Community Service's first campaign enabled towns to build new "war memorial" community center buildings as headquarters for the local chapters. Such "living memorials," unlike the "glacial" sculptures with which towns honored their dead after the Civil War, could also house a variety of other social service and recreational activities, from community sings and teen dances to a job placement bureau for returning veterans.[4] In the early 1920s several hundred towns across the United States built war memorial community centers—described in one Community Service brochure as "power-plant[s] for the generation of civic happiness"—often housing municipal government in the new buildings.[5]

Duplicating the strategy of mobilization campaigns during the war, Community Service maintained that local recreation workers could best transform a "city of strangers" into a "community of neighbors" by creating an infrastructure of small groups, linked through the community center, that would involve all the local residents. "The community should be cross-sectioned in every direction," Professor Jay B. Nash of New York University told a national recreation conference in Memphis, Tennessee, "so that every member of the community belongs to at least one activity group." One Community Service brochure argued that only through such total participation could the "residents of a community get together and truly become *members* of a community." It reasoned, "If you were building a house or running a factory, how many idle hands would you want? Idle people on the sidelines without interest or stake in things are just as bad in a community as in a factory—if not worse." The pamphlet concluded that "Community Service leaves no idle hands, no lookers-on in civic affairs."[6]

In part, the recreation workers' advocacy of organized recreational activities stemmed from a decade-long interest in offering alternatives to commercial dance halls, drinking, and prostitution. "Leisure time may become a curse," remarked one brochure, "Community Service makes it a blessing." An issue of the journal published by New York City's Community Service chapter, while condemning "puritanical pestiferocities" dictating how people should behave, lauded the establishment of a new community center because it "counteracts the use of [Riverside] Park as a place of rendezvous for young girls and sailors." Community Service's call for towns to erect war memorial buildings as

year-round recreation centers grew even more urgent with the enactment of national Prohibition, as many neighborhoods suddenly experienced an acute shortage of legal gathering places.[7]

The recreation workers' drive to involve every local resident in a
formally organized group reflected the belief that the small group
furnished an invaluable source of moral values to a transient population less likely to be influenced by customs of church and neighborhood. Joseph Lee, head of Community Service in 1922, noted that
with the constant migration of population "people do not stay long
enough [in one neighborhood or town] to get rooted in the group
sense." Formal recreational organizations could provide an "intensity
of tradition to make up in some measure for a population less fixed
than that of the old village communities" and thus help local residents
"make up by intensity of participation for brevity of stay" in much the
same way that colleges inculcated values and traditions in their transient populations. Concern with molding individual values through
group participation, evident before World War I in the child study
movement's claim that only proper "social education" would prevent
"misfits" in later life, became institutionalized in Community Service
recreation programs in the 1920s, along with the growing influence of
psychological theory within the social work profession.[8]

The vehemence of the recreation workers' call for the participation
of all citizens in one or another community activity also, however,
reflected the Red Scare immediately following World War I. Officially,
Community Service's national leaders remained opposed to the extreme "100% Americanism" campaigns launched by the American
Legion to purge the nation of dissent. Joseph Lee, though an out-
spoken advocate of immigration restriction, felt that one could not
"Americanize" immigrants by "clubbing them." Executive Secretary
Howard S. Braucher declared in 1919 that "not a dollar would be
accepted for Community Service which came on the understanding
that it was to be used to combat any special political group or special
philosophy of life or of government." But against a background of
bloody Socialist revolution in Russia and a wave of violent labor protest, increasing unemployment, and high inflation at home, leaders of
local Community Service chapters promoted the value of intensive
community organization through recreation explicitly as an antidote
to class warfare and social unrest. Community Service of Boston circu-
lated a fund-raising letter over Governor Calvin Coolidge's signature
stating that "all of us in Massachusetts deplore the so-called 'class
consciousness' which it seems is being persistently created in the minds
of the employees of our industries." In July 1919, the New York City
chapter observed that "the inevitable answer to the decline of commu-

nity feeling in any people is the rise of some sort of 'communism' in the lower economic strata of that people"; it concluded that this could be counteracted only by fostering the individual's active participation in community groups. Another Community Service brochure pictured American society as a tinderbox: "A Sarajevo starts a World War; a Seattle strike rocks a continent. A local blaze may set the world on fire tomorrow. We need insurance against that fire. Community Service is social insurance on a national scale applied locally."[9]

Community Service recommended the continuation of historical pageants as a means of building new permanent local community organizations out of the remnants of wartime mass enthusiasm and of bringing disparate community groups into closer collaboration. Constance D'Arcy MacKay, who headed the Department of Community Drama for both Community Service and its predecessor, War Camp Community Service, insisted that a successful pageant should result in the formation of a permanent community orchestra, chorus, outdoor theater group, indoor theater group, and folk dance group, as well as Boy Scout and Girl Scout troops. Using the historical pageant as a forerunner of permanent groups, noted Kenneth S. Clark of Community Service's Bureau of Community Music, might even have worked for Carol Kennicott, the heroine of Sinclair Lewis's *Main Street*.

> The pageant would begin with the arrival of the pioneer family, such as the Champ Perry's, in their prairie schooner. The history of the town could then be traced down to the arrival of the various Scandinavian and German settlers. This would have led to the participation of the farmers and their families along with the "city folks" in such a way as to bring about a rapprochement between town and countryside. Such participation would also occur in the latter part of the pageant which would represent the farming and industries of Gopher Prairie today. . . . The community-wide co-operation of such a venture as the pageant would have created a community spirit that Carol could have utilized permanently for carrying on other plans for social service.[10]

Viewing historical pageantry primarily as a tool for the creation of permanent community organizations, Community Service's Department of Community Drama distributed manuals on pageant technique and lists of published pageants. It also cosponsored with the Drama League of America "institutes" on community drama, lasting from three days to three weeks, taught by experienced "pageant-masters." Joseph Lindon Smith, Lotta A. Clark, and Virginia Tanner staffed one such workshop for Community Service in Boston in

1920.[11] Percy MacKaye lectured at another institute in Cincinnati in 1922.

Many of the thirteen experts on drama whom Community Service's national office employed full-time as roving field workers to help local chapters establish amateur dramatic programs also had backgrounds in pageantry. Nina Lamkin, who worked for Community Service in Michigan, Florida, South Carolina, and Louisiana in the 1920s, had organized children's pageants on a tent Chautauqua circuit during the previous decade. Percy Jewett Burrell, who worked for Community Service primarily in the Middle Atlantic states, had made his reputation in the 1910s directing religious pageants.[12]

But Community Service's goal of organizing and sustaining recreation groups on a permanent basis ultimately led its national leaders to downplay historical pageants among the assortment of activities it recommended to local recreation workers. "What significance for a community has a big pageant, a play, or a one-night's entertainment of any other description," asked Ethel Armes in 1922, "if it flits away like a will-o-the-wisp, turns into the stuff of dreams, and tomorrow is forgotten?" Howard Braucher explained that "the pageant is an occasional and temporary form of dramatic art. The special interest of Community Service is not in pageants, but in the use of the dramatic effort continuously throughout the year." Only a "thoroughgoing organization of a permanent dramatic program," he declared, would be an effective use of Community Service's money and energies. Suspecting that his stable of dramatists overemphasized pageantry at the expense of other, less ephemeral activities, at one point Braucher called for Burrell and Lamkin to undergo a "fairly severe" evaluation to discern their "permanent achievements." "What work has [each] started that will continue after [he/she] leaves?" he asked, and required that each undergo special training in community organizing before returning to the field. Summarizing Community Service's attitude toward the pageant-masters, Constance D'Arcy MacKay wrote in 1926, "A pageant nowadays is judged not only by its performance, but by its lasting results."[13]

The problem with historical pageantry, according to the national leaders of Community Service, was that it was too expensive and unwieldy to use as a recurrent community activity. MacKay warned in 1920 of the dangers of "over-pageantizing—of making the pageant monotonous through having one pageant follow too fast on the heels of another." She contrasted pageants and plays: "Pageants may be wearisome if too many are given during the season, but the interest in plays is a quenchless interest." Recreation workers affiliated with Community Service who were concerned with establishing a program of year-round dramatic activities in their towns joined forces with the Drama League of America to promote and distribute easily produced plays that could be staged by "Little Theatre" groups that were organized on a permanent basis.[14]

Although recreation workers complained that the pageant form was becoming stale, they showed little interest in revitalizing it. Their advise focused mainly on increasing the number of permanently organized groups left in a pageant's wake, rather than improving the creative artistry of the pageant performance. Recreation workers considered their activities more as vehicles for fellowship than artistic inspiration. The Playground and Recreation Association of America confessed in a guidebook for *Community Drama* published in 1926 that "the viewpoint of the recreation worker in this field is not aesthetic but sociological." The same year, *Playground* magazine casually summarized a Fourth of July pageant as displaying "the familiar 'Spirit of '76' tableau depicting the major wars, Betsy Ross and the flag, the Boston Tea Party, and many others." While not hostile to artistic innovation in historical pageantry, the recreation workers exhibited far more interest in disseminating well-worn pageant techniques that had proven results for local community organization.[15]

Community Service's rather indifferent stewardship of historical pageantry hampered the pageant work done by its field workers who had a genuine interest in the pageant form and contributed to pageantry's steadily declining artistic reputation. In 1921, Percy Jewett Burrell warned his superiors in the Department of Community Drama that their failure to uphold high standards for pageant performances as well as pageant results would lead to pageantry losing not only the prestige and support of creative artists, but, ultimately, the respect of the general public.[16] The recreation workers' pageant, instead of representing a tool for social and artistic revitalization, would be no better than the commercial amusements, billed as pageants, that flooded the field.

The increased activity of national commercial theatrical companies soliciting local pageant business also contributed to historical pageantry's declining artistic reputation in the 1920s. Commercial pageant producers had always filled the demand of those local celebration planning committees that cared little for social reform and merely wanted to present an entertaining holiday show. While the interest of reform organizations in pageantry waned, commercial producers of amateur indoor theatricals, whose operations had been sharply curtailed by the growing popularity of motion pictures, expanded even further into the outdoor pageant business.

Among the largest of the national commercial producing companies entering the historical pageant market in the 1920s was the John B. Rogers Producing Company of Fostoria, Ohio. John B. Rogers founded the firm in 1903 to furnish costumes, scripts, and directors for indoor amateur musical shows staged by fraternal organizations, women's clubs, and schools. The Rogers Company did not produce its first historical pageant until 1919; by the mid-1920s, the company sent its pageant-masters on jobs throughout the United States and Canada. The firm copied its historical format primarily from the published guidebooks and pageants written by dramatists and recreation workers active in pageantry before World War I, though it hired commercial theater directors rather than academic dramatists or recreation workers to direct the pageants. Historical pageantry developed from an important sideline in the 1920s to the Rogers Company's mainstay in the 1930s, when the indoor amateur show business all but collapsed.[17]

Academic dramatists active in pageantry before the war, already unhappy with the lukewarm treatment War Camp Community Service had given their works during the conflict, in peacetime finally voiced their mounting disgust with the apparent collapse of artistic standards in a field they felt had become overrun with inept playground directors, slick commercial producers, and, in the words of Thomas Wood Stevens, "club-ladies" who took "three week courses." In 1920 Stevens advised a fellow dramatist that, although community pageants had civic benefits, they lacked artistic rewards: "One or two, where the material is good and the opportunity for experiment open, you might enjoy doing. But I have found that they have wasted me, and while I may do more of them, under pressure, I can't help being sorry to contemplate your getting into them. Artistically the rewards are too small for the force expended." Stevens bitterly recalled in 1939 that "after the war the pageant game began to be attacked on one side by commercial racketeers and from below by cheesecloth shows in the high schools. . . . We prepared careful bulletins to guide people; but the rackets could make more money by not following our advice, and the high schools didn't have the skill."[18]

Dramatists who in the 1910s had promoted historical pageantry as a form of expressive art for the masses all but conceded in the 1920s that they had lost their battle against standardization and commercialism in popular entertainment in the wave of mass-produced wartime hoopla and the meteoric rise of Hollywood. Moreover, dramatists in the twenties found themselves locked in an aesthetic conflict between their long-held interest in reaching the general public with their art and the claims of an increasingly vocal counterculture that scorned mainstream American life as embodied in the small town and epitomized in the local historical pageant. The national media increasingly identified pageantry not with artistic innovation and dynamic reform but rather with the cultural conservatism, aesthetic indifference, and saccharine moralizing of the YMCA, chambers of commerce, and women's clubs. The images employed in pageantry and other public art since the 1890s to represent the ideal of a responsibly led common civic culture were ridiculed by those who attacked that ideal in subsequent decades. Works such as George Kelley's *Torch Bearers* parodied the Little Theatre movement, while the Marx Brothers on stage (and later screen) derided the art-loving society matron characters played by Margaret Dumont.[19] Hackneyed pageant features—the Colonial teas, the prancing "Spirits of the Community"—became easy targets for lampoon not only in novels, such as Sinclair Lewis's *Arrowsmith*, generally critical of the small-town culture pageantry seemed to celebrate, but even in stories in the *Saturday Evening Post*. In one *Post* story, "Mrs. Blossom Pottle" insists that her husband must don a cheesecloth toga to impersonate the "Spirit of History" in the local community pageant because "spirits never wear pants." In 1921, promoters in Atlantic City, New Jersey, could exploit this wholesome image by calling their new Miss America beauty contest a "pageant," bathing their seaside urban enterprise in the air of small-town moral respectability. But these same associations compromised pageantry's aesthetic respectability for artists and dramatists who wished to be taken seriously by their professional peers. Historical pageantry's vitality in the 1910s lay in its creators' syntheses of a variety of genteel, popular, counter, and ethnic cultural elements. Many dramatists believed that pageantry's synthetic potential was exhausted by the 1920s and that their experiments to revitalize the American stage required new directions.[20]

Forced to choose between their devotion to public art and aesthetic respectability, dramatists who had been active in community pageantry in the 1910s redoubled their efforts within legitimate theater as their primary arena of artistic innovation in the next decade. Although Thomas Wood Stevens continued to write and direct historical pageants over the next twenty years until his death in 1942—they paid much better than teaching summer school—he devoted most of his creative energies to building up the fledgling Carnegie Institute School of Drama and then, between 1924 and 1930, the new Goodman Theatre Company associated with the Art Institute of Chicago. Within the field of drama, Stevens clearly remained more comfortable in the role of acquainting the general public with what he regarded as the well-established classics of the theater than in advancing the more experimental works of modernists such as Eugene O'Neill. Stevens's popular history of *The Theatre from Athens to Broadway* appeared in 1932. Between 1935 and 1936 he supervised the Federal Theater Project in the Midwest. Stevens won perhaps his greatest national acclaim in the 1930s for his productions of Shakespeare plays in replica Globe theaters constructed at the Chicago Century of Progress Exposition in 1934, in San Diego in 1935, and as part of a "merrie old England" exhibit at the New York World's Fair in 1939. These dramas employed professionals or highly trained amateurs rather than the general public as actors. Similarly, Stevens's historical pageants in these years—among them works for St. Louis (1921), Richmond (1922), Charlotte (1925), Santa Fe (1927), Yorktown (1931), and Albuquerque (1940), as well as for conventions of the National Safety Council (1923) and the American Bar Association (1928)—resembled formal plays more than his sprawling works of the previous decade. Each pageant had lengthy episodes filled with extensive dialogue, only rarely relieved by crowd-pleasing spectacular and mass effects.[21]

Percy MacKaye also concentrated his talents on plays instead of historical pageants, but not before several more attempts at staging massive communal ritual. In May 1919, he joined Harry Barnhart, a chorus director from New York City, to produce *The Will of Song: A Dramatic Service of Community Singing.* The production set to music selections from Walt Whitman, among other poets, for citizen choruses to chant. Although unable to stage the songfest in New York City's Central Park, as originally planned, Barnhart and MacKaye mounted performances in Buffalo, New York, and the Oranges, New Jersey. The Oranges program proclaimed that *"The Will of Song* seeks to reveal intimations of the subconscious rhythmic life whose will is the natural law of human brotherhood." The next year MacKaye tried unsuccessfully to persuade the Community Service chapter in Cincinnati to stage a $150,000 *Masque of Music* similar to *The Pageant and Masque of St. Louis.* On this mammoth municipal extravaganza, proposed as part of the city's celebration of the Pilgrim tercentenary, MacKaye would have collaborated with stage designer Norman Bel Geddes. MacKaye's projects in the period immediately after the war reflected his continued interest in promoting a sense of emotional communion among heterogeneous urban residents through elaborate, if obscure public ritual.[22]

But MacKaye's vision of a spontaneous yet disciplined community life integrating the "new worlds" of modern social organization and the "ancient fires" of primordial emotional bonds increasingly unraveled in the 1920s. The coercive war mobilization and the Red Scare heightened his awareness of the contradictions between local residents who were formally organized from the outside by agencies employing standard images of mass persuasion and local residents who expressed a genuine emotional solidarity and the unique folk traditions embedded in the rhythm of their daily lives. MacKaye slowly came to realize that the fate of his massive public enterprises lay in the hands of local chambers of commerce and civic officials who cared little for his noble ideals. Intellectually, he could no longer collaborate with official representatives of a culture that had exercised such a hypnotism toward destruction; physically, several nervous breakdowns and, after 1927, heart attacks made his involvement in large-scale public enterprises increasingly difficult. Much of his energy in these years turned inward, to family matters: his son's recovery from an automobile accident, the completion of a two-volume biography of his father, and the arrangement and disposition of family papers.[23]

Yet by temperament MacKaye could not abandon his optimistic vision of a democratic art of and for the people grounded in Native American themes. Unlike literary colleagues such as H. L. Mencken, MacKaye did not believe that contemporary American artists were forever cut off from genuine folk traditions by Puritanism and from the larger public by philistinism. Unlike colleagues in the theater such as Eugene O'Neill, MacKaye did not believe that Freudian psychology and the world war had demonstrated conclusively the tragic inevitability of human conflict rooted in unconscious motivation. MacKaye's dissent from American mass culture in the 1920s ultimately found expression neither in the cynicism of Mencken nor in the modernism of O'Neill or the expatriate counterculture of Ernest Hemingway and F. Scott Fitzgerald, but rather in the assertion that an alternative, "untamed" America still existed deep within the American character. Percy MacKaye sought a way to explore this America, an America that revealed itself not in massive demonstrations of national patriotism but rather in quiet, everyday expressions of local art and drama.[24]

Though MacKaye continued to follow national politics in the 1920s—he contributed a sonnet (as a "non-socialist," he insisted) to Upton Sinclair's anthology honoring the imprisoned Eugene Debs and submitted a poem to the *Nation* on the deaths of Sacco and Vanzetti—his dramatic work focused not on the situation of large heterogeneous groups in urban areas, but rather on that of tiny, relatively homogeneous settlements of the Kentucky mountains. Resuming the quest for unique local expressions of an American folk identity, a quest that had been present in the historical pageantry movement before the war but had been drowned out in the extensive wartime mass mobilization, MacKaye wrote plays that celebrated what he regarded as the primordial "Anglo-Saxon" and "Celtic" folk heritage of rural Appalachia. His interest in English, Scottish, and Celtic folklore extended back to his studies at Harvard in the 1890s with Francis J. Child, pioneering collector of ballads. In 1912, MacKaye wrote *Yankee Fantasies*, five one-act plays based on tales and holiday customs of rural New England. Four years later, he had prevailed upon Cecil Sharp, coauthor with Olive Dame Campbell of *English Folksongs of the Southern Appalachians*, to help prepare the Elizabethan "Sumer is y-cumen in" dance interlude for *Caliban*, the Shakespeare tercentenary pageant he produced for New York City. MacKaye's World War I play, *Washington: The Man Who Made Us*, also featured musical interludes incorporating ballads that Sharp and Campbell identified with Appalachia between scenes of Washington preparing to cross the Delaware.[25]

MacKaye's special interest in Appalachia as an example of the nation's folk culture developed further in the early 1920s with his intermittent position as "artist in residence" at Miami University in southern Ohio and with the publication of his brother Benton's studies of the area as a regional planner and his proposal for the creation of the Appalachian Trail.[26] Using the Pine Mountain Settlement School in Kentucky as a base, Percy and Marion MacKaye rode up and down the hills of eastern Appalachia, filling up volumes of notebooks with traditional tales and songs. Out of these visits, Percy MacKaye wrote plays, poems, and short stories mimicking the dialect spoken in what he assumed were isolated mountain villages. In 1923, his play *This Fine Pretty World* premiered in New York City. *Napoleon Crossing the Rockies* premiered in Pittsburgh the following year under the direction of Thomas Wood Stevens at the Carnegie Institute. In 1926, MacKaye published a collection of *Tall Tales of the Kentucky Mountains*, some of which he later told in performance at the White Top Folk Festival in southwestern Virginia. Though in the vicinity of the Pine Mountain School MacKaye probably encountered a more polite than authentic version of mountain culture, his publications on mountain folklore attracted national attention. In 1930, Professor Ben Botkin of the University of Oklahoma, the future head of the folklore program for the Federal Writers Project and the Library of Congress, invited MacKaye to serve as advisory editor for his journal *Folk-Say*.[27] It was in the guise of a folk dramatist that MacKaye returned briefly to large-scale historical pageantry, writing *Wakefield: A Folk-Masque of the Birth of Washington* for the George Washington Bicentennial Celebration in Washington, D.C., in 1932.

Through these plays, the antimodernism implicit in Percy MacKaye's work of the 1910s emerged more fully. His Kentucky mountain folk plays stemmed from his growing sense of the irreconcilability of traditional culture and modern technology. He expressed particular concern that the standardizing effect of national mass communications would eventually destroy the unique but dwindling folk heritage of Appalachia. Authentic local culture would be "rooted out by the penetrating magneto, the thin revolving disk, the coils of radio and telephone" in a confrontation in which the "world of Isaiah stands confounded by the world of Marconi."[28] Unlike MacKaye's earlier poetry in praise of recent technological achievements, or his drama of progressive reform, the world- and future-embracing *Masque of St. Louis*, *Napoleon Crossing the Rockies* portrayed the outside world and modernity as a threat to local traditions. Its plot concerns a rural family that does not eventually triumph over "Gold," but rather is mercilessly swindled out of its land by invading coal and railroad companies. Even though much of the play's material came from MacKaye's stay in Harlan County, Kentucky, a region with a heritage of violent labor conflict that only a few years later would again erupt, attracting national attention, the idealist MacKaye pictured the battle between local families and national corporations not primarily as an economic struggle but rather as a drama of "cultural conservation," a microcosm of the larger battle between the "Pioneer Spirit of America" and the "Machine of Modernism." He argued that the nation should practice a "new conservation" by somehow maintaining the diversity of its traditional local and ethnic cultures and learning from them.[29] Although MacKaye insisted that he advocated a new pluralistic American civilization rather than a return to the rural isolation of the past, his folk dramas make clear that he regarded local culture and tradition more as a bulwark against, than as a springboard to, the local community's connection with the rest of the nation.

Although Percy MacKaye enjoyed a greater reputation with the general public, the major figure in American folk drama in the 1920s was Frederick Henry Koch, a pageant-master, dramatist, and professor at the University of North Carolina at Chapel Hill. Born in Covington, Kentucky, in 1877, Koch grew up in Peoria, Illinois, where his father August worked as a cashier for the Aetna Insurance Company. His mother, Rebecca Julian, grew up in Mississippi. Koch returned to the Ohio Valley to attend Central Methodist College in Cincinnati and Ohio Wesleyan University. Intent on a career in academics, he found a position teaching English at the University of North Dakota, interrupting his stay at Dakota between 1907 and 1909 to obtain a master's degree under George Pierce Baker at Harvard University. Koch indulged his interest in theater and drama, and encouraged his students at North Dakota to write plays based on local history. His *Pageant of the Northwest*, produced at the University of North Dakota at Grand Forks in 1914, reworked Amerindian and pioneer tales from throughout the state into dramatic form.[30]

Soon after joining the faculty of the University of North Carolina in 1918, Koch resumed his work in historical pageantry by writing *Raleigh: The Shepherd of the Ocean* for the Raleigh Women's Club. Described by the *Raleigh Times* as North Carolina's first community pageant, Koch's dramatic account of Sir Walter Raleigh's ill-fated attempts to found a colony in the New World was staged in a local baseball park in 1920. The next year, Koch helped his students to write historical pageants for the North Carolina towns of Wilmington and Halifax. He established a Bureau of Community Drama as part of the University of North Carolina's Extension Division and, in 1923, hired Ethel Theodora Rockwell, a veteran pageant director and former student of Thomas H. Dickinson at the University of Wisconsin, to introduce drama into high schools, start permanent community dramatic groups, and advise these groups on the production of original local plays. Rockwell encouraged pageantry as part of a local dramatic program. Her standard historical pageant, *Children of Old Carolina*, was published and distributed by the university's Extension Division and performed in two dozen towns throughout the state.[31]

Koch devoted most of his efforts, however, to the Carolina Playmakers, a student dramatic group he founded to write and produce original one-act plays based on North Carolina life and people. In 1924, Koch described his Playmakers as "contributing to the state a fresh consciousness of itself—its lore and its legends, its romantic history, and its stirring new life of today." In an article for *Playground* magazine the following year, he wrote that the Playmakers tapped "the folk consciousness of the people." Koch published three volumes of collected *Carolina Folk Plays* in 1922, 1924, and 1928, and arranged for his Playmakers to perform in Chapel Hill as well as on annual tours to both northern and southern cities. By the middle of the decade the Playmakers were clearly Koch's major priority. After Ethel T. Rockwell left North Carolina to return to Wisconsin in 1927, historical pageantry disappeared from the topics scheduled for discussion at the annual meetings of the Carolina Dramatic Association, the federation of local community dramatic groups under the university's Bureau of Community Drama. The bureau instead concentrated on establishing permanent dramatic groups in North Carolina towns and on sponsoring an annual statewide tournament of high school drama clubs.[32]

The transition by MacKaye and Koch from pageant-master in the 1910s to folk dramatist in the 1920s reflected the belief that native folk expressions required translation into "higher" forms of art. As early as 1915, Thomas H. Dickinson had observed that pageantry's limitations were already "becoming apparent" and that it was time for pageantry to "give way to other forms" of community dramatic expression. Yet the folk play that MacKaye, Koch, and other dramatists created in the

Frederick Henry Koch. Koch's Bureau of Community Drama at the University of North Carolina promoted historical pageantry throughout the state in the 1920s. (North Carolina Collection, University of North Carolina Library, Chapel Hill)

1920s was not an indigenous form of performance in the Kentucky mountains or in the hills of rural North Carolina. Just as composers such as Arthur Farwell translated exotic black, Amerindian, and cowboy music into European-style harmonies for symphony orchestras, dramatists like MacKaye and Koch wove mountain dialect and folk tales into one-act plays performed by professionals or highly trained amateurs for audiences in New York City, Philadelphia, and Baltimore—far removed from the locale of their subjects. One folk play about Abraham Lincoln performed in 1925 by students from the Carney Creek Community School in Pippapass, Kentucky, reportedly did draw a large audience from the surrounding mountain region—but the crowd might have been attracted not by the prospect of seeing the "natural acting" of their fellow mountaineers, but by the play's presentation in the local movie house on a Saturday night immediately after a showing of the latest feature film from Hollywood. Folk drama represented less an attempt to communicate indigenous culture than to create a highly stylized version of that culture for modern audiences. What Koch had termed as "the folkways of our less sophisticated and more elemental people, living simple lives apart from the responsibilities of a highly organized social order" became raw material for the dramatists' own efforts at artistic innovation.[33]

The third group that had promoted historical pageantry in the 1910s, members of patriotic and hereditary societies, also lost interest in the form in subsequent decades. Like the recreation workers and dramatists, these self-appointed guardians of local tradition now preferred to make their presence felt through smaller, more easily managed activities.

The hereditary societies continued to assert their public presence in the 1920s through historic preservation and museums. In 1926, the elite Woman's Committee of the Philadelphia Sesquicentennial International Exposition declined Ellis Paxson Oberholtzer's offer to organize them in a massive historical pageant. Leaving the historical pageantry in the hands of commercial producers and professional actors, the Woman's Committee instead erected "High Street," a collection of twenty homes along a replica Colonial Philadelphia street. The Colonial-style exteriors were built in collaboration with the local chapter of the American Institute of Architects and architectural historian Fiske Kimball, the new director of the Pennsylvania Museum (later renamed the Philadelphia Museum of Art), while responsibility for furnishing the interior of each building went to a different women's organization, such as the Daughters of the American Revolution. Sponsoring organizations also staffed their houses with members in Colonial costume.[34] The decade's most influential display of history in a museum got underway in 1924, when the relics originally assembled by prominent New Yorkers and displayed as part of the Hudson-Fulton Celebration of 1909 were installed permanently in the new American Wing of the Metropolitan Museum of Art. In language nearly identical to that of genteel writers of a half century earlier, curators R. T. H. Halsey and Elizabeth Tower prefaced the guidebook for the wing by emphasizing the collection's value for communicating the conservative moral values they associated with the past: "Much of the America of today has lost sight of its traditions. The stage settings have largely passed away, along with the actors. Many of our people are not cognizant of our traditions and the principles for which our fathers struggled and died. The tremendous changes in the character of our nation, and the influx of foreign ideas utterly at variance with those held by the men who gave us the Republic, threaten, and unless checked, may shake its foundations."[35] In the 1920s, members of patriotic and hereditary societies believed that the times required them to create and maintain permanent institutions dedicated to the preservation of items they identified with the purity of their Anglo-American heritage, rather than to join in activities such as community historical pageants that would merge that heritage with those of other classes and ethnic groups in the projection of a common present and future.

The gulf between the three principal groups that had promoted historical pageantry in the 1910s widened in the 1920s as the recreation workers, dramatists, and patriotic and hereditary societies more clearly demarcated their different social, aesthetic, and political agendas. None of the groups placed the large, ephemeral, polyglot, artistically unwieldy historical pageant high on its program of recommended activities. To recreation workers, there were better tools for community organization; to dramatists, better forums for exploring folk art; to the hereditary elite, better vehicles for conserving and disseminating their version of patriotic, Anglo-American values.

Consequently, the American Pageant Association (APA), created in the 1910s by a coalition of recreation workers, dramatists, and members of patriotic societies specifically to promote historical pageantry for cities and towns across the nation, lapsed into inactivity in the 1920s. The association failed to reclaim its role, ceded to War Camp Community Service during World War I, as the national clearinghouse for information about pageantry and pageant-masters. Members lost track of one another. Thomas Wood Stevens, APA president from 1916 to 1921, confessed to Frank Chocteau Brown in 1920, "I am so completely in the woods that I don't know whether there is still an association or not."[36] Brown, among the association's most active correspondents in the 1910s, began to devote more time to other, more vital organizations. He served on the national board of the Drama

League of America and became a leading preservation architect with the Society for the Preservation of New England Antiquities, a career that culminated in his direction of the Historic American Building Survey for Massachusetts in the 1930s. When William Chauncy Langdon succeeded Stevens as president of the American Pageant Association in 1921, he could not even locate the addresses of its directors.

Even though the veteran publicist Langdon talked for a while of bringing about the organization's "resurrection," apparently he did nothing.[37] Langdon spent the war year of 1918 in residence at the University of Illinois; the following two years took him to Europe for a Memorial Day pageant for American troops in France, pageants for the International Boy Scouts Jamboree in London (repeated in Paris and Brussels), and back to the Midwest for pageants at Marietta College in Ohio and Indiana University at Bloomington. He finally returned home to Bronxville, New York, in 1921. Turning fifty, and having been on the road constantly for ten years directing historical pageants, Langdon decided to seek steady employment in one place so that he could provide a stable home for his wife and two young children. Langdon did not want to return to teaching, which he had abandoned nearly two decades before; he tried, but failed, to find a job in his second career of social work.[38] Hopes that his book on *The Coming of the Pilgrims,* timed to coincide with the three hundredth anniversary of their arrival in North America, would be accepted for publication faded, as did his hopes that the Pilgrim manuscript would be purchased for production by a motion picture company. Finally in the spring of 1922, almost a year after his last job as a pageant-master, Langdon landed a position in the Advertising Department of the American Telephone and Telegraph Company (AT&T) in New York City. He soon convinced AT&T management of the importance of establishing an archives and historical library pertaining to the founding of the firm and of interviewing the early members of the company before they died (Alexander Graham Bell had died in August 1922). Within a year after Langdon's arrival, he published a narrative, *Early Corporate Development of the Telephone,* and his new career as business archivist was underway.

Langdon remained at AT&T for the next fifteen years, apparently quite happily, until his retirement.[39] With a growing family and a demanding job that he did not want to jeopardize by periodic absences, Langdon declined the historical pageant offers that still found their way to his office in the 1920s. In the decade since *The Pageant of Thetford* in 1911, Langdon's interest in historical pageantry had been inextricably linked with his participation as a pageant-master; unwilling to continue in this exacting role, he soon lost interest in reviving the flagging American Pageant Association. Although Langdon remained the association's president through the 1920s, he ignored Lotta Clark's repeated pleas for action to prevent its demise and neither issued a *Bulletin* nor called a meeting of its board of directors.[40] Langdon's personal interest in social history continued, however; on his retirement from AT&T in 1936, he began writing *Everyday Things in American Life*, a three-volume study of the evolution of American material culture and society. He completed the first two volumes, covering 1607 to 1776 and 1776 to 1876, respectively; the third volume, chronicling Langdon's lifelong interest, the changes in American communities that had occurred during his own lifetime, remained unfinished at his death in 1947.[41]

The final appearance of the American Pageant Association occurred in 1930, when members who lived in the Boston area issued a second edition of *Who's Who in Pageantry* under its name as a guide for Massachusetts towns that might be choosing directors for historical pageants celebrating the tercentenary of the Commonwealth's founding. Many of the pageant-masters listed in the new *Who's Who* had worked for Community Service in the 1920s as community drama experts.[42] But after 1930, with the Massachusetts tercentenary over and the worsening depression diminishing the ability of towns to hire professional directors for local holiday celebrations, the long-dormant American Pageant Association once again, and apparently permanently, entered oblivion.

The disintegration of the American Pageant Association underscored the differences between the various versions of historical pageantry available to local celebration committees that were trying to determine the appropriate way to commemorate civic holidays in the decade after the war. Community Service, through its national network of local playground associations, professional recreation workers, and schoolteachers, probably enjoyed the widest distribution for its concept of historical pageantry as a tool of community organization. Commercial producing companies, whose livelihood depended on beating the bushes for pageant business, were close behind in outreach. The few well-publicized historical pageants produced by professional dramatists as folk art or by patriotic and hereditary societies as vehicles for the transmission of conservative values also offered scenes for local officials planning less elaborate public celebrations to imitate. Nevertheless, despite these divergent influences and the lack of consistent guidelines, representations of history in pageants of the 1920s were remarkably similar, sharing common features which subtly distinguished them from pageants of the previous decade. And by the mid-1930s, a new pageant historical formula had emerged.

Some uses of tradition in historical pageants remained unchanged from the 1910s to the 1920s. Pageants in the twenties, like those of the previous decade, exhibited the idealized behavior of past generations for present generations to emulate. Pioneers conquered the wilderness and repulsed Indian attacks; Revolutionary and Civil War soldiers, even in the aftermath of the world war, unhesitatingly marched off to battle; closely knit town residents of the past punctuated their work routines with lively dances and elaborate receptions for visiting dignitaries. Each historical pageant produced by the John B. Rogers Company featured a standard "Pioneers versus the Wilderness" scene, where a man and a woman fend off "Fever," "Famine," and "Death." Episodes in the Montgomery, Alabama, historical pageant of 1926 duly noted that both Indian attacks in the town's history were precipitated by outsiders giving the Indians liquor—a suitable warning for Prohibition times. Historical pageants in River Falls, Wisconsin, in 1924 and Elizabeth, New Jersey, in 1926 honored the courage of local veterans of World War I in episodes respectively entitled "Crawling through No Man's Land" and "Over the Top." Scenes of husking bees, barn dances, and stately minuets in historical pageants of the twenties, like those of the previous decade, rounded out the idealized portrait offered local residents of their hard-working, though occasionally playful ancestors.[43]

That the town, past and present, be shown as a cohesive unit free of internal discord was a second historical pageant theme that remained essentially unchanged from the 1910s to the 1920s. A scene in the Gastonia, North Carolina, pageant in 1924 depicted representatives of Gaston County's ninety-seven textile mills paying homage to "Queen Cotton"—five years before their bitter strike. Pageant finales highlighted the myriad local groups that by pitching together constituted the modern community, giving an especially prominent place to organizations established after World War I. In the grand finale of *The Gateway*, a historical pageant of Kansas City, Missouri, in 1921, symbolic figures representing the "American Legion," "P.T.A.," and "Father's Club" band together with the "Boy Scouts" on stage to vanquish "Evil" and his cohorts. The Conway County, Arkansas, centennial historical pageant of 1925 concluded with a stately procession of various "Spirits"—not only of the "Arts," of the "Community," and of "Play," but also of the "Spirit of the Kiwanis Club." As a further demonstration of local community cohesion, many pageant organizers inserted musical interludes for the "Band and Audience" to perform between historical episodes, a feature held over from community singing in wartime, when local residents were asked to demonstrate their loyalty and unity through song.[44]

Some historical pageant directors of the 1920s also retained militant elements of the postwar Red Scare, going beyond the solely affirmative display of local solidarity to depict explicit menaces to the community's cohesion. The author of a historical pageant in Miami, Ohio, in 1920 pitted the community represented on stage against "Red Cap . . . chief of the gnomes who wander about in the dark, stirring up trouble and unrest, and feeling that the light will destroy them." Sue Ann Wilson wrote a model *Yankee Doodle Festival* distributed by Community Service, which as performed in Nassau, Long Island, in 1921, included a scene where police put a suspected member of the "Black Hand" with concealed explosives through the "Third Degree." In the allegorical finale of *The Pageant of Stoughton*, Massachusetts, in 1926, "Anarchy," clad in a red mantle, surreptitiously circulates among groups of recent immigrants, offering them a red flag, until the "New England Spirit" summons "Liberty" to remove him forcefully with the help of a uniformed soldier and sailor. Such historical pageants displayed local residents as mobilized against the forces that would corrode their solidarity.[45]

One of the decade's most prominent historical pageants nearly fell victim to the Red Scare. *Lexington: A Pageant-Drama of the American Freedom*, staged in Lexington, Massachusetts, in 1925, depicted the evolution of the idea of freedom through four historical episodes: the Minutemen, George Washington and the Continental Army, the Civil War, and "Our Own Day." In the latter section the symbolic figure "Freedom," played by Ruth St. Denis, weeps at a vision of workers and farmers manipulated by greedy capitalists and insensitive politicians. The scarlet "Fan of Unrest" also attempts to manipulate the workers and farmers—but they instead follow Freedom's exhortation, delivered in the words of Lincoln's Gettysburg Address, to act as individuals democratically and not as revolutionary masses. Though the pageant's plot was hardly revolutionary, national patriotic and hereditary societies attacked it as "the reddest possible Communist propaganda" and lumped it together with other dramatic works through which Communists purportedly sought to influence the American public. The Lexington historical pageant probably came under attack less for its content than for its author, Sidney Coe Howard, who had excoriated the same organizations the previous year in an eight-part series in the *New Republic* entitled "Our Professional Patriots."[46]

Despite the strong nativist sentiments in the early 1920s, which culminated in the passage of immigration restriction legislation and the resurgence of the Ku Klux Klan, the bulk of ethnic images in the decade's historical pageants reflected the same cosmopolitan stance toward recent immigrants commonly displayed in pageants from before the war. The local Community Service chapter in Chester, Pennsylvania, billed its League of Nations pageant in 1919 as an "official welcome for immigrants." A historical pageant in Reading, Pennsylvania, in 1923 spotlighted "Our New Americans." National recreation experts recommended that playground workers allocate time and space in pageant finales for each local ethnic group to assert its contributions and loyalty to the community as a whole. Percy Jewett Burrell's historical pageant for Lancaster, Pennsylvania, in 1926 included a section of episodes depicting the Pennsylvania German community's loyalty to the American cause in the Revolutionary War—from Moravians caring for soldiers wounded at the Battle of Brandywine to the Pietist brotherhood of Ephrata Cloister sacrificing pages of their religious books for gun wadding. Such demonstrations of loyalty gained additional significance in the wake of suspicions of German-Americans' disloyalty during World War I.[47]

After focusing almost exclusively on national history during World War I, civic officials resumed the display of primarily local and regional historical imagery that had been the mainstay of pageantry before the war. Both recreation workers and folk dramatists believed that local and regional loyalties were easier to nurture and maintain than the more diffuse, national ties. Echoing John Dewey's assertion in 1920 that "the locality is the only universal," an editorial reprinted in *Playground* magazine in 1921 declared that "local patriotism" and "regionalism" were the best forms of Americanism. Frederick Koch, the maker of Carolina folk plays, wrote in 1925 that "the only way we can be truly national is by being loyally local." While not ignoring local ties to the nation, organizers of historical pageants in the 1920s devoted renewed attention to asserting the town's place within a distinctive region.[48]

Nowhere was this regionalism more evident than in the South. With the greater penetration of national recreation organizations southward during World War I and the example and promotional efforts of Frederick Koch's Bureau of Community Drama at the University of North Carolina, states of the Old Confederacy presented far more historical pageants in the 1920s than in the 1910s.[49] Southerners organized historical pageants most often at the county level, in the spring as part of school commencements or in the fall in conjunction with county fairs. Although wartime pageants in the South, as in other parts of the United States, had submerged distinctive sectional images in favor of those depicting the national war effort, southern historical pageants of the twenties embodied sectionalism in both its progressive and reactionary forms.

The South in the 1920s, perhaps more intensely than any other part of the nation, witnessed the clash of progressive and reactionary elements. It was home both to civic uplift campaigns to move the "New South" into the forefront of modern life and to Ku Klux Klan rallies and fundamentalist religious movements condemning that life.[50] Historical pageants in southern towns reflected the desire of civic officials to merge these two images, to assert a progressive image to the rest of the nation while fostering renewed appreciation of their unique Confederate past. As Mrs. L. P. Hollis, executive chair of a pageant committee in Greenville, South Carolina, in 1921, explained, "It has often been said that history has been made in the South and written in the North. The purpose of our pageant is to create interest among the people of our section in our own history, thus increasing their pride in their own towns, communities, and in their section." Folk dramatists asserted the South's distinctive contribution to the nation's art and culture. Edwin Greenlaw of the University of North Carolina, the man who hired Frederick Koch from North Dakota, declared that "the foundations of America are not to be found solely in the England of Cromwell, but also in the England of Elizabeth," and that the nation's Elizabethan heritage had developed most fully in the South.[51]

Southern sectionalism in historical pageants of the 1920s juxtaposed images of the "Lost Cause" that had been present in public holiday celebrations since the late nineteenth century with the progressive iconography that had been disseminated by national recreation organizations in the previous decade. Civil War episodes in pageants in Macon in 1923 and Montgomery in 1926 proudly reenacted the inauguration of Jefferson Davis. In the latter production, a symbolic figure representing the "Spirit of the South" sends Confederate troops bravely off to battle, led by "Chivalry," who later returns to again lead southern troops in World War I. Another pageant in 1926, sponsored by the United Daughters of the Confederacy of Lexington, Kentucky, featured a spirited Civil War episode reenacting "Raiding with Morgan" down to the last rebel yell. In 1929, the tableau form proved an especially appropriate way for the United Confederate Veterans in Charlotte to depict the Confederate army's victory at Manassas; in the pageant program, the scene was captioned, "There stands Jackson like a stone wall." Atlanta's historical pageant in 1920 displayed a triumphal scene from the end of Reconstruction when the Ku Klux Klan (playing themselves) chased carpetbaggers and their black followers out of town, with music from the score to *The Birth of a Nation* sounding in the background. During a similar scene in a Morgantown, North Carolina, pageant in 1925, the audience reportedly burst into applause when Ku Kluxers rode on stage. Southern historical pageants in the 1920s, as in World War I, included episodes of

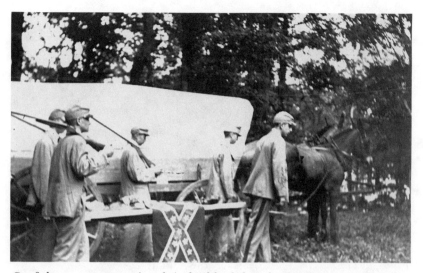

Confederate troops carrying their dead back from battle. This scene from Our Heritage, *a pageant held in Rocky Mount, North Carolina, in 1919, differed little from the "departure and return" formula prevalent in historical pageantry elsewhere before the world war. It asserted a unique Confederate heritage alongside that of town and nation. (Photo collection, North Carolina Collection, University of North Carolina Library, Chapel Hill)*

sectional reconciliation—the final scene of a historical pageant in Halifax County, North Carolina, organized with the help of the University of North Carolina's Bureau of Community Drama, depicted the "Spirit of the Roanoke" and "Columbia" leading a long line of soldiers in khaki, headed by a Union and a Confederate soldier. But they also portrayed sectional hostility. A pageant scene in Rocky Mount, North Carolina, showed Yankee soldiers looting a local farm, drinking whiskey and stealing hams. Still absent from pageant versions of Civil War history, as in the 1910s, were treatments of the political events leading up to the conflict. The historical pageant presented by students at Winthrop College in Rock Hill, South Carolina, in 1921, which recapitulated the debate over slavery in a scene depicting abolitionist Angelina Grimké's visit to a local plantation in 1857, was the exception.[52]

Along with elegies to the Confederate past, southern historical pageants of the 1920s, as those in the rest of the nation, celebrated local economic progress. *The Pageant of Wilmington*, North Carolina, in 1921 included both a "Spirit of Loyalty" carrying a Confederate flag and a grand finale of the modern Wilmington of the future made prosperous by oceangoing vessels from around the world navigating the Cape

In the days of the Old South, from Visions Old and New.

Fear River. In the finale of the pageant sponsored by the Eastern Carolina Chamber of Commerce in Kinston, North Carolina, in 1924, residents of the twelve surrounding counties portrayed the present "Eastern Carolina in Action"—civic, industrial, and commercial. Participants dressed as symbolic figures representing not only the area's agricultural crops—tobacco, cotton, and sweet potatoes—but also the spirits of "Good Roads" and "Manufactures," surrounded by "Joy Maidens" and the "Citizens of the Future."[53]

Along with more historical pageants in southern towns came more depictions of blacks. Frederick Koch encouraged his drama students writing plays about North Carolina history to make use of the literature on black music and folklore being collected at the university by sociologist Howard W. Odum. Several of these students, including DuBose Heyward and Paul Green, produced sympathetic portraits of black culture (though in 1920 Koch acquiesced in the suppression of Green's play about race relations, *White Dresses*, because the time was not yet "ripe" for it). For the most part, however, southern historical pageants, mimicking the decade's popular entertainment, portrayed blacks as comic buffoons who had been happy under slavery. Three North Carolina pageants offered absolutely no apologies for slavery—in the Wilmington pageant of 1921, slaves beg to accompany their masters off to fight the Civil War; in a pageant in Hickory in 1925, a slave protests to his master that he really does not want his freedom; and a Charlotte pageant in 1929 titled one of its antebellum scenes "Slave Contentment." In most of these pageants, the role of slaves was

For home and country, from Visions Old and New.

probably played by whites in blackface. The John B. Rogers Company produced amateur indoor minstrel shows as well as outdoor pageants and kept "Old South" wigs and costumes readily available for rental. Yet in at least a few historical pageants blacks apparently played themselves. In 1921, hardly two generations after emancipation, organizers of the Wilmington pageant featured "real darkies" as slaves singing at a "Plantation Wedding," perhaps beside the descendants of their ancestors' former owners. At another pageant in Wilmington nine years later, blacks sat in a segregated section in the grandstand in order to view their friends and relatives singing traditional songs as they picked cotton—but significantly, perhaps, they appeared in a scene displaying the textile industries of "modern Wilmington" and not as slaves. The "Negro Spiritual" scene became a circumscribed role for blacks in southern historical pageants, much as Eastern and Southern European immigrants performed folk dances in pageants of the Northeast and Midwest. Spirituals also figured prominently in the decade's several pageants of black history staged outside the South. Among the largest were W. E. B. DuBois's *Star of Ethiopia*, which was revived in Los Angeles in 1925, and the musical *Loyalty's Gift*, which premiered in 1926 on the grounds of the Sesquicentennial International Exposition in Philadelphia. The latter pageant, organized with the help of the Playground and Recreation Association of America, featured the Hampton and Fisk University Quintets, a five-hundred-voice chorus, and soloist Marian Anderson.[54]

These attempts in the twenties to express distinctive local, regional,

"Gastonia" and "Queen Cotton." On July 4, 1924, the town of Gastonia staged Visions Old and New, *a historical pageant written by Pearl Setzer, a student of Frederick Koch at the University of North Carolina. The above scenes illustrate both the progressive and reactionary features typical of historical pageantry in the South after the world war: the idealization of plantation days and the tribute to the men who fought for the "Lost Cause, as well as the elevation of the modern city and its most important product, cotton. (North Carolina Collection, University of North Carolina Library, Chapel Hill)*

Slave cabin, High Point, North Carolina, 1923. This float from High Point's Pageant of Progress, *like most scenes depicting blacks under slavery, was peopled by whites in blackface—in this case, members of the United Daughters of the Confederacy, Rotary Club, and Children of the Confederacy. (High Point Historical Museum)*

and ethnic cultural identities through historical pageantry continued to rely, as in the world war, on national organizations and corporations for their realization. Producers of *The Spirit of the South* pageant in Montgomery, Alabama, rented costumes from firms in Philadelphia and Chicago, electrical effects from a firm in Columbus, Ohio, and fireworks from a firm in Chicago. When the producers of the Atlanta historical pageant wanted to depict the Ku Klux Klan during Reconstruction, they used the music from *The Birth of a Nation,* a motion picture filmed in suburban Los Angeles that played throughout the United States. The John B. Rogers Company's central office in Fostoria, Ohio, supplied its client towns nationwide with nearly identical sets of costumes, sets, and lights. The firm's directors created pageant scripts for towns that plugged local historical episodes into the company's standard formula, which also included near-identical symbolic dance interludes. Community Service, Incorporated, sought to foster "local patriotism" by maintaining a centrally administered national bureau of pageant experts and by publishing model historical pageants in *Playground* magazine. Although organizers insisted that their pageants illustrated their towns' unique histories, the experience of producing a historical pageant more than ever betrayed the influence of national media and organizations, which furnished not only technical expertise but also standard "local" imagery and costumes. Such help enabled local celebration committees to declare their cultural autonomy without sacrificing the convenience that came with national connections.[55]

The dual images of a modern community linked with national organizations and a folk community enacting its unique local traditions had coexisted within the historical pageant form as disseminated by the American Pageant Association and adopted, however imperfectly, by local celebration committees in the early 1910s. The pageant formula of the 1910s, like the historical oration of the late nineteenth century, integrated these two images of community as successive stages of local progress—that is, a town's development, past, present, and future, was inevitably tied to its increasing linkage with a national and even international network of agencies and markets. But by the end of the 1920s, the representation of a smooth, nearly organic development from forest primeval to City Beautiful had given way to an increased demarcation of locale and nation, of the town of the past, the present, and the future. Although pageant writers and directors emphasized that a town's past remained an essential anchor for its residents' present and future identity and values, and labored mightily to make the pageant episodes reenacting that past more detailed and accurate than ever, "past" and "present" historical imagery appeared less woven into a single coherent story of successive stages of local community development than in the pageants of the previous decade.

Historical pageants of the 1920s were more likely than those of the 1910s to display images of the past in contexts that made the past appear fundamentally different from the present. Sometimes the language of pageant promoters made this difference explicit. Milton Fletcher, one of the organizers of a historical pageant in Jamestown, New York, in 1927, explained that its historical episodes "will make vivid the contrast in the mode of life a generation or more ago and at the present time." Language in pageant programs indicating how the audience should interpret pageant scenes also betrayed a dissociation of past and present. The adjective "old-fashioned" seldom appeared in pageant programs of the 1910s but was common in those of the 1920s. *The Torchbearer*, commemorating the seventy-fifth anniversary of Illinois Women's College at Jacksonville, Illinois, entitled one pageant episode simply "The Good Old Days." Community Service suggested that local recreation workers stage "An Old Fashioned Party" where guests would imitate the poses in "old-style photographs." Such delineation of "old" and "new" emphasized the gulf, rather than the continuities, between the lives of past and present generations.[56]

Pageants of the twenties were also more likely to isolate the behavior of past generations in terms of present values. In 1914, those in charge of a historical pageant in Salem, Massachusetts, reportedly dropped a proposed episode dealing realistically with the prosecution of witches in favor of a vague symbolic scene. No such inhibitions appeared in the Salem historical pageant of 1926, which author Nellie Stearns Messer introduced with the following echoes of the decade's literary attack on Puritanism: "Locally, Salem was unfortunate in being the home of a group of neurotic children and the focus of religious zealots. These ministers and judges must appear bigoted to us in this year of 1926. Two hundred years hence, what will our successors write of us?" One of Community Service's recommended recreation activities, a costume party called "Echoes of Yesterday," advised participants, "You can wear a dress of five years or one hundred years ago. Some of our own costumes of five or ten years ago are very funny now." Such language minimizes the differences between historical periods, while accentuating the differences between past and present; it assumes that each generation is destined to think of previous generations, whether five or one hundred years past, as equally foreign.[57]

Demarcation of the community of the past, present, and future in the 1920s appeared less evident in the language of historical pageant programs and guidebooks, which—the above examples notwithstanding—generally urged continued veneration of the moral principles associated with the past, than in changes in the pageant structure itself. Whereas pageants of the 1910s presented realistic historical reenactments linked by abstract symbolic interludes within an overarching civil-religious framework of local community development, pageants by the late 1920s tended to present each realistic historical episode as a discrete, self-contained entity. Pageants employed abstract symbolism in dance interludes and grand finales for variety or for spectacular visual effect, but not for its thematic contribution.

Allegory remained in historical pageantry of the 1920s although its importance diminished. The abstract symbols employed to make lofty ideals and heartfelt emotions appear tangible in the 1910s suffered from overexposure in the world war and became targets for parody by the late 1920s—though the popularity of allegory, and the essentially religious historical framework associated with it, persisted in southern pageants longer than in those of the Northeast and Midwest.[58] Academic dramatists who were active in the pageantry movement, such as Robert Withington, Thomas H. Dickinson, and George Pierce Baker, had always been skeptical of abstract symbolism. Hermann Hagedorn, the biographer of Theodore Roosevelt and poet who worked with Baker on a dramatic historical pageant for Plymouth, Massachusetts, in 1921, complained that "pageants, as a rule, seem to me only an

The Wheel of Life. This standard feature of Rogers Company pageants placed the "Queen" at the hub of the action in the finale. (Courtesy of John B. Rogers Company, Pittsburgh; Smithsonian Institution)

appeal to the eye, and the appeal to the spirit which they attempt to make through allegory is to me generally inexpressively tedious." By the late 1920s, even recreation workers' advice to towns staging historical pageants downplayed any potential thematic contribution abstract symbolic interludes could make. *Playground* magazine told its readers in 1928 that symbolic interludes "are highlights of the pageant and are spectacular and entertaining. Their purpose is to relieve the strictly historical episodes."[59]

Commercial producing companies, in particular, relied heavily on abstract symbolism to provide crowd-pleasing spectacle between episodes of historical reenactment. Each of the John B. Rogers Company's productions in the mid-1920s—whether in Ellsworth, Maine; Columbia, South Carolina; or Edmundton, Alberta—displayed identical spectacular interludes: the "Creation Ballet," the "Ballet of Fertility," the "Melting Pot of Nations," and the "Wheel of Life." In the latter drill, all pageant participants form a living wheel, rotating on an

axis with the pageant queen at its hub. Rogers Company officials claimed to have derived these fantastic mass routines from the symbolic interludes popular in historical pageants before the war. But divorced from the representation of a particular historical theme, the extravaganzas more resembled the spectacular ballet of Imre Kiralfy's grand entertainments of the late nineteenth century or the mass dance routines that would be featured in Busby Berkeley's motion pictures of the 1930s. One dance interlude in the Rogers Company's pageant for Kalamazoo, Michigan, in 1929 displayed "Celery, Queen Product of Kalamazoo County, disporting herself in a modernistic mood."[60]

Following the lead of the Miss America pageant, Rogers Company directors cast as the "Spirit of the Community" the young winner of a beauty contest rather than a middle-aged woman personifying the community's maturity and experience. Upon arriving with her court on the pageant grounds, the young queen ceremonially opened the proceedings. But then, instead of appearing on stage throughout the performance as a symbol of continuity with which local residents could identify their evolving community, she remained on the sidelines, not emerging until her literally pivotal role in the "Wheel of

A pageant queen and her court, Boise, Idaho, 1934. Rogers Company pageants featured a young woman as pageant queen, echoing the Miss America pageant and other beauty contests of the period. (Courtesy of John B. Rogers Company, Pittsburgh; Smithsonian Institution)

Life" finale. In the historical pageant of Canton, Missouri, the audience did not even learn the identity of the beauty contest winner "Queen Cantonia" until her coronation in the spectacular finale.[61]

Employing the latest technological innovations in artificial lighting and amplification, Rogers Company directors staged their historical pageants at night, when the dazzling costumes they furnished local participants, such as iridescent lavender satin "Indian" outfits, appeared to best effect.[62] These pageants contained no dialogue, only narration over a loudspeaker introducing pantomimed scenes set to music.[63] The directors thought that battle scenes, as well as mass dance routines, played especially well as spectacle. A program from *The Pageant of Point Pleasant*, West Virginia, described the giant reenactment of the Battle of Point Pleasant as "*the* feature episode" of the pageant. In the St. Augustine, Florida, Ponce de León celebration of 1925, Rogers Company directors departed from custom by staging most of the historical episodes in the daytime—but saved the spectacular reenactment of Oglethorpe's attack on the Castillo de San Marcos for evening, immediately preceding the final fireworks display. History in such works served as no more than a loose background for a succession of special effects.[64]

In part to distinguish themselves from the directors of commercial historical spectacles, professional dramatists and recreation workers involved in historical pageants in the 1920s ostentatiously displayed heightened concern with demonstrating the accuracy of detail in each of the episodes they dramatized. Thomas Wood Stevens especially prided himself on the depth of his historical research, which he felt enabled him to explore the dramatic nuances of historical events. His *Pageant of Virginia* in Richmond in 1922 included lengthy reenactments of the debates over whether Virginia should join the Revolution in 1775 and the Confederacy in 1861, complete with direct quotations from the original speakers. Stevens cited the source of each quotation in footnotes published in the pageant libretto. The Amerindians in his "Pocahontas and John Smith" scene spoke an Indian language. Constance D'Arcy MacKay published footnotes attributing the "Indian Corn Dance" episode of her pageant *America Triumphant* to Harvard University's Peabody Museum of Ethnology, though she did not specify the Indian nation from which the dance was taken. Nina Lamkin cited the Smithsonian Bureau of American Ethnology as the source for the "Green Corn Dance" she used in pageants throughout the South. Ethel T. Rockwell associated the black dialect she wrote for *Children of Old Carolina* with the research of Natalie Curtis Burlin, a musicologist who had explored black communities of the Sea Islands—though apparently in Dunn, and probably in

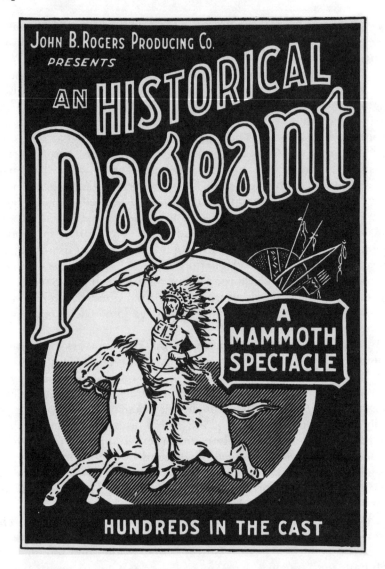

A standard Rogers Company pageant poster. This poster appeared in a souvenir volume for a pageant the company produced in Schuylerville, New York, in 1926 in commemoration of the 150th anniversary of the Declaration of Independence and the Battle of Saratoga. While the pageant did contain an Indian attack—a reenactment of the French and Indian "massacre" of the Colonists in 1745—the attack was not by Sioux on horseback in full headdress, as depicted in the poster. (Courtesy of John B. Rogers Company, Pittsburgh; Schuylerville Public Library)

the other North Carolina towns where it was performed, the black characters were played by whites. In the drive to appear more historically accurate, background music, employed as a symbol of continuity between historical eras in pageants of the 1910s, was confined more to its proper historical period. Civic officials tried to demonstrate to their audiences that the period scenes, dialogue, and music in their historical pageants were authentic according to the canons of scientific history, rather than staking public acceptance of the truth of their representations solely on their word as guardians of local tradition. Sometimes, however, they assumed this word was sufficient; the official program for the Gastonia, North Carolina, pageant in 1924, in place of a footnote to the source of a scene reenacting the Tryon County Declaration of 1775, declared flatly, "Note: This scene is actual history."[65]

The trend toward conspicuous attention to accuracy of detail appeared in historical motion pictures as well as pageants. When D. W. Griffith made *America* (1924), the million-dollar-story of the American Revolution, he abandoned the blend of history and allegory displayed in *The Birth of a Nation* (1915) and *Intolerance* (1917) in favor of realism alone. With the cooperation of the Daughters of the American Revolution and several other patriotic and hereditary societies, Griffith filmed in actual battlefields and houses from the Revolutionary period and insisted on genuine period furniture and costume. But the film's action, particularly in the second half which featured spectacular battle scenes of the war in the Mohawk Valley, overwhelmed any cinematic ambitions Griffith might have had to explore more subtle historical issues.[66]

Although the increased prominence of broad spectacle and accuracy of detail in historical pageants of the 1920s at first seems contradictory, both trends highlight the individual episode at the expense of the historical sequence. As pageant productions grew more historically and technically sophisticated, audiences looked to each episode for the accuracy of its details or for the power of its special effects but not for an overall historical interpretation. Even pageant directors who set out to develop an interpretation of a historical event over several dramatic episodes were judged in terms of the effect of each scene. George Pierce Baker traveled to Holland and Great Britain to conduct original research for his Pilgrim tercentenary pageant of 1921, but those critics present at the performance in Plymouth had more to say about the lighting—300 kilowatts flowing in 500 separate lines through 15 miles of wire—than about Baker's dramatic story of the Pilgrims' struggles in the Old and the New World. Norreys J. O'Connor remarked in the *Bookman* that "the spectacular scenes were

Rehearsal, The Pilgrim Spirit, *Plymouth, Massachusetts, 1921. The grand background and crowd scenes of the Pilgrim tercentenary pageant overwhelmed the dramatic ambitions of its creator, George Pierce Baker. (Courtesy of the Pilgrim Society, Plymouth)*

the only ones that really carried; the pictorial overshadowed the dramatic." Ludwig Lewisohn of the *Nation* noted that Baker's meticulously researched and crafted sequence of dramatic episodes looked "helpless," and that only the "rhythm of larger masses" came through. Concentration on the effect and accuracy of individual episodes at the expense of an overall theme contributed to the sense of discontinuity between historical periods evident in the pageants of the 1920s.[67]

The growing popularity during this period of the type of historical pageant that resembled a formal play in its detailed depiction of a limited chronological period, generally the town's early years, rather than a larger sweep of the town's past, further accentuated the gulf displayed in public between communities of the past and the present. Thomas Wood Stevens's *Pageant of St. Louis* of 1914 covered local events up to the Civil War; his Missouri centennial pageant of 1921 reenacted nothing after 1821, the year Missouri was admitted to statehood. Seventeen of the twenty-one historical episodes in Stevens's *Pageant of Virginia* in Richmond in 1922 depicted events that occurred before 1825. Historical pageants in Bennington, Vermont, in 1911 and Saratoga, New York, in 1913 reenacted events from local history until at least the Civil War; historical pageants in these towns in 1927 depicted incidents only until the Revolutionary War battles each pageant commemorated. In 1911, Virginia Tanner worked alongside William Chauncy Langdon on *The Pageant of Thetford*, which displayed a dozen episodes of local history up to the present. In 1924, she directed a twelve-episode historical pageant in Albany, New York, that stopped with the founding of the city in 1686. Her thirteen-episode pageant for Portsmouth, New Hampshire, in 1923 stopped in 1789; her twelve-episode pageant for Bath, Maine, in 1928 ended with Maine's admission to statehood in 1819. Unlike the final scene of Langdon's pageant for Indiana University in 1920, which addressed what he termed "The Present Crisis in the Country," depicting businessmen luring young graduates away from the field of education at a university commencement, his pageant for Michigan State University in 1927, entitled *The Beginnings*, stopped in 1857. The pageant in Newburyport, Massachusetts, commemorating the Commonwealth's tercentenary in 1930—the one on which W. Lloyd Warner based his observations about the uses of the past in "Yankee City"—placed thirty-one of its forty-two scenes before 1800. The bias toward reenacting episodes from a town's early years rather than the recent past, evident in historical pageants of the 1910s, grew more prominent in the 1920s. Scenes of Colonial history or the first fifty years of white settlement, which had comprised approximately two-thirds of the scenes in a typical pageant of the 1910s, comprised five-sixths of the episodes in pageants of the 1920s, while pageants that depicted exclusively a town's early years grew more common.[68]

Except for scenes celebrating local veterans' departure and return from World War I, the events pageant directors and their clients chose to reenact as "history" in the 1920s grew more remote in time. Concentrating their reenacted episodes in an earlier and shorter time span, pageants depicted a past that appeared to recede from the present rather than lead toward it. Pageants divided local history into scenes portraying a distant, almost static past, in which time moved slowly between episodes, and a grand finale displaying scenes of a dynamic present and future, in which time moved at an accelerated pace that compressed, or more likely ignored, the events immediately preceding the present. Unlike the prevailing pageant formula of the 1910s, the sequence of historical episodes reenacted in pageants of the 1920s offered little in the way of a rhythm of social evolution between past and present that local residents could imaginatively project into their future.

The trend toward representing only a single period of history in public appeared not only in historical pageants that increasingly re-sembled formal plays, but also in the growing popularity of restored villages and annual historical festivals as tourist attractions. Though the preservation of individual homes remained primarily the domain of patriotic and hereditary societies, the idea of restoring an entire village to a particular historical period as an "outdoor museum" gained attention through the 1920s and 1930s with several large, well-publicized projects. In 1923, Henry Ford created Old Sudbury, Massa-chusetts, a collection of buildings restored to the eighteenth century; the village extended over 2,500 acres surrounding the Wayside Inn, made famous by Henry Wadsworth Longfellow. Six years later, Ford dedicated the larger Greenfield Village, Michigan, a collection of buildings and artifacts mostly dating from the mid-nineteenth cen-tury.[69] The popularity of Colonial High Street, the ersatz block from eighteenth-century Philadelphia that was reconstructed on the fair-grounds of the Sesquicentennial International Exposition in 1926, also promoted national interest in museum villages. Three period villages sprouted in 1930 for the Massachusetts tercentenary—Pio-neer Village in Salem, Fort Massachusetts in North Adams, and Aptuxcet Trading Post in Bourne, on Cape Cod. By then, plans for opening Colonial Williamsburg, Virginia, to the public were well un-derway. All of these villages featured guides in period costume who demonstrated obsolete industrial, agricultural, and domestic arts and handicrafts. Pioneer Village in Salem re-created thirty scenes of life in the seventeenth century, including the crafts of thatching, smithing, and salt-making as well as the Puritans' exotic social practices, such as placing a woman suspected of witchcraft on the dunking stool, a woman who wore "gay clothing" in the stocks, and a drunken man in the pillory. Such displays fanned interest in preindustrial material culture while carefully delineating past and present social behavior.[70]

Local chambers of commerce could mimic the period village con-cept by staging annual festivals focusing on one period of their history. These types of historical celebrations gained special popularity in the West. As early as 1911, a group of businessmen in Santa Fe, New Mexico, resurrected the *Fiesta* as a celebration each fall re-creating the Spanish city of the seventeenth century.[71] Thomas Wood Stevens wrote a pageant for the group in 1927, tacking onto the nine scenes of the city from 1536 to 1680 episodes reenacting local celebrations when Mexico won independence in 1822 and when the territory joined the United States in 1846. Beginning in 1925, the citizens of Wicksburg, Arizona, reenacted the *Days of '49*, while Deadwood, South Dakota, residents staged the *Days of '76*. Beginning in 1929, the *Helldorado* celebration in Tombstone, Arizona, provided tourists with a basically pulp novel and movie version of the wild West of the 1880s, complete with stagecoach holdups, lynchings, and dances. A more genteel version of the annual local historical festival began in Natchez, Mississippi, in 1931, when the women of the local garden club dressed in antebellum costume and opened their historic houses to the public, capping off the week with a Confederate ball. While the historical pageants of the 1910s—usually performed only once—assumed a metaphoric rite-of-passage quality for local residents as a community, celebrating their town in transition, the annual historical festival performed repeatedly for tourists assumed something of a rite-of-passage quality for local residents as individuals, coming of age to play the various roles.[72]

The restored village and annual historical festival offered a view of past communities as separate worlds far removed from the complexities of life in the present. Whereas visitors to the Chicago World's Columbian Exposition in 1893 could visit exotic locales such as the "Streets of Cairo," visitors to the Philadelphia Sesquicentennial Exposition in 1926 could visit Colonial High Street—remote in time if not in place. A promotional brochure issued in conjunction with George Pierce Baker's Pilgrim tercentenary pageant in 1921 advertised the charms of Plymouth, Massachusetts, as any other product to restore health and well-being, claiming that visitors to the extensively restored landscape of the seventeenth century would "gain refreshment in body and spirit." The Victor Talking Machine Company's series of advertisements in *Playground* magazine in 1926 promised that, by purchasing phonograph records by "Henry Ford's Old Time Orchestra," the house band at the automaker's period barn dances in Dearborn, Michigan, one could "Recapture the Old-Time Communal Joy in Music" at any place and time. The company advertised that the recorded music and dance tunes culled from the past would "charm old and young alike into a camaraderie spirit," offering a means for "the forgetting of loneliness and thwarted aspirations" in a "communal intoxication of fun." Such imagery represented history primarily as an opportunity to escape temporarily to a world depicted as different from the present, one where the emotional feelings of community had not been overtaken by a purportedly impersonal modern mass society. The antimodern image of the past as a stable refuge brimming with authentic expressions of communal joy had been present in historical pageants of the 1910s—indeed, since the costume balls of the late nineteenth century. But in the 1920s it grew more prominent, while the religious historical framework that assumed that the past had serious moral lessons to teach the present, and the progressive historical framework that assumed that the past offered ways to understand

and thus guide the direction of future social and economic evolution, declined.[73]

Much as the theme of timeless moral principles uniting past and present in the historical oration of the late nineteenth century paralleled the structure of a minister's jeremiad sermon, and the framework of social and technological evolution in historical pageants of the 1910s paralleled the structure of academic historians' "New History," the emphasis on technological discontinuities over continuous traditions between generations in the historical pageants, restored villages, and festivals of the 1920s paralleled sociologists' pronouncements about cultural lag. Social scientists had expressed the theme of dramatic discontinuity between generations since the turn of the century—E. R. A. Seligman cautioned the American Economic Association in 1902 that modern industrial society was qualitatively different from "all its predecessors" and that "the American of the future will bear but little resemblance to the American of the past"—but it was not until the 1920s that William F. Ogburn, a sociologist at the University of Chicago, coined the term "cultural lag" and it was echoed in the popular press. Cultural lag theory asserted that the rate of technological innovation always exceeded the rate of change in human values, attitudes, and beliefs. Sweeping technological changes required adjustments in social institutions and values; in a period when technology and society were changing rapidly, clinging to the values of past generations only worsened feelings of social and psychological dislocation. Thus Americans could look to history for reminders of their past identity but not for principles that could guide their present public policies. Robert and Helen Lynd's famous study of Middletown, which depicts a town under stress from the incomplete adjustment of its social institutions and values to rapid technological change, uses history solely as a way to ground its contrast of "past" and "present" conditions. The Lynds portrayed the Muncie, Indiana, of only thirty years before as another world, reporting that the environment had changed so drastically between the 1890s and 1920s that parents no longer knew what kinds of advice would best prepare their children for the future. Interestingly, a historical pageant performed in Muncie in 1927 produced by the John B. Rogers Company paralleled the Lynds' formula of history as dramatic discontinuity, contrasting eleven realistic episodes of the past—a "little pioneer school," a church, and a wedding scene—with a triumphant finale marveling at how "from a small village Muncie has sprung into a flourishing modern city . . . within the memory of a single generation."[74]

Recreation workers most influenced by this use of history as a means of contrasting the communities of past and present emphasized the need to break free from, rather than to uphold, the values they associated with the past. Whereas recreation workers in the 1910s sought to reform Americans' use of leisure by encouraging them to embrace a robust play tradition evolving from Elizabethan England through the barn dances of the nineteenth century, a writer in *Playground and Recreation* magazine in 1930 argued that, before Americans could change their leisure habits, they first must "recognize how much the values of another day are ruling us. . . . We are living up to the code of some dead ancestor near or remote, who worked out a philosophy of life of his own, while we do not take the same liberty of fitting our working and living values to our own particular needs."[75] At the heart of reform movements in the 1910s had been the projection of new institutions as continuous with those of the past through historical rhetoric and imagery—that old and new belonged in the same tradition and were part of a continuous process of social evolution. By contrast, many advocating reform in the late 1920s, echoing social scientists of the period, insisted that the solution to present problems lay more in inculcating modern values adapted to modern circumstances than in promoting adherence to the antiquated values of past generations.

Public historical imagery in the 1920s reflected the quest for solid historical ground, a baseline for comparison with the present and a foundation for local identity, yet also a tacit repudiation of the applicability of "timeless" moral or continuous social and economic principles derived from the past for the modern age. By omitting the present and future from their conception of appropriate historical imagery to put before the public, civic officials assumed that history remained extremely usable as long as it was confined to depicting the past.[76]

The disruptive experience of the stock market crash and the Great Depression of the 1930s reinforced the tendency to represent history in public primarily as a stable refuge insulated from present crises, rather than also as a way to comprehend how those crises developed. Severe shortages of public and private funds virtually brought the production of historical pageants to a standstill during the depression. Towns overburdened by the demand to assist the rising numbers of local poor in 1930, 1931, and 1932 found elaborate civic celebrations a luxury. Towns laid off professional recreation workers, much to the chagrin of Playground and Recreation Association leaders who argued that the swelling numbers of unemployed Americans intensified the need for experts who could lead the public in constructive leisure activities.[77] Nevertheless, New Brunswick, New Jersey, went ahead with Percy Jewett Burrell's historical pageant as part of the city's 250th anniversary celebration in 1930, declaring that the nearly $60,000 spent was "entirely in accordance with recovery principles." In 1931, the Concord, North Carolina, Women's Club sought to use its pageant, *The Voice of Cotton*, to stimulate demand for the town's local product. If not accelerating economic recovery, explained those behind the Massachusetts Bay tercentenary celebration, such celebrations of the past offered the public "reassurance" amid present crises. Congress promoted patriotic pageants as part of the bicentennial celebration of George Washington's birth in 1932 in much the same manner, as an occasion for local civic groups and schools to reaffirm the soundness of the republic's foundations.[78]

Many artists and writers in the 1930s abandoned the critical stance toward American mass culture and provincial traditions that they had assumed in the 1920s and again created historical representations that could offer the public a usable past. In works such as *The Ground We Stand On*, by John Dos Passos, or the compilation *I'll Take My Stand*, artists and writers reaffirmed a concept of the past as "firm ground" on which to anchor a present sense of local and regional identity. Historical and biographical plays such as Robert Sherwood's *Abe Lincoln in Illinois* promised the long-awaited emergence of an American drama based on American themes. Nevertheless, the public uses of tradition in the thirties were extremely limited compared to those of the decade before World War I. Repeated proclamations that history indeed had relevance for the present—a claim that went without saying two decades earlier—betrayed anxiety that nothing in the nation's experience was really relevant to solving the current breakdown of modern industrial organization, that some vast gulf separating past and present needed to be overcome. Even the post office murals of the decade displayed primarily untroubled communities of the remote past as a contrast to present crises, rather than successive generations confronting problems and working out solutions. William Chauncy Langdon's "New Country Life" pageants of the 1910s bridged past and present, town and nation, depicting the economic hardships and triumphs of past generations as inspiration and guidance for present generations in pursuit of tangible future goals; historical pageants of the 1930s, despite the rhetoric trumpeting adherence to the values of the past continuously handed down from generation to generation, depicted past communities as "reassurance" for the present and avoided any reference to present economic problems and their possible solution in the future.[79]

A few historical pageants of the depression, however, explicitly contrasted past security and present insecurity. Thomas Wood Stevens,

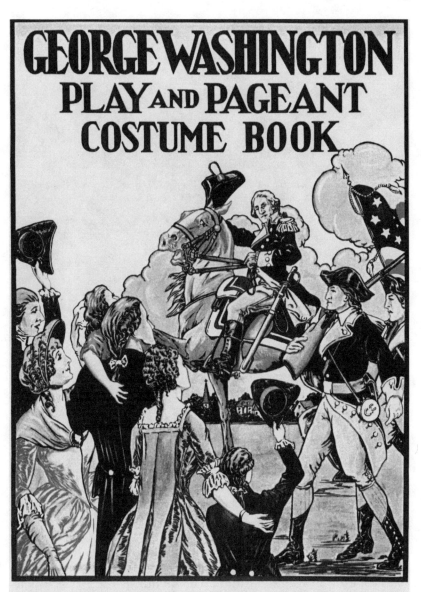

A 1931 publication of the U.S. George Washington Bicentennial Commission, which attempted to promote pageantry throughout the nation in 1932. Such pageants focused on the Colonial past to the exclusion of the present Great Depression. (Courtesy of University of Maine, Presque Isle)

*Yorktown Sesquicentennial pageant, 1931. The U.S. Army joined the cast of the three-day celebration, which culminated in the reenactment of Cornwallis's surrender. (*The Yorktown Sesquicentennial: Proceedings of the U.S. Yorktown Sesquicentennial Commission, *ed. Schuyler Otis Bland [Washington, D.C.: U.S. Government Printing Office, 1932], p. 14)*

who had worked on the forward-looking *Pageant of St. Louis* in 1914, wrote a pageant for Yorktown, Virginia, in 1931 that re-created several dozen scenes of Colonial and Revolutionary Virginia, then leapt 150 years in the finale to a scene depicting the present, in which "music blares a mad medley, punctuated by automobile horns, shots, bombs, and discordant voices over the radio. . . . Stock brokers rush about their tickers . . . automobiles rush into traffic jams, break loose, and strew their wreckage." Percy MacKaye's contribution to the George Washington Bicentennial Celebration in 1932, *Wakefield: A Folk-Masque of the Birth of Washington*, set the "Folk Age" against the "Machine Age," the "Spirits" of George Washington, Davy Crockett, and Paul Bunyan against "Drift" and his muddled "Fog Spirits." Wakefield was George Washington's birthplace; MacKaye explained that he wrote his masque (he vehemently denied that it was a historical pageant) to give the "American folk spirit" a locale and a name, to make it tangible. Such imagery portrayed the folk past as a bulwark against the forces of modernity, rather than as the period of its origins, and represented an extreme statement of the basic framework that would characterize public historical imagery in the future.[80]

One historical pageant of the 1930s became the model for towns wishing to stage historical pageants in subsequent decades. In 1937, Paul Green's *The Lost Colony* opened in Manteo, North Carolina, in commemoration of the 350th anniversary of the Roanoke settlement. Green had studied drama with Frederick Koch at Chapel Hill before embarking for Hollywood and a career in screenwriting. The Carolina Playmakers performed Green's folk plays regularly in North Carolina and on tour; one of them, *In Abraham's Bosom*, won the Pulitzer Prize in drama in 1927. With this background, Green built his pageant of the first English attempt to settle the New World along the lines of a formal play. *The Lost Colony* was produced with the help of the Federal Theater Project of the Works Projects Administration (WPA) and performed by unemployed professional actors, Frederick Koch's Carolina Playmakers, and local residents. Young men from a nearby Civilian Conservation Corps camp built the outdoor theater and sets and played the Indians; women from a WPA sewing workshop in Durham made the costumes. After its initial run in the summer of 1937, *The Lost Colony* became an annual production, attracting enough tourists to be subsidized by the North Carolina legislature beginning in 1940 and inspiring scores of imitators in North Carolina and throughout the nation (though mostly in the South) in succeeding decades. Green in the 1940s and 1950s followed up *The Lost Colony* with *The Highland Call* for Fayetteville, North Carolina, *The Common Glory* for Williamsburg, Virginia, and several others. Kermit Hunter, another student of Frederick Koch at the University of North Carolina, wrote two North Carolina productions: *Horn in the West* for Boone and *Unto These Hills* for Cherokee. The proliferation of these outdoor historical dramas for tourists in the decades after World War II led to the creation of the Institute for Outdoor Drama at the University of North Carolina in 1963. Echoing the role the American Pageant Association saw for itself a half century earlier, the institute has served as a clearinghouse for information and expert consultants for towns wishing to stage outdoor historical dramas. As of 1989, fifty-five of them were still in annual production, mostly in the South.[81]

While North Carolina since the 1930s has advanced its version of historical pageantry as a tightly woven dramatic production, commercial producing companies have continued to produce their version as a loose succession of special effects. The John B. Rogers Company remained in the pageant business after World War II, though the number of directors it sent on the road diminished from twenty-five in 1948 to six in 1988. The company added the "Gay Nineties" and "Roaring Twenties" to the standard historical periods around which it built its spectacular episodes. For a while the firm integrated its re-

Baptism of Virginia Dare, The Lost Colony, *1938. Paul Green's drama of the first English settlement in North America went into annual production and became a model for other towns wanting to present their history for tourists. (Courtesy Roanoke Island Historical Association; North Carolina Division of Archives and History, Raleigh)*

enactments with dazzling fireworks displays—including one standard scene depicting the dropping of the atomic bomb. But realizing that their pageants could not compete with television and film as spectacle, nor even as art, members of the firm's sales force marketed Rogers Company services to local celebration committees by emphasizing the company's ability to stimulate what they claimed towns of the mid-twentieth century lacked most—"mass participation."[82]

Significantly, neither remnant of the historical pageantry craze of the early twentieth century called its shows "pageants." Paul Green labeled *The Lost Colony* and his subsequent works "symphonic dramas." Samuel Selden, the director of *The Lost Colony* and Koch's assistant, then successor as head of the Carolina Playmakers, admitted in 1943 that "the *term* pageant does not always have today a very appealing sound" and blamed the "wretched" commercial companies that dominated the field for the term's demise. The Rogers Company also dropped the term "pageant" in the 1940s, preferring to call its productions "historical spectacles." Adele Gutman Nathan, a pageant director whose career spanned the 1920s through 1950s, noted perhaps the principal reason for the demise of historical "pageantry"—its association with the pageant form of the 1910s and early 1920s, when the historical reenactments were set within an overarching abstract symbolic framework. Such symbolic pageants, Nathan declared flatly in 1950, were "balderdash"—deservedly "poison at the box office." "Those of us embroiled in pageant production today are determined that no such calamities shall happen again."[83]

Indeed, as of the 1980s, the "calamities" of American historical pageantry, the attempts to present the sweep of local community development in symbolic form, integrating past and present, locale and nation, within a single dramatic performance, have not been repeated.

Conclusion:
The Era of
Pageantry

. . . .

The new pageant strives to unite the
body politic by means of the celebration
of its general joy. The Master of the Revels, The Lord of Misrule, has been superseded by a new master, who with the
functions of his forerunner has combined the ambition of the statesman.
—Louise Burleigh, *The Community Theatre*, 1917

Virginia Tanner as the Spirit of Pageantry. (Courtesy of Margaret Langdon; Smithsonian Institution)

In 1950, *Theatre Arts* magazine asked Percy MacKaye to write about his contribution to outdoor festivals and pageantry in America. The seventy-five-year-old poet hesitated at first, then half-heartedly listed a few of the technical innovations he had introduced nearly four decades earlier in his large civic masques, *The Masque of St. Louis* and *Caliban*. MacKaye concluded:

> The most important contribution my masques had to make is the one I find it most difficult to write about. . . . How can I make the present generation understand what it meant when an entire community put its heart and soul into such a production, when in "Caliban" a bootblack played Pericles and a banker carried his train; when the medical student who acted the role of St. Louis asked me to excuse his coming late to rehearsal, explaining that he had just rushed there from his marriage ceremony; when every day 1,000 to 2,000 people came merely to attend rehearsals and watch the thing grow?[1]

We are left with the same problem as MacKaye, trying to understand a social phenomenon so pervasive, yet so ephemeral. What made the historical pageant so popular a form of public holiday celebration in the early years of the twentieth century, yet seem so foreign to us today? Why did members of patriotic and hereditary societies, recreation workers and educators, and artists and dramatists think that they could change society by staging pageants? How did changes in historical pageantry's form and popularity reflect changes in the public uses of tradition in the early twentieth century? And what relevance do these changes in the ways we communicate our understanding of the nature of our history in public have for us today?

We can begin to find the answers to these questions by examining the social and cultural context in which pageantry flourished at the turn of the century. During the era of pageantry, improvements in transportation and communications technology enabled national corporations, as well as media, to reach even the smallest of towns, increasing residents' contacts with the world beyond local boundaries. These contacts, along with increased demand for factory labor, pulled rural families with poor prospects for working in agriculture into towns and cities, where they joined immigrants from overseas. To a greater or lesser extent in different regions of the United States, urbanization, immigration, and the growth of national economic and communications networks meant that residents of the same town were less likely to share the same cultural background and that they had nearly as much contact with people who resided outside their town as with those who resided within. Amid a burgeoning multiplicity of external connections and internal divisions, the town's unique identity and role as a social unit, and civic officials' customary claim to leadership of that unit, required redefinition.[2]

In the nineteenth century, civic officials sought to define local community identity, cohesion, and sense of common purpose through elaborate civic historical celebrations and commemorations. Historical orations and imagery appealed to an ethnically diverse, geographically mobile local population on the basis of historical themes encompassing the town's past, present, and future. Familiar religious metaphor invited nearly all local residents, despite diverse backgrounds, to unite as a congregation fulfilling a unique historical mission in a succession of past and future generations. The comprehensive civic tradition expounded from the speaker's platform, backed by the prestige of the holiday orators, projected overarching themes within which local residents could interpret their particular group traditions and individual experiences.

Yet public holiday celebrations had also been important activities through which local residents expressed their diverse cultural tastes and interests, as well as particular ethnic, occupational, and neighborhood loyalties. The sheer variety of holiday activities mocked civic officials' presumption that they could define a common town character and sense of cohesion. Historical orations had limited appeal among audiences increasingly drawn to public ceremonies by amusing spectacle or by their desire to watch their particular ethnic group march. Civic officials felt in the midst of these displays of cultural diversity that never were town-wide rituals that could unite local residents in the expression of a common civic culture and identity more necessary, but that never were the customary forms for addressing the public so inadequate.

The customary historical ceremony appeared inadequate not only because of limitations with its form in appealing to a diverse audience, but also because of limitations many saw with its usual content. Confidence in the boundless future, a mainstay of historical orations, was accompanied by a sense of unease about the pace of social and technological innovation. Each new institution linking town and nation, cited as evidence of material progress, also pointed to the possibility that the emerging national industrial society would sweep away all local custom and tradition. Modern life, beset with class and ethnic divisions, also appeared drab and emotionally unsatisfying. A different, more overtly nostalgic version of history, emphasizing a picturesque, closely knit communalism attributed to a preindustrial past, increasingly appeared in public alongside the usual sweeping tributes to industrial progress. Many of the same genteel holiday orators who trumpeted from the speaker's platform the creed of modern technology bringing closer the fulfillment of their town's sacred destiny also participated in costume balls and other activities brimming with the same Renaissance and Medieval imagery that had originally been invented by social critics to glorify a romanticized handicraft past.[3]

Historical pageantry appeared in America at a time when local civic officials were casting about for new forms through which to develop public consciousness of a "collective" history and culture in their towns. Prompted by members of national patriotic and hereditary societies who viewed the English import as just the means to teach the moral principles they associated with the past to a heterogeneous local population, planners of holiday celebrations envisioned the historical pageant as superseding the popular entertainment elements of holiday celebrations, integrating all into a responsibly led common civic culture. The content of that culture would combine the customary patriotic and religious themes of the historical oration, revised for an age of mass spectacle, with a growing interest in the past as a source of communal traditions that could offer emotional respite from the consequences of modern progress.

Yet reform movements in public recreation and the fine arts did the most to develop and publicize the pageant form. Recreation workers believed that a properly constructed historical pageant could depict past generations not merely as moral exemplars, but as forerunners of a new democratic, cosmopolitan, expressive civilization in the making. Through the restoration of the nation's forgotten preindustrial childhood of color and romance, as well as encouragement of a childlike play spirit, historical pageants could offer every citizen the feeling of emotional completeness that modern industrialism failed to provide. Historical pageantry as a public ritual of communal self-discovery would lead to the integration of the town's various peoples and point to the reforms necessary for their continued future progress. Influenced by the principles of both progressive education and the "New History," pageant-masters such as William Chauncy Langdon insisted that carefully selected historical episodes properly cast would help local residents better comprehend their contemporary position and responsibilities in both local and national society. Through historical pageantry, recreation workers offered an expanded, more pluralistic, and present-oriented view of the public and its history than the Anglocentric and frequently nostalgic vision advanced by patriotic and hereditary societies.

For professional artists and dramatists, pageantry also meant an expanded role for art in modern society, in contrast to the conservative genteel ideal of elite cultural leadership. Participation in the creation of elaborate communal ritual offered not only wholesome expressive public recreation, but also an essential link in the revitalization—from the town up—of moribund American artistic traditions. Through historical pageantry, artists sought to uncover the traditional social and aesthetic forms that would furnish them with, in the words of Van Wyck Brooks, a "usable past." In return, artists felt that their creation of a new American art based on these traditional forms would make articulate the latent folk identity of the nation, giving shape to a society that Percy MacKaye characterized in 1914 as a "formless void" and that Brooks described the following year in *America's Coming of Age* as "a vast Sargasso Sea—a prodigious welter of unconscious life, swept by groundswells of half-conscious emotion."[4] In an era of dramatic social and technological change, historical pageants could give tangible form to the artists' vision of a new American civilization that was being born.

Wrapped in the pageant form from its very inception was a blend of progressivism and antimodernism, customary civic religious ritual and the promise of artistic innovation. American historical pageantry borrowed liberally from earlier forms of presenting history in public—the procession, tableaux vivants, costumed reenactments—and the "plot" tying together the succession of reenacted historical scenes often resembled that of the historical oration. Like the customary civic ceremony, the pageant communicated beliefs about the nature of history and society to an ethnically diverse, geographically mobile local population. Yet it was the pageant's new features—elements of modern dance, the reenactment of scenes from social and domestic as well as political life, and the elaborate grand finales resembling playground holiday festivals—that made pageantry the characteristic form for representing the public history in the Progressive Era. Pageantry's most fervent advocates viewed it as no less than an instrument of communal transformation, able to forge a renewed sense of citizenship out of the emotional ties generated by the immediate sensation of expressive, playful social interaction. Its combination of elite, popular, and ethnic cultural forms depicting images of a "common" past would break down social and cultural barriers between local residents, triggering the release of their underlying emotions and the revitalization of their overarching civic commitments. Artists and recreation workers agreed that society could be transformed by staging historical pageants because they believed that pageants revealed a deeper, more emotional level of local community solidarity and aesthetic expression than the customary forms of holiday celebration.

In this quest for new forms alternately to address and give shape to public sentiment—to find ways to explain the public to itself—historical pageantry was similar to political and social reform movements of the period. Every advocate for reform in the Progressive Era was his or her own pageant-master, placing faith in the new techniques of mass persuasion to inform public opinion, evoke public sentiment, and spur public action on a variety of important issues. Just as the historical pageant was an amalgam of cultural forms, reform appeals in politics and social welfare combined diverse, sometimes conflicting languages to reach the broadest possible audience. Images and rhetoric of a common history, however vague, played a large part in holding these coalitions together, as well as enabling the reform coalitions to justify their proposals for what otherwise would seem unprecedented actions.[5]

The historical pageant form accommodated a widely diverse content, enabling local civic officials who had little interest in the reform ideas of its national promoters to interpret it as they saw fit and impart whatever meaning to it that they wanted. Nevertheless, historical pageants across America did have a characteristic content: the theme of community development, the importance of townspeople keeping pace with modernity while retaining a particular version of their traditions, the rite-of-passage format signifying the town in graceful transition. Historical imagery in pageants set the modern town's unique identity as a social unit amid a matrix of outside organizations, depicting its increasing relations with the outside as an extension rather than a disruption of the emotional ties and shared values that constituted the core of local community life throughout its history. On the pageant stage, local residents' internal divisions were healed and their contacts with outside organizations developed within the context of the natural development of the town. Symbolic interludes placed centuries of social evolution within a single framework, asserting continuity in the midst of change and harmonizing images of past and present, local and national community. Pageant organizers attempted through elaborate public historical ritual to reconcile the new large-scale organizational forms that marked their town's material progress and coming of age with the "traditional" values of a locally based feeling of fraternity and belief in a common future.

Historical pageants became the characteristic form of public historical representation in the Progressive Era not only because they appealed to advocates of reform, but also because they enabled local civic officials to promote an expanded, yet coherent sense of the public and its history. Pageantry grew with civic officials' efforts to create a coherent public out of a hodgepodge of classes, interests, and immigrant groups—though blacks and organized labor usually remained outside of the boundaries of the public that the pageants delineated. It also reflected the attempts of civic officials to create a coherent history out of a succession of recent social and technological changes—though the conflicts that accompanied those changes, especially resistance to the expansion of industrial capitalism, remained outside of the story of inevitable progress that the pageants told. The pageant form, and the peculiar historical consciousness it embodied and helped to shape, combined the new progressive view of history as social and technological evolution with the customary civil-religious view of history as divine revelation. Historical pageants imaginatively situated their audiences on the verge of a new era in which the customary relations between social classes, institutions, and interests would be transformed, while promising that the new society would be no more than the inevitable outgrowth of those of the past.

By the late 1920s, it was clear that the historical pageant could not bear the weight of expectation placed upon it by various groups. Pageants in the 1910s had been expected to reinforce an already active reform impulse, and they had done so. The virtual collapse of that impulse after World War I made expectations of institutional change occurring as a result of the pageant appear even more unrealistic than before the war. Consequently, artists, social workers, and members of patriotic and hereditary societies ceased to promote pageantry. Moreover, if the historical pageant's uniqueness in the Progressive Era depended on the belief that a single public ritual could foster modern social organization and traditional community feeling, popular culture and high art, attachment to locale and loyalty to nation, then the growing conviction that these attributes were impossible to combine—one celebrated either tradition or modernity, popular or high art, locale or nation—limited pageantry's appeal in subsequent decades.

In many towns, historical pageants continued to follow trends in popular culture evident since the late nineteenth century toward more spectacle and shorter, more focused messages—trends that intensified during World War I, when mass media rallied support for the nation's war aims. In 1920, Frank Morton Todd observed that the public's threshold of wonder had steadily increased since the advent of the motion picture, the airplane, and the radio. "There was a time," explained Todd, "when great crowds could be attracted and helped by stereopticons, but it was so no longer. . . . The public imagination had been 'speeded up' and to outrun it things must be swift." In the midst of these trends, "spread-eagled oratory" (in the words of *Playground* magazine) gave way to increasingly spectacular fare. One newspaper columnist in North Carolina noted the differences wrought by changing technology and tastes in the public celebration of the anniversary of the Battle of Kings Mountain, contrasting the reputed 3½-hour oration in 1855 and 1¼-hour oration in 1880 with the 22-minute oration in 1930 by President Herbert Hoover over a national radio network. "There was nothing to set loose the high rebel yells, the prolonged cheering of the typical battleground oration. It was in the new style, even as new styles of transportation enabled the throng to gather here, and new styles in communication enabled the world at its fireside to listen in." Indeed, radio enabled public officials to address a large audience on holidays without having to draw a crowd away from home or family activities. Commercial firms in the business of providing holiday entertainment for towns attempted to make their productions more and more spectacular to compete with other popular amusements—moving pictures, radio, and professional sports—but this was a competition that pageantry clearly could not win.[6]

If historical pageantry after World War I was soon overtaken by trends in popular culture, it was also left behind by trends in elite culture. The experience of war mobilization not only accelerated the ascendancy of a standardized mass culture nationally; it also accelerated the development of a more fully articulated and self-conscious modernist stance in the arts in opposition to that standard national culture. Coercive mobilization in the service of technologically based destruction in the world war reinforced the doubts present since the late nineteenth century that new technological innovations and modern social organization really could further traditional goals of promoting fraternity and idealism in the new century. In response to the war mobilization experience, artists and writers intensified their search for primal authenticity and an American folk historical identity to counter modern mass society and a standardized "middle-brow" national culture.

While artists and dramatists in the Progressive Era claimed that moral and technological progress, though not identical, could be harmonized through the skillful intervention of creative artists, modernist artists by and large believed that the spheres of technology and morality, progress and tradition remained inherently and irreconcilably opposed. Works such as Eugene O'Neill's *Dynamo* (1929) made clear that one celebrated either the machine or the spirit, the dynamo or the virgin, though some intellectuals such as Lewis Mumford continued to push for a new reconciliation of technics and folk civilization. Expatriate writers joined the European avant-garde in claiming that the world war had made them into a distinctive generation isolated in a civilization without precedents. Poets T. S. Eliot and Ezra Pound, contemporaries of Percy MacKaye, attempted to recover a sense of tradition by celebrating the timelessness of the creative process and the artist's eclectic inheritance from all generations simultaneously, outside of any sequence of particular historical contexts or evolving historical themes. The resulting idiosyncratic versions of history produced by modernist writers in the 1920s made little effort to connect with either contemporary social issues or a mass audience.[7]

But most of all, pageantry by the late 1920s was overtaken by a changing public conception of the nature of history. Embedded in the pageant form of the 1910s was an emphasis on historical continuity; other forms of representing history in public were better suited to express the theme of dramatic discontinuity between generations that came into prominence in the 1920s and after. The use of historical imagery as a bulwark against modernity, implicit in pageantry from its inception, grew more prominent and overwhelmed its other uses. Historical pageants that survived in the 1930s and after, such as *The Lost Colony*, eventually took on the form of the folk play, the restored museum village, or the annual historical festival, forms that depicted the past as a separate world from the present.

Historical pageantry as a form of folk play delineating a traditional past from a modern present offered a niche for those dramatists and artists such as Percy MacKaye who rejected both the idiosyncratic modernism of the avant-garde and the standardized commercialism of a national popular culture. MacKaye, who explored the spirit of place embodied in towns such as Wakefield, Virginia, the ancestral home of George Washington, believed that tales from the remote past furnished ground far more fertile than the barren soil of the present for the development of an American folk consciousness. And in the 1930s, these folk images achieved a measure of public prominence they never enjoyed in the Progressive Era.[8]

The folk historical images that appeared in the popular media in the 1930s tended to highlight a gulf not only between past and present but also between America and Europe, in contrast to the transatlantic view of the origins of American traditions that flourished in the decades before the world war. In the nineteenth century, genteel intellectuals had traced the origins of American courtly traditions to the aristocratic minuets and costume balls of Elizabethan England and Renaissance Italy; a new generation of progressive artists and playground workers looked to Europe as well and found folk democratic traditions such as the egalitarian Maypole dance. But in the aftermath of the war, the same nationalism that resulted in drives for 100 percent Americanism and in suspicions that children's history textbooks were pro-British also appeared in popular historical media. The nationalistic "fakelore" of Paul Bunyan and the frontier that emerged by the

1930s in popular versions of American history all but denied European influences on American civilization.[9]

Yet the nationalistic folklore never entered mass culture and politics in the United States in the 1930s as completely as in other Western industrial nations. Not only in England, but also in France, Germany, and Italy, the effort to define a particular version of the public and its history through elaborate civic rituals such as historical pageants flourished during this period. In Europe, as in the United States, public demonstrations on the scale of the *Masque of St. Louis* combined folk imagery and mass participation, and were put to national political purposes in patriotic rallies during World War I. But in Europe in the 1920s and 1930s, antimodern folk symbolism and massive public demonstrations remained linked and developed further in support of a fascist politics; while in the United States in the interwar years, mass political spectacle and folk symbolism split apart.[10] Popular history in America by and large maintained a vision of the place as the hero—that the nation's folk life revolved around the emotional bonds of local community and the products of local artisans which served as a symbol of opposition to mass politics and a bulwark against a standardized national culture. American national folklore created in the 1930s fixed the nation's identity as a nation of diverse neighborhoods and small towns. Even in the midst of a fascination with the "average" American town, itself a folk symbol often manipulated for political purposes, this self-conscious localism has continued well into the late twentieth century, whether in the "pioneer" imagery of local history buffs or in the writings of leftist intellectuals entranced with "community."[11]

The social and cultural transformations that historical pageants both embodied and attempted to bridge in the early twentieth century continue to shape the ways we use the past to inform the present. Like the generations before us, we look to history for public confirmation of our personal experiences, family traditions, and ethnic heritage, as well as some level of collective identity and common culture. When visiting historic sites, museums, or theme amusement parks, we find the images of a "common" past useful for anchoring a sense of our own identity in the currents of social change. By and large, this imagery draws upon one legacy from the era of pageantry—the use of history to offer a respite from the demands of the present, a way of delineating the disjunctions, rather than the continuities, between what it depicts as the close-knit emotional ties of virtually timeless traditional local community and the impersonal bureaucratic links of rapidly changing modern mass society. Modern public historical imagery characteristically displays a static picture of the past, lacking technological or social forces that continue to shape the present. It promotes a persistent sense of disjunction between past and present, present and future, and fosters the belief that there once existed a simple communal past in contrast to our technologically dominated modern society. In restored "Victorian" villages and Disneyland main streets circa 1910, even the complex period we just explored, the turn of the twentieth century, appears as a stable refuge innocent of the problems that continue into our present. And the products of this way of representing history in public are communities of individuals who have little sense of how their local action relates to modern mass society, or of how contemporary problems grew out of a long historical development.[12]

Another legacy of the era of pageantry is the conception, evidenced by the pageant-masters and their clients, of the role of public historical imagery in fostering a sense of connection between past and present, between locale and nation, as a springboard to a particular, if severely circumscribed, vision of an ideal future. Many academic historians at the turn of the century also shared with their audiences a view of history as relevant to contemporary issues. Attempts to reassert a relevant public history in the late twentieth century must transcend contemporary notions of the irrelevance of the past except as solid ground or popular fantasy if they are to help Americans fashion an understanding of the relationship between their locale and nation, their past, present, and future, that enables them to perceive contemporary society as the product not of technological and bureaucratic drift but rather of particular historical circumstances that can be affected by their future collective action.

Notes

· · · · · · · · · · · ·

This book was planned and written to appeal to the general reader as well as to the historian. Accordingly, the scholarly apparatus is presented as simply as possible. To keep the text uncluttered, the sources for quotations and other items are summarized, where appropriate, in notes at the end of the relevant paragraphs. Sources in each note are given in the order in which the information appears in the text. By matching text and notes, the reader should be able to discern readily the source for any particular item.

Introduction. History into Ritual

1. On the importance of a society's conception of history for its ways of legitimizing institutions and guiding present action, see J. G. A. Pocock, "Time, Institutions, and Action: An Essay on Traditions and Their Understanding," in *Politics and Experience: Essays Presented to Michael Oakeshott on the Occasion of His Retirement*, ed. Preston B. King and B. C. Parekh (Cambridge: Cambridge University Press, 1968), pp. 209–37, and Edward Shils, *Tradition* (Chicago: University of Chicago Press, 1981). On the importance of historical imagery for orienting individuals to their immediate surroundings, see David Lowenthal, "Past Time, Present Place: Landscape and Memory," *Geographical Review* 65 (January 1975): 1–36, and Yi-Fu Tuan, *Topophilia: A Study of Environmental Perception, Attitudes, and Values* (Englewood Cliffs, N.J.: Prentice Hall, 1974). On the possible role shared historical imagery plays in structuring individual memory, see John Bodnar, "Power and Memory in Oral History: Workers and Managers at Studebaker," *Journal of American History* 75 (March 1989): 1201–21.

2. On public imagery as furnishing a model of and for reality, see the essays in Clifford Geertz, *The Interpretation of Cultures* (New York: Basic Books, 1973), especially "Religion as a Cultural System." On this public discourse as a mode of power and domination, determining what is included and excluded from public debate, see Stephen Lukes, *Power: A Radical View* (London: Macmillan, 1974), and T. J. Jackson Lears, "The Concept of Cultural Hegemony: Problems and Possibilities," *American Historical Review* 90 (June 1985): 567–93.

3. For an excellent example of an analysis of public imagery in terms of the unequal access to public space of competing groups, see Susan G. Davis, *Parades and Power: Street Theatre in Nineteenth Century Philadelphia* (Philadelphia: Temple University Press, 1986).

4. On the intersection of public culture and various subcultures, see Thomas Bender, "Wholes and Parts: The Need for Synthesis in American

History," *Journal of American History* 73 (June 1986): 120–36. Public historical imagery can also be analyzed in terms of Robert Redfield's concept of how a "great tradition" is interpreted locally. Redfield, *Peasant Society and Culture* (1956; reprinted with *The Little Community* [Chicago: University of Chicago Press, 1967]), pp. 40–59. On the potential for the misunderstanding or deliberate subversion of the meaning of public ritual intended by its creators, see Sally Falk Moore, "Epilogue: Uncertainties in Situations, Indeterminacies in Culture," in *Symbol and Politics in Communal Ideology*, ed. Moore and Barbara Myerhoff (Ithaca, N.Y.: Cornell University Press, 1975), pp. 211–39. Also see the succinct discussion of ritual as a communications process in Sally Falk Moore and Barbara G. Myerhoff, Introduction to *Secular Ritual*, ed. Moore and Myerhoff (Amsterdam, The Netherlands: Van Gorcum, 1977).

5. On how the dialectic between concept and experience changes culture, and especially categories of history, see Marshall Sahlins, *Islands of History* (Chicago: University of Chicago Press, 1985).

6. For a succinct overview of the recent historiography of progressivism, see Daniel T. Rodgers, "In Search of Progressivism," *Reviews in American History* 10 (December 1982): 113–32.

7. On antimodernism, see T. J. Jackson Lears, *No Place of Grace: Anti-Modernism and the Transformation of American Culture, 1880–1920* (New York: Pantheon, 1981).

8. On contemporary Americans' perception of a great distance between their past and present, see David Lowenthal, *The Past Is a Foreign Country* (New York: Cambridge University Press, 1985).

Chapter 1. Influences Felt to the End of Time

1. On the religious aspects of American political rhetoric, see Robert N. Bellah, "Civil Religion in America," *Daedalus* 96 (Winter 1967): 1–21. The following works helped refine my understanding of Bellah's concept: *American Civil Religion*, ed. Russell E. Richey and Donald C. Jones (New York: Harper and Row, 1974); Catherine Albanese, *Sons of the Fathers* (Philadelphia: Temple University Press, 1976); and John F. Wilson, *Public Religion in American Culture* (Philadelphia: Temple University Press, 1979).

2. C. E. DeLong, "Freedom's Grand Review," delivered at Gold Hill, Nev., July 4, 1876, in *Our National Centennial Jubilee*, ed. Frederick Saunders (New York: E. B. Treat, 1877) [hereafter cited as Saunders], p. 874; Robert C. Winthrop, "A Century of Self-Government," delivered in Boston, July 4, 1876, in Saunders, p. 149; Rev. R. S. Storrs, "The Rise of Constitutional Liberty," delivered at the Academy of Music, New York City, July 4, 1876, in Saunders, p. 286; Thomas G. Alvord, "The Nation's Jubilee," delivered in Syracuse, N.Y., July 4, 1876, in Saunders, p. 402.

3. John Watts, "The Fundamental Principles of 1776," delivered in Montgomery, Ala., July 4, 1876, in Saunders, p. 743; Isaac Smith, "The First Century of the Republic," delivered in Manchester, N.H., July 4, 1876, in Saunders, p. 245; William Evarts, "What the Age Owes to America," delivered

in Philadelphia, July 4, 1876, in Saunders, p. 59; John Dillon, "Our Duty and Our Responsibility," delivered in Davenport, Iowa, July 4, 1876, in Saunders, p. 798. Analysis of holiday orators' rhetoric explaining how American progress meant a quantitatively but not qualitatively different future appears in Rush Welter, "The Idea of Progress in America," *Journal of the History of Ideas* 16 (June 1955): 401–15; Welter, *The Mind of America, 1820–60* (New York: Columbia University Press, 1975); and Arthur A. Ekirch, Jr., *The Idea of Progress in America, 1815–60* (New York: Columbia University Press, 1944). On holiday orators' rhetorical assimilation of a cyclical view of human history to a linear belief in American progress, see Fred Somkin, *Unquiet Eagle: Memory and Desire in the Idea of American Freedom, 1815–60* (Ithaca, N.Y.: Cornell University Press, 1967).

4. On Gilded Age versions of the republican ideology historians such as J. G. A. Pocock have described as flourishing in the eighteenth century, see Dorothy Ross, "The Liberal Tradition Revisited and the Republican Tradition Addressed," in *New Directions in American Intellectual History*, ed. J. Higham and P. Conkin (Baltimore: Johns Hopkins University Press, 1979), pp. 116–31.

5. Alvord, "The Nation's Jubilee," p. 403; Rev. Joseph Twitchell, "The Grand Mission of America," delivered in Hartford, Conn., July 4, 1876, in Saunders, p. 130; Rev. Morgan Dix, "The Hand of God in American History," delivered in New York City, July 4, 1876, in Saunders, p. 346. On millennial rhetoric in American political oratory, see Ernest L. Tuveson, *Redeemer Nation: The Idea of America's Millennial Role* (Chicago: University of Chicago Press, 1968). Sacvan Bercovitch suggests that this fusing of sacred and profane is a distinctively American jeremiad form, as opposed to the more purely sacred European versions. Bercovitch, *The American Jeremiad* (Madison: University of Wisconsin Press, 1978), p. 29.

6. For a list of the important components of Victorian character in the nineteenth century, see Daniel Walker Howe, "Victorian Culture in America," in *Victorian America*, ed. D. W. Howe (Philadelphia: University of Pennsylvania Press, 1976), pp. 17–25.

7. Charles Francis Adams, "The Progress of Liberty," delivered in Taunton, Mass., July 4, 1876, in Saunders, p. 212; Lucius E. Chittenden, "The Character of the Early Settlers of Vermont—Its Influence Upon Posterity," delivered in Burlington, Vt., July 4, 1876, in Saunders, pp. 501, 511. Sacvan Bercovitch notes that holiday orators justified their present social prescriptions in terms of the community's future well-being, transforming the jeremiad's customary warnings of doom into promises of deliverance. Bercovitch, "New England's Errand Reappraised," in *New Directions in American Intellectual History*, ed. J. Higham and P. Conkin (Baltimore: Johns Hopkins University Press, 1979), p. 95.

8. The two best general accounts of public holiday behavior as civil religious ritual in the former Confederate states are Charles Reagan Wilson, *Baptized in Blood: The Religion of the Lost Cause, 1865–1920* (Athens: University of Georgia Press, 1980), and Gaines M. Foster, *Ghosts of the Confederacy: Defeat, the Lost Cause, and the Emergence of the New South, 1865 to 1913* (New York: Oxford University Press, 1987). On the "theology" of the southern civil religion and its

dissemination in periodical literature, see Thomas L. Connelly, *The Marble Man: Robert E. Lee and His Image in American Society* (New York: Knopf, 1977); Rollin Osterweiss, *The Myth of the Lost Cause, 1865–1920* (Hamden, Conn.: Archon Books, 1973); and Susan Speare Durant, "The Gently Furled Banner: The Development of the Myth of the Lost Cause, 1865–1920" (Ph.D. dissertation, University of North Carolina, Chapel Hill, 1972).

9. By contrast, centennial celebrations of events of the Revolution were staged as rituals of reconciliation in the North. In 1875, a brigade of former Confederate soldiers from South Carolina marched in the Battle of Bunker Hill centennial procession, then planted a palmetto tree next to a northern pine to symbolize continued friendship between the sections. Two years later, at the centennial celebration of Burgoyne's surrender at Saratoga, each of the three main speakers wore a palmetto leaf badge presented to them by General Stephen D. Kirk of Charleston, S.C.

10. John Mercer Langston, "The National Utterances and Achievements of Our First Century," delivered in the Banneker Lyceum, Portsmouth, Va., July 4, 1876, in Saunders, pp. 257–69. See Philip S. Foner, "Black Participation in the Centennial of 1876," *Phylon* 39 (Winter 1978): 283–96.

Charleston (S.C.) *News and Courier*, June 23, 1876, p. 1. The *Raleigh* (N.C.) *Sentinel*, July 5, 1876, described "The Fourth in Charlotte: The Whites Don't Celebrate Worth A Cent, But the Colored Brothers Threw Themselves Away Upon It." Also see "July Fourth Ignored by Post-Bellum South," Raleigh *News and Observer*, July 5, 1936.

"Fourth of July," *Memphis Daily Appeal*, July 5, 1876, p. 4; "The City: The Fourth," *Mobile Daily Register*, July 5, 1876; "The Fourth At Mobile," *Mobile Daily Register*, July 6, 1876, p. 2.

11. *Celebration of the Municipal Centennial of Morgantown* (Morgantown, W.Va.: New Dominion Steam Printing Co., 1885), p. 37.

12. Statistics on the rise of local historical societies are from David D. Van Tassel, *Recording America's Past* (Chicago: University of Chicago Press, 1960), pp. 181–90. Also see Henry D. Shapiro, "Putting the Past under Glass: Preservation and the Idea of History in the Mid-Nineteenth Century," *Prospects* 10 (1985): 243–78.

13. On the relationship between historians and their audiences in the mid-nineteenth century, see Dorothy Ross, "Historical Consciousness in Nineteenth Century America," *American Historical Review* 89 (October 1984): 909–28; David Levin, *History as Romantic Art* (Stanford: Stanford University Press, 1959); and George Callcott, *History in the United States* (Baltimore: Johns Hopkins University Press, 1970). The theme of history as moral education in the period's schoolbooks is discussed in Ruth Miller Elson, *Guardians of Tradition: American Schoolbooks of the Nineteenth Century* (Lincoln: University of Nebraska Press, 1964), especially chap. 6. On historical themes in American fiction, see Harry Henderson III, *Versions of the Past* (New York: Oxford University Press, 1974).

14. On cities' role as ceremonial centers for their surrounding region, see Robert Redfield and Milton Singer, "The Cultural Role of Cities," *Economic Development and Cultural Change* 3 (1954): 53–73.

15. "Proceedings at Schuylerville in Honor of Burgoyne's Surrender," in *Centennial Celebrations of the State of New York*, ed. Allen C. Beach (Albany: Weed, Parsons, and Co., 1879), p. 236.

16. The committee in charge of the celebration of Marietta's centennial arranged the exhibition categories into "Pioneer," "Old China and Other Articles," "German," "Mound-Builders, Indian and Mineral," "Books and Miscellaneous Relics," and "Foreign Articles." "Centennial Celebration at Marietta," *Ohio Archeological and Historical Quarterly* 2 (June 1888): 245–51. For more on relic displays, see Shapiro, "Putting the Past under Glass."

17. "Proceedings at Schuylerville," p. 252. On the similar role Lafayette played for Americans during his visit in the 1820s, see Fred Somkin, *Unquiet Eagle: Memory and Desire in the Idea of American Freedom, 1815–60* (Ithaca, N.Y.: Cornell University Press, 1967).

18. "Proceedings at Schuylerville," p. 339.

19. Morton Keller states that the demonstration of organizational loyalty was among the central themes of American public life in the decades following the Civil War. Keller, *Affairs of State* (Cambridge: Harvard University Press, 1977). According to one estimate, the number of fraternal organizations in America increased sevenfold between 1880 and 1900. Half of the nearly 5.5 million members of fraternal organizations in America belonged to the Odd Fellows, Free Masons, or Knights of Pythias; the remainder joined smaller, usually ethnically based groups. B. H. Meyer, "Fraternal Beneficiary Societies in the United States," *American Journal of Sociology* 6 (March 1901): 647–61.

20. As many as 10,000 brass bands played in America by 1900, most organized since the Civil War. See Jon Newsom, "The American Brass Band Movement," *Quarterly Journal of the Library of Congress* 36 (Spring 1979): 114–39, and Neil Harris, "John Philip Sousa and the Culture of Reassurance," in *Perspectives on John Philip Sousa*, ed. Jon Newsom (Washington, D.C.: Library of Congress, 1983), pp. 11–42.

21. *History of the Celebration of the 100th Anniversary of the Promulgation of the Constitution of the United States*, ed. Hampton L. Carson, 2 vols. (Philadelphia: J. B. Lippincott, 1889); *Celebration of the Municipal Centennial of Morgantown, West Virginia*, pp. 22–23.

22. On popular historical paintings of the mid-nineteenth century, see Gilbert Tapley Vincent, "American Artists and Their Changing Perceptions of American History, 1770–1940" (Ph.D. dissertation, University of Delaware, 1982), and Thomas H. Pauly, "In Search of 'The Spirit of '76'," in *Recycling the Past: Popular Uses of American History*, ed. Leila Zenderland (Philadelphia: University of Pennsylvania Press, 1978), pp. 29–49. The examples of historical tableaux recommended in guidebooks are from Tony Denier, *Parlor Tableaux: Or Animated Pictures for the Use of Families, Schools, and Public Exhibitions* (New York: O. A. Roorbach, 1868); Josephine Pollard, *Artistic Tableaux* (New York: White, Stokes, and Allen, 1884); Martha Coles Weld, *Illustrated Tableaux for Amateurs* (New York: Harold Roorbach, 1886); and Emma Cecilia Rook, *Tableaux, Charades, and Pantomime* (1889; reprint, Freeport, N.Y.: Books for Libraries Press, 1971).

23. J. A. Hill, *Hill's Book of Tableaux* (1884; reprint, Indianapolis: Fraternity

Publishing Co., 1891), pp. 75–76; Homer L. Calkin, "Iowa Celebrates the Centennial of American Independence," *Annals of Iowa* 43 (Winter 1976): 161–80. For comparison of conservative and revolutionary representations of the figure Liberty in France, see Maurice Agulhon, *Marianne into Battle: Republican Imagery and Symbolism in France, 1789–1880*, trans. Janet Lloyd (New York: Cambridge University Press, 1981).

24. *Celebration of the Municipal Centennial of Morgantown*, p. 22. The growing popularity of Old Home Week in the late nineteenth century is described in Lewis Atherton, *Main Street on the Middle Border* (Bloomington: Indiana University Press, 1954), pp. 207–8.

25. *Celebration of the Bicentennial Anniversary of the Town of Suffield, Connecticut* (Hartford: Wiley, Waterman, and Eaton, 1871), p. 31.

26. On the holiday oration as a prime target for parody by the late nineteenth century, see Barnet Baskerville, "Nineteenth Century Burlesque of Oratory," *American Quarterly* 20 (Winter 1968): 726–43. On the appeal of speculating on the authenticity of relics on display in museums, see Neil Harris, *Humbug* (Boston: Little, Brown, and Co., 1973).

27. *Celebration of the Municipal Centennial of Morgantown*, p. 8.

28. *Celebration of the 100th Anniversary of the Promulgation of the Constitution*, 2:52, 135.

29. Bicentennial Association of Pennsylvania, *Historical Sketches, Illustrations of Philadelphia, and Official Programme of Days, Religious Services, Processions, Pageants, Exercises, Receptions and Entertainments Connected With the Bicentennial Celebration of the Founding of the Commonwealth of Pennsylvania* (Philadelphia: McCalla and Stavely, 1882); *Celebration of the 100th Anniversary of the Promulgation of the Constitution*, 2:70.

30. On the role that the prestige of the presenter plays in legitimating public historical representations, see W. Lloyd Warner, "The Protestants Legitimate Their Past," in *The Living and the Dead* (New Haven: Yale University Press, 1959; reprinted in *The Family of God* [New Haven: Yale University Press, 1961]). Robert Redfield's description of civic leaders as the sole interpreters of important cultural ideas locally, with few alternative media available through which a public would directly encounter competing formulations, seems more appropriate for American towns in the mid-nineteenth century than for the late nineteenth century. See Redfield, *Peasant Society and Culture* (1956; reprinted with *The Little Community* [Chicago: University of Chicago Press, 1967]), pp. 40–59. For the suggestion that many of the audience may not share values extolled in public rituals but lack the ability to formulate coherently articulated alternatives, see Steven Lukes, "Political Ritual and Social Integration," *Sociology* 9 (May 1975): 289–308; Michael Mann, "The Social Cohesion of Liberal Democracy," *American Sociological Review* 35 (June 1970): 423–39; and T. J. Jackson Lears, "The Concept of Cultural Hegemony: Problems and Possibilities," *American Historical Review* 90 (June 1985): 567–93. An excellent overview of the question of how to analyze various groups' attempts to define the "meaning" of public events is Gareth Stedman Jones, "Class Expression versus Social Control? A Critique of Recent Trends in the Social History of 'Leisure'," *History Workshop* 4 (1977): 162–70.

31. "Proceedings at Schuylerville," p. 243; *Bicentennial Souvenir of New Castle, New Hampshire*, comp. Chester C. Curtis (Concord, N.H.: Republican Press Association, 1893); *Celebration of the 250th Anniversary of the Settlement of Hingham, Massachusetts*, ed. Francis H. Lincoln (Hingham: The Committee of Arrangements, 1885).

32. The *Philadelphia Inquirer* reported that the crowd assembled in Philadelphia for evening ceremonies to ring in the centennial year 1876 did not disperse until two in the morning. "1776–1876 National Jubilee," *Philadelphia Inquirer*, January 1, 1876, p. 1. Philadelphia's patterns of holiday neighborhood festivities are described in Susan G. Davis, "Making Night Hideous: Christmas Revelry and Public Order in Nineteenth Century Philadelphia," *American Quarterly* 34 (Summer 1982): 185–99; Davis, "Festive Forms and Popular Politics: The Case of July Fourth in Philadelphia, 1788–1844," seminar paper, Philadelphia Center for Early American Studies, April 1982; and Davis, *Parades and Power: Street Theatre in Nineteenth Century Philadelphia* (Philadelphia: Temple University Press, 1986). Excellent analyses of the "plebeian" Fourth of July celebrations in Pittsburgh and Worcester, respectively, appear in Francis G. Couvares, "Work, Leisure, and Reform in Pittsburgh: The Transformation of an Urban Culture, 1860–1920" (Ph.D. dissertation, University of Michigan, 1980), and Roy Rosenzweig, *Eight Hours for What We Will: Workers and Leisure in an Industrial City, 1870–1920* (New York: Cambridge University Press, 1983). Couvares notes of Pittsburgh, "The plebeian Fourth sought less to define unity than to display diversity," p. 91.

33. "Holidays," *North American Review* 84 (April 1857): 353. For general descriptions of complaints about rowdyism on the Fourth in the mid-nineteenth century, see William Cohn, "A National Celebration: The Fourth of July in American History," *Cultures* 3 (1976): 141–56, and Robert Hay, "Freedom's Jubilee: One Hundred Years of the Fourth of July" (Ph.D. dissertation, University of Kentucky, 1967). Graphic evidence appears in *Ballou's Pictorial* 5 (July 9, 1859): 17, and *Godey's Ladies Book* 5 (July 1864): 13; prints in Library of Congress Prints Division, Washington, D.C.

34. Stephen Hardy, *How Boston Played: Sport, Recreation, and Community, 1865–1915* (Boston: Northeastern University Press, 1982), pp. 154, 159; *Historical Souvenir Programme of the Fourth of July Demonstrations*, (Philadelphia, 1893, 1894, 1895, 1896, 1897, 1899, 1901), Collections of the Historical Society of Pennsylvania, Philadelphia. For Pittsburgh's July Fourth ceremonies, see Francis G. Couvares, "The Triumph of Commerce: Class Culture and Mass Culture in Pittsburgh," in *Working Class America: Essays on Labor, Community, and American Society*, ed. Michael H. Frisch and Daniel J. Walkowitz (Urbana: University of Illinois Press, 1983), p. 134. Also see Couvares, "Work, Leisure, and Reform in Pittsburgh."

35. St. Louis began its Veiled Prophets parade in 1878; Louisville's carnival began in 1887. See His Mysterious Majesty, *The Veiled Prophets' Golden Jubilee: A Short History of St. Louis' Annual Civic Carnival, 1878–1928* (St. Louis, 1928). Also see *Souvenir Program, Louisville Fall Celebration* (Louisville: George G. Fetter Printing Co., 1889). On the evolution of Philadelphia's burlesque New Year's processions, see Charles E. Welsh, *O' Dem Golden Slippers* (New York:

Thomas Nelson, 1970), pp. 36–37, 45. For Mardi Gras parades in New Orleans, see Leonard V. Huber, *Mardi Gras: A Pictorial History of Carnival in New Orleans* (Gretna, La.: Pelican Publishing Co., 1977); Charles L. DuFour, *Krewe of Proteus: The First Hundred Years* (New Orleans: Krewe of Proteus, 1981); and Perry Young, *The Mistick Krewe: Chronicles of Comus and His Kin* (New Orleans: Carnival Press, 1931).

36. On the spectacular theater, see Jack W. McCullough, "Edward Kilanyi and American Tableaux Vivants," *Theatre Survey* 16 (May 1975): 25–41, and McCullough, *Living Pictures on the New York Stage* (Ann Arbor: UMI Press, 1983). Also see Glen Hughes, *A History of American Theatre, 1700–1950* (New York: Samuel French, 1951), and Richard Moody, *America Takes the Stage: Romanticism in American Drama and Theatre, 1750–1900* (Bloomington: Indiana University Press, 1955).

For the Roman Hippodrome and the Mardi Gras, see Leonard V. Huber and Charles DuFour, *If I Ever Cease to Love: One Hundred Years of Rex, 1872–1971* (New Orleans: Upton Printing Co., 1971), and "Barnum's Roman Hippodrome," *New York Times*, April 28, 1874, p. 7. Also see Harris, *Humbug!*, pp. 244–45.

For fairies and forest nymphs in street processions and theater productions, see Mystic Order of the Veiled Prophets of the Enchanted Realm, *Veiled Prophets Sixth Annual Autumn Festival* (St. Louis: Compton Litho. Co., 1883), and Julia Holmes Smith, *The Butterflies' Ball* (Chicago: Hazlitt and Reed, 1878). Images of fairies and butterflies also appeared prominently in the period's fantasy-book illustrations.

Frank P. Pease, *Ali Hassan* (Buffalo, 1877); Pease, *The Queen of Death* (Buffalo, 1883); Pease, *Niagara Falls* (Buffalo, 1884). Pain's "Last Days of Pompeii" appeared at the Louisville Autumn Carnival of 1889. Rettig also designed sets for the Cincinnati Opera. Joseph E. Holliday, "Cincinnati Opera Festivals during the Gilded Age," *Bulletin of the Cincinnati Historical Society* 24 (April 1966): 131–49.

37. *Frank Leslie's Weekly*, May 26, 1877, pp. 203–7, for New York City carnival; *The Veiled Prophet's Golden Jubilee*, list of parades; "Adam Forepaugh Shows: The American Revolution," poster, in *100 Years of Circus Posters*, ed. Jack Rennert (New York: Avon, 1974), pp. 6, 27; Imre Kiralfy, *America: Grand Historical Spectacle* (Cincinnati: Strobridge Litho. Co., 1893). Lewis Atherton notes that by the turn of the twentieth century, urban-style mass amusements traveled into rural areas to take place alongside the customary gambling and drinking at country fairs. Atherton, *Main Street*, pp. 297–98, 308.

38. Doris L. Pullen and Donald B. Cobb, *The Celebration of April the Nineteenth from 1776 to 1960 in Lexington, Massachusetts* (Lexington: Lexington Press, 1960), p. 11. On the prominent role Boston's Ancient and Honorable Artillery Company played in July Fourth celebrations, see Julia Ward Howe, "How the Fourth of July Should Be Celebrated," *Forum* 15 (July 1893): 568.

39. *Philadelphia Inquirer*, July 4, 1876. Masqueraders also marched as part of local centennial celebrations in Prairie City and Burlington, Iowa. Homer Calkin, "Iowa Celebrates the Centennial of American Independence," *Annals of Iowa* 43 (Winter 1976): 161–80.

40. Bicentennial Association of Pennsylvania, *Historical Sketches, Illustrations*

of Philadelphia, and Official Programme, p. 21; *A History of the World's Columbian Exposition*, ed. Rossiter Johnson (New York: D. Appleton and Co., 1897), 1:418, 456.

41. Pullen and Cobb, *Celebration of April the Nineteenth*, p. 17; "A Midway Review," *Dial* 15 (September 1, 1893): 106.

42. A similar working definition of "educational and hereditary elite" appears in E. Digby Baltzell, *Philadelphia Gentlemen* (New York: Free Press, 1958), pp. 6–7, and Baltzell, *Puritan Boston and Quaker Philadelphia* (New York: Free Press, 1979), chap. 2. For a wealth-based methodology for studying urban elites, see Frederic C. Jaher, "Nineteenth Century Elites in Boston and New York," *Journal of Social History* 6 (Fall 1972): 32–77.

43. On the respective rise of amusement parks, nightclubs, and motion pictures as challenges to "genteel culture," see John F. Kasson, *Amusing the Million: Coney Island at the Turn of the Century* (New York: Hill and Wang, 1978); Lewis Erenberg, *Steppin' Out: New York Nightlife and the Transformation of American Culture* (Westport, Conn.: Greenwood Press, 1981); and Lary May, *Screening Out the Past: The Birth of Mass Culture and the Motion Picture Industry* (New York: Oxford University Press, 1980). On the Protestant intellectuals' spiritual crises, see John Tomsich, *A Genteel Endeavor* (Stanford, Calif.: Stanford University Press, 1971); Stow Persons, *The Decline of American Gentility* (New York: Columbia University Press, 1973); and T. J. Jackson Lears, *No Place of Grace: Anti-Modernism and the Transformation of American Culture, 1880–1920* (New York: Pantheon, 1981). Lears notes that the late Victorians' quest for "peace of mind" would ultimately have greater impact than their official public optimism on the emerging "therapeutic" culture of the twentieth century.

44. The increasing public presence of these societies is documented in the "Celebrations and Proceedings" section of the *American Historical Register*, September 1894–May 1897. Also see Wallace Evan Davies, *Patriotism on Parade: The Story of Veterans and Hereditary Organizations in America, 1783–1900* (Cambridge: Harvard University Press, 1955); Wesley Frank Craven, *The Legend of the Founding Fathers* (Ithaca, N.Y.: Cornell University Press, 1956); and Merle Curti, *The Roots of American Loyalty* (New York: Columbia University Press, 1946). Also see the plea for the elite to remain in town on July Fourth in Julia Ward Howe, "How the Fourth of July Should Be Celebrated," pp. 567–74.

45. On the designation of well-publicized historic sites as a stimulus to patriotism, see American Scenic and Historic Preservation Society, *Annual Report* (Albany, N.Y.: Wynkoop Hallenbeck, 1897), 2:3; Pullen and Cobb, *Celebration of April the Nineteenth*, p. 15; *American Historical Register* 2 (August 1895): 1480; *Historical Souvenir Programme of the Fourth of July Demonstrations* (Philadelphia, 1896), in Collections of the Historical Society of Pennsylvania, Philadelphia; George G. Manson, "A Renaissance of Patriotism," *The Independent* 52 (July 5, 1900): 1612–15. For further discussion of the early years of the historic preservation movement in the United States, see Charles Hosmer, Jr., *Presence of the Past: A History of the Preservation Movement in the United States before Williamsburg* (New York: G. P. Putnam's Sons, 1965), and *Keepers of the Past*, ed. Clifford Lord (Chapel Hill: University of North Carolina Press, 1965).

46. For examples of genteel intellectuals' inability to answer Arnold's at-

tacks, see James B. Fry, "Mr. Matthew Arnold On America," *North American Review* 146 (May 1888): 515–19, and "Matthew Arnold's Influence," *American* 7 (October 27, 1883): 37.

47. "Holidays," *North American Review* 84 (April 1857): 360, 353, 348.

48. Barr Ferree, "Elements of a Successful Parade," *Century* 60 (July 1900): 461, 459; *The American Scenic and Historic Preservation Society*, pamphlet, 1907, p. 2. On the meaning of culture to Chicago intellectuals in the late nineteenth century, see Helen L. Horowitz, *Culture and the City: Cultural Philanthropy in Chicago from the 1880s to 1917* (Lexington: University of Kentucky Press, 1976), especially chap. 4, "The Meaning of Culture," pp. 70–92.

49. Superb discussions of Delsartism in America appear in Elizabeth Kendall, *Where She Danced: The Birth of American Art-Dance* (New York: Knopf, 1979), and Nancy Lee Ruyter, *Reformers and Visionaries: The Americanization of the Art of Dance* (New York: Dance Horizons, 1979). For American examples of Delsartism manuals, see Genevieve Stebbins, *The Delsarte System of Expression* (1885; reprint, New York: Edgar S. Werner, 1902), and Stebbins, *Society Gymnastics* (New York: E. S. Werner, 1888). Stebbins was the leading promoter of Delsartism in the United States in the late nineteenth century.

50. "Review of John Gorham Palfrey's *History of New England During the Stuart Dynasty*," *North American Review* 100 (January 1865): 162; "The American Development of Leisure," *Andover Review* 6 (August 1886): 185.

51. Alfred H. Peters, "The Extinction of Leisure," *Forum* 7 (August 1889): 683; Frederick Law Olmsted to Daniel H. Burnham, June 20, 1893, Frederick Law Olmsted Papers, Library of Congress. On the genteel intellectuals' critique of American overwork, see Daniel T. Rodgers, *The Work Ethic in Industrial America, 1850–1920* (Chicago: University of Chicago Press, 1978).

52. These were peak years for picturesque and colorful Medieval imagery in public murals and popular magazine illustrations. See The Brooklyn Museum, *The American Renaissance, 1876–1917* (New York: Pantheon, 1979), and Ann Early Levin, "The Golden Age of Illustration: Popular Art in American Magazines, 1850–1925" (Ph.D. dissertation, University of Pennsylvania, 1980). On the aristocratic appeal of Medieval imagery for wealthy Americans at the turn of the twentieth century, see John Fraser, *America and the Patterns of Chivalry* (New York: Cambridge University Press, 1982), and Mark Girouard, *The Return to Camelot: Chivalry and the English Gentleman* (New Haven: Yale University Press, 1981). Of course, the genteel version was but one of many uses of Medieval imagery popular in the Gilded Age—an age when the largest working-class organization called itself the Knights of Labor. On the appeal of knights for the working class, see Michael Denning, *Mechanic Accents: Dime Novels and Working Class Culture in America* (New York: Verso, 1987), and Robert E. Weir, "Beyond the Veil: Culture and Conflict in the Knights of Labor" (Ph.D. dissertation, University of Massachusetts, 1990).

53. On the arts and crafts movement and its artifacts, see Eileen Boris, *Art and Labor: Ruskin, Morris, and the Craftsman Ideal in America* (Philadelphia: Temple University Press, 1986); Robert Judson Clark, *The Arts and Crafts Movement in America, 1876–1916* (Princeton, N.J.: Princeton University Press, 1972); Rodgers, *Work Ethic in Industrial America*, pp. 78–82; and Lears, *No*

Place of Grace, pp. 60–96. Lears discusses the psychological dimensions of the movement as therapy for neurasthenic intellectuals. For a fascinating case study of one arts and crafts community, see *A Poor Sort of Heaven, a Good Sort of Earth: The Rose Valley Arts and Crafts Experiment*, ed. William Ayers (Chadds Ford, Pa.: Brandywine River Museum, 1983).

54. Lady Blanche Murphy, "Glimpses of Old-Time Pageantry," *Southern Magazine* 9 (February 1875): 134; "Festivals in American Colleges for Women," *Century* 49 (January 1895): 429–44. On the genteel intellectuals' efforts to unearth an Elizabethan play tradition for America, see David Glassberg, "Restoring a 'Forgotten Childhood': American Play and the Progressive Era's Elizabethan Past," *American Quarterly* 32 (Fall 1980): 351–68.

55. R. Fellow, "American History On Stage," *Atlantic Monthly* (1882): 309–16. Perhaps the best example of the period's view of the domestic and social aspects of Colonial America is Alice Morse Earle's *Home Life in Colonial Days* (1898; reprint, Middle Village, N.Y.: Jonathan David Publishers, 1975). On the Colonial revival, see Karal Ann Marling, *George Washington Slept Here: Colonial Revivals and American Culture, 1876–1986* (Cambridge: Harvard University Press, 1988); Harvey Green, "Popular Science and Political Thought Converge: Colonial Survival Becomes Colonial Revival, 1830–1910," *Journal of American Culture* 6 (Winter 1983): 3–24; and *The Colonial Revival in America*, ed. Alan Axelrod (New York: W. W. Norton, 1985), especially Rodris Roth, "The New England, or 'Old Tyme' Kitchen Exhibit at Nineteenth Century Fairs," pp. 159–83. On Colonial revival architecture, see William Rhoads, *The Colonial Revival* (New York: Garland Publishing Co., 1977). On the Deerfield Society of Blue and White Needlework, see Boris, *Art and Labor*, pp. 116–20.

56. Mary Mann Page Newton, "The Association for the Preservation of Virginia Antiquities," *American Historical Register* 1 (September 1894): 9–21; *American Historical Register* 4 (March 1896): 124–25.

57. "Rhode Island Society," *American Historical Register* 4 (June 1896): 338–39; "Rhode Island Days," *Providence Daily Journal*, April 7, 1896, p. 10; *Official Programme, Rhode Island Days of Auld Lang Syne, 1636–1865* (Providence, R.I.: Livermore, Knight, and Co., 1896). Eager's earlier dramatic work included *Toyland: Or Nip and Tuck, the Fairy Toymakers* (Pittsfield, Mass.: J. B. Harrison, 1885).

Old Plymouth Days and Ways, souvenir program (Plymouth, Mass.: Thomas P. Smith, 1897); also presented July 1896 and in the Boston Historical Festival, April 1897.

58. *The National Pageant and Dramatic Events in the History of Connecticut* (Hartford: Clark and Smith, 1889); "The Historical Pageant," *Hartford Courant*, September 25, 1889, p. 8. Pound and Livermore staged *The National Pageant* earlier that year in Newport, R.I., and Boston, Mass., with special historical scenes appropriate for each state as well as standard scenes from national history. Mary A. Livermore, prominent leader of woman suffrage and temperance campaigns, served as "Historian" for all three productions and appeared on stage with brief remarks introducing each scene. "The Pageant," *Boston Daily Globe*, May 10, 1889, pp. 1–2; Robert E. Riegel, "Mary Ashton Rice Livermore," in *Notable American Women, 1607–1950: A Biographi-*

cal Dictionary, ed. Edward T. James (Cambridge: Harvard University Press, 1971), 2:410–13.

59. "Society of Colonial Dames of America," *American Historical Register* 3 (November 1895): 418. The phrase described the society's evening of tableaux and dance in Madison Square Garden, New York City.

Chapter 2. The New Pageantry

1. "Today's Lesson," *Philadelphia Inquirer*, July 5, 1876, p. 4.

2. John Ruskin, *London Globe*, February 15, 1882; *London Daily Telegraph*, February 10, 1882; Art Workers Guild of London, *Beauty's Awakening: A Masque of Winter and of Spring*, published in *Studio* (Summer 1899). Walter Crane chaired the pageant committee.
May Morris, "Pageantry and the Masque," *Journal of the Society of Arts* 50 (June 27, 1902): 669–77.

3. Louis Napoleon Parker, *The Sherbourne Pageant* (Sherbourne, U.K.: F. Bennett, 1905).

4. Louis Napoleon Parker, "Historical Pageants," *Journal of the Society of Arts* 54 (December 2, 1905): 143; Parker, *Several of My Lives* (London: Chapman and Hall, 1928), pp. 285–86, 279; Parker, "Historical Pageants," p. 145. Parker estimated that the Sherbourne pageant cost approximately £2,500 to produce and made roughly £1,200 profit from the sale of tickets. Parker to William Chauncy Langdon, July 23, 1910, William Chauncy Langdon (WCL) Papers, Harris Collection, John Hay Library, Brown University, Providence, R.I. (hereafter cited as WCL Papers). See Parker's description of his works in *Several of My Lives*, and see the pageant texts themselves. The following are available at the Free Library of Philadelphia, Philadelphia: Louis Napoleon Parker, *The Warwick Pageant* (Warwick: Evans and Co., 1906); "Bury St. Edmunds Pageant," Third Special Number, *The Connoisseur Magazine* (London: W. H. Smith and Son, 1907); Louis Napoleon Parker, *Souvenir and Book of Words of the Colchester Pageant* (London: Jarrold and Sons, 1909).

5. George Turnbull, "English Historical Pageants," *World's Work* 15 (1907): 9667, 9670.

6. Oberholtzer's early career is summarized in the biographical volume of *Philadelphia: A History of the City and Its Peoples* (Philadelphia: S. J. Clarke, 1908), 4:594. Membership in the Franklin Inn Club was limited to one hundred men, each of whom had published at least one book. Its world is described in John Lukacs, *Philadelphia: Patricians and Philistines, 1900–50* (New York: Farrar, Straus and Giroux, 1981); E. Digby Baltzell, *Philadelphia Gentlemen: The Making of a National Upper Class* (New York: Free Press, 1966), p. 343; and C. Williams, "Literary Clubland: The Franklin Inn Club of Philadelphia," *Bookman* 21 (1905): 576–80.

7. Poster for Founders' Week pageant, Ellis Paxson Oberholtzer (EPO) Papers, Historical Society of Pennsylvania, Philadelphia (hereafter cited as EPO Papers). At the time of my research (1982), Oberholtzer's papers were not yet

processed and assigned box and folder numbers. The materials I examined were in three boxes labeled "Founders Week"; one box labeled "Historical Pageant Assn."; three boxes labeled "1900–06," "1907–11," and "1912–26"; and ten boxes labeled "Historical Pageant 1912."

In July 1907 Oberholtzer received a letter from his fellow Franklin Inn Club member W. W. Keen describing English historical pageants he had seen and how Philadelphia could scoop the nation by presenting one. Keen to EPO, July 25, 1907, EPO Papers.

8. EPO to Violet Oakley, July 14, 1908, EPO Papers. Floats are described in detail in *The Book of the Pageant* (Philadelphia: George Jacobs, 1908).

9. EPO to A. G. Hetherington, July 31, 1908, EPO Papers.

10. EPO to Mr. Ames, August 31, 1908, EPO Papers.

11. EPO to George W. B. Hicks, June 25, 1908, EPO to Dr. C. J. Hexamer, September 9, 1908, and EPO to White Cloud, July 28, 1908, all EPO Papers. Oberholtzer wanted Chinese for a historical scene representing Philadelphia's China trade of the 1790s.

12. EPO to George W. B. Hicks, June 25, 1908, EPO Papers; *Official Programme, Musical-Historical Drama "Philadelphia"* (October 5–10), in Collection of Prints and Photographs Department, Free Library of Philadelphia; "Outdoor Drama Stirs Spectators," *Philadelphia Inquirer*, October 4, 1908, p. 26; Hicks to EPO (July 20, 1908), EPO to Hetherington (August 25, 1908), EPO to Henry Kabierske (September 10, 1908), EPO Papers.

13. EPO to Mayor John E. Reyburn, October 21, 1908, EPO Papers.

14. John Dewey, "The School as Social Center," *Elementary School Teacher* 3 (1902): 84–85; E. B. DeGroot, General Director, Fieldhouses and Playgrounds, *Annual Report of the [Chicago] South Park Commissioners, 1910*, quoted in Clarence Rainwater, *The Play Movement in the United States* (Chicago: University of Chicago Press, 1921), p. 102. Also see Michael M. Davis, *The Exploitation of Pleasure: A Study of Commercial Recreation in New York City* (New York: Russell Sage Foundation, 1911), and Lillian Betts, "Tenement-House Life and Recreation," *Outlook* 61 (February 11, 1899): 365.

Jane Addams, *The Spirit of Youth and the City Streets* (New York: Macmillan, 1910), p. 103. The social workers' philosophy is described as "counter-attraction" in Paul Boyer, *Urban Masses and Moral Order in America, 1820–1920* (Cambridge: Harvard University Press, 1978).

15. George Romanes, "The Science and Philosophy of Recreation," *Popular Science Monthly* 15 (October 1879): 772; Charles Horton Cooley, *Social Organization* (New York: Scribner's, 1909), pp. 23–31. Also see Marshall J. Cohen, *Self and Society: Charles Horton Cooley and the Idea of the Social Self in American Thought* (New York: Garland Publishing, 1982). Among the better general discussions of the social and psychological ideas behind the playground movement are Bernard Mergen, "The Discovery of Children's Play," *American Quarterly* 27 (October 1975): 399–420; Dominick Cavallo, *Muscles and Morals: Organized Playgrounds and Urban Reform, 1850–1920* (Philadelphia: University of Pennsylvania Press, 1981); and Lawrence Finfer, "Leisure as Social Work in the Urban Community: The Progressive Recreation Movement, 1890–1910" (Ph.D. dissertation, University of Michigan, 1974). Dorothy Ross discusses the

child-study movement in detail in G. Stanley Hall: The Psychologist as Prophet (Chicago: University of Chicago Press, 1972), pp. 279–308. For a thorough discussion of play as training for adulthood by a leader of the playground movement in Boston, and later nationally, see Joseph Lee, Play in Education (New York: Macmillan, 1916).

16. E. A. Ross, "The Mob Mind," Popular Science Monthly 51 (July 1897): 397. A brief but perceptive profile of Ross's intellectual career appears in R. Jackson Wilson, In Quest of Community: Social Philosophy in the United States, 1860–1920 (New York: John Wiley and Sons, 1968), pp. 87–113.

Luther H. Gulick, "Play and Democracy," Charities and the Commons 18 (August 3, 1907): 484. For more on the problem of interdependence and scale in social thought at the turn of the twentieth century, see Thomas Haskell, The Emergence of Professional Social Science: The American Social Science Association and the Nineteenth-Century Crisis of Authority (Urbana: University of Illinois Press, 1977), and Jean Quandt, From the Small Town to the Great Community: The Social Thought of Progressive Intellectuals (New Brunswick, N.J.: Rutgers University Press, 1970).

17. John Dewey, The School and Society (1899; reprint, Chicago: University of Chicago Press, 1974), p. 117. A more complete analysis of the ideas and institutionalization of progressive education appears in Lawrence A. Cremin, The Transformation of the School: Progressivism in American Education, 1876–1957 (New York: Knopf, 1961; reprint, Vintage, 1964); George Ellsworth Johnson, Education by Plays and Games (New York: Ginn and Company, 1907).

18. The best overview of the organization of the national movement to reform public recreation and children's play are Rainwater, Play Movement in the United States, and Richard Knapp, "Play for America: The National Recreation Association, 1906–50" (Ph.D. dissertation, Duke University, 1971), published serially in Parks and Recreation magazine, August 1972 et seq. On the play movement's efforts to gain professional status for its members as well as reform recreation, see Roy Lubove, The Professional Altruist: The Emergence of Social Work as a Career (New York: Atheneum, 1972). On the role of the working class in movements for more playgrounds, see Roy Rosenzweig, Eight Hours for What We Will: Workers and Leisure in an Industrial City, 1870–1920 (New York: Cambridge University Press, 1983). Rosenzweig demonstrates that in Worcester, Mass., residents of working-class neighborhoods allied with movements that promised to provide them with more recreational space, but did not necessarily accept those movements' prescriptions for how they should use the space. The playground movement offers a prime example of the type of urban reform in the Progressive Era that depended on mobilizing working-class support for its success, as described in John Buenker, Urban Liberalism and Progressive Reform (New York: Scribner's, 1973).

19. G. Stanley Hall, "The Value of Dancing and Pantomime," in Educational Problems (New York: D. Appleton, 1911), p. 61.

20. William Orr, "An American Holiday," Atlantic Monthly 103 (June 1909): 785; "Fourth of July" box, WCL Papers. Also see Wallace Evan Davies, Patriotism on Parade: The Story of Veterans and Hereditary Organizations in America, 1783–1900 (Cambridge: Harvard University Press, 1955), p. 218; John M.

Glenn, Lillian Brandt, and F. Emerson Andrews, *The Russell Sage Foundation, 1907–46* (New York: Russell Sage Foundation, 1947), pp. 73–75; and Raymond W. Smilor, "Creating a National Festival: The Campaign for a Safe and Sane Fourth, 1903–16," *Journal of American Culture* 2 (1979): 611–22.

21. Orr, "American Holiday," p. 786; "Report of the Committee on Festivals," read before the Fourth Annual Congress of the Playground Association of America, June 10, 1910, published in *Playground* 4 (February 1911): 372; Luther H. Gulick, "Folk and National Dances," in *Proceedings of the Second Annual Playground Association of America Conference* (Philadelphia: William Fell, 1908), p. 437.

22. Orr, "American Holiday," p. 788.

23. Luther H. Gulick, *The Healthful Art of Dancing* (New York: Doubleday, Page, and Co., 1910), p. 104. Gulick initiated a Girls Branch of the New York City Public Schools Athletic League in 1905 to provide additional recreational opportunities. Gulick, the son of missionaries, first got interested in physical education through the YMCA. He turned his attention to private, then public schools at the turn of the century before joining the Russell Sage Foundation full-time as head of its Child Hygiene Department. See Ethel Dorgan, *Luther Halsey Gulick, 1865–1918* (New York: Teachers College, Columbia University, 1934).

24. Hall, "Value of Dancing and Pantomime," p. 56. Hall praised "the pure lightheartedness of the Old English dances in the day of Sir Roger deCoverly, until Puritanism called the way to heaven too narrow for men to dance in." Ibid., p. 57; Addams, *Spirit of Youth*, pp. 13, 99.

25. Charles A. McMurry, *Special Method in History: A Complete Outline of a Course of Study in History for the Grades Below the High School* (New York: Macmillan, 1903), p. 13. McMurry's interest in teaching history through play reflected his belief in Herbartian theory that teachers above all should select educational materials and techniques that interest the child. See Dorothy McMurry, *Herbartian Contributions to History Instruction in American Elementary Schools* (New York: Teachers College, Columbia University Contributions to Education No. 920, 1946).

26. Eugene C. Gibney, "The Mission of Our Brooklyn Playgrounds," in *An Historical Pageant: Century Steps in Brooklyn's Progress*, official program, August 18, 1914. On the use of history outside of schools, see "Local History and the Civic Renaissance in New York," *American Monthly Review of Reviews* 16 (October 1897): 446–49. On Scouting's use of the reenactment of pioneer and Indian lore as a form of moral training, see David I. Macleod, *Building Character in the American Boy: The Boy Scouts, the YMCA, and Their Forerunners, 1870–1920* (Madison: University of Wisconsin Press, 1983).

27. Charles A. McMurry, *Special Method in History*, pp. 3, 6, 9, 17. Also see John Dewey, "The Aim of History in Elementary Education," in *The School and Society*, pp. 150–59. An account of Dewey's efforts to promote local history appears in Katherine Camp Mayhew and Anna Camp Edwards, "Local History," in *The Dewey School: The Laboratory School of the University of Chicago, 1896–1903* (1936; reprint, New York: Atherton, 1966), pp. 141–65. For an extremely perceptive analysis of the merging of the "New History" and the

"New Education" for citizenship, see Thomas M. Jacklin, "Progressives and the Usable Past: Historical Themes in the Literature of American Reform, 1880–1915" (Ph.D. dissertation, Johns Hopkins University, 1981).

28. See, for example, Elizabeth Burchenal, *Folk Dances and Singing Games* (1909; reprint, New York: Schirmer, 1933). Burchenal, born in 1877, taught folk dancing in the New York City public schools and was the first chair of the Playground Association of America's Folk Dance Committee. She became a major organizer of folk festivals in the 1920s and in 1928 founded the Folk Art Center in New York City as a national clearinghouse for folk art exhibitions from the United States and abroad. I am grateful to Jane S. Becker for information on Burchenal's later career.

29. Percival Chubb, *Festivals and Plays* (New York: Harper and Brothers, 1912), p. 126. For examples of model children's programs and skits, see Mary Master Needham, *Folk Festivals: Their Growth and How to Give Them* (New York: B. W. Heubsch, 1912), and Constance D'Arcy MacKay, *Patriotic Plays and Pageants for Young People* (New York: Henry Holt, 1912). One discussion of the utility of Duncan's art for the playground appears in Gulick, *Healthful Art of Dancing*, p. 224. Also see Lucia Gale Barber, "The Significance of the Present Dance Movement," *New England Magazine* (November 1909): 272–79. The connections between progressive education and modern dance are analyzed in Nancy Lee Ruyter, *Reformers and Visionaries: The Americanization of the Art of Dance* (New York: Dance Horizons, 1979).

30. The Playground Association of America held Play Congresses in Chicago in June 1907, in New York City in September 1908, in Pittsburgh in May 1909, and in Rochester in June 1910. See the *Proceedings* of the Congresses and their description in *Playground* magazine. Also see Ida Tarbell, "An Old World Fête in Industrial America," *Charities and the Commons* 20 (August 1, 1908): 546–48; "The Festival of Play and Folk Dance," *Outlook* 90 (September 28, 1908): 145–46; and three articles by Graham R. Taylor: "The Chicago Play Festival," *Charities and the Commons* 20 (August 1, 1908): 539–45, "A Play Festival," *Outlook* 92 (May 29, 1909): 252–53, and "Ten Thousand at Play," *Survey* 22 (June 5, 1909): 365–73.

31. See Jeannette E. C. Lincoln, "Selected National Folk Dances Adapted for Maypole Festivals," in *The Festival Book* (New York: A. S. Barnes, 1912), and David Glassberg, "Restoring a 'Forgotten Childhood': American Play and the Progressive Era's Elizabethan Past," *American Quarterly* 32 (Fall 1980): 351–68.

32. Mary Fanton Roberts, "The Value of Outdoor Plays to America," *Craftsman* 16 (August 1909): 494; Mary Master Needham, "The Fiesta in America," *Outlook* 99 (October 28, 1911): 528; "Festival Week: Festival and Pageant of Nations," New York City, 1914, press release, New York Public Library Theatre Collection, for Bohn quotation; Luther H. Gulick, "Folk and National Dances," in *Proceedings of the Second Annual Playground Asssociation of America Conference*, p. 438; Gulick, *Healthful Art of Dancing*, p. 197.

33. John L. Gillin, "The Sociology of Recreation," *American Journal of Sociology* 19 (May 1914): 832; Luther H. Gulick, "The New and More Glorious Fourth," *World's Work* 18 (July 1909): 11787.

34. Chubb, *Festivals and Plays*, p. 127; Mari R. Hofer, "The Folk Game and

Festival," *Proceedings of the First Annual Playground Congress* (1907), p. 88. The reminder that the folk dance represented a selective revival of tradition for immigrants as well as the native born appears in John Bodnar, *The Transplanted* (Bloomington: Indiana University Press, 1985).

35. Orr, "American Holiday," p. 788; E. A. Ross, "The Mob Mind," p. 397.

36. Lee F. Hamner to John Bradford of Pensacola, Fla., March 16, 1911, WCL Papers; "Tentative Report of the [Festivals] Committee," delivered May 1909 at the PAA Congress in Pittsburgh and published in *Proceedings of the Third Annual Playground Congress* (Philadelphia: William Fell, 1909), p. 444; E. B. Mero, "The Holiday as a Builder of Citizenship," *Playground* 8 (June 1914): 102.

37. Orr, "American Holiday," p. 783. For other descriptions of the Springfield celebration, see Luther H. Gulick, "The Vacant Fourth," *Survey* 22 (July 3, 1909): 482–85, and "Glorious, if Damp," *Springfield Republican*, July 5, 1908, pp. 1, 4, 6.

Mary Vida Clark, "An International Fourth of July," *Charities and the Commons* 20 (July 11, 1908): 469–70; Orr, "American Holiday," p. 789.

38. On the progressive reformers' search for a "new citizenship" that transcended class and ethnic lines as a response to the social upheavals of the 1890s, see David Thelen, *The New Citizenship: The Origins of Progressivism in Wisconsin, 1885–1900* (Columbia: University of Missouri Press, 1972).

39. Lee F. Hamner, *How the 'Fourth' Was Celebrated in 1911: Facts Gathered from Special Reports* (New York: Russell Sage Foundation Department of Child Hygiene Pamphlet No. 105, 1912?), p. 1; "The Fourth of July in Two Cities," *American Monthly Magazine* 37 (August 1910): 137. On the impact of the Safe and Sane movement in Worcester, see Rosenzweig, *Eight Hours for What We Will*, pp. 162–67.

40. *Hudson-Fulton Celebration, 1909*, ed. Edward Hagaman Hall (Albany: J. B. Lyon Co., 1910); "The Historic Pageant," *St. Louis Republic*, October 9, 1909, p. 8; Maurice Anderson, "San Francisco Discovers Portola," *World Today* (December 1909): 1320–23. Charles Ware declared in 1909: "The modern carnival, as the progressive businessman has defined and engineered it, is not entirely an amusement institution. It is a commercial project, an industrial tonic, an educational exhibit. The twentieth century city must advertise. This is a new thought, but it has already become a municipal axiom. It must attract new population, new business, new wealth. It must show what it has done, what it can do. It must prove its attractions as a home and a business center. Reduced to bold facts, the carnival is one form of modern civic advertising." Ware, "King Wamba Rules Toledo," *World Today* (October 1909): 1099.

41. Gustav Stickley, "The People and the Pageant," *Craftsman* 17 (1909): 223, 225.

42. Paul Pinkerton Foster, "Reviving the Elizabethan Pageant," *World Today* 15 (August 1908): 833; "Revival of Pageantry," *Dial* 47 (October 16, 1909): 271–72; Needham, *Folk Festivals*, p. 26; Frances Maule Bjorkman, "A Nation Learning to Play," *World's Work* 18 (September 1909): 12045; "Pageants Better than Gunpowder," *Century* 58 (July 1910): 476.

Chapter 3. The Place Is the Hero

1. Langdon's father's missionary activity in Europe stemmed from his belief in the eventual reunion of the Protestant and Catholic churches. "Reverend William Chauncy Langdon," *Dictionary of American Biography* (New York: Charles Scribner's Sons, 1933), 10:589–90; "William Chauncy Langdon," obituary, *New York Tribune*, October 30, 1895; *Providence Journal*, October 30, 1895. Langdon mentioned being a pupil of J. Franklin Jameson in a letter to Mrs. Jessie Palmer Weber, Illinois Centennial Commission, November 20, 1916, William Chauncy Langdon (WCL) Papers, John Hay Library, Brown University, Providence, R.I. When I first encountered Langdon's papers (1979), they were not yet processed and many items were still in the possession of Margaret Langdon. Since then, the papers have been cataloged—beautifully, by Barbara Filipac—and Ms. Langdon has donated the materials I saw at her home to Brown University, where they form a supplement to the original Langdon collection. I have designated the materials I examined at Brown before they were assigned box and folder numbers "WCL Papers" and those I examined at Ms. Langdon's home, since donated to Brown, "WCL Papers, Supplement."

2. WCL to Luther H. Gulick, November 10, 1902, WCL Papers. Langdon recounted his early years in a letter to Homer Folks of the New York State Charities Aid Association, March 22, 1910, WCL Papers. Also see WCL to Arthur J. Baldwin, who was compiling a "Who's Who of [Cornell] '92," May 18, 1917, WCL Papers, Supplement.

3. For a discussion of the Citizens Union and New York City reform politics, see Gerald Kurland, *Seth Low: Reformer in an Urban and Industrial Age* (New York: Twayne Publishers, 1971).

WCL to Folks, March 22, 1910, WCL Papers; R. S. Simons, "A History of the Juvenile Street Cleaning League," report to John G. Woodbury, New York City Commissioner of Street-cleaning, February 21, 1903, WCL Papers.

4. William Chauncy Langdon, "Ideas for Civic Education from the Juvenile City League," address before American Civic Association, Cleveland, Ohio, October 4, 1904; later published in *The Chautauquan* (June 1906): 374 (ms. of address is in box 24, folder 1, WCL Papers).

5. Langdon's sister Florence remained in Alaska from 1904 to 1919. Gulick's career in the YMCA, heading the Pratt Institute, directing physical education for the New York City public schools, and helping found the Playground Association of America is described in Ethel J. Dorgan, *Luther Halsey Gulick, 1865–1918* (New York: Bureau of Publication, Teachers College, Columbia University, 1934). Langdon's background as a minister's son who entered a secular social service profession most nearly approximates the typical biographical profile of progressive social reformers advanced in Robert Crunden's *Ministers of Reform: The Progressives' Achievement in American Civilization, 1889–1920* (New York: Basic Books, 1982).

6. Miscellaneous correspondence between Langdon and various New York charities, 1910, WCL Papers.

7. WCL to Sherbourne (England) Pageant Committee, January 9, 1910, and

WCL to Parker, July 12 and 21, 1910, WCL Papers, Supplement; miscellaneous correspondence between Langdon and various civic celebration associations throughout the United States, 1910, WCL Papers.

8. WCL to Jameson, October 20 and 22, 1910, WCL Papers; "Bureau of American Pageantry," dummy pamphlet, WCL Papers, Supplement.

9. WCL to Braucher of Playground Association of America, September 24 and November 5, 1910, and Braucher to WCL, November 22, 1910, WCL Papers. Gulick helped form the PAA in 1906. The organization received Sage Foundation support from 1907 until 1910, when Gulick formed a separate Playground Committee for the foundation. See Richard Knapp, "Play for America: The National Recreation Association, 1906–50," *Parks and Recreation*, October 1972, pp. 20ff. Also see "PRAA History," manuscript in files of National Parks and Recreation Association, Arlington, Va.

WCL to Russell Sage Foundation President John M. Glenn, November 1910, and Gulick to WCL, October 6, 1910, WCL Papers; WCL to Andrew Carnegie, John D. Rockefeller, E. H. Harriman, et al., Fall 1910, WCL Papers. For more on the Westchester County pageant, which was directed by Violet Oakley, see *Book of Words: Pageant of Westchester County* (New York, 1909).

10. WCL to George Pierce Baker, October 6, 1910, WCL Papers.

11. Gulick founded the Girl's Branch of the Athletic League in 1905 while he directed physical education for the New York City schools. See Dorgan, *Luther Halsey Gulick*. Charlotte Farnsworth headed the Horace Mann School in New York City. Her husband pioneered in the teaching of folk songs in elementary schools and was a leading theorist in progressive education in music. See William Ronald Lee, "Education through Music: The Life and Work of Charles Hubert Farnsworth, 1859–1947" (Ph.D. dissertation, University of Kentucky, 1982). Charles Farnsworth's mother, Caroline, had attended Thetford Academy. The girls' camp was named "Hanoum" (Turkish for "Lady"), the town where Farnsworth had spent his childhood as the son of missionary parents.

WCL to Charlotte Farnsworth, December 6, 1910, WCL Papers. Also see correspondence between Charlotte Farnsworth and Langdon, November 1910, WCL Papers.

Charlotte Farnsworth to Mrs. Mary Slade, December 1910, WCL Papers. Mrs. Farnsworth paid for Langdon's train ticket to Thetford. WCL Diary, January 11, 1911, WCL Papers, Supplement.

12. John M. Glenn to WCL, January 16, 1911, box 26, folder 11, WCL Papers. Langdon's $2,500 grant from the foundation was supposed to have been matched by $2,000 that he raised himself from private philanthropists, and to have covered not only his Thetford work but also his "Bureau" activities. Langdon, however, never raised the matching funds, and the Sage Foundation ended up waiving the matching fund requirement, though refusing to give him the extra $2,000. Langdon, "Report of Work in Pageantry to the Russell Sage Foundation, January 1–May 10, 1911," WCL Papers, Supplement. Also see WCL Diary and his manuscript "History of the Thetford Pageant," WCL Papers.

13. The program of *The St. Gaudens Masque* appears in Percy MacKaye, *The*

Civic Theatre in Relation to the Redemption of Leisure (New York: Mitchell Kennerly, 1912), pp. 306–8; George P. Baker, *The Peterborough Pageant* (MacDowell Memorial Association, 1910); St. James Church, Woodstock, Vt., "Program, Back to the Past, Down to the Future," October 18, 1910, WCL Papers.

14. Charles Latham, Jr., *A Short History of Thetford, Vermont, 1761–1870* (Thetford Historical Society, 1972).

15. Ibid., p. 23.

16. "The Pageant of Thetford," January 6, 1911, WCL Papers, Supplement. Also see Langdon, "Report of Work," p. 2.

17. U.S. Commission on Country Life, *Report of the Commission on Country Life* (1909; reprint, New York: Sturgis and Walton, 1911), p. 23; Nathan Shaffer, "The Rural School," in *Proceedings of the Pennsylvania Rural Progress Association* (Williamsport, Pa.: Grit Press, 1912), p. 26. William L. Bowers pointedly argues that the Country Life movement's emphasis on modern organization helped break down the rural society it attempted to preserve. Bowers, *The Country Life Movement in America, 1900–1920* (Port Washington, N.Y.: Kennikat Press, 1974). Yet much of the movement's literature was devoted to preserving rural folk traditions as long as they did not obstruct other efforts to further economic progress. The U.S. Country Life Commission believed that festivals, fairs, and pageants helped broaden rural social life. In March 1911, former commission chair Liberty Hyde Bailey extolled the social value of presenting historical dramas acted by local talent and "grounded in the lives of the people in the community." Bailey, *The Country Life Movement in the United States* (1911; reprint, New York: Macmillan Co., 1919), p. 215.

18. WCL to U.S. Secretary of Agriculture, December 8, 1910, WCL Papers; miscellaneous correspondence, Langdon to various agricultural experts and to the Thetford Grange, February–April 1911, WCL Papers. See especially WCL to Grange Master Charles Cook in March 1911, cajoling that if Thetford residents could become sufficiently organized to ask for help, the federal government was now, but not for long, disposed to give it to them. Also see WCL Diary, March 27, 1911, and Langdon, "Report of Work," WCL Papers, Supplement.

19. The actual founding of the Campfire Girls dates from a dinner attended by Langdon, Mrs. Farnsworth, and Gulick on March 22, 1911. All three remained active in the early years of the organization. As well as giving the group its name, Langdon also devised many of its ceremonies. See Helen Buckler, Mary F. Fiedler, and Martha F. Allen, *Wo-He-Lo: The Story of the Campfire Girls, 1910–1960* (New York: Holt, Rinehart and Winston, 1961), pp. 8–18; also see WCL Diary, March 22, 1911, WCL Papers, Supplement.

20. William Chauncy Langdon, "The Pageant of Thetford," *The Vermonter* 16 (June–July 1911): 192.

21. William Chauncy Langdon, "Pageantry as Public Recreation," manuscript of an address given April 10, 1912, at the Springfield, Mass., Recreation Conference, pp. 8, 10, WCL Papers; William Chauncy Langdon, "The Prophetic Pageant," manuscript for *Suburban Life*, 1913, box 24, folder 5, WCL Papers.

22. Langdon stated this definition over and over in his writings, beginning

with his dummy pamphlet, "Bureau of American Pageantry," WCL Papers, Supplement.

23. William Chauncy Langdon, "The Pageant Grounds and Their Technical Requirements," *American Pageant Association (APA) Bulletin*, no. 11, December 1, 1914.

24. William Chauncy Langdon, "The Pageant in America," *American Monthly Magazine* 38 (March 1911): 102–3; dummy pamphlet, "Bureau of American Pageantry," WCL Papers, Supplement; WCL to Walter Hines Page, December 25, 1911, WCL Papers. Langdon told Lady Gregory that American pageantry and the Irish theater were "sister movements." WCL to Lady Gregory, December 17, 1911, WCL Papers.

25. "Originality in Pageant Work," manuscript, February 1915, published as *APA Bulletin*, no. 40, September 15, 1916, WCL Papers.

26. Langdon, "The Prophetic Pageant," p. 5.

27. William Chauncy Langdon, "The Creative Power of Pageantry," *Atlantic Educational Journal* (December 1912): 15–17; Langdon, "Report of Work," WCL Papers, Supplement.

28. William Chauncy Langdon, "A Fundamental Principle in Civic Education," manuscript (1906?), WCL Papers.

29. Boston—1915, "Program, Cave Life to City Life: The Pageant of a Perfect City," November 10–12, 1910. Also see William Chauncy Langdon, "The Pageant of the Perfect City," *Playground* 5 (April 1911): 2–16, and Frank Chocteau Brown, "Symbolism in the Pageant of the Future," *Atlantic Educational Journal* (May 1914): 343–47.

30. William Chauncy Langdon, "The Pageant in America," book manuscript, never published, WCL Papers.

31. Roosevelt to WCL, June 24, 1911, WCL Papers. The letter read:

My Dear Mr. Langdon,
   I cordially wish you well, and am much pleased to learn that the people of the town of Thetford are doing all they can to develop their resources under the direction of the University of Vermont, and of the United States Department of Agriculture. What is necessary is to endeavor to take advantage of the American power of individual initiative, by uniting all the people of the town together in a spirit of absolute cooperation, a cooperation which shall be made efficient in large part by getting all possible benefit out of the agricultural experts from Burlington and Washington.
   Very sincerely yours
   [signed] Theodore Roosevelt

32. Langdon describes local opposition to pageants in a letter to Nelson H. Porter, March 13, 1911, Thetford Historical Society.

33. William Chauncy Langdon, "Pageant of Thetford, Historical Preparation," January 10, 1911, and WCL to Slade, February 1, 1911, WCL Papers. Langdon visited Thetford three times: initially to secure the job in December 1910, again in April 1911 to persuade the Thetford Grange to invite the

outside agricultural experts, and finally from June through August 1911 to rehearse and direct the pageant.

34. Among the period's romantic-tone poems associated with Native Americans was Edward MacDowell's *Indian Suite for Orchestra* (1891–95). See Gilbert Chase, *America's Music: From the Pilgrims to the Present*, rev. 3d ed. (Urbana: University of Illinois Press, 1987), p. 346.

35. Langdon, "Report of Work," WCL Papers, Supplement. One biographical profile of Tanner concluded, "She is thoroughly intellectual, but, providentially, does not look it." "College Education Helps Dancer," *Boston Herald*, October 6, 1912.

36. Duncan gave abstract symbolic dancing its first widespread exposure, though her overt sensuality was shunned by her imitators. Aesthetic dancing, in fact, combined the idealistic art of the late nineteenth century with the expressive motion of Delsartism and the fantasy of spectacular ballet. For a brilliant discussion of how modern dance grew out of nineteenth-century precedents to become part of the progressive education curriculum, see Nancy Lee Ruyter, *Reformers and Visionaries: The Americanization of the Art of Dance* (New York: Dance Horizons, 1979). Also see Clare de Moriani, "Loie Fuller, the Fairy of Light," *Dance Index* 1 (March 1942): 40–51, and Lucia Gale Barber, "The Significance of the Present Dance Movement," *New England Magazine* (November 1909): 272–79.

37. Langdon's diary lists purchases of tickets to see Duncan perform. WCL Diary, WCL Papers, Supplement. Langdon entered his complaint about classical ballet's lack of civic value in March 16, 1911, after seeing Pavlova dance at the Metropolitan Opera House. He pointed to dramatic dancing's superiority to "evil possibilities of the current Barbary-Coast type of dances" in a letter to the executive committee of the St. Louis Pageant Drama Association, September 28, 1913, St. Louis Pageant Drama Association Papers, Missouri Historical Society, St. Louis.

38. Langdon, "Pageant of Thetford," *The Vermonter*, p. 192.

39. William Chauncy Langdon, *Book of Words: The Pageant of Thetford* (White River Junction, Vt.: Vermonter Press, 1911), p. 192.

40. William Chauncy Langdon, "The Pageant of Thetford," *Playground* 5 (December 1911): 309. It was in this article that Langdon explained the division of episodes into Thetford's "making," "development," "depletion," and "future."

41. Langdon, *Book of Words: Pageant of Thetford*, p. 57.

42. Ibid., p. 59.

43. Langdon, "Pageant of Thetford," *The Vermonter*, p. 194; Langdon, "The Pageant of Thetford: A Study of the Rural Problem in the Form of the New Community Drama," *Journal of American History* 6 (January–March 1912): 217.

44. Langdon, "Pageant of Thetford," *Journal of American History*, p. 230.

45. Langdon, "Pageantry as Public Recreation," p. 3.

46. William Chauncy Langdon, lecture notes for a course on pageantry given at the University of Illinois, 1918, WCL Papers.

47. Latham, *Short History of Thetford*, pp. 23–24.

48. Ibid., pp. 45–48.

49. Hal S. Barron, *Those Who Stayed Behind: Rural Society in Nineteenth Century New England* (New York: Cambridge University Press, 1984), pp. 98–99.

50. William Chauncy Langdon, "Pageant of Thetford," January 6, 1911, WCL Papers, Supplement. The same year as the Thetford pageant, the Vermont legislature established a separate Bureau of Publicity, relieving responsibility for promoting tourism from the railroads and the Board of Agriculture. See Andrea Rebek, "The Selling of Vermont: From Agriculture to Tourism, 1860–1910," *Vermont History* 44 (Winter 1976): 14–27. On the commercial importance of urban dwellers believing that the rural areas they visited remained unspoiled, pastoral landscapes, see Peter J. Schmitt, *Back to Nature: The Arcadian Myth in Urban America* (New York: Oxford University Press, 1969).

51. The Campbells had been funded by the Sage Foundation since 1908. Langdon corresponded with them about their interests in mountain folklore and later, as pageant-master for the state of Indiana in 1916, explicitly identified his research with that of this early generation of American folklorists. Through Langdon, Olive Dame Campbell met Cecil Sharp, her collaborator on *English Folk Songs of the Southern Appalachians* (1917). Charles Farnsworth also collaborated with Sharp on a collection of *Folk Songs, Chanteys, and Singing Games* (1916). For more on the Sage Foundation and the Campbells, see David E. Whisnant, *All That Is Native and Fine: The Politics of Culture in an American Region* (Chapel Hill: University of North Carolina Press, 1983), and Henry D. Shapiro, *Appalachia on Our Mind: The Southern Mountains and Mountaineers in the American Consciousness, 1870–1920* (Chapel Hill: University of North Carolina Press, 1978).

52. Langdon received $275 as payment of his one-third share of pageant profits. WCL Papers. Estimates of pageant attendance based on the Bradford (Vt.) *United Opinion*, August 18, 1911, and on Reverend and Mrs. William Slade, "The Pageant of Thetford," *The Vermonter* 17 (March 1912): 475–90.

53. Bradford *United Opinion*, July 21 and August 4, 1911; Rutland *Daily Herald*, August 10, 1911.

54. Latham, *Short History of Thetford*, p. 23.

55. Slade to WCL, December 8, 1930; Minutes, Thetford Pageant Committee, Thetford Historical Society. In 1912, the Campfire Girls held a summer festival in Thetford. In 1914, the local summer camps staged a new pageant, "Drudgery Transformed," WCL Papers. Langdon attended a tenth anniversary cast reunion in 1921. In 1937, the town staged Langdon's "Pageant of the Church in Thetford," a church service in historical dress, which also incorporated music from the pageant of 1911. WCL Papers, Supplement. Thetford today appears prosperous. With Interstate 91 linking the town with the other Connecticut River Valley towns and Hanover, N.H., only twenty minutes away, Thetford now faces problems caused by rapid population growth rather than depletion. In 1980, its population was 2,188, a 54 percent increase over 1970 and the largest in the town's history.

56. WCL to John M. Glenn (November 1911), WCL to M. L. Hanson, concert promoter (September 19, 1911), and WCL to Louis Napoleon Parker, (September 22, 1911), all WCL Papers.

57. Langdon wrote articles on the Thetford pageant for *Playground* maga-

zine, *The Vermonter*, the *National Municipal Review*, and the *Journal of American History*.

58. Among the schools that taught pageantry as part of their extension programs in the 1910s were Cornell and the universities of Illinois, Indiana, Wisconsin, Massachusetts, North Dakota, and North Carolina.

59. John M. Glenn and Lillian Brandt, *The Russell Sage Foundation, 1907–46* (New York: Russell Sage, 1947), p. 75. The Sage Foundation made Langdon a guaranteed loan of $3,000, but he had to forfeit all pageant fees except $600. WCL Diary, November 27, 1911, and Langdon, "Report of Work," WCL Papers, Supplement. Langdon's model July Fourth pageant for the foundation included not only a realistic dramatization of the signing of the Declaration of Independence, but also a "future" scene, dated 1912, depicting "The Struggle for a Better National Life." Langdon, *The Celebration of the Fourth of July by Means of Pageantry* (New York: Russell Sage Foundation, 1912), p. 11.

60. William Chauncy Langdon, "The Pageant of St. Johnsbury: Pageantry as a Constructive Force in Community Betterment," *American City* 8 (May 1913): 481–87. Also see Langdon's *Book of Words: The Pageant of St. Johnsbury* (St. Johnsbury, Vt.: Caledonian Press, 1912).

Langdon, *Book of Words: The Pageant of Meriden, New Hampshire* (Hanover, N.H.: Dartmouth Press, 1913). Also see Langdon's "Pageant of Meriden, N.H.: Education in the New Country Life," *American City* 10 (April 1914): 355–61.

Langdon, *Book of Words: The Pageant of Darien, Connecticut* (New York: Clover Press, 1913). Also see *Darien, 1641–1820–1970: Historical Sketches* (Essex, Conn.: Pequot Press, 1970).

Langdon, *Book of Words: The Pageant of Cape Cod* (Boston: Blanchard Printing Co., 1914). Also see Boston *Sunday Globe*, August 9, 1914, p. 53. The Amherst pageant, planned to commemorate the fiftieth anniversary of the establishment of Massachusetts Agricultural College in 1917, was postponed when the United States entered World War I; it was never held after the war. See Langdon, "The Fiftieth Anniversary Pageant," *Massachusetts Agricultural College Alumni Quarterly* 1 (April 1917): 2–7, and the correspondence between Langdon and the college, box 11, folder 142, Kenyon Butterfield Papers, University of Massachusetts Archives, Amherst.

61. WCL to George M. McCallum of Northampton, Mass., February 11, 1917, WCL Papers.

62. Langdon felt that pageants were best supported by ticket sales. Pageants subsidized by the government were apt to be political, and pageants subsidized by business were apt to be commercial advertising. Langdon, "The Financing of Pageants," manuscript, March 1, 1911, WCL Papers.

63. Farwell (1872–1952) supervised municipal concerts for the New York City Department of Recreation. His special interest was American folk music. In 1910, he founded the Wa-Wan Press to publish American composers and "Indian," "Negro," "Cowboy," and "Spanish-American" music. Farwell's own compositions, such as the "Navaho War Dance," featured Native American folk tunes in a romantic, symphonic setting.

64. Langdon, *Book of Words: Pageant of St. Johnsbury*; Costume book, WCL Papers, Supplement.

65. William Chauncy Langdon, "Originality of Pageant Work," *APA Bulletin*, no. 40, September 15, 1916; Langdon, "Pageant of Thetford," *Journal of American History*, p. 221.

Chapter 4. Community Development Is the Plot

1. John Collier quoted in *American Pageant Association (APA) Bulletin*, no. 1, May 15, 1913. Collier's words originally appeared in the program for a pageant of Irish history held in New York City, May 7–8, 1913.

Walter Hines Page to William Chauncy Langdon, December 2, 1910, William Chauncy Langdon (WCL) Papers, Harris Collection, John Hay Library, Brown University, Providence, R.I. (hereafter cited as WCL Papers; see Chapter 3, n. 1); Adelia B. Beard, "The American Pageant," *American Homes and Gardens* 9 (July 1912): 239. Lotta A. Clark described G. Stanley Hall's rapture sitting cross-legged on the grass in the front row watching her Worcester, Mass., pageant in 1913. Clark to WCL, WCL Papers. Ida Tarbell served on the advisory committee for Constance D'Arcy MacKay's Portland, Maine, pageant in 1913. Official program, May 27, 1913, Percy MacKaye (PMK) Papers, Baker Library, Dartmouth College, Hanover, N.H. (hereafter cited as PMK Papers).

Booth Tarkington, "Penrod and the Pageant," *Everybody's Magazine* 28 (June 1913): 738–51.

2. On Bryn Mawr, see "The Spectator," *Outlook* 95 (May 21, 1910): 108–12; on Sing Sing, see *New York Times*, September 17, 1916. On the Christmas pageant in Los Angeles, see Paul Henry Dowling, "The Masque of the Nativity: A Triumph in Municipal Pageantry," *American City* 15 (December 1916): 649–57. On the Chautauqua circuit, see "Chautauqua Stars," *Everybody's Magazine* 33 (September 1915): 329. On *The Pageant of Darkness and Light*, see "The World in Chicago," *The Survey* 30 (July 19, 1913): 529–32. On issue-oriented pageants, see *Woman's Suffrage Procession*, official program, ed. Harriet Connor Brown (Washington, D.C.: Sudworth Co., 1913); *Pageant of the Paterson Strike* (New York: Success Press, 1913); Percy MacKaye, *Sanctuary, a Bird Masque* (New York: Stokes, 1914). The plot of the Fresno pageant concerns a princess, on her deathbed, who is revived by a handful of raisins. *The Princess and the Magic Raisins: A Pageant Presented by the People of Fresno in Honor of the Raisin*, official program, April 28, 1916.

3. "Industrial and Historical Pageant Corporation," flyer, PMK Papers; Van Horn and Son, "Why Not Produce a Historical Pageant in Connection with Your Celebration," flyer, box 21, folder 6, WCL Papers.

4. William Chauncy Langdon, marginal pencil notes on manuscript of "History of Thetford Pageant," WCL Papers; Hazel MacKaye, "The Promise of the Peterborough Pageant," *The Independent* 69 (September 8, 1910): 528; Ellis Paxson Oberholtzer, "Historical Pageants in England and America," *Century* 58 (July 1910): 422; "Reforming the Fourth," *Nation* 89 (July 15, 1909): 47; WCL to Ford, March 2, 1913, James Ford Papers, Harvard University Archives, Cambridge.

5. On the "promiscuous" use of the term "pageant," see Mary Porter Beegle,

"The Fundamental Essentials of Successful Pageantry," *APA Bulletin*, no. 7, September 15, 1914. On the need for the Russell Sage Foundation to help guide pageantry's "right development," see WCL to John M. Glenn of the Russell Sage Foundation, November 2, 1911, WCL Papers.

6. Frank Chocteau Brown, "The American Pageant Association: A New Force Working for the Future of Pageantry in America," *Drama* 9 (February 1913): 178, 181. Also see *APA Constitution*, 1913. The composition of the first APA board demonstrated the organization's focus in the northeastern United States as well as its mix of genteel intellectuals, progressive educators, and professional dramatists. The members were William Chauncy Langdon; Peter Dykema, Director of Music and Festivals, Ethical Culture School, New York City; Lotta Clark, high school history teacher, Boston; Howard Davenport, Somerville, Mass.; Arthur Farwell, Director of Municipal Concerts, New York City; Percy MacKaye, dramatist, Cambridge; Frank H. Brooks, St. Johnsbury, Vt.; Vesper George, artist, Boston; Ellis P. Oberholtzer, historian, Philadelphia; George F. Kunz, American Scenic and Historic Preservation Society, New York City; Frank Chocteau Brown, architect, Boston; Marian MacDowell, widow of composer Edward MacDowell, Peterborough, N.H.; Margaret M. Eager, pageant director, Deerfield, Mass.; Virginia Tanner, dancer, Dorchester, Mass.; George Pierce Baker, drama professor, Harvard; and Thomas Wood Stevens, art professor, Chicago.

7. APA, Annual Convention Programs, 1914–16, in Pageantry Ephemera, Library of Congress. For more on the M.I.T. pageant, held on June 13, 1916, to celebrate the school's move across the Charles River, see Massachusetts Institute of Technology, *The Technology Pageant and the Masque of Power* (Boston: George F. Ellis Co., 1916).

8. Retroactive listings appeared in five "Record Lists of American Pageants," *APA Bulletin*, no. 10, November 15, 1914; no. 12, December 14, 1914; no. 14, February 1, 1915; no. 22, July 15, 1915; and no. 24, August 15, 1915. Several institutions own complete sets of the *APA Bulletin*, including the Vassar College Library, Poughkeepsie, N.Y., from which I obtained my photocopy.

9. For a description of these courses, see Lotta A. Clark, "The Development of American Pageantry," *APA Bulletin*, no. 9, November 1, 1914; "Summer Instruction in Festivals and Pageants," *Atlantic Educational Journal* (May 1914): 346–47; and Charles H. Farnsworth, "The Festival Course at Dartmouth," *The Independent* 73 (August 15, 1912): 371–74.

10. Brown, "American Pageant Association," p. 184; APA, *Who's Who in Pageantry*, 1914; APA, flyer soliciting potential listings for *Who's Who in Pageantry*, included with *APA Bulletin*, n.d., Vassar College Library Collection, Poughkeepsie, N.Y.

11. Ralph Davol, *A Handbook of American Pageantry* (Taunton, Mass.: Davol Publishing Co., 1914), pp. 9–10; Percy MacKaye, *The Civic Theatre in Relation to the Redemption of Leisure* (New York: Mitchell Kennerly, 1912), p. 68. For more on women, see Martin S. Tackel, "Women and American Pageantry: 1908 to 1918" (Ph.D. dissertation, City University of New York, 1982).

12. Figures based on a letter from Frank Chocteau Brown to WCL, September 11, 1917, WCL Papers.

13. George Pierce Baker, "The Theater: An Enterprise or an Institution?" in St. Louis Pageant Drama Association (SLPDA), *Proceedings of the Conference of Cities* (St. Louis, 1914), p. 12. The academic dramatists' professional background is surveyed in Clifford Eugene Hamar, "College and University Theatre Instruction in the Early Twentieth Century," and Paul Kozelka, "Dramatists in the High School, 1900–25," both in *History of Speech Education in America: Background Studies*, ed. Karl R. Wallace (New York: Appleton-Century Crofts, 1954), pp. 572–94 and 595–616, respectively. Also see Wilson Payne Kinney, *George Pierce Baker and the American Theatre* (Cambridge: Harvard University Press, 1954), and the biographical sketch and reminiscences of Thomas Wood Stevens, the first head of the Drama Department at the Carnegie Institute, collected by Melvin White in *Educational Theatre Journal* 3 (December 1951): 280–321.

14. See Frank Chocteau Brown, "Pageantry as a Means of Improving American Standards of Dramatic Art," *APA Bulletin*, no. 45, July 15, 1917. Brown, an architect, was active in both the APA and the Drama League of America. Also see Mrs. A. Starr Best, "The Drama League of America," *Drama* 4 (February 1914): 135–50. Head of the Drama League, Best declared: "We should never have clean, wholesome, clever, worthwhile drama until we secure an educated, awakened audience which should support and demand it." Best, *The Drama League of America: Its Inception, Purposes, Wonderful Growth, and Future* (New York: Doubleday, Page, and Co., 1914), pp. 2–3.

15. Drama League of America, *Proceedings of the First Drama League of America Annual Convention*, 1911, p. 3; Hazel MacKaye, "The Pageant's Place in the Life of the People," in Drama League of America, *Report of the Third Annual Convention* (Chicago: Rogerson Press, 1913), pp. 77–78.

16. Thomas H. Dickinson, *The Case of American Drama* (New York: Houghton-Mifflin, 1915), pp. 197, 163–64, 180; Baker quoted in Kinney, *George Pierce Baker*, p. 143. For a contemporary view of how Yeats's Abbey Theatre in Ireland and Wagnerian opera festivals in Germany could serve as models for a folk theater in America, see Percy MacKaye, *Yankee Fantasies* (New York: Duffield and Co., 1912), p. xi. As early as 1903, Romain Rolland suggested that each French town perform dramatic versions of local and national history, and he wrote *The Fourteenth of July* as a model. His colleague Firmin Gémier directed the production of *The Fourteenth of July*, as well as a festival in Vaud, Switzerland, where a cast of 2,400 acted out episodes from local history from the Middle Ages to the present. See Oscar G. Brockett and Robert R. Findlay, *Century of Innovation: A History of European and American Theatre and Drama since 1870* (Englewood Cliffs, N.J.: Prentice-Hall, 1973), pp. 224–27. For more on the connections between folk drama and nationalism in Europe at the turn of the twentieth century, see George L. Mosse, *The Nationalization of the Masses: Political Symbolism and Mass Movements in Germany from the Napoleonic Wars through the Third Reich* (New York: New American Library, 1975). On the connection between the arts and crafts movement and nationalism in Europe, see Carl Schorske, "The Quest for the Grail: Wagner and Morris," in *The Critical Spirit: Essays in Honor of Herbert Marcuse*, ed. Kurt Wolff and Barrington Moore, Jr. (Boston: Beacon Press, 1967), pp. 216–32.

17. Dickinson, *The Case of American Drama*, p. 70; "The Rise of the Curtain," *Playbook* 1 (April 1913): 3; "The Pageant," *Playbook* 2 (September 1914): 5; and *The Case of American Drama*, p. 205.

18. Randolph Bourne, "Pageantry and Social Art," in *The Radical Will: Selected Writings, 1911–18*, ed. Olaf Hansen (New York: Urizen Books, 1977), pp. 515–19.

19. Farwell described his civic activities and beliefs in "The Democratization of Music," *Current Literature* 49 (1910): 317–19. Also see Edward Waters, "The Wa-Wan Press: An Adventure in Musical Idealism," in *A Birthday Offering to Carl Engel*, ed. Gustave Reese (New York: G. Schirmer, 1943), pp. 214–33; Gilbert Chase, "The Wa-Wan Press: A Chapter in American Enterprise," in *The Wa-Wan Press, 1901–11*, ed. Vera Brodsky Lawrence (New York: Arno Press and New York Times, 1970), pp. ix–xix; and Edgar Lee Kirk, "Toward American Music: A Study of the Life and Music of Arthur George Farwell" (Ph.D. dissertation, Eastman School of Music, 1958). Farwell's four-part series on ragtime for *Musical America*, vol. 16, consisted of "The Popular Song Bugaboo" (July 6, 1912), p. 2; "The Popular Song Bugaboo: No. 2" (July 27, 1912), p. 2; "Apaches, Mollycoddles, and Highbrows" (August 17, 1912), p. 2; and "Where Professors and Socialists Fail to Understand Music" (August 31, 1912), pp. 26–27. It was summarized in "The Ethics of Ragtime," *Literary Digest* (August 10, 1912), p. 225. Edward Berlin analyzes the debate over ragtime in *Ragtime: A Musical and Cultural History* (Berkeley: University of California Press, 1980).

20. Margaret MacLaren Eager, "The Building of the Pageant," *APA Bulletin*, no. 25, September 9, 1915; *Official Program, Pageant of Newburgh-on-Hudson* (Newburgh, N.Y.: News Co., 1915); Clara Fitch, "Suggestions for Year of American Pageantry," *Drama League Monthly* 1 (October 1916): 157.

21. Katherine Lord, "To Give a Pageant in a Small Town," *Ladies Home Journal* 30 (February 1913): 24.

22. Eager, "The Building of the Pageant."

23. The suggestion that Italians made good "Indians" appeared in Myra Emmons, "Pageantry for Children," *Outlook* 98 (July 1911): 662.

24. Virginia Tanner, "The Dances of American Pageantry: Realistic," *APA Bulletin*, no. 64, November 1, 1919.

25. William Chauncy Langdon, "The Financing of Pageants," typescript dated March 1, 1911, WCL Papers; "Poor Man Will Pay for Jubilee," *Norristown Register*, March 28, 1912. The Norristown Borough government paid $1,140 of the total $2,700 spent. Theodore Heysham, *Norristown, 1812–1912* (Norristown, Pa.: Norristown Herald, 1913), pp. 62–63. For more on the Philadelphia historical pageant of 1912, see David Glassberg, "Public Ritual and Cultural Hierarchy: Philadelphia's Civic Celebrations at the Turn of the Twentieth Century," *Pennsylvania Magazine of History and Biography* 107 (July 1983): 421–48.

26. Mary Porter Beegle and Jack Randall Crawford, *Community Drama and Pageantry* (New Haven: Yale University Press, 1916), p. 256; APA, "Graphic Chart of Pageant Organization Scheme," supplement to *APA Bulletin*, no. 11, December 1, 1914.

27. Florence Magill Wallace, *Pageant-Building* (Springfield, Ill.: Schnepp

and Barnes, 1918), p. 18; Robert Withington, "A Manual of Pageantry," *Indiana University Bulletin*, no. 13 (June 15, 1915): 15; Ethel T. Rockwell, "Historical Pageantry: A Treatise and a Bibliography," *State Historical Society of Wisconsin Bulletin of Information* 84 (July 1916): 10. For a model budget, see Virginia Tanner, *The Pageant of the Little Town of X*, Massachusetts Civic League Leaflet, no. 10, 1914, p. 15.

28. Eager, "The Building of the Pageant"; Tanner, *Pageant of the Little Town of X*, p. 17. An elaborate scenario of children adopting lonely senior citizens in order to learn about the past for a historical pageant appears in Mary Master Needham, *Folk Festivals: Their Growth and How to Give Them* (New York: B. W. Heubsch, 1912), pp. 30–41.

29. Withington, "Manual of Pageantry," p. 11; Frank Chocteau Brown, "The Possibilities of the Pageant as Local Historian," *APA Bulletin*, no. 50, October 15, 1917.

30. WCL to SLPDA Executive Committee, September 28, 1913, in Executive Committee Folder, SLPDA Papers, Missouri Historical Society, St. Louis. A similar plea for dramatic continuity between historical episodes appears in Frank Chocteau Brown, "The Book of the Pageant and Its Development," *Drama* 4 (May 1915): 261–83.

Francis Howard Williams, "The Pageant as a Form of Dramatic Literature," *APA Bulletin*, no. 17, May 1, 1915; Thomas Wood Stevens, "The Spoken Word in Pageantry," *APA Bulletin*, no. 23, August 1, 1915; Arthur Farwell, "Pageant Music," *APA Bulletin*, no. 43, December 1, 1916; Mary Porter Beegle, "Pageant Dancing," *APA Bulletin*, no. 34, June 1, 1916.

31. Pageant-master Ellis P. Oberholtzer took an active role in the regulation for public benefit of motion pictures as well as historical pageantry. Between 1915 and 1921, he headed the Pennsylvania State Board of Motion Picture Censors and belonged to the Society for Visual Education, a national organization dedicated to using motion pictures for educational rather than commercial purposes. Myron Lounsbury, "Flashes of Lightning: The Moving Picture in the Progressive Era," *Journal of Popular Culture* 3 (1970): 769–97, surveys film criticism in the 1910s. Also see the progressive social workers' response to the motion picture in Lary May, *Screening Out the Past: The Birth of Mass Culture and the Motion Picture Industry* (New York: Oxford University Press, 1980); Robert Sklar, *Movie-Made America: A Social History of American Movies* (New York, 1975); and Garth Jowett, *Film: The Democratic Art* (Boston: Little Brown, 1976), pp. 74–107.

32. Thomas Wood Stevens, "The Making of a Dramatic Pageant," *Atlantic Educational Journal* (September 1912): 15. For examples of the music pageant-masters recommended to accompany each type of pageant scene, see Roland Holt, *A List of Music for Plays and Pageants* (New York: D. Appleton and Co., 1925). Holt was a leader of the New York City chapter of the Drama League of America and the husband of pageant director Constance D'Arcy MacKay.

33. William Chauncy Langdon, "The Pageant in America," unpublished manuscript, p. 19, WCL Papers; Ralph Davol, *A Handbook of American Pageantry* (Taunton, Mass.: Davol Publishing Co., 1914), p. 38; Frank Chocteau Brown, "Boston Sees the First American Civic Pageant," *Theatre* 13 (February 1911): 43–44. For the outdoor craze for hiking, eating, and camping at the

turn of the century, see Peter Schmitt, *Back to Nature: The Arcadian Myth in Urban America* (New York: Oxford University Press, 1969). On the importance of appearing "natural," see T. J. Jackson Lears, "From Salvation to Self-Realization: Advertising and the Therapeutic Roots of the Consumer Culture, 1880–1930," in *The Culture of Consumption: Critical Essays in American History, 1880–1980*, ed. Richard Wightman Fox and Lears (New York: Pantheon, 1983), pp. 1–38.

34. WCL to Percy MacKaye, February 26, 1914, PMK Papers.

35. Langdon, "The Pageant in America," p. 25; Davol, *Handbook of American Pageantry*, p. 38.

36. Beard, "The American Pageant," p. 239; Frank Chocteau Brown, "Symbolism in the Pageant of the Future," *Atlantic Educational Journal* (May 1914): 346. The manifesto of this transatlantic avant-garde dramatic movement was Edward Gordon Craig, *On the Art of the Theatre* (London: William Heinemann, 1911). Robert Edmond Jones's greatest acclaim came in the 1920s as the designer for many of Eugene O'Neill's productions. For more on Craig, Jones, and the international context of the new art drama, see Susan Valeria Harris Smith, *Masks in Modern Drama* (Berkeley: University of California Press, 1984), pp. 49–88.

37. Davol, *Handbook of American Pageantry*, p. 68; Thomas H. Dickinson, "The Pageant," *Playbook* 2 (September 1914): 28; Robert Withington, *English Pageantry: An Historical Outline*, 2 vols. (Cambridge: Harvard University Press, 1918), 2:296; Withington, "Manual of Pageantry," p. 11.

38. Complaints about the APA's inability to define the word "pageant" appear in Lotta Clark to WCL, November 29, 1916, WCL Papers; Frank Chocteau Brown to Ellis P. Oberholtzer, November 2, 1914, Ellis Paxson Oberholtzer (EPO) Papers, Historical Society of Pennsylvania, Philadelphia (hereafter cited as EPO Papers; see Chapter Two, n. 7). No less than eight different types of pageants are classified in Jack Randall Crawford, "Pageant Study Course #9," *Drama League Monthly* 1 (1916): 226–36. The APA eventually published a list of "tentative" definitions distinguishing among "pageant," "community drama," "masque," "festival," and "parade," but allowed that these boundaries could be crossed by those possessing "artistry and understanding." "A Set of Tentative Definitions of the Principal Types of Modern Community Celebrations," *APA Bulletin*, no. 53, December 1, 1917.

39. William Chauncy Langdon, "America, Like England, Has Become Pageant-Mad," *New York Times*, June 15, 1913, part 5, p. 5; Beegle and Crawford, *Community Drama and Pageantry*, pp. 11–12.

40. William Chauncy Langdon, *The Celebration of the Fourth of July by Means of Pageantry*, Russell Sage Foundation Department of Child Hygiene Publication, no. 114, 1912, p. 38; Langdon, "The Necessity for Originality in Pageant Work," *APA Bulletin*, no. 40, September 15, 1916; Davol, *Handbook of American Pageantry*, p. 127; George Pierce Baker, "What the Pageant Can Do for the Town," *Ladies Home Journal* 31 (April 1914): 44.

41. APA, "Graphic Time Analysis of Three Typical Pageant Plans," supplement to *APA Bulletin*, no. 19, June 1, 1915; Tanner, *Pageant of the Little Town of X*, p. 17; Eager, "The Building of the Pageant."

42. Parades and pageantry, along with catastrophes and sports, appeared as mainstays of the new weekly newsreels that began to appear in the fall of 1911. Raymond Fielding, *The American Newsreel, 1911–67* (Norman: University of Oklahoma Press, 1972), pp. 48–57.

43. My understanding of how genre theory can help formulate useful generalizations about hundreds of diverse local performances comes primarily from studies of popular fiction, especially Northrop Frye, *Anatomy of Criticism* (1957; reprint, Princeton, N.J.: Princeton University Press, 1973); John Cawelti, *Adventure, Mystery, and Romance* (Chicago: University of Chicago Press, 1976); and Janice A. Radway, *Reading the Romance: Women, Patriarchy, and Popular Literature* (Chapel Hill: University of North Carolina Press, 1984). Although at the most profound level many of these images represent timeless archetypes neither specifically American nor twentieth century, at another level we can characterize the conventions, disseminated nationally, that distinguished American historical pageantry between 1910 and 1916 from those of other places and times.

44. Lotta A. Clark, "Pageants and Local History," *History Teachers Magazine* 5 (November 1914): 287.

45. See, for example, the representation of the Puritans going to church in Colonna P. Dallin, *The Arlington* (Mass.) *Pageant* (Boston: Stetson Press, 1913).

46. Caldwell Board of Trade, *Program of the Pageant and Folk Dances in Celebration of the 225th Anniversary of the Settlement of Caldwell, New Jersey, "The Borough Beautiful"* (New York: Vechten-Waring Co., 1915); Ethel T. Rockwell, *Freeport Pageant of the Blackhawk Country* (Freeport, Ill.: n.p., 1915); Frances Gilchrist Wood, *The Book of the Pageant of Ridgewood, New Jersey* (Paterson: Paterson Press, 1915); Adriana S. Kolyn, *Pageant of Hope* (Holland, Mich.: n.p., 1916). The scene in the Lincoln pageant, of course, could not be depicted realistically. Instead, scores of local residents dressed as grasshoppers descended upon the pageant grounds. Hartley B. Alexander, *The Pageant of Lincoln, Nebraska* (Lincoln, Nebr.: State Printing Co., 1915). See Chapter Six for additional discussion of the image of war in community historical pageants.

47. Margaret MacLaren Eager, *Historical Pageant of Bennington, Vermont* (Troy, N.Y.: Troy Times Art Press, 1911); Rockwell, *Freeport Pageant*; Dallin, *Arlington Pageant*. A variation on the Elizabethan versus Puritan scene depicted the Puritans passing a festival of Elizabethan folk dances as they bid farewell to England. See, for example, Eager's historical pageant for Ipswich, Mass., August 25–27, 1910. In a Pennsylvania variation of Merry Mount, the Elizabethan dancers are disrupted by Quakers and cry out, "Too long have we been repressed in our innocent pleasures by such thees and thous as you. Simple pleasures are as necessary to life as long faces and holy smiles." *Father Penn: A Pageant Presented by the Summer School at Penn State College* (State College, Pa.: n.p., 1915), p. 10. For more on Elizabethan versus Puritan imagery in the period, see David Glassberg, "Restoring a 'Forgotten Childhood': American Play and the Progressive Era's Elizabethan Past," *American Quarterly* 32 (Fall 1980): 351–68.

48. Langdon, *Celebration of the Fourth*, p. 16.

49. Robert Withington, quoted in Rockwell, "Historical Pageantry," p. 11; WCL to Raymond P. Kaighn, August 27, 1911, WCL Papers; Rockwell, *Freeport Pageant*, pp. 45–47; Colonna P. Dallin, *A Pageant of Progress* (Lawrence, Mass.: Boothby Press, 1911); Hazel MacKaye, "The New Vision," staged by several hundred Larkin Company employees in Delaware Park, Buffalo, N.Y., June 29, 1916, described in "Larkin Forces in Park Masque," *Buffalo Express*, June 30, 1916, p. 5.

50. Rose Pastor Stokes, "Tonight's Red Pageant at Garden," *New York Call*, June 7, 1913, p. 1. Despite the IWW leaders' intention to use the Paterson pageant for fund-raising, most of the seats were sold at too low a price to cover its expenses and the production lost $2,000. Discussions of the pageant and its finances appear in Anne Huber Tripp, *The IWW and the Paterson Silk Strike of 1913* (Urbana: University of Illinois Press, 1987), pp. 130–54, and Steve Golin, *The Fragile Bridge: Paterson Silk Strike, 1913* (Philadelphia: Temple University Press, 1988), pp. 157–78. A copy of the pageant program, two contemporary reviews, and Elizabeth Gurley Flynn's account of the event appear in *Rebel Voices: An IWW Anthology*, ed. Joyce L. Kornbluh (Ann Arbor: University of Michigan Press, 1964), pp. 197–226. For examples of the reaction to the pageant in the national press, see "Paterson Strike Pageant," *The Independent* 74 (June 19, 1913): 146–47; "Pageant of the Paterson Strike," *Survey* 30 (June 28, 1913): 428; "The I.W.W. Pageant," *Outlook* 104 (June 21, 1913): 352–53; and "The Pageant as a Form of Propaganda," *Current Opinion* 55 (July 1913): 32. On artists' contributions to the pageant, see Linda Nochlin in "The Paterson Strike Pageant of 1913," *Art in America* 62 (May–June 1974): 64–68. On John Reed's involvement in the Paterson pageant, see Granville Hicks, *John Reed: The Making of a Revolutionary* (New York: Macmillan, 1936), pp. 40–45, 101, and Robert Rosenstone, *Romantic Revolutionary: A Biography of John Reed* (New York: Knopf, 1975), pp. 117–32. It is interesting to contrast the IWW drama in Paterson with an example of French Socialists' theater of the previous decade such as "La Pâque Socialiste" (Socialist Passover) described by Joan Wallach Scott. Both depicted workers on strike—but the French also incorporated tableaux vivants of the ideal future society free of class warfare and much more explicit religious symbolism of death and resurrection. Scott, "Popular Theatre and Socialism in Late Nineteenth Century France," in *Political Symbolism in Modern Europe: Essays in Honor of George L. Mosse*, ed. Seymour Drescher, David Sabean, and Allan Sharlin (New Brunswick, N.J.: Transaction Books, 1982), pp. 197–215.

51. Heysham, *Norristown*, p. 18; Lotta A. Clark, "The Boston—1915 Civic Pageant," *New Boston* (December 1910): 335–43. Also see Boston—1915, *Official Program: Cave Life to City Life*, November 10–12, 1910.

52. *Official Program: Pageant of the Nations* (Newburyport, Mass.: Herald Publishing Co., 1913), in WCL Papers; Langdon, *Celebration of the Fourth*, p. 12. Also see J. Stanley Lemons, "Black Stereotypes as Reflected in Popular Culture, 1880–1920," *American Quarterly* 29 (1977): 102–16.

George Pierce Baker, *The Peterborough Memorial Pageant* (Peterborough, N.H.: MacDowell Memorial Association, 1910); W. E. B. DuBois, "The Drama among Black Folk," *Crisis* 12 (August 1916): 173.

53. "The Great Pageant," *Washington Bee*, October 3, 1915, p. 1. DuBois

wrote Ellis P. Oberholtzer for pageant advice shortly before staging the New York production. DuBois to EPO, June 20, 1913, EPO Papers. On the Washington production, see DuBois, "The Star of Ethiopia," *Crisis* 11 (December 1915): 90–94. On the Philadelphia production, see DuBois, "The Drama among Black Folk." DuBois recalled his historical pageant activities in a letter to S. L. Smith, May 10, 1932, published in *The Correspondence of W. E. B. DuBois*, ed. Herbert Aptheker, 3 vols. (Amherst: University of Massachusetts Press, 1973), 1:457–58. More on DuBois's pageant activities can be found on reel 87 of the microfilm edition of the W. E. B. DuBois Papers, Archives and Manuscripts Department, University of Massachusetts, Amherst.

54. Heysham, *Norristown*, p. 18.

55. Hazel MacKaye, "Wake Up Woman!—To This Man-Made World," n.d., PMK Papers, quoted in Martin S. Tackel, "Women and American Pageantry, 1908 to 1918" (Ph.D. dissertation, City University of New York, 1982), p. 202. See *Official Program: Woman's Suffrage Procession*, ed. Harriet Connor Brown (Washington, D.C.: Sudworth Co., 1913). This massive demonstration attracted enormous publicity, in large part because the Washington police failed to keep order among the bystanders watching the women march, resulting in a near riot as the women shoved their way up Pennsylvania Avenue. A comparison of the procession of 1913 with other demonstrations for woman suffrage appears in Sidney Bland, "Techniques of Persuasion: The National Woman's Party and Woman Suffrage, 1913–19" (Ph.D. dissertation, George Washington University, 1972), and Bland, "New Life in an Old Movement: Alice Paul and the Great Suffrage Parade of 1913 in Washington, D.C.," in *Records of the Columbia Historical Society of Washington, D.C., 1971–72* (Baltimore: Waverly Press, 1973), pp. 657–78.

56. For an example of how a civic image matured during a pageant performance, see *The Pageant of Elizabeth, N.J.* (1914), described in Beegle and Crawford, *Community Drama and Pageantry* (New Haven: Yale University Press, 1916), p. 202. On idealized female imagery at the turn of the century, see Lois Banner, *American Beauty* (New York: Knopf, 1983), pp. 154–74.

57. See, for example, the chapter on "Chivalry" in Boy Scouts of America, *The Boy Scout Handbook* (Garden City, N.Y.: Doubleday, Page, and Co., 1913). Among the recent works that attempt to analyze the popular appeal of classical and Medieval imagery in America at the turn of the century are John Fraser, *America and the Patterns of Chivalry* (New York: Cambridge University Press, 1982), and the essays collected in the Brooklyn Museum, *The American Renaissance, 1876–1917* (New York: Pantheon, 1979). On the parallels between neoclassical imagery in historical pageantry and mural painting, see Trudy Baltz, "Pageantry and Mural Painting: Community Rituals in Allegorical Form," *Winterthur Portfolio* 15 (August 1980): 211–28.

58. William Chauncy Langdon, *The St. Johnsbury Pageant* (St. Johnsbury, Vt.: Caledonia Press, 1912). Local pageant producers in Indiana in 1916 were told that "The Indian, like nature, belongs in the scenic as well as the historic background of the state." Charity Dye, "Pageant Suggestions for the Indiana Statehood Centennial Celebration," *Indiana Historical Commission Bulletin*, no. 4 (1916): 4.

59. Thomas Wood Stevens, *Book of Words: A Pageant of the Old Northwest*

(Milwaukee: J. S. Bletcher, 1911), p. 75; Joseph Mills Hanson, *Book of the Pageant of Yankton* (Yankton, S.Dak.: Yankton Printing Co., 1916). Historical pageants held on Indian reservations may have offered a notable exception to the representation of Indians painlessly fading away with the arrival of white settlers. One such pageant held in Chilocco, Okla., in 1924 vividly depicted the "Trail of Tears." *A Pageant of Oklahoma* (Chilocco: Indian Print Shop, 1924).

60. Haddonfield Celebration Committee, *The 200th Anniversary of the Settlement of Haddonfield, New Jersey* (Philadelphia: Franklin Printing Co., 1913); Isabella F. Conant, *The Pageant of the Charles River* (Wellesley, Mass.: Margus Printing Co., 1914); Constance D'Arcy MacKay, *The Pageant of Schenectady* (Schenectady, N.Y.: Gazette Press, 1912), p. 62; William Chauncy Langdon, *The Pageant of Indiana: The Drama of the Development of the State as a Community from Its Exploration by LaSalle to the Centennial of Its Admission to the Union* (Indianapolis: Hollenbeck Press, 1916).

61. Eva Winnefred Scates, *Historic Pageant of Fort Fairfield and the Aroostook Valley, Maine* (Fort Fairfield: Review Press, 1916); performed August 8–10, 1916.

62. William Chauncy Langdon, "Music in Pageantry," *Drama* 8 (November 1918): 502. Also see Langdon, notes for "Chapter Six: Music in Pageantry," in "The Pageant in America," unpublished ms., WCL Papers, Supplement, and Arthur Farwell, "Pageant Music," *APA Bulletin*, no. 43, December 1, 1916. Among the better-known composers who wrote original scores for historical pageants were George Chadwick (1854–1931), Frederick S. Converse (1871–1940), Arthur Farwell (1872–1952), and Daniel Gregory Mason (1873–1953). For more on this "Second New England School," see H. Wiley Hitchcock, *Music in the United States: A Historical Introduction* (Englewood Cliffs, N.J.: Prentice-Hall, 1969), pp. 127–47, and Gilbert Chase, *America's Music: From the Pilgrims to the Present*, rev. 3d ed. (Urbana: University of Illinois Press, 1987), pp. 353–56, 379–94.

Compare Edward MacDowell's "New England Idylls" (1902) and Charles Ives's "Three Places in New England" (1903–14) for contemporaries' radically different musical treatment of regional and historical themes. For more on Ives's vision of American history, see Frank Rossiter, *Charles Ives and His America* (New York: Liveright, 1975), pp. 87–109.

63. Duncan appeared in the opening performance of Percy MacKaye's *Caliban* in New York City in 1916; Ruth St. Denis and Ted Shawn used one hundred students from their school in Los Angeles to create their own pageant, *Egypt, Greece, and India*, which played in Berkeley, Long Beach, and San Diego in 1916. Aesthetic dance numbers also found their way into Broadway revues such as Florenz Ziegfeld's *Follies*, which began in 1907. Elizabeth Kendall, *Where She Danced: The Birth of American Art-Dance* (New York: Knopf, 1979), pp. 128–29, 178.

64. Virginia Tanner, *The Masque of Rockport* (Rockport, Mass.: n.p., 1914), p. 5; Wood, *Book of the Pageant of Ridgewood.*

65. On the differences between the progressive history of Frederick Jackson Turner, Charles Beard, and James Harvey Robinson, who portrayed social conflict as the engine of historical change, and that of the "conservative evolutionists," see John Higham, *History* (1965; reprint, New York: Harper and

Row, 1973), pp. 150–82; Richard Hofstadter, *The Progressive Historians: Turner, Beard, and Parrington* (New York: Knopf, 1968); and Thomas M. Jacklin, "Progressives and the Usable Past: Historical Themes in the Literature of American Reform, 1880–1915" (Ph.D. dissertation, Johns Hopkins University, 1981).

66. WCL to Frank Chocteau Brown, August 24, 1917, WCL Papers.

67. Francis Howard Williams describes Penn's treaty scene in a letter to Ellis P. Oberholtzer, September 6, 1911, EPO Papers. The bearded Lincoln in the Freeport pageant's debate scene is described in Christian Moe, "From History to Drama: A Study of the Influence of the Pageant, the Outdoor Epic Drama, and the Historical Stage Play upon the Dramatization of Three American Historical Figures" (Ph.D. dissertation, Cornell University, 1958), p. 93. Lincoln began a beard after his election in November 1860 and it had grown in by the time of his inauguration in March 1861. Russell Freedman, *Lincoln: A Photobiography* (New York: Clarion Books, 1987), pp. 64–65.

68. On public ritual's "traditionalizing" role, depicting the unknown in familiar actions and imagery, see Sally Falk Moore and Barbara G. Myerhoff, Introduction to *Secular Ritual*, ed. Moore and Myerhoff (Amsterdam, The Netherlands: Van Gorcum, 1977). The historical pageant form combined what Sherry Ortner calls "elaborative symbols" and "summarizing symbols." Elaborative symbols (such as the moral lessons embedded in the plot of a realistic historical reenactment) offer "key scenarios" that help formulate specific orientations to action, whereas summarizing symbols (such as the abstract representations of home and community in the pageant interludes) "catalyze feeling" and evoke a strong emotional response. See Ortner, "On Key Symbols," *American Anthropologist* 75 (October 1973): 1338–46.

69. For a superb overview of rites of passage, see Barbara Myerhoff, "Rites of Passage: Process and Paradox," in *Celebration: Studies in Festivity and Ritual*, ed. Victor Turner (Washington: Smithsonian Institution, 1982), pp. 109–35. On communitas and liminality during transitions in status, see Victor Turner, *The Ritual Process* (1969; reprint, Penguin Books, 1974), and *Dramas, Fields, and Metaphors: Symbolic Action in Human Society* (Ithaca, N.Y.: Cornell University Press, 1974).

70. Lotta A. Clark, "The Development of American Pageantry," *APA Bulletin*, no. 9, November 1, 1914. Frances M. Bjorkman remarked that, while British historical pageants were held to give thanks for the past, American pageants were designed to "throw light upon the present and the future." Bjorkman, "A Nation Learning to Play," *World's Work* 18 (September 1909): 12039.

Davol, *Handbook of American Pageantry*, p. 92.

71. *The Stonington Battle Centennial* (Stonington, Conn.: Palmer Press, 1915), pp. 13–15.

72. For more on the Philadelphia pageant of 1912, see Glassberg, "Public Ritual and Cultural Hierarchy," 421–48. For *The Pageant of Indianapolis*, see "Pageant Arouses Local Residents," *Indianapolis Star*, September 17, 1916, p. 33. Also see newspaper descriptions of the pageant, which was held October 2–7, 1916, and Langdon's pageant script.

73. Frank J. Wilsatch, "Putting a Town on the Map" and "What a Pageant

Does for a Town," press releases in scrapbook, "The Pageant of Darien, Connecticut," 1913, New York Public Library Local History Collection; Untitled press release in scrapbook, "Pageant of Darien."

74. Francis R. North, "The Celebration of Columbus Day in Boston," *Playground* 7 (May 1913): 76–78. The Italian fraternal organization's floats were described in the *Norristown Register*, May 8, 1912.

75. This scene is described in Louise Burleigh, *The Community Theatre* (Boston: Little, Brown and Co., 1917), pp. 46–51.

76. For the conventions of historical plays for the commercial stage, such as *The Girl of the Golden West*, see Lise-Lone Marker, *David Belasco: Naturalism in the American Theater* (Princeton, N.J.: Princeton University Press, 1975). Commercial motion pictures based on events from American history were common enough by 1913 that one writer boldly predicted that film would eventually replace written history as the primary way the mass of Americans learned about their past. W. Stephen Bush, "History on the Screen," *Moving Picture World*, February 22, 1913. A few public agencies responded to this educational challenge by producing historical films to supplement public historical commemorations. Massachusetts displayed filmed reenactments of a half-dozen episodes from its past as part of its exhibit at the Panama-Pacific exposition in San Francisco in 1915. The next year the Indiana Historical Commission produced a seven-reel history of Indiana for the state's centennial celebration. But historical filmmaking, like other types of filmmaking, remained primarily in the hands of commercial producers in the decade before World War I.

77. Griffith's *Intolerance* also follows historical pageant form with its allegorical interludes linking realistic reenactments. Most Civil War films between 1908 and 1917 revolved around domestic themes, especially a courtship that successfully crossed regional lines—a convention of popular fiction and drama of the period as well. Jack Spears, *The Civil War on the Screen and Other Essays* (New York: A. S. Barnes, 1977). Though historians have identified the "historical" film as a popular film genre, like the Western, the mystery, or the domestic comedy, no one has analyzed the structure and content of these films or how they changed over time. One rather weak attempt to do so across all of Western culture is Pierre Sorlin's *The Film in History: Restaging the Past* (New York: Oxford, U.K.: Basil Blackwell, 1980), which includes a discussion of *The Birth of a Nation*.

78. Withington, *English Pageantry*, p. 296; Helen Thoburn, "Pageants of Girlhood," *Good Housekeeping* 57 (August 1913): 231.

Chapter 5. To Explain the City to Itself

1. Robert Withington, "A Manual of Pageantry," *Indiana University Bulletin*, no. 13 (June 15, 1915): 19; George McReynolds, "The Centennial Pageant for Indiana: Suggestions for Its Performance," *Indiana Magazine of History*, September 1915, p. 3.

2. William Chauncy Langdon to Hermann Hagedorn, October 17, 1910,

William Chauncy Langdon (WCL) Papers, Harris Collection, John Hay Library, Brown University, R.I. (hereafter cited as WCL Papers; see Chapter Three, n. 1). On the financial failure of the Philadelphia historical pageant of 1912, see David Glassberg, "Public Ritual and Cultural Hierarchy: Philadelphia's Civic Celebrations at the Turn of the Century," *Pennsylvania Magazine of History and Biography* 107 (July 1983): 421–48.

3. William LaBeaume, "The Historic Pageant a People's Diversion: St. Louis Will Give the World's Largest," *Pageant and Masque of St. Louis Bulletin*, no. 1 (February 1914): 5. A complete set of these bulletins exists in the St. Louis Pageant Drama Association (SLPDA) Papers, Missouri Historical Society, St. Louis (hereafter cited as SLPDA Papers).

4. *St. Louis Republic*, July 9, 1913; "Pageant to Depict St. Louis History," *St. Louis Republic*, July 3, 1913; *St. Louis Republic*, August 1, 1913.

5. On the social background of those behind the centennial celebration of 1909, see Donald Bright Oster, "Community Image in St. Louis and Kansas City" (Ph.D. dissertation, University of Missouri, 1969).

6. Lincoln Steffens, "Tweed Days in St. Louis," *McClure's Magazine* 19 (October 1902): 577–86; Steffens, "The Shamelessness of St. Louis," *McClure's Magazine* 20 (March 1903): 545–60; "Lost Centennial Opportunities," *St. Louis Republic*, October 5, 1909, p. 8.

7. For more on St. Louis' sultry reputation, see Oster, "Community Image in St. Louis and Kansas City."

8. SLPDA Finance Committee to Julius S. Walsh, Mississippi Valley Trust Co., April 22, 1914, SLPDA Papers. On the differences between the 1904 and 1914 celebrations, see Henry Kiel, "Educational Value of the Pageant and Masque One of Its Most Impressive Features," *Pageant and Masque of St. Louis Bulletin*, no. 2 (March 1914): 5.

9. See Charlotte Rumbold, *Housing Conditions in St. Louis: Report of the Housing Committee of the Civic League of St. Louis* (St. Louis, 1908). Dwight F. Davis, incidentally, was the wealthy sportsman who donated the Davis Cup. For a more complete description of the social and professional backgrounds of SLPDA Executive Committee members, see Donald Bright Oster, "Nights of Fantasy: The St. Louis Pageant and Masque of 1914," *Bulletin of the Missouri Historical Society* 31 (April 1975): 175–205. Both Oster and Paul Boyer discuss the St. Louis pageant as a reflection of the values of the middle-class urban reformers who promoted the event. Boyer, *Urban Masses and Moral Order in America, 1820–1920* (Cambridge: Harvard University Press, 1978).

10. Charles Stix to George E. Steadman, Curtis and Co. Mfg., February 18, 1914, SLPDA Papers; SLPDA, "An Awakened City," brochure, ca. 1914, SLPDA Papers.

11. Charlotte Rumbold, "Municipal Recreation: A School for Democracy," in SLPDA, *Proceedings of the Conference of Cities* (St. Louis, 1914), p. 28; SLPDA, "An Awakened City."

12. WCL to William LaBeaume, July 22, 1913, SLPDA Papers.

13. Quoted in *St. Louis Republic*, September 23, 1913.

14. WCL to William LaBeaume, September 5, 1913; WCL to SLPDA Executive Committee, September 28, 1913, SLPDA Papers.

15. Charlotte Rumbold to John Gundlach, September 16, 1913, SLPDA Papers.

16. Ibid.

17. WCL to William LaBeaume, September 5, 1913, SLPDA Papers; William LaBeaume to Ellis P. Oberholtzer, October 7, 1913, Ellis Paxson Oberholtzer (EPO) Papers, Historical Society of Pennsylvania, Philadelphia (hereafter cited as EPO Papers; see Chapter Two, n. 7).

18. *St. Louis Republic*, December 15 and 18, 1913.

19. Biographical information on Stevens is based on the Thomas Wood Stevens (TWS) Collection, University of Arizona Library, Tucson (hereafter cited as TWS Papers); William Robert Rambin, Jr., "Thomas Wood Stevens: American Pageant-master" (Ph.D. dissertation, Louisiana State University, 1977); and the essays recalling Stevens, collected by Melvin White, that appeared in a special issue of *Educational Theatre Journal* 3 (December 1951): 280–321.

20. Thomas Wood Stevens, *Book of Words: A Pageant of the Italian Renaissance* (Chicago: Alderbrink Press, 1909). Several newspaper articles describe the elite's participation in the pageant: "Grand Pageant Ready," *Chicago Tribune*, January 24, 1909; "Pageantry and Pomp in Italian Spectacle," *Chicago Record-Herald*, January 27, 1909; and "Society Flocks to Italian Pageant," *Chicago Inter-Ocean*, January 27, 1909. Stevens's confession that he wanted to be a professional playwright appeared in a letter dated June 28, 1909, vol. 2, TWS Papers.

21. On the Illinois pageant, which raised $9,000 for Northwestern University's settlement fund, see "Pioneers in Pageant," *Chicago Daily News*, October 2, 1909, p. 11; Thomas Wood Stevens, *Book of Words: A Historical Pageant of Illinois* (Chicago: Alderbrink Press, 1909); Stevens, *Book of Words: A Pageant of the Old Northwest* (Milwaukee: I. S. Bletcher, 1911); *Souvenir Program, Historical Pageant of Madison County*, Madison County (Ill.) Centennial Association, 1912. Stevens describes his use of Parkman in a flyer advertising his Old Northwest pageants, vol. 31, TWS Papers.

22. Program, Chicago Municipal Art League, vol. 54, TWS Papers; Stevens, Lecture Notes for Course on Civic Art, vol. 46, TWS Papers.

23. In 1913, the Chicago Society of Etchers elected Stevens its president. Stevens annually etched his own Christmas cards, and he judged the category in 1915 at the San Francisco Panama–Pacific Exposition. While lecturing on civic art and pageantry, Stevens continued to write plays that he hoped would be produced on Broadway. In 1908 he collaborated with Wallace Rice on *The Chaplet of Pan* and in 1912 with Kenneth Sawyer Goodman on *Ryland*. These efforts, along with his familiarity with costume and set design, led to Stevens's appointment to the faculty of the Carnegie Institute in 1913.

24. Stevens to WCL, August 20, 1910, TWS Papers.

25. Ibid.

26. MacKaye's half brother Arthur—Steele's son by a previous marriage—also was an author and journalist. Biographical information on MacKaye is based on the MacKaye Family Collection, Percy MacKaye (PMK) Papers, Baker Library, Dartmouth College, Hanover, N.H. (hereafter cited as PMK

Papers); the Percy and Marian MacKaye Collection, Harvard Theatre Collection, Cambridge; Percy MacKaye's daughters, Christy MacKaye Barnes and Arvia MacKaye Ege, interviews with author, Hillsdale, N.Y., August 1984; and Arvia MacKaye Ege, "The Power of the Impossible: The Life Story of Percy and Marion MacKaye" (unpublished ms., 1984). A concise sketch of Mac-Kaye's career appears in Claude Dierolf, "The Pageant Drama and American Pageantry" (Ph.D. dissertation, University of Pennsylvania, 1953). An exhaustive list of nearly everything written by or about the MacKaye family as of 1932 appears in *Annals of an Era: Percy MacKaye and the MacKaye Family*, ed. E. O. Grover (Washington, D.C.: Pioneer Press [for Dartmouth College], 1932).

27. On Steele MacKaye and the Spectatorium, see Percy MacKaye, "Steele MacKaye: Dynamic Artist of the American Theatre," Part One, *Drama* 4 (November 1911): 138–61, and Part Two, *Drama* 5 (February 1912): 158–73. Also see Percy MacKaye, "The Theatre of 10,000: Steele MacKaye's Spectatorium," *Theatre Arts* 7 (April 1923): 116–26, and a full-length biography, Percy Mac-Kaye, *Epoch: The Life of Steele MacKaye, Genius of the American Theatre*, 2 vols. (New York: Boni and Liveright, 1927).

28. Percy MacKaye, "Steele MacKaye," Part Two, p. 172.

29. The text of MacKaye's Harvard commencement speech appears in Ege, "The Power of the Impossible." References to his dramatic career at Harvard appear in *Annals of an Era*.

30. It is likely that the connections of MacKaye's wife—as a first cousin of Winslow Homer and a piano student of Edward MacDowell—also helped him gain access to the circle at Cornish. A roster of the Cornish art colony appears in Frances Duncan, "The Gardens of Cornish," *Century* 72 (May 1906): 3–19.

31. "Percy MacKaye on the Poetic Drama," *Theatre Magazine* 20 (November 1914): 222–25. An important introduction, if not manifesto, for the symbolist dramatists is Edward Gordon Craig, *On the Art of the Theatre* (London: William Heinemann, 1911). For more on Craig and MacKaye, see Susan Valeria Harris Smith, *Masks of Modern Drama* (Berkeley: University of California Press, 1984), pp. 49–84.

H. L. Mencken, *Smart Set* (September 1910); Thomas H. Dickinson, *Playwrights of the New American Theatre* (New York, 1925); *Percy MacKaye: A Symposium on His Fiftieth Birthday* (Hanover, N.H.: Dartmouth Press, 1928).

32. *Collier's Weekly*, February 25, 1911. Of all MacKaye's dramatic works of the period, *The Scarecrow* proved the most enduring. Based loosely on Hawthorne's tale "Feathertop," about a scarecrow given life by the devil, it was revived off-Broadway as recently as 1978 (again to mixed reviews).

New York Times, September 23, 1910; *Chicago Record*, January 15, 1912.

33. A complete list of the places where MacKaye's "Poems of Public Events and Inventions" were read, then published, appears in *Annals of an Era*, pp. 77–92.

34. Percy MacKaye, *The Civic Theatre in Relation to the Redemption of Leisure* (New York: Mitchell Kennerly, 1912), pp. 15–20. MacKaye specifically discussed the new pageantry in "American Pageants and their Promise," *Scribner's Magazine* (July 1909), and "The New Fourth of July," *Century* (July 1910), both reprinted in his *Civic Theatre*. Also see MacKaye's earlier lectures and essays,

especially "The Dramatist as Citizen" and "The Drama of Democracy," collected in Percy MacKaye, *The Playhouse and the Play* (New York: Macmillan, 1909).

35. Percy MacKaye, "The Wisconsin Idea in Theatre," *Playbook* 1 (April 1913): 10. MacKaye described community drama as a "ritual of democratic religion" in an address before the American Civic Association in 1916, published in his *Community Drama: Its Motive and Method of Neighborliness* (New York: Houghton Mifflin, 1917), p. 11.

36. MacKaye sent Croly a note praising *The Promise of American Life*, and Croly invited MacKaye to stay with him in New York. PMK Papers. On MacKaye's relationship with John Reed, see reminiscences contained in the correspondence from MacKaye to Granville Hicks, September 21, October 29, and November 25, 1935, Granville Hicks Papers, George Arents Research Library, Syracuse University. MacKaye appears in the memoirs of Mabel Dodge as well as Hutchins Hapgood. Mabel Dodge Luhan, *Movers and Shakers* (1936; reprint, Albuquerque: University of New Mexico Press, 1985); Hutchins Hapgood, *A Victorian in the Modern World* (1939; reprint, Seattle: University of Washington Press, 1972). Still useful as overviews of literary radicalism in Greenwich Village before World War I are James B. Gilbert, *Writers and Partisans: A History of Literary Radicalism in America* (New York: John Wiley and Sons, 1968), and Henry F. May, *The End of American Innocence: A Study of the First Years of Our Own Time, 1912–17* (New York: Knopf, 1959). Correspondence between MacKaye and Woodrow Wilson is collected in the Ray Stannard Baker Papers, Manuscripts Division, Library of Congress. Despite MacKaye's admiration for these writers and politicians, he later expressed frustration that his fellow "progressive" reformers who wrote for the *New Republic*, *The Masses*, and the *Nation* did not take civic pageantry seriously enough. Preface to Louise Burleigh, *The Community Theatre* (Boston: Little, Brown, and Co., 1917), pp. xvii.

37. MacKaye quoted in Mary Fanton Roberts, "The Dramatic Engineer and the Civic Theatre: A New Idea for Bringing the Stage Back to the People," *Craftsman* 26 (May 1914): 139. In another scrapbook, MacKaye pasted a publisher's announcement for ten books on advertising, circling J. Angus MacDonald's *Successful Advertising: How to Accomplish It* and Walter Dill Scott's *The Theory of Advertising*. PMK Papers.

38. On Percy MacKaye and woman suffrage, see Percy MacKaye, "Art and the Woman's Movement," *Forum* 49 (June 1913): 680–84; also see *Official Program: Woman's Suffrage Procession*, ed. Harriet Connor Brown (Washington, D.C.: Sudworth, 1913). On MacKaye's possible involvement in the Paterson pageant, Granville Hicks reports that MacKaye assisted Reed. Hicks, *John Reed: The Making of a Revolutionary* (New York: Macmillan, 1936), p. 101. Hutchins Hapgood also recalled dining with MacKaye and Bill Haywood at Mabel Dodge's home. Hapgood, *A Victorian in the Modern World*, pp. 293–95. But Dodge's memoirs do not mention MacKaye's involvement in planning the pageant. Luhan, *Movers and Shakers*, pp. 186–212. Moreover, correspondence between Reed and MacKaye surviving in the MacKaye Papers at Dartmouth and in the John Reed Papers at Harvard neither refer to MacKaye's involve-

ment at Paterson nor contain any specific dramatic advice. One letter in the Reed Papers describing a meeting of artists in New York City to plan the pageant does not list MacKaye among those present. E. E. Hunt to his wife, June 9, 1913, John Reed Papers, Houghton Library, Harvard University. MacKaye's letters to Hicks in 1935 also do not mention the Paterson pageant, though possibly MacKaye discussed the pageant with Hicks during the personal interviews they had that year. Granville Hicks Papers.

39. Percy MacKaye, *Sanctuary: A Bird Masque* (New York: F. A. Stokes, 1914). A children's version of MacKaye's masque appeared as part of Redpath Tent Chautauqua circuit for 120 performances over 17 weeks in 1916. See *Annals of an Era*, pp. 106–8.

40. For a detailed blueprint of MacKaye's plans for the Pittsburgh civic celebrations, see Percy MacKaye, *Civic Theatre*, pp. 288–305. The Pittsburgh scandal concerned bankers bribing city officials in return for city money being deposited in their banks. Philip S. Klein and Ari Hoogenboom, *A History of Pennsylvania* (New York: McGraw-Hill Book Co., 1973), p. 378.

41. TWS to Thomas H. Dickinson, November 20, 1913, vol. 3, TWS Papers.

42. "St. Louis: A Civic Masque," *Bookman* 39 (June 1914): 376–77. Lighting consisted of four 24-inch spotlights mounted on the Art Museum roof; four 18-inch spotlights, one on each tower and wing; and two hundred and seventy-five 250-watt footlights. SLPDA, *Report of the Chairmen of the Committees* (St. Louis, 1916), pp. 78–86. For more description of the grounds, see "'A World Site' Is Location of Great Stage for the Pageant and Masque," *Pageant and Masque of St. Louis Bulletin*, no. 2 (March 1914): 4, and the dozens of photographs of the pageant amphitheater and stage under construction in the collections of the University of Missouri at St. Louis, the Missouri Historical Society, and the St. Louis Public Library.

43. Another 4,000 spectators could cram into the "Free" side, raising the total seating capacity of the amphitheater to 47,000. SLPDA, *Report of the Chairmen*, p. 108.

44. Converse, founder of the New England Opera Company, had collaborated with MacKaye on the music for *Sanctuary*, the proposed Pittsburgh celebrations, and several indoor operas. His *Pipe of Desire* (1910) was the first work by an American composer performed at the Metropolitan Opera House. Gilbert Chase, *America's Music: From the Pilgrims to the Present*, rev. 3d ed. (Urbana: University of Illinois Press, 1987), p. 543.

45. SLPDA Papers. Also see SLPDA, *Report of the Chairmen*.

46. Figures reported in *New St. Louis Star*, June 2, 1914, and in SLPDA, *Report of the Chairmen*.

47. Charlotte Rumbold to Luther Ely Smith, February 16, 1914, SLPDA Papers; Arthur Proetz, *I Remember St. Louis* (St. Louis: Zimmerman-Petty Co., 1963), pp. 205–6. Proetz was assistant stage manager for the pageant. *New St. Louis Star*, June 2, 1914; SLPDA, *Report of the Chairmen*; Luther Ely Smith to Owen Miller of the American Federation of Musicians, January 31, 1914, SLPDA Papers.

48. Charles Stix to Julius Walsh, April 27, 1914, SLPDA Papers.

49. *The St. Louis Pageant and Masque: What It Is and Why It Is Produced*,

pamphlet (1914), pp. 4, 6, SLPDA Papers. The advertising firm was the Western Publicity Bureau, St. Louis.

Invitation to the Conference of Cities, March 21, 1914, EPO Papers.

50. Luther Ely Smith to William LaBeaume, April 13, 1914, SLPDA Papers. St. Louis already had Sunday professional baseball in 1914.

51. The department store was Scruggs, Vandervoort, and Barney. "Exhibit of Articles of Historic Interest in Conjunction with the St. Louis Pageant and Masque, May 25–30, 1914," SLPDA Papers.

52. Charles Stix, "Citizens of St. Louis 'Boss' of Pageant," *SLPDA Bulletin*, no. 2 (March 1914): 2.

53. *St. Louis Republic*, July 27, 1913; Casting Committee Files, May 12, 1914, SLPDA Papers.

54. "The Italians and the Pageant," *St. Louis Globe-Democrat*, May 25, 1914, p. 10.

55. "Can't Find Leader for the Irish," *New St. Louis Star*, December 16, 1913; Luther Ely Smith to William LaBeaume, April 13, 1914, SLPDA Papers. Of all the nationalities in St. Louis listed in the U.S. Census of 1910, only the Germans and Irish counted more second-generation American than foreign-born residents. U.S. Government, *Thirteenth Census, 1910, Population*, 2:1118.

56. Eugene Wilson to William Hole-in-the-Day, March 23, 1914, SLPDA Papers; *St. Louis Globe-Democrat*, May 29, 1914, p. 9.

57. Totaling the first- and second-generation American population for each nationality in St. Louis, blacks were the second largest minority in the city after the Germans. U.S. Government, *Thirteenth Census*, p. 1118.

58. James L. Usher to Luther Ely Smith, April 17, 1914, SLPDA Papers. I have not found Smith's reply to Usher. MacKaye's claim to have solicited black participation in the St. Louis pageant appeared in Joyce Kilmer, "Percy MacKaye Predicts Communal Theatre," *New York Times*, May 14, 1916, section 5, p. 12. Unfortunately, no copy of the *St. Louis Argus*, the city's black newspaper, survives for the year 1914. In 1980, Julia Davis of St. Louis tried to ascertain black participation in the pageant by checking with her oral sources and putting an advertisement in the *Argus*. Luther Ely Smith might have tried to solicit the participation of the "Colored Waiter's Club." On February 5, 1914, the club's secretary, William Wilson, referred to a letter from Smith when requesting casting cards for members from Eugene Wilson, chair of the pageant casting committee. No evidence exists that the SLPDA sent the cards or that the black waiters participated in the pageant. William Wilson to Eugene Wilson, February 5, 1914, Casting Committee Files, SLPDA Papers.

59. "Central Trades and Labor Union," *St. Louis Labor*, March 14, 1914, p. 5; Otto Paul, "Life as It Is," *St. Louis Labor*, January 24, 1914 (p. 4), March 14, 1914 (p. 8).

60. A facsimile cast registration card appeared in "7,500 St. Louisians Are to Be Stars in Great Play of the City's History," *SLPDA Bulletin*, no. 2 (March 1914): 6.

61. "Society in Pageant: Men and Women Leaders Take Part in Cosmopolitan Cast," *St. Louis Globe-Democrat*, June 2, 1914. Stevens originally hoped to hire actor Donald Robertson, the trusty "White Cloud" from his earlier pag-

eants, to come down from Chicago to play the narrator, but, bowing to the SLPDA, he chose a local man instead.

62. "How 7,500 Actors Are Made Ready for Pageant," press clipping, May 29, 1914, vol. 40, TWS Papers.

63. Thomas Wood Stevens, "Making the Romantic History of St. Louis into a Great Play," *SLPDA Bulletin*, no. 1 (February 1914): 1.

64. Thomas Wood Stevens, *Book of Words: Pageant of St. Louis* (St. Louis: Nixon-Jones, 1914), p. 21.

65. Ibid.

66. Casting figures from *Pageant and Masque of St. Louis: What It Is and Why It Is Produced*, pamphlet.

67. "Scenes of Civil War Barred from Pageant," *St. Louis Republic*, December 15, 1913. Also see correspondence between Stevens and the SLPDA in the Luther Ely Smith Papers, Missouri Historical Society, St. Louis.

68. William LaBeaume to Luther Ely Smith, May 27, 1914, SLPDA Papers.

69. Percy MacKaye, *St. Louis: A Civic Masque* (New York: Doubleday, 1914), p. xi.

70. Ibid., p. xiii. Smith described his temple as a copy of the Mayan Chichen-Itza. Ibid., pp. xiii, 85.

71. Ibid., p. xiii; Proetz, *I Remember St. Louis*, p. 188. Reginald B. Powell, "the man with the bass drum voice," spoke Cahokia's lines. *St. Louis Globe-Democrat*, May 26, 1914.

72. Percy MacKaye, *St. Louis*, pp. 10, 34.

73. Ibid., p. xii.

74. Ibid., p. 58. It is difficult to discern whether or not the actors who played "Asia" and "Oceania" were genuine Asians and Pacific Islanders. Their names—J. Floyd Alcorn and Clarence M. Fleming—suggest not, but it is nearly impossible to tell from existing photographs. During one performance, "War" burst too vigorously and crashed from his mount to the stage, fracturing his knee. Percy MacKaye, *St. Louis*, p. 61.

75. The "Poverty" figure might have been based on Charlotte Rumbold's early suggestion that "The Slum" be included as one of the characters in the pageant. Rumbold to John Gundlach, September 16, 1913, SLPDA Papers.

76. Percy MacKaye, *St. Louis*, pp. 78, 80–81.

77. The SLPDA canceled plans for the plane to fly over the pageant stage when it discovered that the Wright Brothers had never heard of the pilot. The masque plane was said to have inspired two members of the cast who in 1927 backed Charles Lindbergh to name his plane the "Spirit of St. Louis." Lindbergh landed in St. Louis after his flight in 1927 on the site of the *Pageant and Masque* of 1914. "Lindy Alights in St. Louis," *New York Evening Post*, June 18, 1927; *Annals of an Era*, pp. 37–38.

78. "The Historical Pageant," *St. Louis Globe-Democrat*, October 9, 1909. On the history of St. Louis' changing civic symbols, see Oster, "Community Image in St. Louis and Kansas City."

79. "Sun-worshippers of Monks Mound," *St. Louis Globe-Democrat*, September 12, 1909.

80. Miscellaneous newspaper clippings, vol. 40, TWS Papers.

81. Charlotte Rumbold, "St. Louis Pageant and Masque," *Survey* 32 (July 4, 1914): 372; also see *St. Louis Republic*, May 29, 1914; Lindsay and Teasdale's remarks from *Percy MacKaye: A Symposium on His Fiftieth Birthday*, pp. 30, 47; Arthur Farwell, "Community Music Drama," *Craftsman* 26 (July 1914): 419; William Marion Reedy, "The Color of a City's Soul," *Reedy's Mirror*, June 5, 1914, p. 1.

82. George Pierce Baker, "The Pageant and Masque of St. Louis," *World's Work* (August 1914): 389–99.

83. The *St. Louis Globe-Democrat*, on June 5, 1914, estimated that the crowd consumed 400,000 sandwiches, 300,000 hot dogs, and 250,000 gallons of lemonade, leaving behind 50 wagon loads of broken glass and 300 wagon loads of paper and refuse.

84. The Cubs won 4–3 in sixteen innings.

85. *St. Louis Globe-Democrat*, May 31, 1914.

86. John McCully, "Pageant Impressions by Police Reporter," *St. Louis Globe-Democrat*, June 2, 1914.

87. St. Louis Chamber of Commerce, *Forest Park and Its History* (St. Louis, 1943).

88. SLPDA, *Report of the Chairmen*, p. 16.

89. Oster, "Community Image in St. Louis and Kansas City."

90. John Gundlach to Jesse McDonald, January 24, 1914, SLPDA Papers; miscellaneous newspaper clippings, Scrapbook, vol. 40, TWS Papers; "Big Cinch Charter Carried by 2681 Votes Majority," *St. Louis Labor*, July 4, 1914, p. 1.

91. "Charter of the City of St. Louis, Missouri," adopted June 30, 1914. The new charter resulted from a compromise between the advocates of "at large" and "ward" representation. The original proposal to change the St. Louis charter in 1911, which was defeated, called for a single fifteen-member city council elected at large. Civic League of St. Louis, *An Abstract of the Provisions of the Old and New Charters of St. Louis, with Explanatory Comment*, pamphlet (January 1911). The new charter of 1914 retained the principle of ward representation while changing representatives' election to at-large. It required that each of the twenty-eight members of the new council reside in and represent a different district of the city, even if the representative was not elected exclusively by that district. Missouri state law prohibited the election of single legislative bodies on bases other than at-large; St. Louis civic reformers agreed that, if the state law changed, each ward would again vote solely for its own representative.

"The New Charter Campaign Situation," cartoon, *St. Louis Labor*, June 13, 1914, p. 1. Samuel P. Hays notes that, when Pittsburgh adopted similar charter reforms in 1909, the variety of class backgrounds of city officials lessened considerably and the locus of power tilted toward a professional managerial elite that had the best chance of obtaining civil service positions and being elected at-large. Hays, "Politics of Reform in Municipal Government in the Progressive Era," *Pacific Northwest Quarterly* 55 (October 1964): 57–69. Also see Hays's more comprehensive treatment of this issue in "Changing Political Structure of the City," *Journal of Urban History* 1 (November 1974): 6–38.

92. Lawrence Christensen, "Black St. Louis: A Study in Race Relations, 1865–1916" (Ph.D. dissertation, University of Missouri, 1972).

93. The pageant film, shot in daylight, reportedly included more detail than the evening performances. SLPDA Papers; TWS Papers. Apparently no prints of the film version of *The Pageant and Masque of St. Louis* have survived.

94. In June 1915, Converse performed the "Chant of the River Spirits" from the *Masque of St. Louis* with the Boston Harvard Alumni Chorus. "Program, June 6, 1915," PMK Papers. H. W. Gray Company of New York City published Converse's pageant score, and portions were recorded for phonograph on the "New York" label.

95. Invitation to the Conference of Cities, March 21, 1914, EPO Papers.

96. Ibid.; Henry Bruere, "Humanizing City Government," in SLPDA, *Proceedings of the Conference of Cities* (St. Louis, 1914), p. 34. At first Bruere was skeptical of the pageant idea. Back in February 1914, he had warned the SLPDA that pageants "cost a great deal of money and leave an intangible result. Doesn't St. Louis need the money for other things?" Three weeks before the pageant, Bruere commented, "It seems to me that your [Conference of Cities] program looks upon life in a city as a series of happy entertainments, festivals, fetes, and theatres." Bruere to SLPDA, February 19 and May 6, 1914, SLPDA Papers. His talk at the Conference of Cities during pageant week, however, referred to these civic entertainments in glowing terms.

Percival Chubb, "The Development of a Civic Folk Culture," in SLPDA, *Proceedings of the Conference of Cities*, pp. 65, 68. The League of Cities meeting in San Francisco in August 1915 with the annual convention of the National Education Association was apparently its last. Letter to Percy MacKaye, September 6, 1915, PMK Papers.

97. Luther Ely Smith, "Municipal Pageants as Destroyers of Race Prejudice," paper delivered at the Sagamore, Mass., Sociological Conference, July 1914, reprinted in Appendix to Percy MacKaye, *A Substitute for War* (New York: Macmillan, 1915), p. 52. Inspired by the pageant, Smith became a major figure in the drive for the creation of the Jefferson National Expansion Memorial and the St. Louis Arch. I am grateful to John Bodnar for information about Smith's activities after the pageant.

Arthur Farwell, "The Pageant and Community Auto-Suggestion," *Musical America*, June 27, 1914, pp. 14–15.

98. SLPDA, *Proceedings of the Conference of Cities*, p. 54.

99. On Wagnerian festivals in Germany during this period, see George L. Mosse, *The Nationalization of the Masses: Political Symbolism and Mass Movements in Germany from the Napoleonic Wars through the Third Reich* (New York: New American Library, 1975).

100. Percy MacKaye, *St. Louis*, p. x.

Chapter 6. Organizing the Soul of America

1. Forty-five new peace organizations were founded in the United States between 1901 and 1914, a spurt unequaled in any other decade of American history. Charles DeBenedetti, *The Peace Reform in American History* (Bloomington: Indiana University Press, 1980), p. 79.

2. Beulah Marie Dix, *A Pageant of Peace* (Boston, 1915); Frederick A. Wilmot, *Somerville Pageant of World Peace* (West Somerville, Mass.: Gage Printing Co., 1915); Mrs. Milton Perry Smith, "A Peace Pageant," *American City* 13 (October 1915): 334.

3. On the preparedness movement, see John Patrick Finnegan, *Against the Specter of a Dragon: The Campaign for American Military Preparedness, 1914–17* (Westport, Conn.: Greenwood Press, 1974), and Michael Pearlman, *To Make Democracy Safe for America: Patricians and Preparedness in the Progressive Era* (Urbana: University of Illinois Press, 1984). On the disorganization of U.S. fighting forces in the Spanish-American War, see Gerald Linderman, *The Mirror of War: American Society and the Spanish-American War* (Ann Arbor: University of Michigan Press, 1974), pp. 77–84.

4. Herbert Croly, "The Effect on American Institutions of a Powerful Military and Naval Establishment," *Annals of the American Academy of Political and Social Science* 66 (July 1916): 162.

5. "The Plattsburg Idea," *New Republic* 4 (October 9, 1915): 247–49; *New York Times*, May 14, 1916; also see American Scenic and Historic Preservation Society, *Report for 1916* (Albany: J. B. Lyon, 1917), pp. 204–7. For a more thorough analysis of the social and regional background of preparedness advocates, see Pearlman, *To Make Democracy Safe*, and Finnegan, *Against the Specter*, p. 92

6. "The Plattsburg Idea," p. 247.

7. Leonard Wood, "Heat Up the Melting Pot," *The Independent* 87 (July 1916): 15; Croly, "Effect on American Institutions," p. 167; "The Plattsburg Idea," p. 248; Walter Lippmann, "Integrated America," *New Republic* 6 (February 19, 1916): 65. For more on how "liberals" such as Croly and Lippmann related preparedness to their agenda for domestic reform, see Charles Forcey, *The Crossroads of Liberalism* (New York: Oxford University Press, 1961). Also see Charles Hirschfeld, "Nationalist Progressivism and World World One," *Mid-America* 45 (July 1963): 139–56.

8. William James, "The Moral Equivalent of War," *Popular Science Monthly* (October 1910): 400–410; Percy MacKaye, *A Substitute for War* (New York: Macmillan, 1915), p. 40. MacKaye's essay first appeared in the *North American Review* 201 (May 1915): 719–26.

Percy MacKaye to Crystal Eastman Benedict, August 25, 1915, box 49, Percy and Marian MacKaye Papers, Harvard Theatre Collection, Cambridge; Violet Oakley, "The Spirit of Pageantry," *American Pageant Association (APA) Bulletin*, no. 39, September 1, 1916. Oakley (1874–1961), a Philadelphia artist, remained active in the international peace movement even after America entered the war. Between 1911 and 1927, she created a giant mural, *International Understanding and Unity*, as part of her decoration for the chambers of the

Pennsylvania state senate in Harrisburg, then spent the remainder of the 1920s at The Hague as the United States' unofficial representative to the League of Nations. "Violet Oakley," *Philadelphia Museum of Art Bulletin* 75 (June 1979): 18–20.

9. MacKaye, *Substitute for War*, pp. 25–26, 29, 32.

10. Albert H. Gilmer, "The Place of Pageantry and Drama in the Program of National Preparedness," *APA Bulletin*, no. 37, July 15, 1916. Gilmer referred to Percy MacKaye's masques in St. Louis (1914) and New York City (*Caliban*, 1916).

11. *The Pageant of Saratoga* (Saratoga Springs, N.Y.: The Saratogan, 1913), performed July 28–August 2, 1913; *The Pageant of Old Deerfield* (Deerfield, Mass.: Montague Press, 1913), performed August 15–16, 18–19, 1913; Thomas Wood Stevens, *Book of Words: A Historical Pageant of Illinois* (Chicago: Alderbrink Press, 1909); Stevens, *Book of Words: A Pageant of the Old Northwest* (Milwaukee: I. S. Bletcher, 1911); Madison County (Ill.) Centennial Association, *Souvenir Program, Historical Pageant of Madison County*, 1912.

Southampton New York Colonial Society, *Celebration of the 250th Anniversary of the Founding of the Town of Southampton, N.Y.* (Sag Harbor, N.Y.: John H. Hunt, 1915), performed June 12, 1915. Michael Kammen argues that, by the late nineteenth century, the American Revolution had long lost its "revolutionary" character in popular historical consciousness. Kammen, *A Season of Youth: The American Revolution and the Historical Imagination* (New York: Alfred A. Knopf, 1978).

12. William Chauncy Langdon, *Book of Words: The Pageant of Darien, Connecticut* (New York: Clover Press, 1913), pp. 51–52. In Theodore Viehman's historical pageant for the centennial celebration in Tuscaloosa, Alabama, in 1916, it was the Confederates who bravely marched off to battle in response to news of a "Yankee" raid. "Centennial at Tuscaloosa Great Affair," *Montgomery Advertiser*, May 31, 1916, p. 3, describes all of the pageant episodes. Viehman was a student of Thomas Wood Stevens at the Carnegie Institute, Pittsburgh.

13. Excelsior (Minn.) Women's Club, *Pageant of Lake Minnetonka* (Minneapolis: Great West Printing Co., 1915), July 27–29, 1915; *Programme, the Brooklyn Historical Pageant* (New York: Brooklyn Eagle Press, 1915), May 21–22, 1915. The fiftieth anniversary of the Civil War spawned several large commemorative ceremonies of reconciliation between North and South. One of the largest occurred in July 1913, when thousands of Confederate and Union veterans gathered at Gettysburg; one of the speakers was President Woodrow Wilson. Local newspapers across the nation carried dispatches from the reunion. See, for example, *Boston Globe*, July 1, 1913. For more on the corresponding historiographical current at the turn of the century that blamed neither side for starting the conflict, see Thomas Pressly, *Americans Interpret Their Civil War* (Princeton, N.J.: Princeton University Press, 1954), pp. 187–92.

14. Caldwell Board of Trade, *Program of the Pageant and Folk Dances in Celebration of the 225th Anniversary of the Settlement of Caldwell, New Jersey, the Borough Beautiful* (New York: Vecten and Waring Co., 1915).

15. Croly, "Effect on American Institutions," p. 162. On Americans' unrealistic image of war at the turn of the century, see Thomas C. Leonard, *Above the

Battle: War-making in America from Appomattox to Versailles (New York: Oxford University Press, 1978).

16. "List of Pageants for 1916," *APA Bulletin*, no. 41, September 1, 1917. See the text of Percy MacKaye, *Caliban by the Yellow Sands* (New York: Doubleday, Page, 1916). On the participation of New York City's public schools, settlement houses, and drama clubs in MacKaye's masque, see "New York Gets Ready to Honor Shakespeare," *New York Times*, March 19, 1916, section 6, p. 12. Also see reviews of *Caliban* by Ernest Hamlin Abbott, "A Masque of Masques," *Outlook* 113 (June 7, 1916): 308–18; John Collier, "Caliban of the Yellow Sands," *Survey* 36 (July 1, 1916): 343–50; and "The Community Masque," *Nation* 102 (June 1, 1916): 586. MacKaye hoped to take *Caliban* on the road through the creation of a national "Civic Drama Association," organizing local casts to perform his masque in various cities across the United States. *Caliban* was performed in Cambridge at Harvard Stadium in 1917 but the subsequent war mobilization prevented its performance elsewhere. "Scrapbook: Civic Drama Association, 1916," Percy MacKaye (PMK) Papers, Baker Library, Dartmouth College, Hanover, N.H. (hereafter cited as PMK Papers). MacKaye's other public project in 1916 was *The New Citizenship* (New York: Macmillan, 1915), a ritual designed to accompany naturalization ceremonies, performed in New York City, St. Louis, and Denver.

17. Thomas Wood Stevens, *The Pageant of Newark* (Newark, N.J.: Essex Press, 1916); William Chauncy Langdon, *The Pageant of Indiana: The Drama of the Development of the State as a Community from Its Exploration by LaSalle to the Centennial of Its Admission to the Union* (Indianapolis: Hollenbeck, 1916). The Indiana Historical Commission designated Langdon "State Pageant-master" for 1916. See *The Indiana Centennial, 1916*, ed. Herbert Lindley (Indianapolis: Indiana Historical Commission, 1919). Yale University displayed its battery guns as part of its bicentennial pageant in 1916. *Book of the Yale Pageant* (New Haven: Yale University Press, 1916); William Chauncy Langdon, *Bronxville (N.Y.) Christmas Mystery*, 1914.

18. Among the works on federal agencies promoting American mobilization during World War I are David M. Kennedy, *Over Here: The First World War and American Society* (New York: Oxford University Press, 1980); Robert Cuff, *The War Industries Board* (Baltimore: Johns Hopkins University Press, 1973); George Creel, *How We Advertised America* (New York: Harper and Brothers, 1920), and James R. Mock and Cedric Larson, *Words that Won the War: The Story of the Committee on Public Information, 1917–19* (Princeton, N.J.: Princeton University Press, 1939), on the Committee on Public Information; and Raymond Fosdick, *Chronicle of a Generation* (New York: Harper and Brothers, 1958). Fosdick headed the U.S. War Department's Commission on Training Camp Activities. A contemporary survey of War Camp Community Service's activities in wartime appears in Martha Candler, "The Better Cities which the War Camp Community Service Is Building," *American City* 19 (October 1918): 262–65. Also see Richard Knapp, "The Playground and Recreation Association of America during World War One," *Parks and Recreation*, January 1972, pp. 27–31, 110–12.

19. The American peace movement split when America entered the war. Some pacifists, like Jane Addams, who opposed the conflict, insisted that the

nation should exert its might on behalf of nonviolent arbitration rather than taking the side of one of the belligerents. Others in the peace movement went along with American military intervention in Europe as a forceful means of restoring the peace. See DeBenedetti, *Peace Reform in American History*, and David S. Patterson, "An Interpretation of the American Peace Movement, 1898–1914," in *Peace Movements in America*, ed. Charles Chatfield (New York: Schocken Books, 1973), pp. 20–38.

20. Robert Woods, "The Regimentation of the Free," *Survey* 40 (July 1918): 395. Allen F. Davis discusses social workers' support for war mobilization in "Welfare, Reform, and World War One," *American Quarterly* 19 (Fall 1967): 516–33.

21. Woods, "Regimentation of the Free," p. 399; *Report of the Connecticut State Council of Defense, December 1918* (Hartford: Bond Press, 1919), p. 10. Also see "Neighborhood Councils of Defense," *Bulletin of the National Community Center Association*, November 9, 1917, records of the Committee on Public Information, RG 63, box 90, National Archives. David M. Kennedy notes that the federal agencies' direct public campaigns often bypassed the state and local councils. Kennedy, *Over Here*, pp. 116–17.

William Chauncy Langdon, "American Pageantry and the War," *Brown University Alumni Monthly* 18 (June 1917): 7. Langdon urged American intervention in the war before 1917. He joined the American Legion in March 1916 and sent to the Pennsylvania National Guard for the "Marksman" and "Sharpshooter" bars that he had earned in high school thirty years earlier. Langdon confessed, six months after the nation's declaration of war, that he had "no sympathy whatsoever for the standpoint of 'conscientious pacifism' if there is such a thing." October 4, 1917, William Chauncy Langdon (WCL) Papers, Harris Collection, John Hay Library, Brown University, Providence, R.I. (hereafter cited as WCL Papers; see Chapter 3, n. 1).

22. Ibid., p. 7.

23. Pageantry's role in "organizing the soul of America" for war was proclaimed in Edward Greenlaw, "The Significance of the Community Pageant," in *The Community Pageant: An Agency for the Promotion of Democracy*, University of North Carolina Extension Leaflets, War Information Series, no. 16, 1918, p. 13. Greenlaw was a professor of English at the University of North Carolina.

24. WCL to Brooks Peters, August 4, 1917, and WCL to Virginia Tanner Green, November 1, 1918, WCL Papers.

25. "Statement to War Camp Community Service from the American Pageant Association, September, 1918," in vol. 43, Thomas Wood Stevens (TWS) Collection, University of Arizona Library, Tucson (hereafter cited as TWS Papers). Also see "Pageantry in War Service," *APA Bulletin*, no. 58, September 15, 1918, and Langdon's response to the plan, WCL to Virginia Tanner Green, November 1, 1918, WCL Papers. The statistics on the size of War Camp Community Service come from Knapp, "Playground and Recreation Association."

26. Knapp, "Playground and Recreation Association"; "Plan Followed in Subdividing Work of Many Local Committees, August, 1917," Commission on Training Camp Activities (CTCA) Papers, RG 165, National Archives (hereaf-

ter cited as CTCA Papers); WCCS materials, National Parks and Recreation Association headquarters, Arlington, Va.; WCCS, *Keep 'Em Smiling* (handbook of activities, December 1918); Howard Braucher, "Organizing the Social and Recreational Life of Communities near Camps," *Drama League Monthly* 2 (October 1917): 474–75; Guy Lewis, "World War One and the Emergence of Sport for the Masses," *Maryland Historian* 4 (Fall 1973): 109–22.

For a more detailed description of Liberty Theatre programs, see Fosdick, *Chronicle of a Generation*, p. 153. Franklin Sargeant quoted in Liberty Theatre Bulletin, October 2, 1917 (or 1918?), RG 165, box 400, CTCA Drama Department, National Archives.

WCL to Virginia Tanner Green, November 1, 1918, WCL Papers. Thomas Wood Stevens did get a chance to entertain the troops in France in 1918 with his play *Joan of Arc*; Langdon got over to Europe in time to produce his *Poilu and Yank* for Memorial Day, 1919.

27. Creel, *How We Advertised America*, and Mock and Larson, *Words that Won the War*, describe the activities of the Committee on Public Information's Motion Picture Division during World War I. The motion picture industry describes its contributions to the war effort in articles such as "Paramount Reviews War Work," *Motion Picture News* 18 (September 21, 1918): 1840; "Liberty Loan Unites Duty and Opportunity," *Motion Picture News* 18 (September 28, 1918): 2006–7; and "The Screen in Wartime," *Moving Picture World* 38 (October 19, 1918): 371–72. Also see Michael T. Isenberg, *War on Film: The American Cinema and World War One, 1914–41* (Rutherford, N.J.: Farleigh-Dickinson University Press, 1981).

28. "Red Cross Pageant Fills Metropolitan," *New York Times*, October 26, 1917, p. 13; Nina Lamkin, *America, Yesterday and Today* (Chicago: T. S. Denison, 1917), p. 5; Percy MacKaye, *The Roll Call: A Masque of the Red Cross* (New York: Williams Printing Co., 1918).

29. Clara Fitch, "Festival Committee Plans and Suggestions for 1918," *Drama League Monthly* 2 (1917): 491; Thomas Wood Stevens, Preface to *The Drawing of the Sword* (Boston: C. C. Birchard, 1918).

30. William Chauncy Langdon, *The Sword of America* (Champaign, Ill.: Twin City Printing Co., 1917), p. 15; "Red Cross Pageant Fills Metropolitan," *New York Times*, October 26, 1917, p. 13; also Percy MacKaye, *Roll Call*; Constance D'Arcy MacKay, *A Patriotic Christmas Pageant*, in RG 165, CTCA Papers. My description of typical pageant formats and historical themes during World War I is also based on my readings in the collections of the Library of Congress and the New York Public Library, New York City.

31. Maud May Parker, *A Pageant of Yesterday and Today* (New Orleans: Hauser Printing Co., 1917), p. 57; Wallace Rice, *The Masque of Illinois* (Springfield: Jefferson's Printing Co., 1918).

32. WCL to Percival Chubb, October 25 and 27, 1916, WCL Papers.

33. National Pageantry Corporation, *The Glory of Old Glory* (Cedar Rapids, Iowa: Torch Press, 1917).

34. One of Langdon's not too subtle historical parallels: "Again the Men of '76 Advance to Meet the Hessians." Langdon, *Masque of the Titans of Freedom* (Champaign, Ill.: Twin Cities Printing, 1918), p. 19.

35. Percy MacKaye, *Washington: The Man Who Made Us* (New York: Alfred A.

Knopf, 1918). MacKaye prepared both indoor and outdoor versions of this work. It was never performed outdoors, but the indoor version premiered in Washington, D.C., on Washington's Birthday, 1920. The greatest public exposure to MacKaye's *Washington* occurred on July 4, 1926, when WGBS radio in New York City broadcast the "Washington at the Delaware" episode as part of its program commemorating the 150th anniversary of American independence.

Linwood Taft, "The Progress of Liberty," reprinted in his manual, *The Technique of Pageantry* (New York: A. S. Barnes, 1921), pp. 163–66; performed in Jefferson City, Mo., June 19–20, 1918. Federal agencies in wartime so suppressed vivid depictions in film and literature of the nation's past conflicts with Great Britain that pageant writers remained wary of too realistic treatment of the events surrounding the American Revolution—with the exception of Colonists battling Hessians. For more on the official suppression of anti-British imagery in American mass media during the war, see Horace C. Peterson and Gilbert C. Fite, *Opponents of War, 1917–18* (Madison: University of Wisconsin Press, 1957), pp. 92–93, and George T. Blakely, *Historians on the Homefront* (Lexington: University of Kentucky Press, 1970), p. 88.

36. Joseph Lee, "Fourth of July Special Exercises, 1918," WCCS materials in Papers of National Recreation and Parks Association headquarters, Arlington, Va.

37. Ibid.

38. Connecticut State Council of Defense, "Liberty Choruses and Community Singing," memo, November 1918. The Committee on Public Information's "Four Minute Men" established a "Four Minute Singing" branch that prepared slides with the words to popular songs so they could be projected on movie screens between features. Carol Oukrop, "The Four Minute Men Became National Network during World War One," *Journalism Quarterly* 52 (Winter 1975): 634–36. For a description of the American community singing movement during the war, see *Fifty-Five Songs and Choruses for Community Singing* (Boston: C. C. Birchard, 1917); "To Nationalize Community Music as War Measure," *Musical America* 28 (July 27, 1918): 1, 3–4; and "Community Singing Grows in Popularity," *Playground* 12 (1919): 427–28.

39. J. R. Jones, "Community Singing," *Playground* 12 (June 1918): 122; Robert D. Dripps, "The Liberty Sing Idea," *Playground* 12 (1918): 238; also see the compilation of "Liberty Songs" distributed by the Connecticut State Council of Defense, Library of Congress.

40. Connecticut State Council of Defense, "Instructions to War Workers," document among miscellaneous collections of Connecticut State Council of Defense materials, Library of Congress; Illinois Centennial Commission, "Children of the Civil War," in *Six Centennial Plays* (Springfield, Ill.: Schnepp and Barnes, 1918); "Are You an Apathist?," *Hartford Times*, March 6, 1918.

41. Wood, "Heat Up the Melting Pot," p. 15. The U.S. Bureau of Education issued its first "Americanization Bulletin" in September 1918. For more on Americanization during World War I, see John Higham, *Strangers in the Land: Patterns of American Nativism, 1860–1925* (1955; reprint, New York: Atheneum, 1972), pp. 190–220.

Constance D'Arcy MacKay, *Patriotic Drama in Your Town* (New York: Henry Holt, 1918), pp. 10, 69, 120.

42. P. P. Claxton, "Americanization," *U.S. Department of the Interior Bureau of Education Americanization Bulletin*, no. 1, September 15, 1918, p. 1. Claxton, the U.S. Commissioner of Education, extolled the "Americanization" potential of public celebrations. For a description of one such parade in Springfield, Mass., see "Mighty Column Marches through City," *Springfield Republican*, July 5, 1918, pp. 1–2.

43. American Scenic and Historic Preservation Society, *Report for 1918* (Albany: J. B. Lyon, 1919), p. 128; Frances R. Grant, "Negro Patriotism and Negro Music: How the Old 'Spirituals' Have Been Used at Penn School, Hampton, and Tuskegee to Promote Americanization," *Outlook* 121 (February 26, 1919): 341–46; Constance D'Arcy MacKay, "Christmas Pageantry for Camp and Community," *Drama League Monthly* 3 (April 1919): 5–7. The phrase "a parallel of hospitality" appeared in "War Camp Community Service—A Retrospect," p. 16, WCCS materials, National Parks and Recreation Association headquarters, Arlington, Va. Material describing War Camp Community Service's strictly segregated recreational activities for black soldiers and residents near training camps during World War I also appears in RG 165, E393, folder 33373, CTCA Papers. On race riots during World War I, see Elliott Rudwick, *Race Riot at East St. Louis, July 2, 1917* (New York: Atheneum, 1972), and Kennedy, *Over Here*.

44. "The Happiest Fourth since the First," WCCS Newsletter, July 24, 1919 (CS 42), pp. 4–5, from box 60, National Recreation Association records, Social Welfare History Archives, Minneapolis. On the victory pageant in the nation's capital, see Martha Candler, "Washington's Community Pageant," *Theatre* 30 (1919): 247, 274; on the victory celebration in New York City, see American Scenic and Historic Preservation Society, *Report for 1919* (Albany: J. B. Lyon, 1920). Also see U.S. Government Loan Organization, Second Federal Reserve District, Liberty Loan Committee, *A List of Plays and Pageants for Victory Loan Festivals of Spring and the Seed-time* (compiled by the New York City branch of the Drama League of America and the Playground and Recreation Association of America), 1919.

Linwood Taft, "Pageant of Thanksgiving," reprinted in Taft, *The Technique of Pageantry*, pp. 109–38, performed in Savannah, Ga., November 29, 1919; Esther Willard Bates, *A Pageant of the League of Free Nations* (Boston: Massachusetts Joint Committee for the League of Free Nations, 1919).

45. Isenberg, *War on Film*, p. 53.

46. John Milton Berdan, "American Songs of the War," *Connecticut State Council of Defense Bulletin*, April 19, 1918, p. 2.

47. "Preparedness and Playgrounds" was proposed as a topic for the Playground and Recreation Association of America Conference in Grand Rapids, Mich., in October 1919. *Playground* 10 (July 1916): 119.

48. Percy MacKaye, *Community Drama: Its Motive and Method of Neighborliness* (New York: Houghton-Mifflin, 1917), p. vii. MacKaye insisted on p. 41 of the essay that "Community Drama must be organized with the permanency and trained efficiency of the regular army."

Chapter 7. The Receding Past

1. Cameron quoted in *Official Souvenir Program—Fostoria Centennial: One Hundred Years of Progress, 1832–1932*, John B. Rogers Co. (JBR) Collection, Fostoria, Ohio (hereafter cited as JBR Collection).

2. Weaver Pangburn, "The War and the Community Movement," *American Journal of Sociology* 6 (July 1920): 86, 91–92.

3. "Community Service in the United States," pamphlet, Playground and Recreation Association of America (PRAA) Files, National Parks and Recreation Association, Arlington, Va. (hereafter cited as PRAA Files). Community Service, Incorporated, was one of three national recreation organizations in the 1920s with nearly identical boards of directors; the other two were War Camp Community Service (WCCS) and the Playground and Recreation Association of America. Community Service had difficulty raising funds beyond the initial $200,000 grant from the Laura Spelman Rockefeller Memorial and folded back into the Playground and Recreation Association by the end of 1922. War Camp Community Service remained in existence officially until 1930, when the funds it raised during World War I (which legally could not be transferred directly to Community Service, Incorporated) finally were exhausted. The Playground and Recreation Association of America used the WCCS surplus (as much as $1.5 million as late as 1922) to subsidize its activities in the 1920s. These confusing institutional arrangements are explained in greater detail in Richard Knapp, "Play for America: Part IV, Community Service: The Aftermath of War," and "Part V, Prosperity Decade: The 1920s," *Parks and Recreation* (February 1973): 30–32, 49–52, and (April 1973): 33–37, 56–67.

4. Albert S. Bard wrote of Civil War memorials, "It was the golden age of the monument man and the local stonecutter, but the glacial period of American sculpture." Bard, "What Sort of War Memorial," one in a series of pamphlets, *Community Buildings as War Memorials*, Community Service, Inc., 1919, p. 6.

5. Bard, "Existing Community Houses," same series, 1919, p. 3.

6. Jay B. Nash, "How Can a City Recreation System Increase the Sum Total of Unorganized, Individual, and Small Group Play and Recreation?" *Playground* 21 (March 1928): 646; *A Positive Force in Reconstruction—Community Service, Inc.*, pamphlet (1919), PRAA Files.

7. "A Positive Force in Reconstruction"; *New York War Camp Community Service Journal of Information* (July 1919): 9; Raymond Calkins, "Substitutes for the Saloon," *Playground* 13 (August 1919): 176–78.

8. Joseph Lee, "The Permanents," *Playground* 16 (December 1922): 406, 408. Ironically, colleges in the 1920s nurtured new peer cultures removed from those of family and community. On the importance of college students "fitting in" to one or another peer group in the 1920s, see Paula Fass, *The Damned and the Beautiful: American Youth in the 1920s* (New York: Oxford University Press, 1977).

Mary M. Russell, *Drama as a Factor in Social Education* (New York: Doran, 1924), p. 80. On the influence of psychological theory on the playground movement and social work, see Dominick Cavallo, *Muscles and Morals: Orga-*

nized Playgrounds and Urban Reform, 1880–1920 (Philadelphia: University of Pennsylvania Press, 1981), and Clark Chambers, *Seedtime of Reform: American Social Service and Social Action, 1918–33* (Minneapolis: University of Minnesota Press, 1963).

9. On the Red Scare, see Robert Murray, *Red Scare: A Study in National Hysteria, 1919–20* (Minneapolis: University of Minnesota Press, 1955); Stanley Coben, "A Study in Nativism: The American Red Scare of 1919–20," *Political Science Quarterly* 79 (March 1964): 52–75; and Burl Noggle, *Into the Twenties* (Urbana: University of Illinois Press, 1974), pp. 84–121.

The American Legion organized as a veterans group in May 1919, taking its name from the preparedness organization that flourished before America entered the war. By 1920, the Legion claimed 843,000 members, over one-fifth of those eligible to join, in posts throughout the United States. Richard S. Jones, *A History of the American Legion* (Indianapolis, 1946), p. 344. Community Service entered into a brief, uneasy alliance with the American Legion to use the Legion's extensive network to further its goals of fostering wholesome recreation and community solidarity. Community Service pumped a half-million dollars into joint activities with the American Legion from November 1919 to February 1920, but it seems to have targeted the money for recreational activities at the post level and not to support the Legion's "100% Americanism" national political program. "Three Emblems: War Camp Community Service, Community Service, and the American Legion," pamphlet, PRAA Files.

Lee to Braucher, November 29, 1919, PRAA Files. Lee admitted to Braucher that he was "a little scared" of Community Service's relationship with the American Legion and suggested that Community Service seize the initiative in all joint projects, "putting things up to them so that they won't have time to put the wrong things up to us."

Braucher to WCCS Workers, WCCS Letter 10, March 6, 1919, PRAA Files. Braucher proclaimed in the same message that "Community Service, in bringing both employers and workers together in fraternal relationships, is doing much to steady public sentiment throughout America at this critical time."

Fund-raising letter, September 5, 1919, PRAA Files; *New York War Camp Community Service Journal of Information* (July 1919): 10; "A Positive Force in Reconstruction," p. 3.

10. Constance D'Arcy MacKay, "Imaginative Rural Recreation," *Playground* 14 (September 1920): 374–75; Kenneth S. Clark, "If Main Street Had Community Service," *Playground* 15 (January 1922): 613.

11. Ethel Armes, "Dramatic Activities Fostered by Community Service," *Theatre Magazine* 32 (October 1920): 202. Also see Maud Howell Smith, "The War Camp Community Service and the Drama League—A Plan for United Effort," *Drama League Monthly* 4 (May 1919): 17–19.

12. The organization and work of the Department of Community Drama is profiled in Percy J. Burrell, "Suggestions and Recommendations regarding Policies and Future Program of Community Service, Inc., in Relation to Dramatics and Pageantry," March 19, 1921, PRAA Files. Lamkin's Chautauqua work is described in "Chautauqua Stars," *Everybody's Magazine* 33 (September

1915): 329. A description of Lamkin's pageant activities for Community Service in Greenville, S.C., appears in Ethel Armes, "Away Down South in Dixie: A Little Study of Community Values in a Pageant," *Playground* 15 (February 1922): 663–65.

13. Ethel Armes, "Community Drama Activities," *Theatre Magazine* 35 (March 1922): 179, and (January 1922): 44; Braucher, "Memorandum regarding Dramatic Work of Community Service," November 20, 1921, PRAA Files; "For Mr. Dickie," cover letter to Braucher, "Memorandum"; Constance D'Arcy MacKay, *America Triumphant* (New York: D. Appleton and Co., 1926), p. 66.

14. Constance D'Arcy MacKay, "Imaginative Rural Recreation," p. 374; MacKay, *Community Drama* (New York, 1921), p. 77.

15. PRAA, *Community Drama: Suggestions for a Community-Wide Program of Dramatic Activities* (New York: Century Co., 1926), p. vii; "That Glorious Fourth," *Playground* 20 (June 1926): 174.

16. Burrell, "Suggestions and Recommendations."

17. Among the other large commercial firms that produced amateur indoor shows and outdoor pageants were the Wayne P. Sewell Producing Company of Atlanta, Ga.; the Empire Producing Co. of Kansas City, Mo.; and the Universal Producing Company of Fairfield, Iowa. On the fortunes of the latter company, which hired exclusively female directors, see Lorelei F. Eckey, "Pilgrims of the Impossible," *Palimpsest* 61 (February 1980), and Lorelei F. Eckey, William T. Schoyer, and Maxine Allen Schoyer, *1001 Broadways: Hometown Talent on Stage* (Ames: Iowa State University Press, 1982). My understanding of John B. Rogers Company activities comes from examining pageant scripts and ephemeral materials housed in the firm's former headquarters in Fostoria, Ohio (JBR Collection); an interview with Phil Frable, president of the Rogers Company, Pittsburgh, Pa., October 1979; and two rather puffed-up histories of the firm: Webb Waldron, "Nothing Amateur but the Cast," *Reader's Digest* (condensed from *Kiwanis Magazine*), July 1939, pp. 74–76; and David Dempsey and Dan Herr, "Everybody Gets in the Act," *Saturday Evening Post*, November 27, 1948, p. 35ff. One former Rogers Company director acknowledged the debt the firm's standard formula owed to Constance D'Arcy MacKay's book of model pageants, *Plays of the Pioneers* (1915). Correspondence with Lorelei F. Eckey, (November 7, 1980).

18. Thomas Wood Stevens (TWS) letter, August 16, 1919, vol. 9, TWS to Stuart Walker, October 9, 1920, vol. 10, and Stevens, "On Pageants: Personal Notes, 1939," vol. 46, all in TWS Collection, University of Arizona Library, Tucson (hereafter cited as TWS Papers).

19. One example of Sinclair Lewis's rather harsh treatment of typical pageant elements was his portrait of Dr. Pickerbaugh's Nautilus Health Fair in *Arrowsmith* (1925). Consider also Meredith Willson's recollection of the mayor's wife directing the women of River City as "Grecian Urns" in *The Music Man* (1957).

20. Richard Connell, "Mr. Pottle and Pageantry," *Saturday Evening Post*, January 14, 1922, pp. 10–11, 34, 36. On the origins of the Miss America pageant, see Lois Banner, *American Beauty* (New York: Knopf, 1983), p. 268.

21. Thomas Wood Stevens, *The Theater from Athens to Broadway* (New York: Appleton Century, 1932). On Stevens's career in the 1920s and 1930s, see William R. Rambin, Jr., "Thomas Wood Stevens: American Pageant-Master" (Ph.D. dissertation, Louisiana State University, 1977). For a complete list of Stevens's pageants of the 1920s, see Rambin, "Thomas Wood Stevens," or the special issue dedicated to Stevens, *Educational Theatre Journal* 3 (December 1951): 280–321. On intellectuals in the interwar years who saw their role as spanning elite and popular culture, see Joan Shelley Rubin, "'Information Please': Culture and Expertise in the Interwar Period," *American Quarterly* 35 (Winter 1983): 500–01.

22. Percy MacKaye, *The Will of Song: A Dramatic Service of Community Singing* (New York: Boni and Liveright, 1919), p. 62; Norman Bel Geddes to PMK, shortly after October 6, 1921, PMK Papers. MacKaye also negotiated with Geddes to produce *A Masque of Modernity* for Detroit in 1928, and with Percy J. Burrell to create a *Masque of the Erie Canal* in Schenectady in 1925. Neither was produced. See *Annals of an Era: Percy MacKaye and the MacKaye Family*, ed. Edwin Osgood Grover (Washington, D.C.: The Pioneer Press [for Dartmouth College], 1932), p. xxxiii.

23. Although Percy MacKaye's physical reasons for not undertaking large-scale public celebrations in the 1920s seem compelling, he had overcome similar nervous breakdowns and bouts of poor health since the early 1900s to create his civic masques. It was not his infirmities that led MacKaye to abandon pageantry for folk drama in the 1920s as much as his feeling that large-scale pageants were no longer worth the exertion involved. Arvia MacKaye Ege and Christy MacKaye Barnes, interviews with author, Hillsdale, N.Y., August 1984.

24. On American intellectuals' doubts in the 1920s that they could use the American past to redeem mass culture and their place as interpreters of genuine American artistic traditions, see David Glassberg, "Restoring a 'Forgotten Childhood': American Play and the Progressive Era's Elizabethan Past," *American Quarterly* 32 (Fall 1980): 351–68. For a concise discussion of what separates the "Victorian" from the "Modernist" temperament, see Daniel Joseph Singal, *The War Within: From Victorian to Modernist Thought in the South* (Chapel Hill: University of North Carolina Press, 1982), p. 8, and Singal, "Towards a Definition of American Modernism," *American Quarterly* 39 (Spring 1987): 7–26.

25. Percy MacKaye, "The Three Guardsmen at Atlanta," in *Debs and the Poets*, ed. Ruth Le Prade (Pasadena, Calif.: Upton Sinclair, 1920), p. 54. Debs was imprisoned in Atlanta. "At the Break of Light," MacKaye's poem about the execution of Sacco and Vanzetti, was submitted to the *Nation* on August 23, 1927, but was not published. A complete list of MacKaye's poetry in the 1920s appears in *Annals of an Era*, pp. 89–92. MacKaye's daughters recall their father expressing sympathy with a variety of causes in the 1920s but not engaged in any sustained political activity. Ege and Barnes, interviews with author. Corresponding with Granville Hicks concerning Hicks's biography of John Reed, MacKaye identified himself as a forerunner of the radical writers of the 1930s, though they regarded him as "terribly confused." Katherine

Buckles to Granville Hicks, July 5, 1935, Granville Hicks Papers, George Arents Research Library, Syracuse University.

MacKaye expressed his view of Appalachia's "Anglo-Saxon" and "Celtic" folk heritage in his *Kentucky Mountain Fantasies* (New York: Longmans, Green and Co. 1928), p. xi. MacKaye's interest in the Anglo-Saxon and Celtic heritage of the region over that of other ethnic groups might have been stimulated by his exploration of his own Scottish background in the 1920s while he prepared the biography of his father. During a trip to Europe in 1869, Steele MacKaye had changed the spelling of the family name from McKay to MacKaye to remind acquaintances that he pronounced his name in the Scottish manner to rhyme with sky, not hay. See *Epoch: The Life of Steele MacKaye* (New York: Boni and Liveright, 1927), 1:131. MacKaye described his association with Cecil Sharp in *Wakefield: A Folk-Masque of the Birth of Washington* (Washington, D.C.: U.S. George Washington Bicentennial Commission, 1932), p. 119.

26. Percy MacKaye was "artist in residence" at Miami intermittently between 1920 and 1924, one of the first creative artists to be so appointed by an American university. Benton MacKaye described his Appalachian Trail idea in much the same terms as his brother Percy had extolled community pageantry in the previous decade. Among the reasons Benton gave for the creation of the trail was the value of conservation and hiking outdoors as a moral equivalent of war. See Benton MacKaye, "An Appalachian Trail: A Project in Regional Planning," *Journal of the American Institute of Architects* 9 (October 1921): 325–30.

27. Percy MacKaye's appearance at the White Top Folk Festival in 1933 is discussed in David E. Whisnant, *All That Is Native and Fine: The Politics of Culture in an American Region* (Chapel Hill: University of North Carolina Press, 1983), p. 193. My sense of what MacKaye might have encountered at Pine Mountain Settlement in the 1920s relies on the description of the school in Whisnant, pp. 122–24. The volume of *Folk-Say* that MacKaye edited also contained contributions by his wife Marian and three children Robert, Arvia, and Christy, as well as Carl Sandburg, Mary Austin, and several other American writers interested in American folklore. See *Folk-Say: A Regional Miscellany* (Norman: University of Oklahoma Press, 1930), and Ben Botkin, "The Kentucky Mountain Cycles of Percy MacKaye," *American Speech*, 1931.

28. On the "penetrating magneto," see Percy MacKaye, *The Gobbler of God* (New York: Longmans, Green and Co., 1928), p. xii; MacKaye's comments on the "world of Marconi" appeared in his *Kentucky Mountain Fantasies*, p. xi.

29. Percy MacKaye, "Untamed America: A Comment on a Sojourn in the Kentucky Mountains," *Survey* 51 (January 1, 1924): 328, 362. MacKaye's conception of American culture, though racialist, remained pluralistic; he felt that American culture consisted of the sum of its ethnic groups as a mosaic, and he did not express a belief common among nativist artists of the period such as composer John Powell of Virginia that the "Anglo-Saxon" was the true or superior American folk culture. For more on Powell, see Whisnant, *All That Is Native and Fine*, pp. 237–44.

30. My discussion of Koch's career is based on my reading of his papers in

the Southern Historical Collection, University of North Carolina, Chapel Hill, and Samuel Selden, *Frederick Henry Koch: Pioneer Playmaker* (Chapel Hill: University of North Carolina Library, 1954).

31. *Raleigh, the Shepherd of the Ocean* (Raleigh: Edwards and Broughton, 1920); Susan Iden, "The Raleigh Pageant," *East Carolina Teachers' Training School Quarterly* 8 (October–December 1920): 15–19. Much of the material documenting the activities of the Bureau of Community Drama is contained in "Bureau of Community Drama Scrapbook, 1923–30," North Carolina Collection, Wilson Library, University of North Carolina, Chapel Hill. Also see Ethel Theodora Rockwell, "Children of Old Carolina," *University of North Carolina Extension Bulletin* 4 (1925); the program to *Children of Old Carolina*, initial performance, Dunn, N.C., October 7, 1924, North Carolina Collection; and Rockwell, "Harlequinading in North Carolina," *Theatre Magazine* 45 (January 1927): 42–43.

32. Frederick H. Koch, "Making a Folk Theater," in *Carolina Folk Plays*, ed. Frederick H. Koch (New York: Henry Holt, 1924), 2:xiii. Also see Koch, "Folk-Play Making in Dakota and Carolina," *Playground* 18 (January 1925): 599–600. On the history of the Carolina Playmakers, see Walter Spearman, *The Carolina Playmakers* (Chapel Hill: University of North Carolina Press, 1970).

"Bureau of Community Drama Scrapbook, 1923–30," North Carolina Collection.

33. Thomas H. Dickinson, *The Case of American Drama* (New York: Houghton Mifflin, 1915), pp. 180–81; Harriett L. Jones, "Dramatics in the Kentucky Mountains," *Playground* 19 (November 1925): 446; Frederick H. Koch, "American Drama in the Making," *Carolina Play Book* 8 (September 1935): 80. On the imposition of folk drama in the 1920s upon more indigenous Appalachian cultural forms, see Whisnant, *All That Is Native and Fine*, p. 204.

34. See Sarah D. Lowrie and Mabel Stewart Ludlum, *The Sesqui-centennial High Street* (Philadelphia: J. B. Lippincott, 1926). Also see William W. Matos, "Pageantry, Drama, and Spectacle," in *The Sesquicentennial International Exposition*, ed. E. L. Austin and O. Hauser (Philadelphia, 1929), pp. 238–48.

35. R. T. H. Halsey and Elizabeth Tower, *The Homes of Our Ancestors as Shown in the American Wing of the Metropolitan Museum of Art* (Garden City, N.Y.: Doubleday, Page, and Co., 1925), p. xxii.

36. TWS to F. C. Brown, April 3, 1920, vol. 10, TWS Papers.

37. William Chauncy Langdon (WCL) to F. H. Koch, November 17, 1922, and WCL to Lotta Clark, December 6, 1922, WCL Papers, Harris Collection, John Hay Library, Brown University, Providence, R.I. (hereafter cited as WCL Papers; see Chapter Three, n. 1).

38. Langdon discussed these ambitions in letters to his brother-in-law. WCL to Conrad P. Hatheway, February 26, 1921, WCL Papers.

39. Langdon's daughter reports that her father seemed quite absorbed in AT&T work in the 1920s. Margaret Langdon, interview with author, Bronxville, N.Y., May 1979.

40. Lotta Clark identified herself as secretary of the American Pageant Association in *The Drama of American Independence* (1926), a guidebook distributed by the National Education Association for schools staging historical pageants to commemorate the U.S. Sesquicentennial.

41. William Chauncy Langdon, *Everyday Things in American Life*, vol. 1, *1607–1776* (New York: Scribners, 1937); vol. 2, *1776–1876* (New York: Scribners, 1941).

42. For the APA's activities surrounding the Massachusetts tercentenary, see Lotta Clark to George F. Kunz, January 6, 1930, George F. Kunz Papers, New-York Historical Society; *Who's Who in Pageantry*, 2d ed., 1930.

43. JBR Collection; *Official Program of Ceremonies and Pageant of Alabama Homecoming Week*, ed. Peter A. Brannon Montgomery, May 5–6, 1926; *Sesquicentennial Celebration of River Falls*, Wisconsin State Normal School, 1924; *Official Program, Elizabeth, New Jersey, U.S. Sesquicentennial Pageant* (Elizabeth: E. G. Gommel Print Shop, 1926).

44. Pearl Setzer, *Visions Old and New: A Historical Pageant of Gaston County, N.C.* (Gastonia: Carolina Printing Co., 1924). Setzer, a student of Frederick Koch at the University of North Carolina, worked for the Bureau of Community Drama.

Florence Magill Wallace, "The Gateway," *State Centennial Souvenir and Program, Missouri Valley Historical Society* 1 (October 1921): 130–36. Margaret Ehresman, *Pageant of Arkansas* (Morrilton: Living Message Publishing Co., 1925), p. 34. For an example of the alternating "Band and Audience" pageant format, see *Bicentennial Celebration of the Settlement of Litchfield, Connecticut*, ed. Alan C. White (Litchfield: Litchfield Enquirer, 1920).

45. Margaret Brandenburg, "Drama at Miami University," *Theatre* 32 (November 1920): 292; Sue Ann Wilson, *Yankee Doodle Festival*, given on Long Island, July 4, 1921, in Library of Congress; *Two Hundredth Anniversary in Commemoration of the Town of Stoughton, Mass.*, ed. Edward H. Ewing (Stoughton, 1926).

46. "New York Paper Finds Radicalism in Pageant," *Lexington Times*, July 3, 1925, p. 1; reprinted from *New York Commercial*, June 18, 1925. In 1925, Sidney Coe Howard won the Pulitzer Prize in drama for *They Knew What They Wanted*; among his later achievements was the screenplay for the motion picture *Gone with the Wind*. His eight-part series, "Our Professional Patriots," appeared in the *New Republic* 39 (August 20, 1924): 346–52; 40 (September 3–October 15, 1924): 12–16, 37–41, 71–75, 93–95, 119–23, 143–45, 171–73. For more on the Lexington pageant, see Sidney Howard, *Lexington: A Pageant-Drama of the American Freedom* (Lexington Historical Society, 1924), performed June 15–20, 1925; *Program, Lexington: Birthplace of American Liberty* (Cambridge: Banta Press, 1925), Harvard Theatre Collection; and Ann Marie Shea, "Community Pageants in Massachusetts, 1908–32" (Ph.D. dissertation, New York University, 1984).

47. "A League of Nations," *Playground* 13 (July 1919): 143–51; Marguerite Block, *Pageant of Reading, Pennsylvania* (October 1–3, 1923); Percy J. Burrell, *A Pageant of Liberty* (Lancaster, Pa.: Lancaster Press, 1926), held July 5–7, 1926.

48. John Dewey, "Americanism and Localism," *Dial* 68 (June 1920): 684–88; "The Heart of Life," *Playground* 15 (August 1921): 316–18, reprinted from "Regionalism in America," *Nebraska State Journal* (December 26, 1920); Koch, "Folk-Play Making in Dakota and Carolina," p. 599.

49. Pageants in states of the Old Confederacy composed only 5.5 percent of the total sample of seventy-three pageants from 1910 to 1919, but 21.1 per-

cent of the sample of seventy-one pageants from 1920 to 1929. Samples were drawn primarily from the local history collections of the Library of Congress. Only two local historical pageants in the North Carolina Collection and the Southern Historical Collection of the University of North Carolina at Chapel Hill dated from before World War I.

50. On the progressive reform efforts of southern women in the decade, see Anne Firor Scott, "After Suffrage: Southern Women in the 1920s," *Journal of Southern History* 30 (1964): 298–318. The characterization of southern politics in the 1920s in terms of a confrontation between progress and reaction appears in George B. Tindall, *The Emergence of the New South, 1913–1945* (Baton Rouge: Louisiana State University Press, 1967), pp. 208–24, and Dewey Grantham, *Southern Progressivism: The Reconciliation of Progress and Tradition* (Knoxville: University of Tennessee Press, 1983), pp. 410–22. It can also be found in Lawrence W. Levine, *Defender of the Faith: William Jennings Bryan, the Last Decade* (New York: Oxford University Press, 1965). On Confederate memorials and veterans' rituals in the South, see Charles Reagan Wilson, "The Religion of the Lost Cause: Ritual and Organization of the Southern Civil Religion, 1865–1920," *Journal of Southern History* 46 (May 1980): 219–38; Wilson, *Baptized in Blood: The Religion of the Lost Cause, 1865–1920* (Athens: University of Georgia Press, 1980); and Gaines M. Foster, *Ghosts of the Confederacy: Defeat, the Lost Cause, and the Emergence of the New South, 1896 to 1913* (New York: Oxford University Press, 1987).

51. Hollis quoted in Ethel Ames, "Community Dramatic Activities," *Theatre* 35 (February 1922): 112; Greenlaw, Foreword to *Raleigh: Shepherd of the Ocean.*

52. *Official Program, Macon, Ga., Centennial Celebration,* May 1923; *Official Program of Ceremonies,* Montgomery, Ala., May 5–6, 1926; *Official Souvenir Program of Lexington, Kentucky, Sesquicentennial Jubilee Celebration,* May 31–June 6, 1926; Eloise Bernheim Burkhimer, *The Rise and Fall of the Confederacy Historical Pageant,* United Confederate Veterans, Charlotte, N.C., June 5, 1929. Burkhimer and her sister ran a dance studio in Charlotte and staged several other historical pageants in the southwestern Carolinas.

"An Atlanta Pageant," *Drama* 11 (May 1921): 288–89; *The Birthright: A Pageant Portraying the History of Burke County,* official program (Morgantown: News Herald, 1924); John A. Livingstone, "Historic Past of Burke County Is Seen in Pageant," Raleigh *News and Observer,* May 23, 1925. The audience applause for the Klan is mentioned in John A. Livingstone, "Loge Patton's Spirit Still Lives in Burke County," Raleigh *News and Observer,* May 25, 1925.

The Spirit of the Roanoke (Roanoke Rapids, N.C.: Herald Publishing Co., 1921); Belle Doub, Effie Newton, and Margaret Adeline Wright, *Our Heritage: A Pageant of Local History Comprising the Counties of Nash and Edgecomb* (Rocky Mount, N.C.: Evening Telegraph Press, 1919), performed June 5, 1919; James Elliott Walmsley, *The Making of South Carolina: A Historical Pageant* (Rock Hill, S.C.: Record Printing Co., 1921).

53. *Book of Words: Pageant of the Lower Cape Fear* (Wilmington, N.C.: Wilmington Printing Co., 1921). Also see "Official Program, a Pageant of the Lower Cape Fear," June 7–9, 1921, and "Pageant of Cape Fear Begins June 6th," *Wilmington Dispatch,* May 31, 1921.

Eastern Carolina in Action (New Bern, N.C.: O. G. Dunn, Printer, 1924).

54. Koch's reaction to the suppression of the Green play quoted in Walter Spearman, *The Carolina Playmakers*, p. 19; *Book of Words: Pageant of the Lower Cape Fear*; Pearl Setzer, *The Building of Catawba*, performed October 2, 1925, at Hickory, N.C., under the auspices of the Catawba County Fair Association; Burkhimer, *Rise and Fall of the Confederacy*; "Pageant Greatest Show Ever Seen in Wilmington," *Wilmington Dispatch*, May 31, 1921, p. 2; "Bicentennial Pageant Shows Here Tonight," *Wilmington Dispatch*, October 9, 1930. DuBois recalled his pageant activities in a letter to S. L. Smith, May 10, 1932, published in *The Correspondence of W. E. B. DuBois*, ed. Herbert Aptheker (Amherst: University of Massachusetts Press, 1973), 1:457–58. A description of *Loyalty's Gift* at the Sesquicentennial International Exposition in Philadelphia appears in Matos, "Pageantry, Drama, and Spectacle," pp. 246–47. Another black history pageant, *The Answer: A Symbolic Pageant Showing the Contribution to America's Growth and Greatness Made by Negroes*, presented in Boston on November 29, 1921, the 110th anniversary of Wendell Phillips's birth, featured a "Spirit of Africa" as a source of strength for blacks on stage depicting the history of their race's oppression in America.

55. *Official Program of Ceremonies*, Montgomery, Ala., 1926; Phil Frable, John B. Rogers Company, interview with author, Pittsburgh, Pa., October 1979.

56. *Centennial of the Incorporation of Jamestown, New York* (Jamestown: Journal Press, 1927), p. 5; *The Torch Bearer*, Jacksonville, Ill., September 9, 1921; Community Service, Inc., *Rural and Small Community Recreation* (New York, 1921), pp. 71–72.

57. Salem historical pageant of 1914 described in Frank Chocteau Brown, "Symbolism in the Pageant of the Future," *Atlantic Educational Journal* (May 1914): 343; Nellie Stearns Messer, *A Pageant-Drama of Salem* (Salem, Mass.: Newcomb and Gruss, 1926), p. 14; Community Service, Inc., *Fun for Everyone* (New York, 1922).

58. On the decline of allegorical ritual among Masons in the 1920s, see Lynn Dumenil, *Freemasonry and American Culture, 1880–1930* (Princeton, N.J.: Princeton University Press, 1984).

59. Hermann Hagedorn to WCL, February 15, 1922, WCL Papers; "The Question Box," *Playground* 22 (August 1928): 292.

60. *Program, Kalamazoo Centennial*, June 19–23, 1929. For another example of the Rogers Company format and symbolic interludes during these years, see *Official Program, A Historical Pageant of Delaware County, Indiana*, September 27–28, 1927, JBR Collection.

61. The Rogers Company historical pageant for Columbia, S.C., in 1925 called the figure personifying the United States "Miss America." *An Historical Pageant of South Carolina* (Columbia: The State Co., 1925), performed October 23–24, 1925. The Canton, Mo., historical pageant, though apparently not produced by the Rogers Company, employed a similar combination beauty and historical pageant format. William Elien Schultz, *Cantonia: A Historical Pageant* (Canton, Mo.: Canton Press-News and Canton Record, 1930).

62. See, for example, the iridescent lavender satin "Indian" costume do-

nated by the Rogers Company in the collections of the Division of Community Life, National Museum of American History, Smithsonian Institution.

63. The earliest reference I found to the use of an electrical public address system in a civic celebration was the ceremony dedicating the Lincoln Memorial in Washington, D.C., on May 30, 1922. U.S. Office of Public Buildings and Public Parks of the National Capital, *The Lincoln Memorial* (Washington, D.C.: U.S. Government Printing Office, 1927).

64. *Historical Battle and Homecoming, Point Pleasant, West Virginia* (Charleston: Tribune Printing Co., 1925); *Official Souvenir Program, Ponce De León Celebration*, St. Augustine, Fla., April 2–4, 1925, JBR Collection. St. Augustine and the Rogers Company repeated the battle reenactment in 1927 and 1930.

65. Thomas Wood Stevens, *Book of Words: The Pageant of Virginia* (Richmond: Williams Printing Co., 1922); Constance D'Arcy MacKay, *America Triumphant*, 1926; Rockwell, "Children of Old Carolina." See Natalie Curtis Burlin, "The Negro's Contribution to the Music of America," *Craftsman* 23 (March 15, 1913): 660. Burlin (1875–1921), a musician from New York City, specialized in the recording, transcription, and publication of black and Amerindian traditional music in the early twentieth century.

Pearl Setzer, *Visions Old and New*, p. 18. Among the pageants in which Nina Lamkin used the "Green Corn Dance" were Jacksonville, Fla., Community Service, *Florida Historical Pageant* (Jacksonville: Tutewiler Press, 1922), and Lafayette Parish, Louisiana Community Service, *The Attakapas Trail* (Morgan City, La.: King-Hannaford Co., 1923).

66. The conclusion that Griffith expended more effort on obtaining accurate costume details than on interpreting the forces behind the Revolution appears in Lawrence L. Murray, "History at the Movies during the Sesquicentennial: D. W. Griffith's 'America' (1924)," *Historian* 41 (May 1979): 450–66. For more on Griffith's filming of *America*, see Richard Schickel, *D. W. Griffith: An American Life* (New York: Simon and Schuster, 1984), pp. 486–94. The film, which I saw at the Historical Society of Pennsylvania in 1983, is divided into a first part that resembles little more than a succession of well-worn tableaux vivants from the coming of the Revolution (except for the action-packed re-creation of Paul Revere's ride), and a second part that essentially alternates between one long violent battle scene and a tawdry melodrama of white women threatened with violation by Indians.

67. *Official Program, The Pilgrim Spirit* (Plymouth, Mass., 1921), p. 16. The pageant included original poetry from Edward Arlington Robinson and Robert Frost, as well as Baker's dialogue. Frost, when asked later about his contribution to the pageant, replied "Hate to be reminded of it." Quoted in Shea, "Community Pageants in Massachusetts," p. 187.

Norreys J. O'Connor, "The Plymouth Pageant," *Bookman* 54 (October 1921): 167; Ludwig Lewisohn, "The Plymouth Pageant," *Nation* 113 (August 24, 1921): 210–11.

68. Thomas Wood Stevens, *Missouri One Hundred Years Ago* (St. Louis: St. Louis Centennial Association, 1921); Stevens, *Book of Words: Pageant of Virginia*; Virginia Tanner, *150th Anniversary of the Battle of Bennington* (Concord, N.H.: Rumford Press, 1927); Josephine W. Wickser, *150th Anniversary of the*

Battle of Saratoga and Surrender of Burgoyne (Albany, N.Y.: J. B. Lyon, 1927); Tanner, *Albany's Tercentenary* (Albany, N.Y.: J. B. Lyon, 1924); *A Pageant of Portsmouth* (Concord, N.H.: Rumford Press, 1923); *A Pageant of the State of Maine* (Augusta: Charles Nash, 1923).

William Chauncy Langdon, *Centennial Pageant of Indiana University* (Bloomington, 1920); "The Beginnings: An Historical Pageant," *Michigan History Magazine* 12 (April 1928): 212–51. Langdon undertook the Michigan State University pageant as a favor to President Kenyon Butterfield, whose first invitation to Langdon to create a pageant in 1917 when he was president of the University of Massachusetts was withdrawn on account of America's entry in World War I.

W. Lloyd Warner, "The Protestants Legitimate Their Past," in *The Living and the Dead* (New Haven: Yale University Press, 1959), reprinted in Warner, *The Family of God* (New Haven: Yale University Press, 1961), pp. 89–154. Observations were based on a group of forty-six local community historical pageants performed between 1912 and 1916 and thirty-eight pageants performed between 1923 and 1927, drawn primarily from the local history collections of the Library of Congress. The number of pageants in each sample that portrayed exclusively the town's early years increased from 13 percent to 42 percent, respectively. Although the celebration of the sesquicentennial anniversary of the American Revolution might account for the emphasis on Colonial history in the pageants of the 1920s, it does not explain why similar anniversaries in the previous decade depicted a broad sweep of local history rather than a narrow concentration on solely the period commemorated, nor why the pageants of the twenties began their historical accounts with the same forest primeval and early settler scenes as in earlier pageants, omitting only events occurring after the American Revolution but not before.

69. On the origins and history of Ford's Greenfield Village, see Geoffrey Upward, *A Home for Our Heritage: The Building and Growth of Greenfield Village and the Henry Ford Museum* (Dearborn, Mich.: Henry Ford Museum Press, 1979), and Reynold Wik, *Henry Ford and Grass Roots America* (Ann Arbor: University of Michigan Press, 1973).

70. Lowrie and Ludlum, *Sesqui-centennial High Street*. The Philadelphia exposition also presented the pageant *Freedom*, which covered in twenty-four scenes the period from Columbus's discovery of America to George Washington's inauguration. See Matos, "Pageantry, Drama, and Spectacle."

Tercentenary Conference of City and Town Committees, Inc., *Celebrating a Three Hundredth Anniversary: A Report of the Massachusetts Bay Tercentenary of 1930* (Boston: Anchor Lino., 1931); Massachusetts Bay Tercentenary Commission, *Guide to Salem, 1630* (Salem: Berkeley Press, 1930). A detailed account of the movement in the 1920s and 1930s to restore period villages rather than solely the structures associated with famous Americans appears in Charles B. Hosmer, Jr., *Preservation Comes of Age: From Williamsburg to the National Trust, 1926–49* (Charlottesville: University of Virginia Press, 1981); also see his earlier volume, *Presence of the Past: A History of the Preservation Movement in the United States before Williamsburg* (New York: G. P. Putnam's Sons, 1965). For an alternative explanation of the craze for period villages, see

Michael Wallace, "Visiting the Past: History Museums in the United States," *Radical History Review* 25 (Winter 1981): 63–96, reprinted in *Presenting the Past: Essays on History and the Public*, ed. Susan Porter Benson, Stephen Brier, and Roy Rosenzweig (Philadelphia: Temple University Press, 1986), pp. 135–61. A perceptive analysis of the ironies of performers "restoring" the behavior of the past in period villages for tourists appears in Richard Schechner, *Between Theater and Anthropology* (Philadelphia: University of Pennsylvania Press, 1984), chap. 2.

71. Information on the Santa Fe and other annual historical festivals of the late 1920s and early 1930s appears in Pearl Ott Weston, "Pageantry in the United States" (Ph.D. dissertation, Duquesne University, 1935). For an anthropological analysis of the contemporary Santa Fe Fiesta, see Ronald Grimes, *Symbol and Conquest: Public Ritual and Drama in Santa Fe, New Mexico* (Ithaca, N.Y.: Cornell University Press, 1976).

72. Weston, "Pageantry in the United States," pp. 39–40, 45–47, 42–45. Also see Hosmer, *Preservation Comes of Age*, pp. 365–71. According to Hosmer, Tombstone so resembled a movie set in the mid-1930s that, when the National Park Service declined to purchase the former mining town as a federal historic site, local business people reportedly offered the entire town for sale as is to a Hollywood motion picture company.

Weston, "Pageantry in the United States," p. 91; Hosmer, *Preservation Comes of Age*, pp. 306–12.

73. *The Pilgrim Tercentenary*, brochure (Plymouth Cardage Company, 1921), p. 11. T. J. Jackson Lears observes that advertisements in the 1920s for a wide range of products promised to restore health and well-being. Lears, "From Salvation to Self-realization: Advertising and the Therapeutic Roots of the Consumer Culture, 1880–1930," in *The Culture of Consumption: Critical Essays in American History, 1880–1980*, ed. Lears and R. W. Fox (New York: Pantheon, 1983), pp. 1–38.

Victor Talking Machine Company, "Recapture the Old-Time Communal Joy in Music," *Playground* 20 (May 1926): 73; "Revive Old Dances and the Roundels of Joyous Games," *Playground* 20 (November 1926): 421.

74. E. R. A. Seligman, "Economics and Social Progress," in American Economic Association, *Papers and Proceedings of the Fifteenth Annual Meeting* (New York: Macmillan, 1903), p. 59. Dorothy Ross argues that academic social thought, primarily "idealist" in the Gilded Age, became historicist by the turn of the century, then gave way in the 1920s to analyses oriented solely to contemporary "processes" and abandoned study of the evolution of institutions over time. Ross, "The Liberal Tradition Revisited and the Republican Tradition Addressed," in *New Directions in American Intellectual History*, ed. J. Higham and P. Conkin (Baltimore: Johns Hopkins University Press, 1979), pp. 125–28.

William F. Ogburn, *Social Change* (New York: B. W. Heubsch, 1922). Cultural lag theory proved especially influential in the essays prepared for the President's Research Committee on Recent Social Trends (which Ogburn chaired), *Recent Social Trends* (New York: McGraw Hill, 1933).

Robert and Helen Lynd, *Middletown: A Study in American Culture* (1929;

reprint, New York: Harcourt, Brace, and World, 1956); *Official Program, a Historical Pageant of Delaware County, Indiana*, September 27–28, 1927, JBR Collection.

75. Henry Suzallo, "The Use of Leisure," *Playground and Recreation* 24 (June 1930): 161.

76. The rejection of the customs of the immediate past in the 1920s was also noted in Stanley Coben, "The Assault on Victorianism in the 20th Century," in *Victorian America*, ed. D. W. Howe (Philadelphia: University of Pennsylvania Press, 1976), pp. 160–81, and Lawrence W. Levine, "Progress and Nostalgia: The Self-Image of the 1920s," *The American Novel and the 1920s*, ed. M. Bradbury and D. Palmer (London: Edward Arnold, 1970), pp. 35–56. Levine interprets the increased bifurcation of popular images of the past and present in the 1920s as symptomatic of a longing for both the material benefits of modernity and the simple verities of an idealized past.

77. For an overview of the activities of the Playground and Recreation Association in the depression, see Richard Knapp, "Play for America: Part VI: The 1930s," *Parks and Recreation* (July 1973): 23–28, 42–52.

78. William H. S. Demarest, *The Anniversary of New Brunswick, New Jersey, 1680–1730–1930* (New Brunswick: J. Heildingsfield, 1930), p. 65; Mary Frix Kidd, *Nature's Child: The Voice of Cotton: A Community Pageant* (Concord, N.C.: Stonewall Jackson Manual Training and Industrial School, 1931); Tercentenary Conference of City and Town Committees, *Celebrating a Three Hundredth Anniversary*, p. 19; U.S. George Washington Bicentennial Commission, *Pageants and Plays Depicting the Life of George Washington and His Time for the Nationwide Celebration* (Washington, D.C.: U.S. Government Printing Office, 1932). Also see Esther Willard Bates, *How to Produce a Pageant in Honor of George Washington* (Washington, D.C.: U.S. Government Printing Office, 1932).

79. Among the writers who declared the need for the "firm ground" of the past in times of crisis, see John Dos Passos, *The Ground We Stand On* (New York: Houghton Mifflin Co., 1941), p. 3, and Twelve Southerners, *I'll Take My Stand* (1930; reprint, New York: Harper and Row, 1962). Among the secondary works that survey the use of history as stable national myth for artists and writers in the 1930s are Alfred H. Jones, "The Search for a Usable Past in the New Deal," *American Quarterly* 23 (December 1971): 710–24; Warren Susman, "The Thirties," in *The Development of an American Culture*, ed. L. Ratner and S. Coben (Englewood Cliffs, N.J.: Prentice-Hall, 1970), pp. 179–218, reprinted in Susman, *Culture as History: The Transformation of American Society in the Twentieth Century* (New York: Pantheon, 1984), pp. 150–83; and Joan Shelley Rubin, *Constance Rourke and American Culture* (Chapel Hill: University of North Carolina Press, 1980). For a discussion of how the search for firm ground translated into a renewed attachment to place in the decade, see Michael Steiner, "Regionalism in the Great Depression," *Geographical Review* 73 (October 1983): 430–46.

On the popularity in the 1930s of plays based on historical figures, see Christian H. Moe, "From History to Drama: A Study of the Influence of the Pageant, the Outdoor Epic Drama, and the Historical Stage Play upon the

Dramatization of Three American Historical Figures" (Ph.D. dissertation, Cornell University, 1958). Also see Alfred H. Jones, "Search for a Usable Past," and Charles C. Alexander, *Here the Country Lies: Nationalism and the Arts in Twentieth Century America* (Bloomington: Indiana University Press, 1980).

Karal Ann Marling argues that the historical imagery of post office murals in the 1930s depicted either the remote past or the modern future but omitted scenes of the immediate past or present. Marling, "A Note on New Deal Iconography: Futurology and the Historical Myth," *Prospects* 4 (1979): 421–40, and Marling, *Wall to Wall America: A Cultural History of Post Office Murals in the Great Depression* (Minneapolis: University of Minnesota Press, 1982); also see Marlene Park and Gerald Markowitz, *Democratic Vistas: Post Offices and Public Art in the New Deal* (Philadelphia: Temple University Press, 1984). Wanda Corn observes that Grant Wood's juxtaposition of anachronistic images in his paintings of the 1930s reflected a disjunction he perceived between past and present. Corn, *Grant Wood: The Regionalist Vision* (New Haven: Yale University Press, 1983).

80. Thomas Wood Stevens, *Yorktown Sesquicentennial Pageants* (Washington, D.C.: U.S. Government Printing Office, 1933), p. 42; Percy MacKaye, *Wakefield: A Folk-Masque of the Birth of Washington* (Washington, D.C.: U.S. Government Printing Office, 1932).

81. Paul Green, *The Lost Colony* (Chapel Hill: University of North Carolina Press, 1937; reprint, 1954); *The Roanoke Colony Memorial Association Presents the Lost Colony*, official program, July 4–September 6, 1937, North Carolina Collection. Also see clippings in the North Carolina Collection on *The Lost Colony* and the Roanoke 350th anniversary celebration from the Raleigh *News and Observer* through summer 1937. For accounts of earlier efforts to dramatize the Lost Colony story outdoors, see "Story of Lost Colony Told in Historical Film," *Greensboro Daily News*, November 13, 1921, and Edith Russell Harrington, *O' Brave New World: The Pageant of Roanoke*, performed August 17–19, 1934 (typescript, North Carolina Collection). For more on Paul Green's pageant career, see Claude Dierolf, "The Pageant Drama and American Pageantry, 1905–52" (Ph.D. dissertation, University of Pennsylvania, 1953). The Federal Theater Project compiled lists of published historical pageants but did not promote pageantry as a form of drama in the 1930s, preferring to support professional rather than amateur theater. The Federal Theater Project's relation to local community dramatic efforts in the 1930s is described in Hallie Flanagan, *Arena* (New York: Duell, Sloane, and Pearce, 1940), and Jane DeHart Mathews, *The Federal Theater Project, 1935–39* (Princeton, N.J., 1967).

For a list of outdoor historical dramas currently in production, send a self-addressed, stamped envelope to the Institute of Outdoor Drama, CB 3240 Graham Memorial, University of North Carolina, Chapel Hill, N.C. 27599–3240.

82. The number of directors the Rogers Company hires each year varies, depending on both the number of celebrations it manages and when they occur. In recent years it has hired between eight and ten directors; from six in 1988, the company hired fourteen in 1989 because so many of its celebrations were scheduled for the same dates. Phil Frable, telephone interview with

author, June 20, 1989. Frable summarized the benefit accruing to towns that hire the Rogers Company to manage their local celebrations with the following phrase: "We market mass participation." Phil Frable, interview with author, Pittsburgh, Pa., October 1979. One technique employed to break down inhibitions about participating in the pageant is to have the local celebration committee insist that all local men grow beards or else pay a "fine." This technique, as well as others employed by Rogers Company directors in the years immediately following World War II, is described in Vance Packard, "America's Biggest Birthday Parties," *American Magazine*, March 1951. Also see the historical pageant staged in Lusk, Wyo., in 1947 by the Rogers Company or one of its imitators, described in Sally F. Griffith, "Legend of Rawhide Pageantry as Vivid Memory," *Lusk Herald*, September 9, 1971.

83. Samuel Selden, "The Production of Local History Plays and Pageants," *Bulletin of the American Association for State and Local History* 1 (April 1943): 158; Adele Gutman Nathan, "Pageant Parade," *New York Times*, July 30, 1950, section 2, p. 1.

Conclusion. The Era of Pageantry

1. "A Letter from Percy MacKaye," *Theatre Arts* 34 (July 1950): 52.

2. The argument that the extension and subsequent coalescence of individuals' kinship, occupational, intellectual, and professional affiliations beyond the borders of their towns into functionally organized regional and national bureaucracies inevitably distended patterns of local community interaction and affection can be found in Robert Wiebe, *The Segmented Society* (New York: Oxford University Press, 1975), pp. 24–25; his earlier *Search for Order, 1877–1920* (New York: Hill and Wang, 1967); and Samuel Hays, "The New Organizational Society," in *Building the Organizational Society*, ed. Jerry Israel (New York: Free Press, 1972), pp. 1–16. In contrast, Thomas Bender, employing anthropologist Robert Redfield's view of community life as the interpenetration of both functional and affective, extended and local affiliations, notes that an increase in contacts beyond local borders does not necessarily decrease the importance of those of locale. Bender suggests that all relations, functional and affective, were less likely in the late nineteenth century to be structured within a specific territory; that feelings of "community" occurred in networks no longer contained within local boundaries; that the physical town and community ties no longer coincided. Bender, *Community and Social Change in America* (New Brunswick, N.J.: Rutgers University Press, 1978).

3. On the concept of interdependence—that individuals formerly thought to be autonomous in fact depended on large-scale social institutions beyond their control or even comprehension—in the academic social thought of the Gilded Age, see Thomas Haskell, *The Emergence of Professional Social Science: The American Social Science Association and the Nineteenth Century Crisis of Authority* (Urbana: University of Illinois Press, 1977). T. J. Jackson Lears also uses the emergence among genteel intellectuals of this concept of the loss of individual autonomy in mass society to account for their feelings of spiritual

"weightlessness" and subsequent quest for "genuine" experience and individual peace of mind. Lears, *No Place of Grace: Anti-Modernism and the Transformation of American Culture, 1880–1920* (New York: Pantheon, 1981).

4. Van Wyck Brooks, "On Creating a Usable Past," *Dial* 64 (April 11, 1918): 337–41; Brooks, *America's Coming of Age* (1915; reprint, New York: Farrar, Straus and Giroux, 1975), p. 164.

5. Daniel Rodgers, "In Search of Progressivism," *Reviews in American History* 10 (1982): 113–32.

6. Frank Morton Todd, *The Story of the Exposition* (New York: G. P. Putnam's Sons, 1921), 2:373. Todd was describing the financial failure of the "Joy Zone" at the Panama-Pacific Exposition in San Francisco in 1915.

"Independence Day Programs," *Playground* 22 (May 1928): 71; Charles Parker, "President Hoover Gets Leading Role in Great Day at King's Mountain," Raleigh *News and Observer*, October 8, 1930.

7. Eugene O'Neill's play depicts a youth literally torn between worshipping the religion in which he was raised or the new god of electricity embodied in the dynamo. O'Neill, *Dynamo* (New York: Horace Liveright, 1929). Terming the conflict between technological and moral progress as that of "the dynamo and the virgin" stems from Henry Adams, *The Education of Henry Adams* (1918; reprint, Boston: Houghton-Mifflin, 1973), pp. 379–90. For a discussion of writers affected by Adams's vision, see William Wasserstrom, *The Ironies of Progress: Henry Adams and the American Dream* (Carbondale: Southern Illinois University Press, 1984). On the emergence among European writers of the belief that the world war had been the culmination of a succession of experiences that defined a unique generation, see Robert Wohl, *The Generation of 1914* (Cambridge: Harvard University Press, 1979). In "Tradition and Individual Talent" (1919), T. S. Eliot states that the writer is a product of his or her culture. But he never reached the position of Percy MacKaye, Thomas Wood Stevens, or Frederick Koch that the folk could produce a new Shakespeare. Among the secondary works that offer an introduction to the peculiar historical visions of modernist writers in the 1920s are Warren Susman, "History and the American Intellectual: Uses of a Usable Past," *American Quarterly* 16 (Summer 1964): 243–63, reprinted in Susman, *Culture as History: The Transformation of American Society in the Twentieth Century* (New York: Pantheon, 1984), pp. 7–26; Leland D. Peterson, "Ezra Pound: The Use and Abuse of History," *American Quarterly* 17 (Spring 1965): 33–47; and Alan Holder, "In the American Grain: William Carlos Williams on the American Past," *American Quarterly* 19 (Fall 1967): 498–515. None of the three essays, however, consider these writers in the context of how limited the audiences were for their respective visions.

8. Among the examples of the blossoming of folklore research in the 1930s are Constance Rourke's *American Humor: A Study of the National Character* (New York: Harcourt, Brace and Co., 1931); the myriad works of the Federal Writers Project, especially its Folklore Unit; and the many anthologies of tall tales that have been published. The intellectual context of much of this research is described in Joan Shelley Rubin, *Constance Rourke and American Culture* (Chapel Hill: University of North Carolina Press, 1980).

9. For a contemporary account of the campaign to make school history textbooks "100 percent American" in the 1920s, see Bessie Louise Pierce, *Public Opinion and the Teaching of History in the United States* (New York: Knopf, 1926). On the nationalistic distortions in popular versions of American folklore in the 1920s and 1930s, see Richard Dorson, "Fakelore," in *American Folklore and the Historian* (Chicago: University of Chicago Press, 1971), p. 9; Dorson, "Folklore and Fakelore," *American Mercury* 70 (March 1950): 336; and Tristam P. Coffin, "Folklore in the American Twentieth Century," *American Quarterly* 13 (Winter 1961): 526–33.

10. The use of crowd symbolism and nationalistic folklore in the United States in the 1930s pales beside that described in George Mosse, *The Nationalization of the Masses: Political Symbolism and Mass Movements in Germany from the Napoleonic Wars through the Third Reich* (New York: New American Library, 1977). See also Mosse, "Caesarism, Circuses, and Monuments," *Journal of Contemporary History* 6 (1971): 167–82; Charles Rearick, "Festivals in Modern France: The Experience of the Third Republic," *Journal of Contemporary History* 12 (July 1977): 435–60; and Eric Hobsbawm, "Mass Producing Traditions: Europe, 1870–1914," in *The Invention of Tradition,* ed. Eric Hobsbawm and Terence Ranger (New York: Cambridge University Press, 1983), pp. 263–307.

11. On the fascination with the "average" in the 1930s, see Warren Susman, "The People's Fair: Cultural Contradictions of a Consumer Society," in The Queens Museum, *Dawn of a New Day: The New York World's Fair, 1939/40,* ed. Helen A. Harrison (New York: New York University Press, 1980), pp. 17–27.

12. On the appeal of genealogy and ethnic heritage in the late twentieth century, see Tamara Hareven, "The Search for Generational Memory: Tribal Rites in Industrial Society," *Daedalus* 107 (Fall 1978): 137–49. On the contemporary uses of the past, see David Lowenthal, *The Past Is a Foreign Country* (New York: Cambridge University Press, 1985). The argument that Americans view the past as a stable refuge distant from present controversies also appears in John Brinckerhoff Jackson, "The Necessity for Ruins," in *The Necessity for Ruins and Other Topics* (Amherst: University of Massachusetts Press, 1980), pp. 89–102. Jackson's essay identifies two modes of depicting the past in public in American history. He suggests that a "covenant" approach linking past and present flourished until the late nineteenth century, when it was replaced by a vision of history as "dramatic discontinuity" contrasting a golden age with the present. Jackson sees the contemporary craze for historical reenactments as rituals of rebirth and the "necessity for ruins"—that is, we allow things to reach a state of disrepair before restoring them, rather than integrating them into a continuous heritage.

A Note on
the Sources

. . . .

Detailed information on the sources used for this book appear in the notes to each chapter. The following essay is highly selective, recommending only the materials that I found most useful. Concerning published sources, the list is largely confined to books rather than journal articles and leans toward those books that offer good introductions to their subjects and can lead the reader to further sources. It is divided into five sections: (1) manuscript collections and personal interviews; (2) primary works on civic celebrations, public recreation, and the performing arts at the turn of the century; (3) secondary works on these topics; (4) theoretical works on public ritual, popular memory, and historical consciousness; and (5) a discussion of the pageants themselves as sources.

Section 1. Manuscript Collections and Personal Interviews

The most extensive manuscript sources for the history of pageantry are the papers of several pageant-masters: the William Chauncy Langdon Papers in the John Hay Library, Brown University, Providence, Rhode Island; the Percy MacKaye Papers in the Baker Library, Dartmouth College, Hanover, New Hampshire (a guide to the collection was published in *Annals of an Era: Percy MacKaye and the MacKaye Family*, ed. E. O. Grover [Washington. D.C.: Pioneer Press, 1932]); the Percy and Marian MacKaye Collection in the Harvard Theatre Collection, Cambridge, Massachusetts; the Ellis Paxson Oberholtzer Papers in the Historical Society of Pennsylvania, Philadelphia,; the Thomas Wood Stevens Papers in the University of Arizona Library, Tucson; and the Frederick Henry Koch Papers and the Edith Russell Harrington Papers, both in the Southern Historical Collection, University of North Carolina, Chapel Hill. Those interested in pageantry after 1937 can examine the papers of Paul Green, also in the Southern Historical Collection, as well as the records of the university's Institute for Outdoor Drama.

Though no manuscript collection exists for the American Pageantry Association, its organizational history can be pieced together from the papers of the member pageant-masters listed above. Of the other organizations that promoted pageantry, some records of the Playground and Recreation Association of America are with those of its successor, the National Recreation Association, in the Social Welfare History Archives Center, University of Minnesota, Minneapolis. Others remain in the headquarters of the organization, now called the National Parks and Recreation Association, in Arlington, Virginia. This is where I examined the papers of War Camp Community Service and Community Service, Incorporated. Also helpful for the study of War Camp Community Service are the records of the Commission on Training Camp Activities, Record Group (RG) 165, in the National Archives, Washington, D.C. Material documenting the activities of the University of North Carolina's Bureau of Community Drama appears in the "Bureau of Community Drama Scrapbook, 1923–30," North Carolina Collection, University of North Carolina, Chapel Hill. Of the commercial firms involved with pageantry, the records of the John B. Rogers Company stand out. When the company moved from Fostoria, Ohio, to Pittsburgh, Pennsylvania, in 1977, it left behind in its former headquarters-warehouse an extensive collection of pageant costumes, scripts, props, and programs from the past seventy-five years. I was able to examine only a small part of these holdings. When the building was sold a few years ago, much of the collection was transferred to Pittsburgh or discarded.

Manuscript collections also survive for many local pageant committees. I made most extensive use of the records of the St. Louis Pageant Drama Association at the Missouri Historical Society in St. Louis and the Pageant of Thetford Collection in the Latham Library, Thetford, Vermont.

Those interested in reconstructing the story of particular pageants can also interview former participants—though I did not use this source extensively. In the spring of 1979 and 1980, and in the summer of 1984, I talked with Margaret Langdon, daughter of William Chauncy Langdon, in Bronxville, New York. In October 1979, I interviewed Phil Frable, president of the Rogers Company, in Pittsburgh. In August 1984, I spoke with Christy MacKaye Barnes and Arvia MacKaye Ege, daughters of Percy MacKaye, in Hillsdale, New York.

Section 2. Primary Works on Civic Celebrations, Public Recreation, and the Performing Arts at the Turn of the Century

Several bibliographies of works on pageantry, civic celebrations, public recreation, and the performing arts compiled in the early twentieth century offer a guide to what local organizations might have been reading on these subjects. Among these works are Caroline Hill Davis, *Pageants in Great Britain and the United States: A List of References* (New York Public Library, 1916); Ethel T. Rockwell, "Historical Pageantry: A Treatise and a Bibliography," *State Historical Society of Wisconsin Bulletin of Information*, no. 84 (July 1916); Bureau of Pageantry and Drama of the YWCA, *Resources for Assistance and Study in Pageantry and Drama* (1920); and Playground and Recreation Association of America, *Community Drama: Suggestions for a Community-wide Program of Dramatic Activities* (New York: Century and Co., 1926). For contemporary articles on public recreation, see the bibliography in Clarence Rainwater, *The Play Movement in the United States* (Chicago: University of Chicago Press, 1921). *Community Service in Periodical Literature* (1920) lists thirty-five pages of titles and articles on public recreation during 1918 and 1919. For contemporary sources on efforts to reform American drama, see Thomas H. Dickinson, *The Case of American Drama* (New York: Houghton-Mifflin, 1915), and Sheldon Cheney, *The Art Theatre* (New York: Alfred Knopf, 1917).

Journals of the period offer another way to enter the network of published information on civic celebrations and pageantry available to local organizations. "Genteel" views of the proper way to commemorate history in public appeared in the *American Historical Register* (1894–97), a journal serving a federation of patriotic and hereditary societies, and the *American Scenic and Historic Preservation Society Annual Reports* (1895–1930). Recreation workers' views of pageantry appeared in the journals of the Playground and Recreation Association of America: *Playground* magazine (1906–29), *Playground and Recreation* (1930–31), and *Recreation* (1932–65). The views of reformers interested in pageantry as a form of dramatic art appeared in the publications of the Drama League of America: *The Drama* (1911–31) and *Drama League Monthly* (1915–19). *Theatre* magazine is also helpful for the 1910–30 period, especially its regular column on "Community Dramatic Activities."

Finally, there are guidebooks and articles written, published, and distributed by the American Pageant Association (APA). The sixty-nine issues of the *American Pageant Association Bulletin*, published between 1913 and 1921, are full of technical advice, tentative definitions, and exhortation aimed at local celebration committees. The APA also published its *Constitution*, two editions of *Who's Who in Pageantry* (1914 and 1930), and the programs of its annual conventions (1914–17). These works survive in several libraries; I used a set housed at Vassar College Library, Poughkeepsie, New York.

Among the most prominent guidebooks for staging pageants are William Chauncy Langdon, *Celebration of the Fourth of July by Means of Pageantry* (New York: Russell Sage Foundation, 1912); Mary Master Needham, *Folk Festivals: Their Growth and How to Give Them* (New York: B. W. Heubsch, 1912); Percival Chubb, *Festivals and Plays in Schools and Elsewhere* (New York: Harper and Brothers, 1912); Esther Willard Bates, *Pageants and Pageantry* (Boston: Ginn and Co., 1912), and *The Art of Producing Pageants* (Boston: W. H. Baker, 1925); Ralph Davol, *Handbook of American Pageantry* (Taunton, Mass.: Davol Publishing Co., 1914); Robert Withington, "A Manual of Pageantry," *Indiana University Bulletin* 13 (June 15, 1915); Mary Porter Beegle and Jack R. Crawford, *Pageants and Pageantry* (New Haven: Yale University Press, 1916); Constance D'Arcy MacKay, *Patriotic Drama in Your Town* (New York: Henry Holt, 1918); Linwood Taft, *The Technique of Pageantry* (New York: A. S. Barnes, 1921); and Playground and Recreation Association of America, *Community Drama: Suggestions for a Community-wide Program of Dramatic Activities* (New York: Century and Co., 1926). Also interesting is Roland Holt, *A List of Music for Plays and Pageants* (New York: D. Appleton and Co., 1925), which lists where to borrow the appropriate musical passages for each type of pageant scene. Though not guidebooks, also influential in shaping how pageant-masters explained their craft are the collected essays in Percy MacKaye, *The Playhouse and the Play* (New York: Macmillan, 1909), and *The Civic Theatre in Relation to the Redemption of Leisure* (New York: Macmillan, 1912).

*Section 3. Secondary Works on Civic Celebrations, Public
Recreation, and the Performing Arts at the Turn of the Century*

There are very few secondary works on pageantry in America, with the
exception of the Paterson strike pageant of 1913 (see Chapter 4, n. 50).
Among published works, one can turn to Trudy Baltz, "Pageantry and Mural
Painting," *Winterthur Portfolio* 15 (August 1980): 211–28, for a discussion of
pageantry in the context of movements in the fine arts. Donald Bright Oster,
"Nights of Fantasy: The St. Louis Pageant and Masque of 1914," *Bulletin of the
Missouri Historical Society* 13 (April 1975): 175–205, discusses the St. Louis
pageant—though in less depth than I do here. One can also refer to over a
half century of unpublished dissertations by doctoral students in theater or
English departments, beginning with Pearl Ott Weston, "Pageantry in the
United States" (Duquesne University, 1935); Frank George Walsh, "Outdoor
Commemorative Drama in the United States, 1900–50" (Western Reserve
University, 1952); Claude Dierolf, "The Pageant-Drama and American Pag-
eantry, 1900–50" (University of Pennsylvania, 1953); Christian Hollis Moe,
"From History to Drama: A Study of the Influence of the Pageant, the Out-
door Epic Drama, and the Historical Stage Play upon the Dramatization of
Three American Historical Figures" (Cornell University, 1958); William Ram-
bin, Jr., "Thomas Wood Stevens: American Pageant-Master" (Louisiana State
University, 1977); Martin Sidney Tackel, "Women and American Pageantry,
1908 to 1918" (City University of New York, 1982), which contains a ten-page
"production chronology" listing pageants by place, date, and artist; and Ann
M. Shea, "Community Pageants in Massachusetts, 1908–1932" (New York
University, 1984). These works discuss the formal dramatic elements of the
production and script but not pageantry as social history.

The secondary literature on the constituent elements of the pageantry
movement is only a little better developed. On the arts and crafts movement,
we now have Eileen Boris's *Art and Labor: Ruskin, Morris, and the Craftsman Ideal
in America* (Philadelphia: Temple University Press, 1986). Still, no one has
taken patriotic and hereditary societies seriously since Wallace Evan Davies,
*Patriotism on Parade: The Story of Veterans and Hereditary Organizations in America,
1783–1900* (Cambridge: Harvard University Press, 1955), and Merle Curti,
The Roots of American Loyalty (New York: Columbia, 1946). The best of several recent works on the playground movement are Dominick Cavallo, *Muscles
and Morals: Organized Playgrounds and Urban Reform, 1880–1920* (Philadel-
phia: University of Pennsylvania Press, 1981), and Richard Knapp, "Play for
America: The National Recreation Association, 1906–50" (Ph.D. dissertation,
Duke University, 1971), published serially in *Parks and Recreation* magazine
beginning in August 1972. On the effect of efforts such as the "Safe and Sane
July Fourth" movement to reform popular culture, see Roy Rosenzweig, *Eight
Hours for What We Will: Workers and Leisure in an Industrial City, 1870–1920*
(New York: Cambridge University Press, 1983). Superb introductions to the
origins of modern dance appear in Nancy Lee Ruyter, *Reformers and Visionar-
ies: The Americanization of the Art of Dance* (New York: Dance Horizons, 1979),
and Elizabeth Kendall, *Where She Danced: The Birth of American Art-Dance* (New
York: Knopf, 1979).

Little has appeared on the history of movements to reform the American theater in this period, though biographies exist of George Pierce Baker (Wisner Payne Kinney, *George Pierce Baker and the American Theatre* [Cambridge: Harvard University Press, 1954]), Frederick Koch (Samuel Selden, *Frederick Henry Koch, Pioneer Playmaker* [Chapel Hill: University of North Carolina Library, 1954]), Thomas Wood Stevens (Rambin, "Thomas Wood Stevens"), and Paul Green (Vincent S. Kenny, *Paul Green* [New York: Twayne, 1971]). None exists for Percy MacKaye—my work only begins to touch on his multifaceted life. On art theater, see Oscar G. Brockett and Robert R. Findlay, *Century of Innovation: A History of European and American Theatre and Drama since 1870* (Englewood Cliffs, N.J.: Prentice-Hall, 1973), especially chapter 7, "Forging a New Art of the Theatre." On commercial producing firms such as the Rogers Company, there is only Lorelei F. Eckey, *1001 Broadways: Hometown Talent on Stage* (Ames: Iowa State University Press, 1982). There has, however, emerged some excellent work on the early history of the folk revival in America, including Joan Shelley Rubin, *Constance Rourke and American Culture* (Chapel Hill: University of North Carolina Press, 1980); David E. Whisnant, *All That Is Native and Fine: The Politics of Culture in an American Region* (Chapel Hill: University of North Carolina Press, 1983); and the essays collected in *Folk Roots, New Roots: Folklore in American Life*, ed. Jane S. Becker and Barbara Franco (Lexington, Mass.: Museum of Our National Heritage, 1988).

Readers wishing to learn more about the general context of the era of pageantry should examine the following works. The literature on progressivism has been extensive. Among the best places to begin are bibliographical works by Arthur S. Link and Richard L. McCormick, *Progressivism* (Arlington Heights, Ill.: Harlan Davidson, Inc., 1983), and Daniel T. Rodgers, "In Search of Progressivism," *Reviews in American History* 10 (December 1982): 113–32. An excellent introduction to the literature on American mobilization for World War I is David M. Kennedy, *Over Here: The First World War and American Society* (New York: Oxford University Press, 1980). The idea of antimodernism is developed in T. J. Jackson Lears, *No Place of Grace: Anti-Modernism and the Transformation of American Culture, 1880–1920* (New York: Pantheon, 1981). On modernism, see Daniel Joseph Singal, *The War Within: From Victorian to Modernist Thought in the South* (Chapel Hill: University of North Carolina Press, 1982), and the special issue edited by Singal, "Modernist Culture in America," *American Quarterly* 39 (Spring 1987): 3–173. On the changing ideas of "community" at the turn of the century, see Thomas Bender, *Community and Social Change in America* (New Brunswick, N.J.: Rutgers University Press, 1978).

Section 4. Public Ritual, Popular Memory, and Historical Consciousness

Those interested in recent studies of ritual should start with Ronald L. Grimes, *Research in Ritual Studies: A Programmatic Essay and Bibliography* (Metuchen, N.J.: American Theological Library Association and Scarecrow Press, 1985). The theoretical works on ritual most helpful to my thinking are

Sally Falk Moore and Barbara G. Myerhoff, eds., *Secular Ritual* (Amsterdam, The Netherlands: Van Gorcum, 1977); Victor Turner, *The Ritual Process* (New York: Penguin Books, 1974), and *Dramas, Fields and Metaphors: Symbolic Action in Human Society* (Ithaca, N.Y.: Cornell University Press, 1974); Clifford Geertz, *The Interpretation of Cultures* (New York: Basic Books, 1973); and Steven Lukes, "Political Ritual and Social Integration," *Sociology* 9 (May 1975): 289–308. A model study employing ritual theory to analyze a particular historical situation is Susan G. Davis, *Parades and Power: Street Theatre in Nineteenth Century Philadelphia* (Philadelphia: Temple University Press, 1986). On genres in popular culture, I found the following works most helpful: John Cawelti, *Adventure, Mystery, and Romance* (Chicago: University of Chicago Press, 1976), and Janice A. Radway, *Reading the Romance: Women, Patriarchy, and Popular Literature* (Chapel Hill: University of North Carolina Press, 1984). Radway's book is especially suggestive for conceptualizing how national pageant elements might have been rearranged and interpreted locally by civic officials and their audiences.

When I began this book nearly ten years ago there was virtually nothing written on historical consciousness and popular memory in America, save for W. Lloyd Warner's analysis of the "Yankee City" (Newburyport, Mass.) Tercentenary Pageant of 1930, published in *The Living and the Dead* (New Haven: Yale University Press, 1959). But recently there has been an explosion of interest in the subject. The best place to begin is David Lowenthal, *The Past Is a Foreign Country* (New York: Cambridge University Press, 1985), and Warren I. Susman, *Culture as History: The Transformation of American Society in the Early Twentieth Century* (New York: Pantheon, 1984), especially his essay "History and the American Intellectual: The Uses of a Usable Past," pp. 7–26. Then go on to books on popular representations of a particular historical period or event. On the Colonial period, see Karal Ann Marling, *George Washington Slept Here: Colonial Revivals and American Culture, 1876–1986* (Cambridge: Harvard University Press, 1988); on the American Revolution and the Constitution, see Michael Kammen, *A Season of Youth: The American Revolution and the Historical Imagination* (New York: Knopf, 1978), and *A Machine That Would Go of Itself: The Constitution in American Culture* (New York: Knopf, 1986); on the Civil War, see Gaines M. Foster, *Ghosts of the Confederacy: Defeat, the Lost Cause, and the Emergence of the New South, 1865 to 1913* (New York: Oxford University Press, 1987). Also suggestive are articles collected in *Recycling the Past: Popular Uses of American History*, ed. Leila Zenderland (Philadelphia: University of Pennsylvania Press, 1978); *Presenting the Past: Essays on History and the Public*, ed. Susan Porter Benson, Stephen Brier, and Roy Rosenzweig (Philadelphia: Temple University Press, 1986); and "Memory and American History, A Special Issue," *Journal of American History* 75 (March 1989): 1117–1280. Two other works on American historical consciousness I found useful are Dorothy Ross, "Historical Consciousness in Nineteenth Century America," *American Historical Review* 89 (October 1984): 909–28, and Thomas M. Jacklin, "Progressives and the Usable Past: Historical Themes in the Literature of American Reform, 1880–1915" (Ph.D. dissertation, Johns Hopkins University, 1981). On images and uses of tradition in Western Europe in the same period, see Lowenthal,

The Past Is a Foreign Country, as well as George L. Mosse, *The Nationalization of the Masses: Political Symbolism and Mass Movements in Germany from the Napoleonic Wars through the Third Reich* (New York: New America Library, 1975), and *The Invention of Tradition*, ed. Terence Ranger and Eric Hobsbawm (New York: Cambridge University Press, 1983).

Section 5. The Pageants

Evidence of past civic celebrations and historical pageants exists primarily in the form of programs, texts, souvenir albums, and newspaper accounts surviving in local historical societies and public libraries. Sometimes this material is supplemented by scrapbooks of photographs and the manuscript records of local organizations responsible for staging the celebrations. The distribution of the evidence is highly decentralized, because these were events of almost exclusively local interest. No comprehensive guide exists to when and where pageants occurred, though one could compile a fairly large listing from the publications of the agencies that tried to keep track at the time. These include the "List of Pageants" published regularly in the *American Pageant Association (APA) Bulletin*; George F. Kunz, "Historical Pageantry in America," *American Scenic and Historic Preservation Society*, vol. 21 (Albany, N.Y.: J. B. Lyon, 1916), pp. 895–914; Caroline Hill Davis, *Pageants in Great Britain and the United States: A List of References* (New York Public Library, 1916). The largest single listing of pageants by place and date is Catherine Henry, "Bibliography of Pageants in the United States" (Manuscript, New York Public Library Theatre Collection, 1939). Lists of pageants by place and date can also be pulled from the bibliographies of the doctoral dissertations mentioned in the preceding section.

Two different, but overlapping techniques were employed to select the approximately four hundred community historical pageants on which this book is based. First, I used the above lists to track down and read nearly every pageant regarded as significant by those organizations, such as the APA, most active in promoting pageantry. Second, I visited several large repositories and read civic celebrations and pageants independently of the reformers' lists. Most of the pageant texts came from the local history collections of the Library of Congress, supplemented by the New York Public Library, Free Library of Philadelphia, Boston Public Library, and North Carolina Room of the University of North Carolina at Chapel Hill. I pursued several of these pageants further through newspapers, scrapbooks, photo albums, and clipping files available at these large repositories—though even the extensive local newspaper holdings of the Library of Congress rarely matched the location of the pageants I wanted to examine. My selection of pageants is skewed toward the East, and maybe toward reformers' works, both because of their greater likelihood of being published and because librarians in these repositories may have used the reformers' guides, such as those of the APA, in developing their collections—although I was told that the pageant collections at the Library of Congress, the bulk of material examined, were unsolicited donations.

Index

. . . .